Introduction to Cyberdeception

Neil C. Rowe • Julian Rrushi

Introduction to Cyberdeception

 Springer

Neil C. Rowe
US Naval Postgraduate School
Monterey, CA, USA

Julian Rrushi
Western Washington University
Bellingham, WA, USA

ISBN 978-3-319-82288-4   ISBN 978-3-319-41187-3   (eBook)
DOI 10.1007/978-3-319-41187-3

Printed on acid-free paper

This Springer imprint is published by Springer Nature
The registered company is Springer International Publishing AG Switzerland

To Suzanne, who is only occasionally deceptive.

—NCR

To the national hero of Albania, George Castriot, aka Skanderbeg, whose skills in deception helped protect his homeland and the entire Europe from Ottoman conquest.

—JR

Preface

We need new ideas in information security. This book offers a set of interrelated ideas about using deception as a framework for attack and defense of computer systems and networks, and mostly defense. Contrary to popular belief, deception is not always bad and can be a useful tool in cyberspace. Much activity is occurring in regard to cyberdeception, so we try to convey some understanding of what is going on.

This book is intended as an introduction to cyberdeception and can be used in a classroom or for independent study. The intended audience is people who deal with cybersystems in one way or another, especially programmers and people focusing on information security and information assurance. But it also includes managers and policymakers who need to understand the options.

We realize that this book may seem a little cynical. We prefer to think of it as realistic. Deception, like war, is ubiquitous in human society, and it is important to address the world as it is, not as we want it to be. Will this book encourage deception and thus lead to a deterioration of societies? We think not, since there are plenty of books on crime and war, and they have not generally caused higher levels of crime and war. Understanding crime, war, and deception enables doing something about them.

We have tried to provide plenty of references to a variety of work on cyberdeception and supporting topics, for readers who want to further pursue particular topics. (All Rowe's publications are available at http://faculty.nps.edu/ncrowe.) They range from nontechnical to technical. Cyberdeception is an active field of research and development today, so new developments occur frequently. Most of the book does not assume the reader knows much about cybersystems other than the basics of software and architectures. However, the later chapters are more technical for readers who want more details, and appendices are available online to provide examples of implementations.

James Bret Michael and Richard Riehle got us interested in studying cyberde-ception. Especially helpful have been Barton Whaley, Dorothy Denning, Paul Thompson, and Glenn Fink. Partial funding for this work has been provided by the U.S. National Science Foundation under the Cyber Trust program.

Monterey, CA   Neil C. Rowe
Bellingham, WA   Julian Rrushi

Contents

Chapter 1
Introduction

It's a war out there. Security of our computer systems and networks ("cybersystems")
is under serious attack these days from a variety of malicious people: cybercrimi-
nals, spies (both government and industrial), disgruntled insiders within organizations, amateur "hackers" (Poulsen 2012), and terrorists (Colarik 2006). They exploit
flaws in software to misuse it for their own ends of making money, advancing their
agendas, and enjoying power over others.

Deception is so prevalent in attacks in cyberspace today that understanding
deception is quite important to understanding attacks and doing something about
them. The ability to conceal things easily in cyberspace lends itself to deception.
Despite the apparent complexities, the number of possible deceptions is finite and
we can enumerate them systematically. That is what this book will do.

© Springer International Publishing Switzerland 2016
N.C. Rowe, J. Rrushi, *Introduction to Cyberdeception*,
DOI 10.1007/978-3-319-41187-3_1

Cyberdeception can be used either offensively (to attack someone) or defensively (to defend against attacks). Offensive deceptions tend to use a limited set of methods like impersonation repeatedly with slightly different details. Defensive deceptions can and should be more varied. Nearly all the defensive deceptions we will discuss are a form of "active defense" for cybersystems (Wyler 2005). A classic form of active defense is a counterattack, a form of offense, so the distinction between offensive and defensive deceptions is not sharp. In addition as we will see, many deception methods work either offensively or defensively. However, we will spend most of this book discussing defensive deceptions since they are relatively new ideas for cyberspace.

1.1   Deception as a Third Line of Defense

One argument for defensive deception is that other methods of protecting cybersystems do not always work. Access controls (Chapple et al. 2013) are the traditional defense against cyberattacks. These include passwords and login procedures, assigned access privileges (for reading, writing, and running files), firewalls for restricting network access, and methods like encryption and steganography for hiding secrets even with access. But access controls are inadequate today (Lucasik et al. 2003). Attacks that subvert controls are being discovered all the time and are quickly being exploited, so that you cannot always trust an operating system to enforce access controls. Access controls have been studied for a long time, and significant innovations are now rare.

So defenders of cybersystems look to additional techniques once access controls have been breached. Intrusion-detection systems are the most popular second line of defense (Trost 2009). These are systems that watch your cybersystems for evidence of malicious or suspicious behavior. They can then report the suspicious activity to authorities, terminate the user session, or even repair the victim systems. However, intrusion-detection systems look for known "signatures" of malicious and suspicious behavior, specific patterns already known to be associated with known attacks. So most cannot recognize new attacks or new attack variants.

We suggest that a third line of defense could be deliberate deception by cybersystems. Attackers tend to act differently from normal users, and this can be detected even if there are no recognizable signatures. Systems could then lie, cheat, and mislead such anomalous users to prevent them from achieving attack goals, even when they have obtained access and fooled the intrusion-detection system. Since people are so accustomed to digital technology telling them the truth, such deception can be very effective with little effort by the defender. There is a risk of misidentifying legitimate users who are just doing something unusual, but we can reason about probabilities of malicious attack, and useful deception need not block users, just make it difficult for them to do bad things.

1.2   Terminology

Cyberdeception is a new topic and terminology is not always consistent. Some terms we will use frequently in this book:

- Cybersystems (comprising "cyberspace") are computers, digital devices, networks, and the data and software they contain.
- Cyberattackers (or just "attackers" in this book) are people attempting to exploit or hurt our cybersystems (and us) by trespassing on them and manipulating them.
- A hacker is an amateur cyberattacker.
- Attacks, cyberattacks, or exploits are methods the cyberattackers use.
- Cyberdefense is methods for defending cyberspace from cyberattacks. It is a subarea of information security, which in turn is a subarea of computer science.
- Deception is a successful attempt to make someone believe something that is false, either by words or deeds, and either deliberately or unintentionally.
- Cyberdeception is deception in and using cyberspace.
- Lies are deliberate verbal deceptions.
- Camouflage and concealment are two kinds of nonverbal deceptions.
- A scam is a deception for monetary gain.
- A deceiver is the perpetrator of a deception.
- A deceivee is the victim of a deception.

1.3   Why Deceive in Cyberspace?

Deception is an unusual idea for cybersystems (computers, devices, and networks). Most cybersystems try to be very honest about what they are doing. Outside of cyberspace, most societies proclaim that deception is rare even when they are doing plenty of it. Nonetheless, there can be good reasons to deliberately deceive in cyberspace:

- Deception can gather information about a deceivee. Attackers can discover things about defenders by seeing how they react to events. Defenders can pretend to succumb to an attack to learn secrets of attackers (Vidalis and Kazmi 2007), the idea behind "honeypots", computers designed solely as attack targets.
- Since there are many methods of deception, it can be hard for a deceivee to recognize them all if they are varied by the deceiver. Failing to recognize just one deception may be enough for successful deception campaign. Access controls and intrusion-detection systems must be more predictable, and attackers can exploit this.
- Offensive deception is essential to "penetration testing" or "ethical hacking", trying to test defenses of cybersystems by attempting unauthorized entry and malicious modifications (Weidman 2014). Cybersystems won't allow these unless you fool them.

- Because deception can be a third line of defense, it is useful for defending cybersystems that must be highly secure. Power plants and banks are examples of this "critical infrastructure".
- Deceptions can be automated to some extent in cyberspace. Botnets, or networks of computers subverted to be controlled by a cyberattacker, automate a set of offensive deceptive activities on a potentially large scale (Elisan 2012). But defensive deceptions can also be preprogrammed.
- Deceptions often can flexibly adapt to what a deceivee is doing, so deceivers can be experiment to find a deception that works.
- Deception can be a relatively benign activity which is only designed to influence, allowing the deceivee to make decisions themselves. Thus it need not be coercive.
- Deception can also serve positive social goals by smoothing human interactions (Castelfranchi 2000), much as mild human deceptions are essential for social interaction.
- Deception can work especially well against the smarter or better-trained deceivees since it can exploit their ability to reason and encourage them to outthink themselves. (Bodmer et al. 2012) argues that deception is necessary for sophisticated attackers like "advanced persistent threats", footholds gained by nation-state adversaries in cyberwar.

1.4   Goals of Cyberdeception

Deception manipulates people. The manipulation can serve several different purposes:

- Encourage the deceivee to do something the deceiver wants. For instance, a phishing attacker tries to get a victim to go to a malicious Web site where the attacker can steal private information (Berghel 2006).
- Discourage the deceivee from doing something the deceiver does not want.

  - Convince the deceivee that what they want to do is too hard. For instance, a defender can ask repeatedly for passwords from an attacker.
  - Convince the deceiver that what they want to is too dangerous to them. For instance, a defender's system can pretend to be a honeypot when it is not, since most attackers try to avoid honeypots.
  - Convince the deceiver that what they want to do will not be very valuable to them, as when a defender's system pretends to have no interesting files.

- Harass the deceivee, as in a denial-of-service attack designed to slow down a cybersystem.
- Learn something about the deceivee, as with honeypots where the deceivee is the attacker.

Note that some of these are mutually incompatible. When we do cyberdeceptions using the methods of this book, we usually need to choose just one of these goals and build a plan to accomplish it.

1.5   Deception Occurs Everywhere

Deception is common in nature. Many animals and plants use deception to protect themselves from predators and to gain competitive advantages over others of their own species (Bell and Whaley 1991). Protective coloration to blend in with the environment is often used as camouflage. Some species actively deceive as to their identity, as for instance butterflies that imitate the markings of unpalatable species to discourage predation. Other species use deceptive behaviors to manipulate or fool other animals, as some animals in combat that raise their limbs and puff out their chests to appear larger than they really are. Deception is also important in courtship as a way to win a better mate than one deserves, as the unnecessarily elaborate tail of the peacock exemplifies.

Societies could not exist without deception (Smith 2007). People lie to one another to build relationships and gain advantages. Businesses need it to do marketing: Advertising routinely makes misleading claims as to the qualities of products. Contracts could not be negotiated if parties were truthful about their intentions. Politics and diplomacy cannot work without a considerable amount of lying (Bailey 1988). Important issues are often too complex to be understood by the general public, so politicians lie about their intentions to please the public while intending to do something else. Evaluation of businesses and politicians by the public tends to be short-term and results-oriented, and these things encourage deception.

Deception is central in the entertainment industry. Actors must pretend to be someone they are not, and set designers make something artificial appear real. The subfield of stage magic focuses heavily on deception. Games and sports encourage deception to make them more interesting, and good deceivers in them are rewarded. Even a scientific field like medicine sees lying. Doctors tend to act more optimistic about a patient's prognoses than they really believe because they think that patients are more likely to get better that way. Deception is common in games, and has now become automated for computer games with software enabling you to cheat (Hoglund and McGraw 2007).

Deception is essential to religions. The world's religions make many incompatible claims, and they all claim to be completely true thanks to divine guidance. There must be a considerable amount of deception and self-deception to explain these contradictions.

Deception has a long history in warfare (Rothstein and Whaley 2013) for both offense and defense. It can be a potent "force multiplier", a way to gain tactical or strategic advantage with smaller resources than most alternative techniques. Deception is valuable as one of the few good strategies always available to the weaker side in a conflict.

Deception occurs with software because the technology is new and has frequent flaws. So often descriptions and documentation deceptively describe how the designers hope their system works although it rarely works that way. Less scrupulous software vendors go further to claim features that their systems do not possess, such as compatibility with a broad range of operating systems. Software vendors can also deliberately mislead for competitive advantage. For instance, the Microsoft Windows help system claims it has no information about how to remove a file ("remove" is too close to the "rm" command in Unix and Microsoft fought Unix for a long time), and when Microsoft Word converts files to Web pages in Microsoft-independent formats you are asked whether you really want to do that as if there were something wrong about it—yet no such message is provided in converting non-Microsoft formats to Microsoft formats. Deception also occurs with software trying too hard to be nice. For instance, Microsoft Internet Explorer first suggests that an unrecognized name of a Web site might not be available, rather than you might have misspelled it, although the latter is more likely.

1.6   Are You Overconfident About Being Fooled?

One objection made to the idea of cyberdeception is that it won't work on people that are at least moderately intelligent, since cybersystems are rather clumsy and obvious. However, people tend to be overconfident about their ability to detect deception. Studies with trained investigators like police showed that they considerably overestimated their ability to detect, and studies with normal people in social settings were similar (Granhag et al. 2015). People have demonstrated cognitive biases that make them susceptible to a variety of kinds of deception. These results are likely to extend to cyberspace. In fact, people are more easily fooled in cyberspace because they do not have clues from physical appearance and voice inflections that are helpful for detecting deception in the real world.

It is, in fact, amazing what people can believe based on minimal evidence. A classic example is astrology, the theory that when you were born affects your personality. There is no adequate evidence supporting astrological claims in any experiments (see www.astrology-and-science.com). Yet the majority of the people of the world believe in at least one astrological claim despite this lack of evidence. It should be still easier to believe false things in the shadowy world of cyberspace.

1.7   Is Deception Ethical?

When we propose that cybersystems should lie and cheat, a common reaction of many people is that this is unethical. But deception is not necessarily unethical. Its widespread unacknowledged use in the world suggests that there are ethical ways to employ it. If deception is an accepted business practice, then it should be acceptable for individuals to use similar techniques.

One approach to ethics is the utilitarian one. From its perspective, deception is acceptable if it prevents a greater harm from occurring. We argue that this applies to cyberspace because of the seriousness of the threats to cybersystems (Quinn 2006). Destruction of the functionality of a cybersystem is a serious threat. It may require many hours of work to restore the system to the state before an attack, and some damage may become apparent only later, requiring frequent reinvestment of time. Attacks can also cause damage that cannot be restored, such as destroying data that is not available from backup, loss of business while the system was down, or damage to reputation. Next to such serious consequences, a few convenient lies can be insignificant.

Deception can also be justified from classic ethical principles. (Bok 1978) provides an excellent summary of many of the applications of the ethics of lying, and a more recent analysis is that of (Carson 2010). Four of her categories particularly apply to defense of information systems.

- *Lies in a crisis*: Most ethical theories allow lying in acute crises, as when someone would be killed if you did not lie. As discussed above, destruction of a cybersystem could have serious repercussions even though cybersystems cannot die. This does require, however, that one be sufficiently sure one is under attack.
- *Lies for the public good*: Keeping critical-infrastructure systems running can be considered a "public good" in many cases. We depend so much on cyberspace today that its continued operation is an uncontroversial public good.
- *Lying to enemies*: Lying to your enemies in war is considered acceptable since it is essential to many military and diplomatic ploys. For instance, the many deceptions that the Allies used prior to the Normandy landings on D-Day in 1944 are uncontroversial. When cyberattackers are state-sponsored groups making plans against us, they can be considered enemies.
- *Lying to liars*: Cyberattackers almost always deceive the system they are attacking. For instance, attackers masquerade as system administrators or banks, fake their Internet addresses to prevent tracing them, offer free software containing concealed malicious features, and request resources they do not need to slow down Web sites. So it seems fair to respond to attackers with deception as well. However, deceiving them in exchange does make you no better than them, and many ethicists feel uncomfortable with this.

We discuss ethical issues in more detail in the last chapter.

1.8 Plan of the Book

Chapter 2 through Chap. 5 provide general background on deception and its methods. Chapter 6 through Chap. 10 discuss some deception techniques that are especially useful. Chapter 11 through Chap. 15 discuss more technical methods of deception planning, and Chap. 16 considers ethical and legal issues.

References

Bailey F (1988) Humbuggery and manipulation: the art of leadership. Cornell University Press, Ithaca, NY

Bell J, Whaley B (1991) Cheating. Transaction, New York

Berghel H (2006) Phishing mongers and posers. Commun ACM 49(4):21–25

Bodmer S, Kilger A, Carpenter G, Jones J (2012) Reverse deception: organized cyber threat counter-exploitation. McGraw-Hill Education, New York

Bok S (1978) Lying: moral choice in public and private life. Pantheon, New York

Carson T (2010) Lying and deception: theory and practice. Oxford University Press, Oxford, UK

Castelfranchi C (2000) Artificial liars: why computers will (necessarily) deceive us and each other. Ethics Inf Technol 2(2):113–119

Chapple M, Ballad B, Ballad T, Banks E (2013) Access control, authentication, and public key infrastructure, 2nd edn. Jones and Bartlett, New York

Colarik A (2006) Cyber terrorism: political and economic implications. IGI Global, Hershey, PA

Elisan C (2012) Malware, rootkits, and botnets: a beginner's guide. McGraw-Hill Education, New York

Granhag P, Vrij A, Verschuere B (eds) (2015) Detecting deception: current challenges and cognitive approaches. Wiley-Blackwell, Chichester, UK

Hoglund G, McGraw G (2007) Exploiting online games: cheating massively distributed systems. Addison-Wesley, Upper Saddle River, NJ

Lucasik S, Goodman S, Longhurst D (2003) National strategies for protection of critical infrastructures from cyber-attack. London, Oxford

Poulsen K (2012) Kingpin: how one hacker took over the billion-dollar cybercrime underground. Broadway, New York

Quinn M (2006) Ethics for the information age. Pearson Addison-Wesley, Boston, MA

Rothstein H, Whaley B (eds) (2013) The art and science of military deception. Artech House, New York

Smith D (2007) Why we lie: the evolutionary roots of deception and the unconscious mind. St. Martin's Griffin, New York

Trost R (2009) Practical intrusion analysis: prevention and detection for the twenty-first century. Addison-Wesley, Upper Saddle River, NJ

Vidalis S, Kazmi S (2007) Security through deception. Inf Syst Secur 16:34–41

Weidman G (2014) Penetration testing: a hands-on introduction to hacking. No Starch, New York

Wyler N (ed) (2005) Aggressive network self-defense. Syngress, Rockland, MA

Chapter 2
Psychology of Deception

This chapter provides background on deception as a psychological phenomenon.

2.1 Definitions of Deception

Deception involves causing someone or something to have false beliefs. This is often accomplished by lies, verbal deceptive statements. It can also involve nonverbal deceptions from misleading appearances. The purpose of deception is to cause the deceivee to subsequently act on those false beliefs to benefit the deceiver.

© Springer International Publishing Switzerland 2016
N.C. Rowe, J. Rrushi, *Introduction to Cyberdeception*,
DOI 10.1007/978-3-319-41187-3_2

Deception is a kind of persuasion. Persuasion means trying to get someone or something to help you achieve goals that would be costly or impossible for you to achieve on your own. There are many methods of persuasion, including appeal to shared interests, appeal to personal benefits, appeal to avoidance of personal harm, and appeal to laws and ethics (Wilson 2002). Deception differs from other methods of persuasion in that it attempts to manipulate a deceivee without their complete knowledge of facts and motives. It is thus useful when other methods of persuasion do not work, as when your goals oppose those of the deceivee's. Societies generally have particular ethical rules concerning deception. That is because societies are built on trust, and deception undermines it. However, small amounts of deception are essential to the functioning of societies. Evidence from people in relationships like marriages shows they use more deception than do people in less-close relationships (Miller et al. 1986).

This book will especially focus on deception for "negative persuasion", persuading people not to do something, as when we want to persuade cyber attackers not to attack us. Negative persuasion is often easier than positive persuasion, since it is easier to persuade someone to avoid or stop something rather than start it. But it does require that you understand the goals of the person you are persuading.

2.2 The Spectrum of Deception

Deception is ubiquitous in human activity (Eckman 2009). Chapter 4 will discuss taxonomies of deception. A start at a taxonomy is that of (Ford 1996):

- White lies: Social lies to smooth relationships.
- Humorous lies: Obvious lies as jokes, including "practical jokes" (Smith 1953).
- Altruistic lies: Lies for the ostensible good of the deceivee, such as a parent's lies to a child to prevent them from worrying.
- Defensive lies: Lies to protect the deceiver such as lies to get rid of telemarketers.
- Aggressive lies: Lies to manipulate the deceivee to make them do things to the deceiver's advantage, such as email scams.
- Pathological lies: Lies that represent obsessive behavior beyond any need, due to a psychological disorder of the deceiver.
- Nonverbal minimization: Understating a key feature, important in camouflage.
- Nonverbal exaggeration: Overstating a key feature, usually to mask something else.
- Nonverbal neutralization: Avoiding display of normal emotions when asked about something emotional.
- Nonverbal substitution: Replacing a sensitive concept by a less sensitive one as a form of decoying.
- Self-deception: Pushing of reality into the subconscious.

In cyberspace we will be mostly concerned with lies, with some occurrence of the other categories listed above. Again note that deception does not require words nor people since animals and plants do it all the time (Zahavi and Zahavi 1997; Searcy and Nowicki 2005).

2.3   The Sociology of Trust

Deception is a two-party interaction and thus a social phenomenon. The related issue of trust is an important subject recently in social psychology and sociology. It is very relevant in Internet commerce where it is hard to see whom you are dealing with. Observations on virtual communities in cyberspace suggest that trust is hard to build (Donath 1999). Trust is important in management of organizations of people because well-functioning organizations tend to have high levels of trust among their members.

Sztompka (1999) identifies factors important in creating trust of a person or organization P1 in a person or organization P2 regarding a claim C asserted by P2 or a proposed task T for P2 to do:

- Reputation: What people say about the trustworthiness of P2 in regard to C or T. For instance, you trust a Web site more if your friends say they have used it and like it.
- Past performance: Whether P2 was correct on previous claims similar to C, or how P2 did previously on similar tasks to T. For instance, if you have previously ordered tickets from a Web site, you can recall how satisfied you were with your purchase.
- Appearance: Whether observable properties of P2 make them appear trustworthy in asserting claim C or performing task T. For instance, you may judge a lawyer's Web site by how professional it appears.
- Accountability: Whether P1 has a way to get compensation from P2 if P2 is incorrect about claim C or fails to deliver on task T. For instance, you may see money-back guarantees from a Web site, or you may realize you could sue them in small-claims court.
- Precommitment: Whether P2 has already proved part of assertion C to be true, or whether P2 has done initial stages of T. For instance, you trust an online supplier more if you can evaluate the product during a free trial period.
- Context: Whether the environment in which P2 operates tends to be trustworthy. For instance, you can trust medical information from a medical Web site of a university more than information from a commercial Web site because universities tend be more objective. The degree to which you actually know someone's context also increases the trust you have in them, as does the existence of self-policing mechanisms in that context such as policies and laws. And if someone does not trust you, that is a reason not to trust them either.

For example, suppose you are a parent whose teenager asks to go on a date with someone you don't know much about. Teenagers are at an age where they are learning to do convincing deceptions, so you want to be careful. You can assess the proposed person for the date by what other parents say about them (reputation), whether previous dates with them seemed to go well (past performance), whether they appear neat and polite when you see them (appearance), whether you can contact the parents of the date if something goes wrong (accountability), whether the date has been nice to your teenager previously (precommitment), and the success of other dates your teenager has had (context).

Trust factors control the success of deception. To deceive effectively, we need to assess our reputation and past performance, as well as the effect that deceptions may have on it. And the deception can be made more effective if we manipulate appearance, accountability, and precommitment to put it over. We will discuss these issues in a more precise way in Chap. 11.

2.4   Detecting Deception

Deception is hard for people to detect. People have a bias towards belief ("truth bias") since deception is relatively rare, and people have misconceptions about deception clues (Qin et al. 2004). On the other hand, once someone detects deception, they can be very difficult to convince otherwise.

Nonetheless, even though deception is difficult to detect, a variety of clues to it can "leak out" despite conscious efforts to prevent them, and these clues can be recognized by an alert observer. Deception detection has been subject of much research because it has many practical applications to police work, law, business, and psychotherapy (Eckman 2009; Houston et al. 2013). Deception detection can be difficult even for trained professionals when faced with clever and determined deceivers, as in police interviewing suspects. Nonetheless, practice can improve detection rates (Biros et al. 2005). It also helps to be depressed—strangely, depressed people can detect deception better (Lane and DePaulo 1999).

Vrij (2000) and Granhag et al. (2015) distinguish deception clues as physiological, nonverbal, and verbal, and (Houston et al. 2013) provides an enjoyable summary. Physiological clues are body measurements such as increased heart rate, increased blood pressure, and increased sweating. Such clues are associated with increased stress levels, and stress is associated with lying, although other causes create stress too. Polygraphs ("lie detectors") attempt to measure these physiological clues, but they have not been shown to be very accurate (Tavel 2016). New technology such as scans that can detect what parts of a brain are active may work better (Granhag et al. 2015). Deception tends to be more centered on the frontal lobes than normal brain activity. However, such measurements are currently expensive to perform, so we will not see them during routine police interrogations anytime soon.

Nonverbal clues involve visible features of the body, such as fidgeting, holding the body rigid, touching the face, using a higher pitch of the voice, stuttering, pausing in speech, responding overly quickly, smiling excessively, failing to look at the person addressed, and moving legs and the body unnecessarily. So if you are a parent and ask your teenager what they did last night, and they smile and blink, look the other way, and then stoke their cheek, those are bad signs. Many of these clues are also stress-related. There are also nonverbal clues based on inconsistency that are independent of stress, such as stylistic clues to fake art works (Amore 2015). Nonverbal clues are generally weaker clues to deception than physiological ones, so more than one is necessary to have confidence that deception is occurring. But there are many useful nonverbal clues, though the good ones are not necessarily what you might expect (Qin et al. 2004).

Verbal clues involve what a person says (Fitzpatrick et al. 2015). They include:

- Vagueness: Deceivers often need to construct a story, and a story with fewer details is easier to construct.
- Negative statements: These reduce the need for details.
- Hyperbole or exaggerated statements: Deceivers try steer deceivees to a desired idea using strong assertions.
- Implausibilities: Deceivers find it hard to make choices for their story that are all equally plausible. For instance, a teenager may claim they spent the evening at the movies but later have difficulty explaining why the police later stopped them outside a bar.
- Contradictions: Deceivers may forget what they said earlier in telling a long story. Contradictions are a powerful clue in police work, and they are the reason police make suspects repeat their stories many times.

So if you ask your teenager what they did last night, and they say "We went out and went to Joe's house and didn't do anything—it was soooooo boring", that is suspicious since it includes all five of the verbal clues mentioned above.

The limited number of clues to deception in cyberspace makes it easier to do deception there than in the real world. Experiments suggest that deception tends to succeed better the narrower the communications bandwidth between deceiver and deceivee (Miller and Stiff 1993; Burgoon et al. 2003; Sundar 2015). For instance, people communicating in cyberspace with human-like avatars deceived more often than people communicating with their video images (Galanxhi and Nah 2007). Communication in cyberspace still involves a good deal of text, and its bandwidth is narrow. Deception also tends to work well in cyberspace because many of the abovementioned clues do not apply. Digital devices do not generally provide physiological measurement or gestural clues, though video cameras attached to computers might. So to detect cyberdeception, we have only verbal clues plus a few nonverbal clues of technology interaction such as pauses or too-fast responses. For instance, a deceiving computer might respond too quickly or too slowly, give many more negative statements than normal, or claim implausible obstacles to doing what a user wants. Avoiding such clues will thus be an important consideration in the techniques suggested in this book.

So verbal clues to deception are the most useful in cyberspace. A good checklist for detecting verbal deceptions is in the "Statement Validity Assessment" process used by European courts for assessing interviews with witnesses to crimes (Steller and Kohnken 1989). It lists 19 criteria:

1. Logical structure: Truthtellers are more likely to tell a story that makes sense.
2. Unstructured production: Truthtellers structure their stories less.
3. Quantity of details: Truthtellers can provide more details.
4. Contextual enabling: Truthtellers mention more specifics of time and place.
5. Descriptions of interactions: Truthtellers mention more human interactions (providing corroboration).
6. Reproduction of speech: Truthtellers more often use exact quotations rather than paraphrases.
7. Unexpected complications: Truthtellers more often mention unexpected obstacles.
8. Unusual details: Truthtellers more often mention surprising details.
9. Superfluous details: Truthtellers more often mention unnecessary details.
10. Accurately reporting misunderstandings: Truthtellers more accurately mention things they did not understand.
11. Related external associations: Truthtellers more often mention corroborating factors.
12. Accounts of subjective mental state: Truthtellers more often mention past emotions.
13. Attribution of perpetrator's mental state: Truthtellers provide more details of other people's mental states.
14. Spontaneous corrections: Truthtellers more often correct themselves during narration.
15. Admitting lack of memory: Truthtellers more often admit memory failures.
16. Raising doubts about one's testimony: Truthtellers more often raise doubts about their own testimony.
17. Self-deprecation: Truthtellers more often self-deprecate.
18. Pardoning the perpetrator: Truthtellers more often excuse a perpetrator.
19. Details characteristic of the offense: Truthtellers more often describe known common patterns in the crime and criminal.

For cyberspace, we can exclude 2, 5, 6, 7, 11, 12, 13, 14, 15, 16, 17, 18, and 19 because they only relate to human interactions. Digital technology is very consistent, can provide lots of details, can interact with people in restricted ways, is not emotional, and does not volunteer information only vaguely relevant. So, taking all the clues discussed into account, we propose the following principles for a convincing cyberdeception:

- Deceptive cyber-technology should make plausible statements and respond plausibly to events that occur.
- Deceptive cyber-technology should avoid contradictions.
- Deceptive cyber-technology should be able to present plenty of details to support their deceptions.
- Deceptive cyber-technology should be able to provide details of time and place to support their deceptions.

- Deceptive cyber-technology should mention surprises on occasion.
- Deceptive cyber-technology should mention irrelevant details on occasion.
- Deceptive cyber-technology should provide unclear messages on occasion.
- Deceptive cyber-technology should avoid unexpected vagueness.
- Deceptive cyber-technology should minimize negative statements and responses.
- Deceptive cyber-technology should avoid responses faster than expected when deceiving.
- Deceptive cyber-technology should avoid responses slower than expected when deceiving.
- Deceptive cyber-technology should avoid presenting a different appearance or manner when deceiving as opposed to when not deceiving.

Vrij (2000) provides another checklist on "characteristics of a good liar":

- Being well prepared: Cyber-technology excels at this.
- Being original: Cyber-technology can do this with some advance preparation.
- Thinking quickly: Cyber-technology excels at this.
- Being eloquent: Cyber-technology is not especially good at this, although some eloquence can be programmed into it.
- Having a good memory: Cyber-technology excels at this.
- Not experiencing emotions associated with lying: Cyber-technology excels at this.
- Being good at theatrical-style acting: Cyber-technology is not especially good at this.

So cyber-technology is excellent at four of the seven criteria (the first, third, fifth, and sixth), neutral on one (the second), and weak on two (the fourth and seventh). This is encouraging for the prospects of cyberdeception.

2.5   Other Factors in Designing Good Deceptions

Beyond the guidelines already mentioned, some other factors affect the effectiveness of a deception. Let us consider these here from the standpoint of designing an effective deception.

2.5.1   Providing Independent Evidence

Often more than one statement or observation is needed to make a convincing deception. This works best when the statements or observations are somewhat different or "independent" of one another while being consistent with a single possible cause. For instance, suppose we want to fool a malicious user into thinking that the network connection is not working. If we say "Error" when they try to download a file from a network site, refuse access to an external email site, and provide a "Site not found" message on attempting to run a Web browser, all those events could be explained by the single cause that the network connection is not working. The three events could also be explained by three independent errors, but that is less likely than having a single cause. So a goal in designing deceptions should be to provide as much independent evidence as possible that will confirm the deception that we intend, and as little evidence as possible supporting other explanations.

Independent evidence can also be used to help detect a deception. For instance, if a teenager says they were studying with a friend last night, but (1) they do not like to study much, (2) they came home late, (3) you know there was a big party that night, and (4) they look very tired this morning, you have four several reasons to suspect their claim, making you more suspicious than if only one clue occurred. Similarly, if a system claims it cannot download a file when it has downloaded similar files in the past from the same site, and the file has a suspicious name, and it is known that there is increased security recently at the download site, those factors together make it more likely that a user is being deceived about being able to download the file.

2.5.2   Consistency

An important clue to deception is inconsistency (McCormick 2013). Consistency relates to predictability. When an operating system says a file is in a format that cannot be opened, it should say that to anyone anytime, since digital technology is usually predictable. If it sometimes allows users to open the file, that is suspicious because restrictions in an operating system do not usually change much over time. So if we are going to deceive, we must track what we have already said or shown.

But there are exceptions. Even in cyberspace some processes are random, and deceptions involving them should be random too. For instance, the network may be down for a while and then come back up once it gets fixed, and exactly when that happens is hard to predict. Or a publisher's Web site may permit only one person from an institution to log in under their account at a time, and it may be random whether someone else is logged in at any given time. Such unpredictability does not jeopardize deceptions because users know such processes are inconsistent. However, you can deceive someone better about something predictable if you are consistent.

2.5.3   Deception by Commission Versus Deception by Omission

Active deception is often easier to detect than passive deception. For example, suppose a user asks a system to download a file. An active deception (error of commission) would be to say the file was downloaded when it was not, while a passive deception (error of omission) would be to terminate the download without saying why; the first would be more suspicious. Ethical theories often treat deceptions of commission as more serious since they involve more steps by the deceiver, but such distinctions are subtle and not usually important for effectiveness. For instance, if your teenager fails to tell you there were alcoholic beverages at a party they went to, that should be just as bad as lying that there were none. Errors of commission tend to call attention to themselves more and can be detected more easily. But some deceptions of omission do not work unless the deceivee notices them in order to be deceived.

2.5.4   Confirmability of a Deception

Deceptions work best when it is hard to argue with them. For instance, if your teenager says they went to a party, you can confirm that by asking other people who went to the party; but if they say they studied alone with a friend, there may be only one witness. So of two equally convincing deceptions, a deceiver should prefer the one that is the more difficult to deny, a principle apparently employed in many online dating profiles (Toma and Hancock 2010). Difficulty can be related in part to the time to check a deception; even if you could check it, you may not have the time. For instance, if your teenager says they went to the movies when they were unsupervised last night, you can check at the theater to see what times the movies were playing; but that's a bother, so most parents would focus on nonverbal clues to deception.

Cyberspace provides many obstacles to confirming information. If a computer tells you that its network connection is down, how can you argue with it? Maybe you could run a process to analyze the network buffers, or you could check if other users have a network connection, but most people do not have the skills and knowledge to do this. So some things in cyberspace are easy to deceive about. But not everything. For instance, it is harder to deceive about downloads since a user can check by looking at the directory, or by trying to open the downloaded file or use it. Digital technology rarely makes mistakes on downloading, so it's suspicious when downloading does not work.

2.5.5   Cognitive Limitations

An advantage for both cyberdeception and its detection is that the excellent memories of cybersystems easily surpass those of people. People have limits as to what they can remember, and may not be able to catch inconsistencies and contradictions in many cases (Heuer 1982). Cyber-technology can also easily flood people with too many details to remember. Experienced users who focus on the right details can be fooled less easily, since broader experience enables people to learn to "chunk" complex patterns as single units and thus remember more. But everyone has limitations. So a good strategy for a deceiver may be to overwhelm the deceivee with details.

On the other hand, the excellent memory of cybersystems can help with detection of deceptions since a cybersystem can keep all the data a deceiver supplies to it over a perhaps long period of time. It can check for known suspicious details, or just rate the overall level of plausibility, to detect deception.

2.5.6   Emotional Manipulation

A teenager who wants to go to a party can play on a parent's emotions by suggesting they are like a prisoner who can't ever study with anyone and so it falling behind in school. While cybersystems do not have emotions, they can certainly exploit emotions of humans to deceive. For instance, phishing can try to scare you about your bank account so you reveal personal data (Dhamija et al. 2006). Defensive deceptions can try to make the cyberattacker feel superior to a deceivee cybersystem by having the system seem inept; attackers who feel superior are less suspicious.

As another example, hacker-type attackers are often motivated by a desire to exercise power as part of a need to maintain their self-esteem, as well as the thrill of doing something illegal and getting away with it. Such deceivers get a thrill called "duping delight" from the deception alone regardless of whether it accomplishes anything. Guilt is another emotion that can be exploited since most attackers know what they are doing is wrong. This means they may in fact be more willing to accept defender's deceptions since they are deceiving themselves. For instance, when hackers "steal" a fake password to a pay Web site, they will be less likely to report it does not work than if they legitimately paid for the password.

2.5.7   Active Methods of Detecting Deception

Vrij (2000) suggests techniques for a deceivee to actively try to get evidence of deception rather than passively waiting to observe it. One technique is "probing", asking questions to force deceivers to fill in details in the hope of encountering inconsistencies (McCormick 2013). For instance, if your teenager claims to have been studying algebra last night with a friend, ask them who the friend was, where they were studying, how long they were studying, what details of algebra they were addressing, and what homework was aided by the study. Skilled interrogators know that asking several times for the same information and withholding what the questioner knows are ways to improve the consistency-checking of probing (Houston et al. 2013)—though it probably is overkill with teenagers.

Active methods do not apply much against software-based automated deceivers because cybersystems can only answer a limited set of questions, and they have no difficulty being consistent. Nonetheless, deceivees can probe too, as we shall discuss in Sect. 11.6.

2.5.8   Individual Differences in Susceptibility to Deception

Even though deception exploits basic principles of human psychology, different people respond to it differently. Some people are inherently more trusting than others, or at least are more trusting in particular contexts. For instance, someone who frequently helps others may be more liable to provide their password to a deceiver. So a clever deceiver can exploit knowledge of their deceivee to choose deceptions that are more effective for them. This has been important in military deception, to be discussed in the next chapter.

Some of the difference between responses to deception is due to differing abilities to perceive deception clues. Some of this can be learned. People that need to detect deception in their jobs—law enforcement personnel, clinical psychologists, and military intelligence analysts—can do better than the average person using active detection methods. Other differences come from cultural assumptions. For instance, the United States is currently getting many cyberattacks originating in China, both government-sponsored and civilian-sponsored. Currently the Chinese have a high opinion of themselves. Their culture is quite isolated, albeit long-surviving and distinguished, and they have made much economic progress in recent years. They are sure they are the greatest country on earth. And U.S. targets are falling relatively easily to simple-minded cyberattacks. So it should be easier to deceive Chinese cyberattackers that their attacks have succeeded than it would cyberattackers of many other countries.

Personality of the deceivee can also affect their susceptibility to deception. People differ considerably in response to adversity (Lydon and Zanna 1990), and some people get more easily discouraged than other people. However, attackers of computer systems are generally adversity-tolerant, and require more deception than the average person to be scared away. Some people are also more careless than others in checking details. Experienced people are willing to pay attention to details (Bishop-Clark and Wheeler 1994), but nowadays a wide range of people are using cyberspace. People also differ considerably in their desire for risk-taking (Demaree et al. 2008), and cyberattackers are risk-takers. People also differ in the degree to which they are active rather than passive in response to adversity, and cyberattackers are willing to be more active on the average, as in trying to confirm error messages.

Cyberattackers do tend to be more suspicious than the average person. This is because they are deceivers themselves, and deceivers tend to be more sensitive to clues of deception by other people. But once attackers get a certain level of comfort with a system, they think they "own" it, and tend to let down their guard. We can deceive them better then.

Some of these personality differences are due to genetics and some are due to life experiences. Similar factors affect who becomes a conventional criminal, and such factors have been discussed extensively in the criminology literature (Nettler 1974). For instance, certain subcultures have more hackers and others have more scammers.

A problem with exploiting individual differences in response to deception is that they may be hard to predict. In military deception as we shall discuss in the next chapter, there is often only one person to deceive, the opposing general or admiral, who we may know about. But in cyberspace we may have much less knowledge about whom we are dealing with. We may need to try a variety of deceptions to get one that works.

We can get feedback from the deceivee by "experimenting" with them. We get clues to the attacker's personality from the way they respond to obstacles they encounter. Providing such obstacles tests how well they handle adversity, and providing both safe and risky alternatives tests their risk-taking.

2.5.9 Exploiting Self-Deception

Deception works better when the deceivee cooperates. It helps when the deceivee is prone to self-deception. Self-deception is common among attackers in cyberspace, who generally have overconfidence in their skills. We can also exploit their generally high intelligence by giving them metaphorical puzzles to solve. We may also be able to exploit their paranoia by claiming we are reporting their actions to law enforcement, since many realize what they are doing is illegal and immoral. Self-deception also occurs with cyberattack victims who may not realize how vulnerable they are.

2.5.10 Groupthink

Self-deception is particularly interesting when it affects an entire group of people. A false idea, once it gets established in the group's consciousness, can persist a long time, longer than for an individual (something that social networking sites encourage). That is because group members tend to reinforce the ideas of one another, an idea that has been called "groupthink" (Janis 1983). In facing adversaries in particular, groups tend to reinforce myths of their own invincibility and of the ineptness of their opponents, as North Korean hackers do today in their very closed society.

This has several implications for state-sponsored cyberattacks because these are generally accomplished by teams. Very likely cyberattacks produced by a group will not be too creative as it would be hard to get group consensus otherwise. State-sponsored teams also have difficulty recognizing when their methods are failing and making adjustments because of overconfidence. Deception by defenders can exploit both of these tendencies.

2.6 Conclusions

Deception is common phenomenon. Despite all the attempts to decry it, it is ubiquitous in many types of human activity. This is partly because it can accomplish things that others forms of persuasion cannot, and partly because it is difficult to detect even for trained professionals. It would seem thus natural to consider deception as a useful measure in cyberspace in critical circumstances.

2.7   Exercises

1. Negative persuasion is not necessarily easier than positive persuasion. Give an example where negative persuasion is harder than positive persuasion to an alternative goal, where both methods attempt to foil a cyberattack.
2. Give an example of how an altruistic lie could help a legitimate (nonmalicious) user of a cybersystem when the system was simultaneously under attack by a malicious user. Design your example so that an argument can be made for using deception rather than some other technique with the legitimate user.
3. You want decide who to vote for in an election based on information on Web sites. Describe how each of the criteria for evaluating trust could influence your evaluation of the sites.
4. (a) What is the justification for thinking that responding too quickly could be a clue that a computer is deceiving you?
   (b) What is the justification for thinking that responding too slowly could be a clue that a cybersystem is deceiving you? Cybersystems respond too slowly quite often.
   (c) How can we estimate what speed is "just right" for responding to a particular command by a user so as to minimize the perception that we are deceiving them?
5. (a) What does it mean for a deceptive computer to avoid being vague? Give an example where vagueness could hurt the effectiveness of the deception. Suggest an alternative for this case.
   (b) What does it mean for a deceptive computer to avoid being negative? Give an example where negativity could hurt the effectiveness of the deception. Suggest an alternative for this case.
6. Give an example of how cognitive limitations on perceiving deception can be more important when responding to certain sequences of commands by a cyberattacker than with others.
7. Hackers often form groups linked by sharing of information. What kinds of "groupthink" could such loosely coupled hacker groups be susceptible to? How could defenders exploit this with deception?
8. Suppose you are a detective interrogating a suspect. Identify the concepts discussed in this chapter that are exemplified by the following utterances of yours.

   (a) "You say you were home watching television last night at 10 PM? What were you watching?"
   (b) "Shall I check the records of the cable company for what was on?"
   (c) "We know your brother got you into this, so you're not really a criminal."
   (d) "You say you were home watching television at 10 PM, so how do you explain a witness seeing you at the crime scene then?"
   (e) "So do you stretch the truth a bit when you do telephone sales?"
   (f) "You'll feel a lot better if you tell us what really happened."

    (g) "We have a confession from everyone else in your gang."

    (h) "When the suspect visited you at 10 PM, what was he wearing?"

    (i) "It's pretty convenient that you don't remember what he was wearing, isn't it?"

    (j) "You say you were walking in the neighborhood at 10 PM. Did you see anyone you know?"

9. Get two text files of prose of at least 50,000 words each, one that has some amount of deception in it and one that does not. If it comes from the Web, remove any HTML tags. Compute the frequency distributions of words for each document. (A number of software tools can do this, as for instance NLTK at www. nltk.org.) It has been claimed that decreased frequency of first-person words and exception words is a clue to deception (Gupta and Skillicorn 2006). Test this out by comparing the frequency of the following list of words in your text files. Is the hypothesis supported that decreased frequency of the clue words correlates with deception? Analyze the two kinds of clue words separately.

first-person words: *i mine we me my i'm i'll i've i'd myself our ours ourselves*
exception words: *except however but although rather unless whereas nor without besides nonetheless*

References

Amore A (2015) The art of the con: the most notorious fakes, frauds, and forgeries in the art world. St. Martin's, New York

Biros D, George J, Adkins M, Kruse J, Burgoon J, Nunamaker J, Sakamoto J (2005) A quasi-experiment to determine the impact of a computer based deception detection training system: the use of Agent99 trainer in the U.S. military. In: Proceedings of the 38th Hawaii international conference on system sciences, 3–6 Jan, 2005, p. 24a

Bishop-Clark C, Wheeler D (1994) The Myers-Briggs personality type and its relationship to computer programming. J Res Technol Educ 26(3):358–370

Burgoon J, Stoner G, Bonito J, Dunbar N (2003) Trust and deception in mediated communication. In: Proceedings of the. 36th Hawaii international conference on system sciences, Honolulu, HI, 6–9 Jan, 2003, 44.1

Demaree H, DeDonno M, Burns K, Everhart D (2008) You bet: how personality differences affect risk-taking preferences. Personal Individ Differ 44(7):1484–1494

Dhamija R, Tygar J, Hearst M (2006) Why phishing works. In: Proceedings of the Conference on Computers and Human Interaction, 22–27 Apr 2006, Montréal, QB, Canada, pp. 581–590

Donath J (1999) Identity and deception in the virtual community. In: Kollock P, Smith M (eds) Communities in cyberspace. Routledge, London, pp 25–29

Eckman P (2009) Telling lies: clues to deceit in the marketplace, politics, and marriage. Norton, New York, Revised edition

Fitzpatrick E, Bachenko J, Fornaciari T (2015) Automatic detection of verbal deception. Morgan and Claypool, New York

Ford C (1996) Lies! lies!! lies!!! The psychology of deceit. American Psychiatric Press, Washington, DC

Galanxhi H, Nah F (2007) Deception in cyberspace: a comparison of text-only vs avatar-supported medium. Int J Hum Comput Stud 65:770–783

Granhag P, Vrij A, Verschuere B (eds) (2015) Detecting deception: current challenges and cognitive approaches. Wiley-Blackwell, Chichester, UK

Gupta S, Skillicorn D (2006) Improving a textual deception detection model. In: Proceedings of the conference of the Center for Advanced Studies on Collaborative Research, Riverton, NJ, US, p. 29

Heuer R (1982) Cognitive factors in deception and counterdeception. In: Daniel D, Herbig K (eds) Strategic military deception. Pergamon, New York, pp 31–69

Houston P, Floyd M, Carnicero S (2013) Spy the lie: former CIA officers teach you how to detect deception. St. Martin's Griffin, New York

Janis I (1983) Groupthink: psychological studies of policy decisions and fiascos, 2nd edn. Houghton Mifflin, Boston

Lane J, DePaulo B (1999) Completing Coyne's cycle: dysphorics' ability to detect deception. J Res Pers 33:311–329

Lydon J, Zanna M (1990) Commitment in the face of adversity: a value-affirmation approach. J Pers Soc Psychol 58(6):1040–1047

McCormick P (2013) Detecting deception. Looseleaf Law, New York

Miller G, Mongeau P, Sleight C (1986) Fudging with friends and lying to lovers. J Soc Pers Relat 3:495–512

Miller G, Stiff J (1993) Deceptive communications. Sage, Newbury Park, UK

Nettler G (1974) Explaining crime. McGraw-Hill, New York

Qin T, Burgoon J, Nunamaker J (2004) An exploratory study of promising cues in deception detection and application of decision tree. Proc. 37th Hawaii international conference on system sciences, Waikoloa, HI, US, 5–8 January 2004

Searcy W, Nowicki S (2005) The evolution of animal communication: reliability and deception in signaling systems. Princeton University Press, Princeton, NJ

Smith H (1953) The compleat practical joker. Doubleday, Garden City, NY

Steller M, Kohnken G (1989) Criteria-based content analysis. In: Raskin D (ed) Psychological methods in criminal investigation and evidence. Springer, New York, pp 217–245

Sundar S (ed) (2015) The handbook of the psychology of communication technology. Wiley-Blackwell, Chichester, UK

Sztompka P (1999) Trust. Cambridge University Press, London, UK

Tavel M (2016) The lie detector test revisited: a great example of junk science. Skeptical Inquirer 40(1):36–41

Toma C, Hancock J (2010) Reading between the lines: linguistic clues to deception in online dating profiles. In: Proceedings of the ACM conference on computer supported cooperative work, 6–10 Feb, Savannah, GA, US. pp. 5–8

Vrij A (2000) Detecting lies and deceit: the psychology of lying and the implications for professional practice. Wiley, Chichester, UK

Wilson S (2002) Seeking and resisting compliance: why people say what they do when trying to influence others. Sage, Thousand Oaks, CA

Zahavi A, Zahavi A (1997) The handicap principle: a missing piece of Darwin's puzzle. Oxford University Press, New York

Chapter 3
Professional Deception

N.C. Rowe, J. Rrushi, *Introduction to Cyberdeception*,
DOI 10.1007/978-3-319-41187-3_3

Deliberate deception of certain kinds is acceptable to most societies. These examples will not only suggest tactics for cyberspace, but some of the problems and pitfalls deceivers can encounter. We discuss here three prominent areas of acceptable deception by professionals.

3.1 Military Deception

Deception is a key component of military strategy and tactics, and has a long history in warfare (Dunnigan and Nofi 2001; Latimer 2003; Rothstein and Whaley 2013). It is one of several "force multipliers" that can increase the strength or the effectiveness of a fighting force with few additional resources. It is particularly important for the weaker antagonist in a conflict, as it can compensate for forces or weapons. Compared to many of their adversaries in cyberspace, the United States and other developed countries are actually more vulnerable to cyberattacks because of their more extensive cyber infrastructures, and thus deception can be relatively more useful for them in cyberspace than in conventional warfare.

We will use the term "cyberwarfare" for warfare in cyberspace, including both offensive and defensive techniques. Many countries now have cyberwarfare teams in their military organizations (Carr 2010; Andress and Winterfeld 2013). The term "information warfare" is used as a more general term than "cyberwarfare" that includes such things as attacking communications and using propaganda.

A good example of the importance of military deception is the Allied D-Day landings in Normandy in June of 1944 (Breuer 1993; Holt 2010). Landing on beaches controlled by well-prepared German forces was dangerous. Improving the chances of success and reducing possible casualties required a well-orchestrated deception plan. Since the Allies could not hide their massing of forces for an invasion, the main deception sought to convince the Germans as to its location, by providing clues it would occur at the narrowest part of English Channel near Calais, rather than at the true target of Normandy. This is plausible because it is easiest to cross at the narrowest part of a strait. So the forces massed in southeast England near Calais were made to appear larger, while the forces in southwest England were made to appear smaller. This included having in the southeast more outdoor activities, brighter lighting of the facilities, and fake boats and other fake equipment. The deceptions were supported by displays developed for German aerial reconnaissance and by reports sent by blackmailed German spies. But the most effective deception tactic involved fake radio traffic made to convince the Germans that a much larger army existed in the southeast. The German army was so well convinced by these deceptions that they thought the initial Normandy landings were just feints for a true attack to come at Calais, and it took them almost a week to fully realize their error.

Military deception is most effective when it is tailored to a specific adversary and situation. Military adversaries can be:

- Foreign governments: These may or may not be suspicious because they have many things to worry about.

- Military personnel: These are planning for conflict and tend to be suspicious.
- Spies: These are looking for particular kinds of information while operating clandestinely. Since they are experienced deceivers themselves, they are often difficult to deceive.
- Hackers or amateur attackers: These may provide irritation, but can on occasion offer serious threats. Most are not expecting deceit and can be fooled.
- Quasi-government organizations like terrorist groups: These have particular political agendas and are not constrained by international law. Their susceptibility to deception can vary widely.
- Information-warfare specialists for cyberwarfare: These are technical people and thus will require sophisticated methods to combat. Heckman et al. (2015) provides an approach to planning for these people.

Deception in warfare is accepted by nearly all ethical systems. Deception in warfare is also generally legal by international law. But there are exceptions that are illegal such as "perfidy" or impersonating a neutral party.

3.1.1 The Role of Deception in Military Activities

Deception in warfare can serve several purposes (Whaley 2007). First, it can cause an adversary to misjudge our strength or resources in planning for or responding to actions. If we make an adversary think we are stronger than we really are, we may discourage them from attacking or counterattacking us for fear they may lose. We can do this by exhibiting false clues to a stronger potential than we really have. Alternatively, if we make an adversary think we are weaker than we really are, we may be able to encourage them to attack or counterattack and then either learn something about their methods or deal them a crushing and justified counterattack. We can do this by concealing our true strength or by appearing inept and confused. Both these strategies can be useful for defense in cyberspace, because the first can scare away cyber attacks and the second can aid honeypots, systems designed to better learn about attack methods. Deception is particularly suited to military cyber defense as part of its "defense in depth" doctrine (Tirenin and Faatz 1999). Chinese military thinking has long given high importance to deception (Yoshihara 2005).

Deception is also essential for intelligence gathering about an adversary. Naturally an adversary does not want us to know about their resources. So we either need to send spies who conceal their true identities, or collect data in a nonobvious way that we can aggregate to learn something about the adversary. In cyberspace, honeypots and spyware (spying by software) can best collect intelligence if they deceive as to their true purposes. Deception by providing false information can also impede an adversary trying to gather intelligence about us.

Deception is also essential if we are to surprise an adversary during conflict. If we attack them at a surprising place or time, or use surprising weapons, or use surprising tactics, we can benefit from concealing that innovation until the last moment so that we can get more power from the surprise. Deception is also valuable after an attack as a way to conceal the effects of the attack. If an attacking adversary does not know how badly they hurt us, they may fail to take advantage of their gains or waste time in repeated attacks on an already-destroyed target.

For all these reasons, deceptions are a key part of military planning. U.S. military doctrine for many organizations requires making a deception plan for every operations plan, a plan that supports it to make it more effective. For instance, when planning an attack, the deception plan should specify measures to take to conceal the location, time, equipment, and size of the attack.

Military deception can be offensive or defensive. Defenders can use deception to protect themselves and attackers can use it to strengthen their attacks. However, different deceptive techniques are appropriate for defenders than those appropriate for attackers: Defenders need more camouflage and concealment deceptions because they often have more assets to protect, whereas attackers need more lying and misrepresenting deceptions, as we shall discuss in Chaps. 4 and 5. Nonetheless, the range of deceptions available to an attacker is similar to the range available to a defender. This is, in fact, a motivation for this book, since defensive deceptions in cyberspace ought to be much more used than they are currently, judging by the military analogy.

3.1.2   Principles of Military Deception

Fowler and Nesbit (1995) provides six useful principles of deception in warfare that are more directly helpful for cyberdeception than the general principles of Chap. 2. These were developed for targeting in warfare where quick decisions must be made, but the principles extend well to cyberspace.

- Deception should tell the adversary what they want to know. In warfare, it works best to fool the adversary into thinking you will attack in a way that they expect you will attack rather than fool them into thinking you will attack in a way that they do not expect. Similarly in cyberspace, you will have more success if you make the deception something that they wish were true, such as that you are stupid and inept compared to them. On the other hand, you will find it difficult to convince the attacker that their attack tool is malfunctioning when they do not expect it or like to hear that. Note that adversary expectations can be manipulated to some degree in advance by repetition. For instance, if you have a troop exercise every week, they will be expecting a troop exercise and that is what they want to see.
- Deception should involve timely feedback. This is related to the principle in Chap. 2 that deceptive responses should neither be too fast or too slow. If we respond too quickly in cyberspace, it appears we did not seriously try to address the request or command; if we respond too slowly, it appears we are trying to stall. But also, if we respond with irregular delays, that may be suspicious too. The word "feedback" can mean two things here: The feedback we offer a deceivee

to confirm the deception, and the feedback the deceivee offers to us about whether the deception worked; both are important.

- Deception should be integrated with operations. That is, it should be tied to some specific goal rather than just trying to confuse. In warfare, this means there is no sense deceiving until you have some good reason such as an operation that can benefit from it. In cyberspace, this principle argues against focusing too much on honeypots as decoy computers, since honeypots are just collecting data passively. Instead, it could be better to focus on deceiving when being attacked. However, some deceptions only work when we have previously established baseline behavior to compare against.
- Deception should act to conceal or divert attention from critical activities. That means that deception is not helpful unless it protects something important or creates significant trouble for an adversary, since any discovered deception tends to create distrust that makes future deceptions more difficult. So in cyberspace defense we should only deceive on critical things such as the integrity of our operating system and not on minor things such as the wording of a Web site.
- Deception should be tailored to the task so the enemy will notice it, but should not be excessively obvious. If we are trying to deceive an adversary about the number of sites we have, we should leave sufficiently obvious deceptive clues about them that will ensure the adversary will notice, but not so many clues that it looks like we are trying to fool them. For this it is helpful to obtain feedback from the adversary, either from previous deceptions or in real time.
- Deception should be imaginative and not stereotyped. This is because deception patterns can be recognized by adversaries and ignored. This is a problem in conventional warfare because much military training encourages stereotyped behavior. In cyberspace, we can avoid stereotypical behavior by using some randomness in our deception choices, and imagination can be helped by using the artificial-intelligence methods for planning deceptions that Chap. 12 discusses. The many options discussed in this book do suggest that cyberdeception can be highly varied.

3.1.3   Counterintelligence

An important part of military operations is intelligence gathering about the adversary (Shulsky 1993). This includes spying but also less glamorous methods of dogged information collection. "Counterintelligence" means methods to interfere with or stop intelligence gathering by an adversary, often involving procedures to maintain secrecy, and the concept applies to cyberspace as well as the real world. Cyberattackers can be considered adversaries in cyberspace, and counterintelligence for cyberspace can mean trying to figure out what they are up to.

Deception is very helpful for counterintelligence. Deception makes it easier to conceal secrets, and cyberspace offers many places to hide things. But more interestingly, counterintelligence can design fake secrets for spies to find. Fake secrets could cause an adversary to waste resources on fruitless measures, question the effectiveness of their spies that found the fake secrets, and give us valuable intelligence about the adversary's intelligence capabilities. Furthermore, if we label fake secrets in some unique way—such as having slightly different fake secrets stored in different places—that can enable us to identify the copy seen by the adversary. For instance, if we give a slightly different time and place for the attack, we can see for what time and place the adversary makes preparations. This will help us track down vulnerabilities and spies. Fakes can also be built on a larger scale, as when we prepare a decoy cybersystem or an entire fake military network in the hope that an adversary will attack it instead of the real systems and networks.

Doing counterintelligence well requires a special set of skills (Whaley and Busby 2002). Counterintelligence personnel must be suspicious, certainly, but they must also have a flexibility of mind that permits seeing ways the adversary might think. They tend not fit into organizations well because they need to be independent thinkers, since often they need to see past a deception plan of the adversary. People that have these skills are rare and not usually found in military organizations, so recruitment is a key issue. Counterintelligence for cybersystems will require an equally unusual set of skills.

Counterintelligence has a price of decreased efficiency in conducting normal operations. It requires additional planning and work that merely prevents a hypothetical threat. Nonetheless, it is often justified as part of the cost of running a military organization, and should increasingly be considered part of the cost of running a cybersystem.

3.2 Stage Magic

Entertainment in all its forms—artwork, written fiction, theater, radio, and film—usually involves deception in the form of people pretending to be someone else. However, one form of entertainment heavily emphasizes deception, stage magic. It is useful to study its deception techniques, honed by years of experience with what works and what does not (Schneider 2011), to plan cyberdeceptions.

3.2.1 Practices of Stage Magic

Effective stage magic involves much care, since as Chap. 2 points out, deceptions can easily be undone by inconsistent details. In addition, the audience of stage magic knows in advance that it is going to be deceived, which makes the deception even more difficult. Contrary to popular belief, most of the deceptions of magicians are not special apparatus but just good planning based on the psychology of the audience. (Nelms 1969) provides a good introduction to the psychological aspect, usually called "showmanship".

Often the deception is accomplished by small details such as quick motions ("sleight of hand") or use of confederates. Magicians often have many ways to

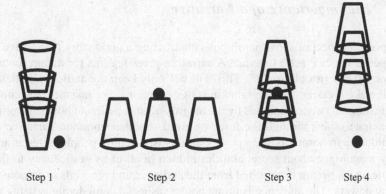

Step 1   Step 2   Step 3   Step 4

Fig. 3.1 The cups and balls trick as perceived

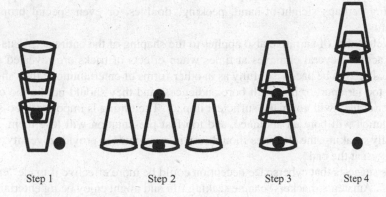

Step 1   Step 2   Step 3   Step 4

Fig. 3.2 The cup-and-balls trick as executed

accomplish a trick based on these details. Exploiting this variety makes it harder for an audience to see how it is being deceived. Variety also provides "outs" or alternatives if something goes wrong with one method. That suggests that cyberdeception should choose among many alternatives too.

A classic example is the "cups and balls" illusion, which is at least 500 years old. While there are many variants on this trick, usually a magician shows the audience a stack of cups nested inside one another, then proceeds to place them upside-down on a table in a row (Fig. 3.1). The magician usually demonstrates how solid the cups are by tapping on them. A ball or some other small object is placed on top of the bottom of one of the cups, then the other cups are nested on top of it. After some "stage business" such as waving a wand, the nested set of cups is pulled up, revealing the ball underneath. It appears to have passed through the bottom of a cup. The main trick is that there is a second ball already hidden in the cups when they are placed, identical in appearance to the other ball (Fig. 3.2). Most people mistakenly think they can see an object falling out of a cup when it is turned over quickly.

3.2.2   The Importance of a Narrative

An important aspect of showmanship is constructing a good story ("narrative") to link a performance ("act") together. A narrative gives reasons for the presentation so it not just a series of "tricks". This will not only keep the audience's attention but will make it easier to do certain kinds of deceptions. For instance, the cup and balls illusion can be accompanied by the magician's discussion of how solid objects can penetrate others through the force of mind. Another common narrative concerns hidden paranormal powers possessed unsuspected by people; after an introductory monologue about secret abilities hidden in all of us (a nice way to flatter the audience), a person is recruited from the audience and proceeds to demonstrate amazing powers. The audience is prone not to suspect a confederate is being used if they are dressed and act like a typical audience member. The flattering of the audience also makes it rather churlish to suspect deception. Of course, other deceptions may be needed to accomplish the demonstration of paranormal powers including perhaps sleight-of-hand, peeking, doubles, or even special props or apparatus.

Development of narrative also applies to the shaping of the entire act. Usually a magic act has several climaxes at times when effects of tricks are revealed. The climaxes need to be paced carefully as in other forms of entertainment; they should not be too far apart or they will bore audiences, and they should not be too close together or they will not make sufficient impact. The timing is important; too-slow presentation will bore an audience, and too-fast presentation will lose them. And generally speaking, the climaxes should vary in magnitude to provide diversity, with the biggest at the end.

This suggests that cyberspace deception could be more effective if made "entertaining". Amateurs (hackers) can be seeking fun and might enjoy being entertained. Timing is important in cyberspace, and in fact even more important than with magic because cybersystems are often predictable. Entertainment also means providing increasingly difficult deceptions for attackers as they penetrate into our systems. We should first try some simpler deceptions, and then increasingly complex ones if attackers do not go away. But consistent with magic, we should intersperse deceptions with plenty of honest responses to attack actions. Alternatively, we could try to construct a narrative which explains why our cybersystem cannot accommodate the attacker, such as it being new or poorly designed.

Another aspect of a narrative is character roles. Magicians usually give themselves a persona such as a paranormal explorer, a scientist, a romantic, or a jokester. The illusions then are tied into motivations for this character, much as the way an actor ties their actions to their character's motivations. A bit of something similar can be done for a cybersystem by giving it a character based on how friendly, reliable, complex, and communicative it is, consistent with the deceptions it practices.

3.2.3 Psychology for Magic

Much of stage magic depends on exploiting human psychology. This can include establishing an atmosphere conducive to suspension of disbelief through development of a world different from our own. This can be a world of paranormal or new kinds of scientific phenomena. It can also involve an element of danger to the magician (as in daring escapes) or other forms of difficulty for the magician (as in discovering secrets). Much of other kinds of effective entertainment involves establishing such worlds or feelings different from our normal ones. There is another reason for danger and difficulty too: It helps to get the audience to identify with the magician by feeling his or her stresses. Cyberspace is its own world, with a different feel from the real world. It may be useful to get an attacker to identify with the site they are attacking by getting them to identify in some way in their target, such as working with it to accomplish goals.

People often think that magic is heavily focused on misdirection and redirection, such as getting the audience to watch one part of the stage when deception is occurring on another part of the stage. Actually, it is desirable to minimize the need for redirection as much as possible, although it is necessary for certain effects. It is hard to ensure that every member of the audience is looking in the desired direction since gaze is evanescent. Similarly in cyberspace, a deception should not depend on the deceivee's failure to notice something because different victims may notice different things. But some misdirection and redirection away from key details in cyberspace can be helpful in accomplishing a cyberdeception.

Magicians also exploit knowledge that the audience does not have. For instance, locks and confinements can open in nonstandard ways that only the magician knows. Hidden wires and mirrors can confuse the senses. There can be copies of objects and people (doubles) where the audience only expects one; the cups and balls illusion depends on presence of a second ball. There can be similar phenomena in cyberspace where deceiver knows more details than it tells a deceivee about, as when a deceiving attacker provides concealed malicious software (a "Trojan horse") to a defender.

Magicians also exploit a cognitive limitation of people, the difficulty of following a lengthy series of events and actions. When too many things happen, the audience gets confused. This is often done with "sleight of hand" illusions. The effect can be intensified by increased speed. Similarly, it is easy for automated systems in cyberspace to overwhelm users with more details than they could conceivably follow within a limited time period.

3.2.4 Minimization of Deception

Although everyone knows that magicians are doing deceptions, is it often desirable for magicians to minimize their number. That is because deception is most effective if used sparingly, the principle of "conservation of effect". So magicians practice a good deal with the goal of minimizing unnecessary deceptions and even the appearance of deception. Serious magicians practice hand feints repeatedly to make them as smooth as possible, since jerky motions are a clue to deception that many people can recognize. The cups and balls illusion benefits from smoothness of practiced motions.

Only when a trick depends on something out of the ordinary that cannot be easily concealed will misdirection or redirection really help. One good strategy is to set up the next trick during the previous trick when people are not expecting it. Generally speaking, it is not a good idea to explain exactly what will happen in advance, to better conceal the deceptions when the audience does not see where the magician is going. But generally speaking, audiences do not like surprises unless they have been somewhat forewarned. Magic is a game and audiences like to feel some degree of control.

In cyberspace, the equivalent of practice by a magician is designing deceptions in advance by software. With plenty of advance planning, deceptions can be analyzed carefully to ensure they are as convincing as possible by being consistent and plausible. Then just like a good magician, cyberspace deceivers need to monitor their "audience" to see if their deceptions are working, and try something else if they are not. Perhaps deceivers can drop some "bait" to assess the deceivee's level of expertise by observing if they exploit them. But the "audience" for defensive cyberdeceptions should not be made comfortable, and a few surprises might be a good idea, unlike with stage magic.

3.3   Marketing

Another legitimate and accepted application of deliberate deception is in the marketing area of business operations (Powell 2014). Every business tries to get consumers to use its products and services. Since often a product or service is not significantly better in quality than similar competing products or services, modest deception is an acceptable business practice to stimulate business (Akerlof and Shiller 2015). Modest deception or "misleading" is acceptable, but stronger deception can be unacceptable or prosecutable as fraud. In the United States, the Federal Trade Commission has oversight on business fraud and makes decisions about the boundary line.

3.3.1   Types of Marketing and Their Deceptions

There are many ways to categorize marketing, and one of the simplest starts from the "four P's" of marketing (McCarthy 1960), to each of which deception can be attached.

- Product: The purveyor tries to explain why the product or service is desirable for purchase. Marketing exaggerates properties of the product, or in the worst cases, alleges false properties of the product. For instance, weight-loss products sold on the Internet are usually fraudulent, but many desperate consumers buy them.

- Place: The purveyor sells from a reputable location in a reputable way. Marketing tries to make the seller look more reputable than they really are. For instance, phishing on the Internet can copy the graphics of legitimate bank Web sites for the purpose of identity theft.
- Price: The purveyor's product is reasonably priced. Marketing can pretend the product is "on sale" or at a discount, add extra charges to the advertised price on a variety of excuses, or require money with no intention of actually delivering the product. For instance, Internet scams often associated with Nigeria repeatedly request victim's money with the lure of a forthcoming large payout.
- Promotion: The public understands the significance of the purveyor's product from disseminated information, especially its comparative advantages over competing products. Marketing can promise features and advantages that it cannot deliver, or make inaccurate comparisons. For instance, drugs sold on the Internet at low prices are usually not the drug claimed, or a credit-card interest rate can be mentioned while failing to mention how long it will be valid.

3.3.2   Deceptive Marketing in Cyberspace

Deceptive marketing is a serious problem in cyberspace. Because consumers lack important kinds of feedback they get with real-world purchases (Sundar 2015)—the building the purveyor operates from, the demeanor of the salesperson, the feel of the goods for sale, the presence of redress mechanisms if they do not get what was promised—cyberspace is more congenial to deception or fraud in marketing (Mintz 2002; Seife 2015). Deception is aided by the size and impersonality of many businesses operating in cyberspace (Penny 2005).

Cyberspace is also well suited to automation of marketing deception. Spam is basically automated marketing and is often deceptive (Spammer 2004). Spam exploits a large volume of mailings in the hope of getting a few responses; since sending it can be very cheap, a purveyor is willing to accept a low response rate. Cyberspace is also a good place for short-term marketing of a few days duration, since it is easy to add and remove new sites for short periods of time. Both these reasons support easy fraud in cyberspace. A typical Internet fraud involves a 1-day spam campaign based in a country with lax cybercrime laws.

Some particular techniques associated with deception in marketing on the Internet (Xiao and Benbasat 2007) include:

- Vagueness: Claims that are hard to disprove because they are overly general or do not have clear evaluation standards. For instance, claims that a product will make you look younger are hard to disprove due to placebo effects.
- Shilling: Saying good things about a product in a supposedly neutral forum. For instance, marketers have logged in anonymously to discussion groups to say good things about their product without identifying their connection to it.
- Negative puffery: Saying bad things about a competing product in a supposedly neutral forum. For instance, restaurants have bad-mouthed their competitors in restaurant discussion groups.

- Steering: Some Internet search engines list results to queries from paid sponsors first, but do not identify which are paid sponsors. Since users are more likely to visit the first-listed sites first, this increases the business of paid sponsors.
- Bait-and-switch: Offering a great deal on one product with the goal of steering the consumer to another product. This can be legitimate (as with "loss leaders") if not too deceptive, but overt forms can be prosecuted as fraud.
- Identity deception: Pretending to be someone or something you are not, such as phishers pretending to be banks.
- Fronts: Internet sites working for only a short time that pretend to be legitimate businesses while they provide no goods or services, just collect money from consumers.
- Counterfeits: Fraudulent documents that are easy to create on computers.
- Embedding: Product references that are embedded in television, movies, magazines, games, etc. This has been increasingly popular recently because consumers get overwhelmed with traditional advertising.

See www.fraudwatchinternational.com for recent trends. All of these can be exploited by cyberattackers. Again, some of these forms are legal and some are not, depending on the jurisdiction and the time.

3.3.3   Deception with Software Marketing

One particular focus of marketing deception is software. Unlike most commercial products, it is often hard to tell if software does what it claims to do. Software can be so complex that it is impossible for the consumer to test it thoroughly, and untested software can demonstrate unexpected bugs that prevent it from functioning properly. So many software vendors market early and buggy versions of their products, then depend on consumers to do much of their necessary testing to discover bugs. Software marketed for security purposes (such as firewalls, malware checkers, cryptographic tools, and intrusion-detection systems) is particularly prone to low quality since it is hard for the consumer to see if it is working at all—only occasionally does an attack trigger the software to test it and make the software noticeable. Most security software needs to be updated frequently as threats change, and not all vendors have the resources to keep it up-to-date.

Updates of software can be done automatically on systems connected to the Internet. But this introduces a new vulnerability since attackers want to update your software too in their own way. In addition, vendors can foist unnecessary features on the consumer by automatic updates. So deception can be involved in updates.

The ubiquity of flaws and loopholes in commercial software means that capitalism is not working well in providing good products. This results in a software industry characterized by low-quality near-monopoly products for which the consumer cannot hope very much. It also means that malicious deceptive software can be hard to recognize, even if poorly designed, considering the many flaws of nondeceptive software. Hence there is a good opportunity for the methods of this book.

3.4   Conclusions

Deliberate deception is an accepted practice already in certain areas of human activity, and in these areas there are professionals whose job is to construct good deceptions. Deception is essential to military operations on both the offensive and defensive sides, and experience has taught military commanders some important principles of deception. Deception is also essential to stage magic, where its use provides useful principles for real-time management of deliberate deception. Finally, deception is essential to the marketing of products as a tool to gain important competitive advantages; much of this involves studying the psychology of the consumer and finding fresh ways to exploit it.

3.5   Exercises

1. The D-Day deceptions were quite elaborate, and elaborate deceptions are more likely to fail since they offer more opportunities for the deceiver to make a mistake. Why was an elaborate deception appropriate for D-Day? Give another situation that justifies an elaborate deception despite its risks.
2. Besides appealing to their ego, what other ways could a deceptive cybersystem tell attackers want they want to hear? Give at least three examples.
3. Give an example of a defensive cyberdeception that is not critical to foiling the plans of a cyberattacker, and give an example that is. Why might noncritical deceptions still be useful?
4. Give examples of deceptions in cyberspace that are very likely for a victim to notice, and give examples of deceptions that are unlikely for an victim to notice.
5. Variants on the cups and balls illusion require betting on which cup the ball is under (or under which "shell", hence the term "shell game"). How could the added concept of betting contribute to the illusion?
6. Suppose you are trying to fool an online victim with whom you are communicating by email. Discuss the advantages and disadvantages of having evenly spaced "climaxes" of your deceptions with them.
7. Give an example of an interesting "narrative" involving alleged problems with a cybersystem that a cyberattacker could create to aid in their offensive deception against a human user of a cybersystem.
8. Give two examples of where an online attacker could be usefully fooled by providing so much detail to them that they cannot follow.
9. Discuss how an online hacker forum could be exploited effectively to encourage attackers to attack a particular site where you try to entrap them. Just mentioning the site is probably not enough.
10. Discuss how a bait-and-switch approach could be used to encourage visits to particular Web sites.

11. Suppose you want people to install your spyware for monitoring their online purchases. What deceptions could you use to get them to install it while not overtly engaging in fraud as defined by the laws of your country?

References

Akerlof A, Shiller R (2015) Phishing for phools: the economics of manipulation and deceit. Princeton University Press, Princeton, NJ

Andress J, Winterfeld S (2013) Cyber warfare, second edition: techniques, tactics, and tools for security. Syngress, Waltham, MA

Breuer W (1993) Hoodwinking Hitler: the Normandy deception. Praeger, London

Carr J (2010) Inside cyber warfare: mapping the cyber underworld, 2nd edn. O'Reilly Media, Sebastopol, CA

Dunnigan J, Nofi A (2001) Victory and deceit, second edition: deception and trickery in war. Writers Club, San Jose, CA

Fowler C, Nesbit R (1995) Tactical deception in air-land warfare. Journal of Electronic Defense 18 (6): 37–44 and 76–79

Heckman K, Stech F, Thomas R, Schmoker B, Tsow A (2015) Cyber denial, deception, and counter deception: a framework for supporting active cyber defense. Springer, New York

Holt T (2010) Deceivers: allied military deception in the Second World War. Skyhorse, New York

Latimer J (2003) Deception in war; the art of the bluff, the value of deceit, and the most thrilling episodes of cunning in military history, from the Trojan Horse to the Gulf War. The Overlook, New York

McCarthy J (1960) Basic marketing: a managerial approach. Richard Irwin, Homewood, IL

Mintz A (ed) (2002) Web of deception: misinformation on the Internet. CyberAge, New York

Nelms H (1969) Magic and showmanship: a handbook for conjurers. Dover, Mineola, NY

Penny L (2005) Your call is important to us. Crown, New York

Powell J (2014) Mind control mastery: successful guide to human psychology and manipulation, persuasion, and deception. CreateSpace, North Charleston, SC

Rothstein H, Whaley B (eds) (2013) The art and science of military deception. Artech House, New York

Schneider A (2011) The theory and practice of magic deception. CreateSpace, North Charleston, SC, US

Seife C (2015) Virtual unreality: the new era of digital deception. Penguin, New York

Shulsky A (1993) Silent warfare: understanding the world of intelligence, 2nd edn. Brassey's, Washington, DC

Spammer X (2004) Inside the spam cartel. Syngress, Rockland, MA, US

Sundar S (ed) (2015) The handbook of the psychology of communication technology. Wiley-Blackwell, Chichester, UK

Tirenin W, Faatz D (1999) A concept for strategic cyber defense. In: Proceedings of the Conference on Military Communications, Atlantic City, NJ, US, 31 Oct–3 Nov, 1999. pp. 1: 458–463

Whaley B (2007) Stratagem: deception and surprise in war. Artech House, Boston, MA

Whaley B, Busby J (2002) Detecting deception: practice, practitioners, and theory. In: Godson R, Wirtz J (eds) Strategic denial and deception. Transaction, New Brunswick, NJ, pp 181–219

Xiao B, Benbasat I (2007) Product-related deception in e-commerce: a theoretical perspective. MIS Q 35(1):169–195

Yoshihara T (2005) Chinese information warfare: a phantom menace or emerging threat? www.strategicstudiesinstitute.army.mil/

Chapter 4
Deception Methods for Defense

There are many ways to deceive, and this provides a rich array of methods for cyberdeceptions. We survey here some deception taxonomies (categorizations) that have been proposed. This framework allows us to systematically seek or develop deceptions. This chapter will focus primarily on defensive deceptions, and the next chapter will survey offensive deceptions.

© Springer International Publishing Switzerland 2016
N.C. Rowe, J. Rrushi, *Introduction to Cyberdeception*,
DOI 10.1007/978-3-319-41187-3_4

4.1   Classic Deception Taxonomies

Bell and Whaley (1991) proposed a popular taxonomy of deception methods with six categories in two groups of three:

*   Masking (hiding things in the background).
*   Repackaging (hiding something as something else).
*   Dazzling (hiding something by having it overshadowed by something else).
*   Mimicking (imitating aspects of something else).
*   Inventing (creating new, often "fake", objects to interest the deceivee).
*   Decoying (using diversions unrelated to the object of interest).

Each of these suggests several defensive deceptions in cyberspace. For instance, consider honeypots, computers designed to attract attacks (Qassrawi and Hongli 2010):

*   Masking could be concealing the monitoring of users by the honeypot by modifying the operating system to hide its traces.
*   Repackaging could be embedding of attack-thwarting software within otherwise innocent utilities of a computer's operating system.
*   Dazzling could be sending many error messages to an attacker when they try to do something malicious.
*   Mimicking could be construction of a fake file directory for a honeypot that looks like the file system of a busy user, with the goal of helping convince the attacker it is not a honeypot.
*   Inventing could be a piece of software left in a honeypot for attackers to download that reports their personal data to authorities when run.
*   Decoying could be planting passwords of honeypot Web sites to encourage attackers to log in there.

Each of these also suggests offensive deceptions as well. Masking can be used to conceal an attack, and repackaging and dazzling could assist a masking. Mimicking and inventing are standard tricks of malware.

The main weakness of the Bell and Whaley taxonomy is that it is too general to be much help in deception planning. There are so many things we could repackage and mimic. Still, it provides a starting point.

4.2   Military Taxonomies

We can also look to the military-studies literature for deception taxonomies. Dunnigan and Nofi (2001) proposed a popular taxonomy with these deception types:

*   Concealment.
*   Camouflage.
*   False and planted information (disinformation).
*   Lies.

- Displays (volunteering misleading information).
- Ruses (tricks).
- Demonstrations (showing capabilities but not using them).
- Feints (pretending to attack).
- Insight (anticipating adversary actions).

We enumerate some possible defensive deceptions in cyberspace for this taxonomy, rating them on a scale of 0–10 where 10 means the most effective (Rowe and Rothstein 2004). We list the best defensive deceptions first.

Lies (10): Lies are distinguished from disinformation by being responses to questions or requests. Users of a cybersystem are told many things by its operating system, and they generally assume these statements are completely true. So an occasionally deceptive operating system could be very effective at deceiving. It could lie to prevent an attacker from accessing files and other resources necessary to their attack. Lies could be more effective than explicitly denying access because they encourage an attacker to continue wasting time trying to access the resource in different ways and at different times.

Insights (10): The best methods of deception require knowledge of how the adversary thinks, and then exploit their expectations and plans. A good deceiver can do systematic "counterplanning", analysis with the objective of thwarting or obstructing the adversary's reasoning (Carbonell 1981). Counterplanning is like putting obstacles along adversary routes in conventional warfare. Counterplanning can provide carefully chosen deceptions that can be more effective than constant or random ones.

Displays (6): Displays can be shown for the benefit of the attacker. A convincing honeypot should have a good such display in the form of its file system, to make it appear it has normal usage. The idea can be extended to "honeynets" (The Honeynet Project 2004) where most or all the nodes of a computer network are honeypots, to encourage the attacker to waste time on useless attacks.

False and planted information (5): Disinformation (false information) could be planted on cybersystems or Web sites to divert or confuse attackers. Planted programs could be attack methods that don't work or that permit concealed monitoring of attackers. However, most false information about cybersystems is easy to check by testing or trying it out, so it will not fool anyone very long. And hackers often quickly communicate their discoveries, so news of disinformation on a site may spread fast and ruin the reputation of its provider, just as one mistake can destroy the illusion in stage magic (Tognazzini 1993).

Camouflage (5): Camouflage can work better than concealment in cyberspace since there are so many objects in cyberspace that there is insufficient time to check them all. Valuable files and programs can be given misleading names so it will take a while for an attacker to find them. However, camouflage can impede legitimate users as well as attackers, and will not protect against many attacks such as buffer overflows.

Concealment (4): Although cyberspace can be searched thoroughly by automated methods, concealment is still possible. Concealment is often used by designers of rootkits (replacement operating systems) to hide the fact they control your computer. For instance, they can modify the normal operating system to disable access controls without your knowledge or prevent their own code from being listed with directory-listing utilities. For defensive purposes, it helps for honeypots to conceal their user-monitoring software so they look more like normal machines (The Honeynet Project 2004). Concealment is easier for less concrete notions like intentions. For instance, a cybersystem can ask unnecessary questions of an attacker to delay them without saying why.

Feints (2): Attackers in cyberspace have so many weapons it is hard to encourage them to respond in a way that the defender wants.

Ruses (1): Ruses usually involve impersonation. But they are not very possible in cyberspace where most everything a defender does looks the same. For instance, it would be difficult for a defender to pretend to be a hacker to gain confidences.

Demonstrations (1): Demonstrations of strength are unlikely to scare away attackers in cyberspace—if anything, they will encourage attacks since many attackers like challenges.

4.3   A Taxonomy from Linguistic Case Theory

Another taxonomy can be made using ideas from computational linguistics. To enable cybersystems to reason about language, understanding of words and how they connect to one another is required. Actions (represented by verbs, verbals, and activity nouns) are usually the central entities in sentences to which other entities are associated. These associates are indicated in English by modifiers, prepositional phrases, participial phrases, relative clauses, infinitives, and other constructs. In other languages they may also be signaled by word suffixes and prefixes. The associates are called "semantic cases" (Fillmore 1968) similarly to the syntactic cases that occur in some languages for nouns.

4.3.1   Linguistic-Case Deception Categories

Every deception action can be characterized by an action and an associated semantic case or set of cases. Often deception changes some aspect of one or more cases. However, cases do vary considerably with the associated action, something documented for English by FrameNet (framenet.icsi.berkeley.edu/fndrupal). Some frequently seen cases are given in (Copeck et al. 1992), which we find useful to supplement with two important relationships from artificial intelligence, the upward type-supertype and upward part-whole links, and two speech-act conditions from (Austin 1975), to get 32 broadly useful cases (Rowe 2006) (Table 4.1).

We now describe the cases in more detail.

Table 4.1 Linguistic-case deception taxonomy

Category	Cases
Spatial	Location-at, location-from, location-to, location-through, direction, orientation
Time	Time-at, time-from, time-to, time-through, frequency
Participant	Agent, beneficiary, experiencer, instrument, object, recipient
Causality	Cause, purpose, result, contradiction
Quality	Accompaniment, content, material, measure, value, order, manner
Essence	Superconcept, whole
Speech-act	External precondition, internal precondition

Spatial cases: Location-at (where something occurred), location-from (where it started from), location-to (where it ended), location-through (where it passed through), direction (of the action), and orientation (of the object performing the action). Actions have associated locations, and deception can apply to them. However, the concept of location is somewhat unclear in cyberspace because people can be using more than one computer or device at the same time. It is thus difficult to deceive in "location-at" or "location-through" in cyberspace. Deception in "location-from" or "location-to" is possible since one can try to conceal one's location in defending against an attack. Deception in direction and orientation can happen with actions that are supposed to be one-way like file transfers.

Time cases: Time-at (when something occurred), time-from (when something started), time-to (when something ended), time-through (duration), and frequency (of occurrence). Attacks and defenses can occur anytime in cyberspace, so it hard to make them surprising. Deceivers can change the times of events recorded in a log file or the directory information about files to conceal records of their activities. Deception in frequency occurs in denial-of-service attacks that greatly increase the frequency of requests or transactions to tie up computer resources.

Participant cases: Agent (who initiates the action, beneficiary (who benefits), experiencer (who observes), instrument (what helps accomplish the action), object (what the action is done to), and recipient (who receives the action). Actions have associated participants and objects by which actions are accomplished. Identification of participants responsible for actions ("agents") is a key problem in cyberspace, and easy to deceive about. Deception in objects is also easy: Honeypots deceive as to the hardware and software objects of an attack, and "bait" data such as credit-card numbers can also deceive. Deception is easy with instruments because details of how software accomplishes things are often hidden in cyberspace. Deceptions involving the beneficiary of an action occur with scams. Deception in the "experiencer" occurs with clandestine monitoring of adversary activities.

Causality cases: Cause (of action), purpose (of action), result (of action), and contradiction (what an action contradicts). Deception in cause, purpose, and result is common in "social engineering" (Chap. 10) where false reasons like "I have a deadline" or "It didn't work" are given for requests for actions or information that aid the adversary.

Quality cases: Accompaniment (an additional object associated with the action), content (what is contained within the action object), material (the units out of which the action is composed), measure (any measurement associated with the action), value (the data transmitted by the action, "value" being the software sense of the term), order (with respect to other associated actions), and manner (the way in which the action is done). These cover the way that actions are accomplished. Deception in accompaniment and content occurs with planted disinformation and Trojan horses (concealed malicious software). Deception in value (or in input to a subroutine) can occur defensively as in a ploy of misunderstanding commands or requests. Deception in measure (the amount of data) occurs in denial-of-service attacks involving swamping the attacker with data. Deception in material does not apply much in cyberspace because everything is represented as bits, though one way is simulating commands rather than executing them. Deception in manner and order do not generally apply to cyberspace.

Essence cases: Supertype (a generalization of the action type), and whole (of which the action is a part). Deception can occur in the type and the context to which the action belongs. Phishing email uses supertype deception where what appears to be a request from a service provider is actually an attempt to steal personal data. Similarly, actions can appear to be part of a different plan than the true one, as when a deceiver asks a deceivee to briefly change their password to "test the system" but instead uses that as a loophole to obtain permanent access.

Speech-act cases: External precondition (some necessary condition not under agent control), and internal precondition (some necessary condition under agent control). Deception can also involve semantic cases related to communication. It helps to distinguish internal preconditions on the agent of the action, such as ability of a user to change their password, and external preconditions on the rest of the world such as the ability of a site to accept a particular password. Both provide useful deceptions since it is hard to check such conditions in cyberspace.

This taxonomy is more precise than the previous two in regard to the deception mechanism. For instance, "mimicking" in the Bell and Whaley taxonomy does not distinguish mimicking the agent (as a defender pretending to be a system administrator), mimicking the object (as a single honeypot pretending to be thousands of sites), or mimicking the cause (as in giving a false error message to an attacker). Similarly, "camouflage" in the Dunnigan and Nofi taxonomy does not distinguish between camouflaging the mechanism that logs attacker actions, camouflaging the logging site, or camouflaging the hidden accompaniment to a free download (as with Trojan horses).

4.3.2 Examples of the Deception Cases

To illustrate use of our taxonomy, consider a magician who shows two vertical boxes on either sides of the stage. He puts his assistant into a vertical box, shuts the lid, and locks it with chains. He shows the other box is empty and locks it with chains as well. He then waves his magic wand, unlocks and opens the other box, and the assistant appears to have been magically moved there. Consider the deception cases that could be used to accomplish this trick:

- Deception in external precondition: The assistant uses a hidden exit in the floor to get out of the first box and get into the second box.
- Deception in recipient: There are two twin assistants and the second enters the second box through a hole in its bottom.
- Deception in location-at: Mirrors are used to make the first box appear at the location of the second box.
- Deception in superconcept: The chains appear to prevent access but they can be easily pushed aside to allow entry or exit.
- Deception in instrument: The magic wand appears to have supernatural powers.

As a cyberspace example, consider defensive deceptions for deliberate obstruction of rootkit installation:

1. An attacker gets access a site through a buffer overflow.
2. The overflow is recognized by software on the site and the session is secretly moved to a safer machine.
3. The attacker tries to copy files from their home site using the FTP file-transfer program, but are told the network is down.
4. They try to copy files using SFTP, another file-transfer program, but the files are garbled in transit.
5. They successfully manage to send files from their home site using email.
6. When they try to copy the files into operating-system directories, they receive an error message that "the directory is protected" although it is not.

Here the initial defensive deception is in object and "location-at" for the site. Then there are two deceptions in external preconditions, one in value, and one in both cause and external precondition. Having multiple deceptions increases the chances of thwarting the attacker.

4.3.3   Rating the Case-Grammar Defensive Deception Methods for Defense

The linguistic cases vary considerably in suitability for defense in cyberspace, and it is helpful to rate them for guidance in deception planning. The following ratings for suitability take into account the statistics of observed attack types from security-survey sites such as www.securitystats.com, and our own literature survey and analysis of feasibility and effectiveness. We are assuming that the major offensive threats in cyberspace are in decreasing order of importance: (1) rootkit installation; (2) viruses and worms; (3) theft of secrets; (4) fraud; (5) sabotage; (6) denial of service; (7) theft of services; (8) site defacement. Besides the issues discussed below, some ways of presenting the deceptions will be more persuasive than others (Fogg 2003), an issue discussed more in Sect. 4.5 and Chaps. 9 and 11. Again, we rate suitability on a scale of 0–10 where 10 means most suitable.

- External precondition (10): Give a false excuse as to why you cannot do something that an attacker wants. Chapter 9 discusses this tactic in detail. Excuses are common tactics (Snyder et al. 1983), and in cyberspace they can exploit the frequent cryptic or erroneous error messages with which we are all very familiar.
- Result (9): Lie about what a command did, as in saying a file was downloaded when it was not, or by saying that a command failed when it was ignored. Chapter 9 gives details of this. A common form is to lie about failure to do a requested action you do not want to do. Users of cybersystems often accept unexplained failures when executables get damaged, so they are often willing to accept outright lies by software. It can also mean simulating a vulnerability so that an attacker thinks they have compromised your system when they have not (Qassrawi and Hongli 2010).
- Content (9): Plant disinformation in computer files for an attacker to find. Chapter 7 discusses more details. Much fake data in cybersystems is easy to build, although fake prose requires skill (Gerwehr et al. 2000). Doctored images can be powerful disinformation, and are increasingly easy to construct (Hutchinson and Warren 2001). Deception in content also includes modifying programs to do unexpected things, as Trojan horses in email attachments that claim useful functions but actually insert malware into cybersystems. Deception in content can also be failure to perform an avowed purpose, such as an ineffective program for encrypting your messages that allows anyone to read them.
- Time-through (8): Delay someone by pretending that a computation is taking a long time. Chapter 6 discusses details. This is especially good against denial-of service attacks since they need speed; delays can also simulate a successful attack while maintaining normal service for other users.
- Purpose (8): Pretend to be a different kind of site than you really are. Honeypots do this, and networks of honeypots can be created using old real data suitably modified. Or ask questions that will help trace an attacker. Chapters 8 and 10 cover aspects of this.
- Experiencer (8): Monitor the attacker through hidden logging to a secure remote site that the attacker cannot erase, as with honeypots, or pretend to report events to law enforcement. Chapter 10 discusses this idea.
- Value (7): Systematically misunderstand commands, as by losing the first character in every command line or by encrypting a file when not asked. Or deliberately follow a procedure incorrectly that has been requested in a social-engineering attack, such as calling the wrong office to get a new password. Chapter 10 discusses this idea.
- Cause (7): Give a false error message such as "segmentation error". This is often coupled to deception in result, and Chap. 9 discusses this idea. Good excuses can refer to causes that a deceivee does not understand, but it can be hard to estimate their degree of understanding.

- Object (7): Camouflage software objects to confuse the attacker or provide Trojan horses. Chapter 8 discusses this. Malicious software can conceal itself from directory-listing programs, but hiding files that should normally be present is suspicious. Phishing-type attacks involving camouflaged sites can trick people into giving information. Bait such as false credit-card numbers and passwords are another form of deception in object (Cohen and Koike 2003).
- Frequency (7): Give too much information to someone to overwhelm them, as a kind of defensive denial-of-service attack. Dazzle the attacker with so many fake sites or files that they cannot find the real ones (Cohen 1999), or ask for confirmation on every command. Chapters 6 and 7 relate to this.
- Measure (6): Create messages or files that are unexpectedly large, analogously to deception in frequency. Chapter 6 relates to this.
- Location-to (6): Deceptively forward attacker commands to a less-dangerous environment ("sandbox"), as in "honeypot farms" (Vrable et al. 2005).
- Internal precondition (6): Give a false excuse for command failure alleging internal problems like overloading or new software. Also, a target of social engineering can pretend to be inept to encourage an attacker to underestimate them. Chapter 9 relates to this.
- Supertype (5): Provide a decoy (unharmable copy) for important site (like a critical-infrastructure one).
- Agent (4): Run a "sting" on a phishing scam by pretending to be a foolable consumer, then trace the money. Or pretend to be a hacker and chat with other hackers to collect intelligence.
- Accompaniment (4): Send a Trojan horse to the attacker by encouraging them to download software containing it.
- Direction (3): Deceptively transfer files with Trojan horses back to the attacker at the same time they send files to you.
- Material (3): "Emulate" (simulate hardware in software) to provide a safe imitation of a target computer, as was done in testing attacks in the DETER testbed (www.deter.org).
- Location-from (2): Try to scare an attacker by fake messages from law enforcement.
- Time-at (2): Falsify directory time information.
- Whole (2): Ask occasional questions of an attacker during chat to help identify them.
- Time-from (1): Falsify directory time information.
- Time-to (1): Similar to the preceding.
- Instrument (1): Do something an unexpected way.
- Location-at (0)
- Location-through (0)
- Orientation (0)
- Beneficiary (0)
- Recipient (0)
- Contradiction (0)
- Manner (0)
- Order (0)

4.3.4   An Example Putting the Deceptions Together

As an example of a full defensive deception plan, suppose we create a "honeynet" (network of honeypots) to fool attackers of a military network. The honeynet could have the names of real military sites (deception in object, supertype, and "location-to") with real-looking data (deception in object and content). Its data could be real data with modified dates and times (deception in "time-from" and "time-to"), and could refer to false locations (deception in "location-at") and fake people (deception in agent). The system could secretly report user commands to a secure remote site (deception in experiencer). If the attacker wants to launch an attack from the honeynet after gaining a foothold on it, the system could lie that the outgoing network connection is down (deception in external precondition) or is being debugged (deception in internal precondition). When the attacker wants to download files, the system could lie that the download software is not working (deception in external precondition); or it could observe that files are not being copied properly today (deception in effect); or it could deliberately damage the files in transit (deception in content); or it could deliberately delay the transfer a long time (deception in "time-through"). To irritate the attacker, it could ask repeatedly for confirmation (deception in frequency) or report unnecessary information about processing status (deception in measure). It could also secretly transfer the attacker to a safer "sandbox" site (deception in "location-to"), or send Trojan horses back to the attacker as the attacker downloads files (deception in accompaniment and direction). Putting deceptions together this way can have a synergistic effect in which they are more effective together than they are individually.

4.4   Second-Order Deceptions

"Second-order" deceptions occur after a first deception is detected by the deceivee, maybe prompted deliberately by the deceiver. They are also called "double bluffing". They primarily involve participant, causal, and speech-act cases, since detection of deception affects perceptions about who participates, why they do it, and the preconditions they recognize. For instance, a defender can do rather transparent external-precondition deceptions in an attempt to seem inept, to better fool the attacker with simultaneous subtler deceptions in material and accompaniment as by transferring Trojan horses back to them. Similarly, an attacker can try an obvious denial-of-service attack, a deception in frequency, to camouflage a subtler attack such as a buffer overflow to get administrator privileges, a deception in measure and value. Third-order and higher-order deceptions do not make much sense, however, much in the way that counter-counter deception is hard to distinguish from plain deception.

Multiple first-order deceptions provide many opportunities for second-order deceptions. For instance, a defender can be quite obvious during file downloads about delaying by asking unnecessary confirmations, while at the same time modifying the executable files in transit to prevent them from working once installed.

This is a second-order deception in internal precondition at the same time as more obvious first-order deceptions in "time-through", frequency, and external preconditions make it appear that the defender is inept.

4.5   Resource Deception

An interesting special kind of deception that arises frequently in cyberspace defense is resource deception, deceiving someone about access to resources. Attackers exploit resources of cybersystems to accomplish their nefarious ends. If we can deceive them into thinking that necessary resources for their attack are not available, they will likely go away without a fight (the best way to win a battle). To study this, we can elaborate upon "deception in object".

The resources associated with commands to an operating system are the "material" of attacks (Templeton and Levitt 2000):

- The directories and files of the computer
- Peripheral devices of the computer
- Connected networks
- Sites accessible by the networks
- The executables (executable files) for the operating system
- Status markers such as "logged-in" and "administrator privileges"
- People (we will mostly ignore this category because they are hard to control, though Chap. 10 considers them.)

Resources associated with commands can be identified in several ways. Some are arguments to commands, like the site "server23" for the command "ftp server23". Resources can persist even when not again mentioned, as the "network" resource over successive commands to a file-transfer utility; and resources can be "released" by particular commands, like an edited file after exiting the editor. In addition, the executable implementing a command is also a resource for it. We can identify both constant resources like computers and networks and created resources like downloaded files and administrator privileges. Resource denial is more convincing for created resources because they are less tested. However, some attacks have few created resources to exploit.

Each resource has six "facets" of its status, each with an associated predicate:

- Existence, exists(X): Whether the resource X exists (or at least is visible).
- Authorization, authorized(X): Whether the user is authorized to use the resource X by passwords and other access controls.
- Readiness, initialized(X,A): Whether the preparation of resource X is sufficient for the action A to be done.
- Operability, working(X): Whether the resource X is functions properly.
- Compatibility, compatible(X,Y): Whether the two resources X and Y are mutually compatible (as for instance whether a text editor is compatible with an image).
- Moderation, moderate(X,A): Whether the action's demands on a resource are within allowed limits.

Defensive deceptions will be most effective on the last four facets since the attacker appears to be closer to success, encouraging them to further waste time. Still, deceptions on the first two can provide variety, and they work very much like traditional access control. The "moderation" facet requires ranges of suitable parameter values which can be inferred. For instance, successful download of a one-megabyte file suggests that a half-megabyte file could also be transferred but not necessarily a two-megabyte file. Some common parameters for cyberspace are:

- Files: size and authorization level
- Peripheral devices: size and bandwidth
- Networks: size and bandwidth
- Sites: load and number of users
- Passwords: length and number of times used

As an example, suppose Tom downloads file "foobar.doc" of size 100,000 bytes from "rsite" to "hsite" across network "lnet" via the FTP file-transfer utility on hsite when lnet has three simultaneous users already. Normal completion of the action says that file systems on rsite and hsite exist, are authorized access by Tom, are initialized for access, and are working. Similarly it says the network lnet exists, is authorized use by Tom, is initialized for file transfers, is working, and is compatible with rsite and hsite. It also says executable FTP exists on hsite, Tom is authorized to use it, it is initialized, it is working, it is compatible with the file system on hsite, it is compatible with lnet, and it is compatible the file system on rsite. Finally, a successful file transfer means that the file system on hsite can hold files of 100,000 bytes, lnet can transfer files of 100,000 bytes, and lnet can handle four simultaneous users.

4.6   Deception Presentation Tactics

A deception planner has some further options once a deception type is selected, what could be called "presentation methods" or "deception tactics". Many of these are analogous to the misdirection methods of magicians. For instance for the resource deception methods:

- To deceive on existence, issue an error message claiming that the resource does not exist. For instance, after a file transfer to the current site, the operating system could say that it cannot find the transferred file.
- To deceive on authorization, either say that the user is not authorized to use the resource, or ask the user to provide credentials (a password or key) and then reject them.
- To deceive on readiness, issue an error message on attempting to use the resource. For instance, after an executable is downloaded, say "Protection violation at location 6349573" when running it.
- To deceive on operability, either halt during execution with an error message, never terminate execution, or create unusable result resources (which is also a deception on their readiness).

- To deceive on compatibility, issue an error message asserting that two particular resources are incompatible. For instance, if the user is doing a network file transfer, claim that the remote site does not recognize our transfer protocol.
- To deceive on moderation, claim that a limit on some parameters of the resource has been exceeded.

Defenders have many choices, but a defensive deception is only effective if it prevents completion of an attacker's inferred goals. For instance, to prevent a rootkit download, we could pretend the network is down so the attacker cannot get it. Ensuring this requires some reasoning about attack plans, but attacker goals are often quite predictable as we shall discuss in Sect. 12.4.1 (e.g. install a rootkit, make a site unusable, steal information, etc.), and many attacks are well documented.

The selection of such deception-presentation tactics is very domain-dependent. In fact, this is a key part of what hackers do: Develop such tactics rather than develop new attack methods. So for each domain for which we want to apply deception, we will need to think carefully to find appropriate such tactics. The rest of this book will examine possible such tactics in more detail.

4.7   Conclusions

We have many options for using deceptions to defend our cybersystems. The reader may find this a daunting set of choices. But actually, we do not need to consider all the options since, as the analysis of the case-grammar taxonomy suggests, some work much better in cyberspace than others. So usually we can pick a few deception methods and work carefully at implementing them well.

4.8   Exercises

1. Give an example of dazzling for camouflage in cyberspace using deception on external preconditions.
2.
   (a) In ordinary English, camouflage is considered a form of concealment. Give an example of concealment which is not a kind of camouflage.
   (b) In ordinary English, disinformation is a kind of lying. Give an example of lying which is not a kind of disinformation.
3. Discuss the different ways a cybersystem can lie about purpose. Note that without human body language, purpose is often more difficult to convey.
4. Give an example of defensive deception in supertype in cyberspace other than that of a decoy.

5. Most deception by amateur hackers of cybersystems involves lies to gain a sense of power, to manipulate the behavior of others, or just for the enjoyment of it. But there are other motivations.

   (a) Give an example of how a lie by a hacker to a cybersystem could be an instance of wish fulfillment.
   (b) Give an example of how a lie by a hacker to a cybersystem could be an instance of trying to avoid punishment.
   (c) Give an example of how a lie by a hacker to a cybersystem could be an instance of legitimately trying to help someone.

6. A magician has a volunteer from the audience select a card from a deck, memorize the card, and return it to the deck. They then shuffle the deck thoroughly. Later the magician pulls a card seemingly at random from the deck, shows it to the volunteer, they appear to be amazed, and they confirm that is the card they selected.

   (a) How could the trick be aided by deception in regard to a result of an action?
   (b) How could the trick be aided by deception in regard to an experiencer?
   (c) How could the trick be aided by deception in regard to an object?
   (d) How could the trick be aided by deception in regard to supertype in an action hierarchy?
   (e) How could the trick be aided by deception in regard to an agent?

7. Several verbs can indicate deception in English: lie, cheat, fool, hoodwink, deceive, misrepresent, delude, lead on, betray, and hoax. Distinguish these words from one another in as precise a way as best you can. Don't just repeat what dictionaries say but try to get at what they really mean.

References

Austin J (1975) How to do things with words, 2nd edn. Oxford University Press, Oxford, UK

Bell J, Whaley B (1991) Cheating. Transaction, New York

Carbonell J (1981) Counterplanning: a strategy-based model of adversary planning in real-world situations. Artif Intell 16:295–329

Cohen F (1999) A mathematical structure of simple defensive network deceptions. all.net/journal/deception/mathdeception/mathdeception.html. Accessed 15 Jan 2016

Cohen F, Koike D (2003) Leading attackers through attack graphs with deceptions. Comput Secur 22(5):402–411

Copeck T, Delisle S, Szparkowicz S (1992) Parsing and case interpretation in TANKA. In: Proceedings of the conference on computational linguistics. Nantes, France, pp 1008–1023

Dunnigan J, Nofi A (2001) Victory and deceit. second edition: Deception and trickery in war. Writers Club, San Jose, CA

Fillmore C (1968) The case for case. In: Bach E, Harms R (eds) Universals in linguistic theory. Holt, Rinehart and Winston, New York

Fogg B (2003) Persuasive technology: using computers to change what we think and do. Morgan Kaufmann, San Francisco, CA

Gerwehr S, Weissler R, Medby J, Anderson R, Rothenberg J (2000) Employing deception in information systems to thwart adversary reconnaissance-phase activities. Project Memorandum, National Defense Research Institute, Rand Corp., PM-1124-NSA, November

Hutchinson W, Warren M (2001) Information warfare: corporate attack and defense in a digital world. Butterworth-Heinemann, London, UK

Qassrawi M, Hongli Z (2010) Deception methodology in virtual honeypots. In: Proceedings of the second international conference on networks security, wireless communications, and trusted computing, Wuhan, China, 24–25 Apr, 2010. pp 462–467

Rowe N (2006) A taxonomy of deception in cyberspace. In: Proceedings of the international conference on information warfare and security, Princess Anne, MD, USA, 15–16 Mar. pp 173–181

Rowe N, Rothstein H (2004) Two taxonomies of deception for attacks on information systems. J Inform Warfare 3(2):27–39

Snyder C, Higgins R, Stucky R (1983) Excuses: masquerades in search of grace. Wiley, New York

Templeton S, Levitt K (2000) A requires/provides model for computer attacks. In: Proceedings of new security paradigms workshop, Cork, Ireland, 19–21 Sept, 2000. pp 31–38

The Honeynet Project (2004) Know your enemy, 2nd edn. Addison-Wesley, Boston, MA

Tognazzini B (1993) Principles, techniques, and ethics of stage magic and their application to human interface design. In: Proceedings of the conference on human factors and computing systems, Amsterdam, Netherlands, 24–29 Apr 1993. pp 355–362

Vrable M, Ma J, Chen J, Moore D, Vadekieft E, Snoeren A, Voelker G, Savage S (2005) Scalability, fidelity, and containment in the Potemkin virtual honeyfarm. In: Proceedings of the ACM symposium on operating system principles. Brighton UK, 23–26 Oct 2005. pp 148–162

Chapter 5
Deception Methods for Offense

Cyberattackers must almost necessarily use deceptions. That is because cybersystems are generally well-designed and robust to most attempts to misuse them. The only way around most of these protections is to deceive someone or some system.

We call deceptions used in cyberattacks "offensive deceptions". Generally speaking, offensive deceptions are unsophisticated. They do not need to be: Often all it takes is one small oversight by the deceivee for the cyberattacker to win. For instance, a single oversight may enable malware to get onto a cybersystem since most have a single layer of defense. So we see a few simple deceptions used repeatedly by cyberattacks, such getting users to run malicious code files by pretending they are something else.

© Springer International Publishing Switzerland 2016
N.C. Rowe, J. Rrushi, *Introduction to Cyberdeception*,
DOI 10.1007/978-3-319-41187-3_5

5.1   Motivation for Offensive Deception

The motivation for offensive cyberdeception usually involves crime. Criminals want to steal money, and cybersystems enable them to automate their crimes. Huge amounts of money can be involved (Poulsen 2012). A range of other crimes including theft, extortion, stalking, and malicious vandalism can also be automated by cybersystems. There are laws against these crimes, but there are always criminals willing to break the law for personal gain. Generally speaking, criminals do not care too much about their targets because they can make money off many kinds of people. Phishing is a typical criminal cyberattack involving deception, where users are persuaded to reveal personal data by deceptive email and Web sites (Jakobsson and Myers 2006).

Offensive cyberdeception is also important in "red teaming", or testing of information security by trying to attack cybersystems. Red teaming is a rather blunt instrument for testing security, however, and is limited in what it can tell you about a cybersystem.

A minority of cyberattacks are by governments to accomplish espionage. Espionage usually involves trying to find secrets, but can also involve sabotage. Espionage-related cyberattacks are quite focused on military and governmental targets. For instance, specially crafted phishing email may go to only the head of a military organization in an attempt to control their computer with a rootkit ("spear phishing"). Espionage-related cyberattacks are difficult to detect because they have the resources of entire governments behind them, and thus their frequency is higher than the very low rates observed. Such attacks generally are considered to be crimes in the victim countries, so they can still be classified as criminal.

Targeted government-sponsored cyberattacks could also try to disable (sabotage) cybersystems of an adversary country during a military attack, as in the 2008 cyberattacks on the country of Georgia during a military operation by Russia against it. Many cyberattack methods used for espionage need only be modified slightly to serve as sabotage, so discovery of espionage machinery on government cybersystems often raises worries. Serious such sabotage could even be considered as an act of war, even if perpetrated by a small group of people within a country, since a country is responsible for policing its citizens and may be legally responsible for such cyberattacks according to international law. Since cyberattacks are hard to prevent and control, cyberwarfare using them has similarities to the use of biological weapons. We have thus argued that international cyberarms limitation agreements are necessary (Rowe et al. 2011).

5.2   The Options in Offensive Deception

Offensive deceptions are well documented in reports of cyberattack methods such as those of the U.S. Computer Emergency Response Team (www.cert.gov). One good way to characterize the possible deception methods is to characterize the options in regard to the agent, object, and ploy. Deception in regard to the agent of some action is often the easiest. Some options are:

- Pretending in a message to be someone you or not. Some popular impersonations:

  - A boss of the person receiving the email.
  - An authority figure such as law enforcement.
  - Information technology personnel who support your cybersystems.
  - A subordinate who needs help.
  - An unfortunate person who needs help (as in the various versions of the Nigerian scam).

- Pretending in a login to a cybersystem that you are a legitimate user (after stealing their password).
- Pretending that you are a legitimate system administrator (after stealing their password), which gives you further powers.
- Pretending that you are a legitimate process running on a computer (the idea behind worms).
- Pretending that your packets are safe when they conceal an attack (Ptacek and Newsham 1998).
- Pretending to have a different Internet (IP) address than you really have ("spoofing") (malicious addresses tend to get blacklisted by servers once their intentions are discovered).
- Pretending to be legitimate hardware when you are not, like a fake automated teller machine.

Object-based offensive deception is also very common. Some options are:

- Messages: These are the chief tool of spam and phishing. A wide range of lies are employed to entice users to do something to further the interests of the attacker. For instance, a message appearing to be from your bank asks you to go to a Web site to confirm your account number.
- Attachments to messages: These are easy way to do bad things to a user if they can be induced to open the attachments. For instance, an email may say "Take a look at this!" If the attachments are malicious software, they can install things on the user's computer or modify it in some other way.
- Web sites: These are often used in spam and phishing. A site can try to persuade the user to do something not in their interests such as revealing their passwords. Or a site can leave malicious software on a visitor's computer. Or it can provide hoax information, intending to increase the believability of a lie (Boese 2006).
- Other Internet sites: More generally, a site can be advertised to be something quite different than it really is. For instance, a phishing site can pretend to be a bank.
- Software: Since users are generally discouraged by vendors from examining software, it is easy for an unscrupulous creator to put something malicious in it. Often software is allowed unnecessary freedom to act on a computer, and this makes it easy to install malware. Malicious software can be installed

surreptitiously (as by exploits) or a user may be persuaded to download it themselves (as after hearing advertisements). Effective malicious software need not only serve malicious purposes, as it is easier to fool users if it also does some useful things.

- Operating system: The ultimate goal of major attackers is to completely control a cybersystem through a "rootkit". This means that key software of the operating system has been replaced by the attacker's version that enables them to do whatever they want with the cybersystem.
- Data: This itself can be malicious. Classic examples are malformed packets sent to an Internet protocol to create problems and enable compromise of a recipient's computer, though this is becoming less possible as protocols are improved. Malicious data can also be sent to software.
- Devices: These can be designed to put malware onto cybersystems to which they are connected. This has been a problem with flash-drive storage devices.
- Input devices like keyboards: These can steal secrets during their use by recording keys that are depressed ("keylogging") when special software is installed. For instance, commercial software claims it can help you track your children.
- Access points for wireless networks: These permit wireless devices to connect to networks. But a malicious access point can steal passwords and other kinds of data.
- Botnets: These are networks of compromised computers that work together to accomplish some task of an attacker such as sending spam or attacking other computers. Often the owners of the victim computers are unaware that their hardware is serving a malicious purpose while still supporting normal tasks.
- Visuals: Graphics can fool a user as to a system state. For instance, a fake login screen can be used to steal a user's password.
- Requests: Most users employ browsers to find information. But a malicious user could try to flood a browser site with information to cause it to crash. Or they could send too-large information to an input buffer, causing an overflow on a poorly designed buffer that could lead to an exploitation.

Since many agent-based and object-based offensive deceptions are well known, they may be unconvincing unless intensified by additional features to help "sell" them (make them effective). Many social-engineering "ploys" can be used (more about these in Chap. 10). Many of these relate to other human persuasion such as advertising. Some examples:

- Exploiting surprise. For instance, the frequent cyberattacks using HTTP (Web) protocol manipulations may make defenders less ready for an attack using a rare protocol, or the rarity of cyberattacks on the BGP protocol may make such a cyberattack more effective. As another example, there are so many cyberattacks coming from the Internet that defenders tend to have trouble recognizing saboteurs within their organization.
- Appeals to urgency (e.g. "Your account will expire unless you confirm your password now").

- Appeals to safety (e.g. "Protect your computer now against new threats by downloading our software").
- Appeals to greed (e.g. "Earn a commission by depositing my check in your bank account").
- Appeals to sex (e.g. "Cheap Viagra").
- Appeals to job responsibilities (e.g. "I'm a system administrator and I need your password for testing").
- Appeals to personal responsibilities (e.g. "I'm your boss and need your password for my records").

In addition, deceptions can exploit human cognitive limitations in interacting with cybersystems (Conti and Sobiesk 2010). Well-known knowledge about design of good interfaces can be inverted and used to confuse and deceive users.

5.3   Applying the Deception Taxonomy to Offense

We can be more systematic about offensive deception using the case-based taxonomy of the last chapter (Rowe 2006). To rate the cases in suitability and effectiveness as we did in the last chapter, we can use the number of mentions in 314 articles randomly selected from the Risks Digest (catless.ncl.ac.uk/Risks), a newsletter on new threat types, as well as other general security-threat Websites. As before, the numbers in parentheses are our overall assessment of the effectiveness of the deception method.

- Agent (10): Identity deceptions are frequent in cyberspace because you rarely can see or hear with whom you are interacting.
- Accompaniment (9): These deceptions conceal something malicious within something innocuous ("Trojan horses"). These work well in cyberspace because it is difficult to view the parts of a software or data object even with special tools, and difficult to understand them even if you view them. If you buy a car in the real world, you can at least look inside it.
- Frequency (9): These deceptions are essential to denial-of-service attacks which attempt to swamp system resources with large numbers of insincere requests. This works well in cyberspace because cybersystems can repeat things easily without getting tired.
- Object (8): Many deceptions are possible with objects, including camouflaged and decoy files, executables, and other software objects. In cyberspace there are often missing supporting details such as handwriting or provenance that occur in the real world (Seife 2015).
- Supertype (7): Deceptions in supertype occur when an attack in disguised as some legitimate activity, a classic strategy of social engineering and other real-world scams and frauds.
- Experiencer (6): An important type is eavesdropping to steal secrets, which can occur in cyberspace when different people share the same resource such as a

network. The need for cybersystems to be efficient means that many resources are shared and could possibly be eavesdropped.

- Instrument (6): Deception involves attacking with surprising tools. Sophisticated attack methods try to do this.
- Whole (6): Deception involves actions that do not appear to be suspicious individually but which together form an attack. This is important in spyware and other Trojan horses, and also in social engineering.
- Content (5): Deception makes some data appear to be something else. This is used by "covert channels" that spies use to sneak secrets out of systems.
- External precondition (5): Deception makes impossible or costly requests.
- Measure (5): Deception sends data too large to handle, as in buffer overflows. The automation of cyberspace makes it easy to create large things.
- Location-from (4): A deception attacks from a surprising site or within unexpected software.
- Purpose (4): Deception gives incorrect reasons during social engineering. The absence of body language makes this easier to do in cyberspace than in the real world.
- Beneficiary (4): Deception makes a deceivee falsely think they are the beneficiary, as in email scams.
- Time-at (4): Deception attacks at a surprising time.
- Value (3): Deception sends different data than expected, as in buffer overflows.
- Location-to (3): Deception attacks a surprising destination.
- Location-through (3): Deception uses a surprising site as an intermediary.
- Time-through (3): Deception takes more than the usual amount of time to do something.
- Internal precondition (2): Deception pretends inability to do something as a reason for failure, or pretends ability to do something bad as a means of extortion.
- Direction (2): Deception attacks in the reverse direction to that expected.
- Effect (2): Deception pretends that something did not work properly.
- Cause (1): Deception gives a false explanation of events.
- Location-at (0).
- Orientation (0).
- Time-from (0).
- Time-to (0).
- Recipient (0).
- Contradiction (0).
- Manner (0).
- Material (0).
- Order (0).

Note that the best offensive deceptions are different from the best defensive deceptions in Chap. 4. All email users are wearily familiar with spam using identity deceptions and Trojan horses, yet identity deception cannot help defenders very much because most attackers do not care who you are. So offensive deception requires a fresh perspective.

5.4 The Ethics of Offensive Deception

The reader who is contemplating the design of offensive deceptions should be warned that many of the ethical justifications for deception mentioned in Chaps. 1 and 16 do not apply to them. Espionage, vandalism, and sabotage are illegal of virtually all countries, and that is what cyberattacks amount to (Spafford 1992). And the laws of war on responding to attacks with counterattacks are quite strict. Most countries put strong restrictions on use of their cyberweapons because of the great difficulties in targeting them precisely, controlling the strength of their effects, and cleaning up the damage afterwards.

One objection raised to the defensive deceptions subsequently discussed in this book is they might encourage more offensive deception. However, this chapter should make clear that is unlikely because offensive deceptions generally look quite different from defensive deceptions. Deception is almost always necessary for any kind of offensive cyber-operation, but it is just one of many techniques for defense.

5.5 Conclusions

The best options for offensive deceptions are different from the best options for defensive deceptions. There overall number and effectiveness is similar, but offensive deceptions are different and simpler. This means a deception planner needs to be in a different frame of mind for creating offensive instead of defensive deceptions.

5.6 Exercises

1. From a philosophical standpoint, why is concealment so effective in offensive methods in cyberspace? Shouldn't our ability to examine everything in a cyber-system in minute detail protect us from attempts to conceal information in cyberspace?
2. Suppose a bank site uses a certificate to authenticate its identity. Suggest three different ways in which a malicious person could deceive users with a fake bank site designed for phishing and copy the legitimate bank site including its certificate machinery.
3. Standard advice in many fields where deception can be practiced offensively is for defenders to "expect the unexpected". Why is this in one sense impossible? Why is this in another sense too costly to be effective?
4. Police sometimes use offensive deceptions such as soliciting drug buys to catch criminals. Such activities are controversial because they can be argued to represent entrapment where a criminal is encouraged to do something they would not do otherwise. How can offensive deceptions in cyberspace run by legitimate agencies avoid entrapment?

References

Boese A (2006) Hippo easts dwarf: A field guide to hoaxes and other b.s. Harcourt, Orlando, FL

Conti G, Sobiesk E (2010) Malicious interface design: exploiting the user. In: Proceedings of international World Wide Web conference, 26–30 Apr 2010, Raleigh, NC, US. pp 271–280

Jakobsson M, Myers S (eds) (2006) Phishing and countermeasures: understanding the increasing problem of electronic identity theft. Wiley-Interscience, New York

Poulsen K (2012) Kingpin: how one hacker took over the billion-dollar cybercrime underground. Broadway, New York

Ptacek T, Newsham T (1998) Insertion, evasion, and denial of service: eluding network intrusion detection. Technical Report. Secure Networks Inc. Available at www.dtic.mil/dtic/tr/fulltext/u2/a391565.pdf

Rowe N (2006) A taxonomy of deception in cyberspace. In: Proceedings of the international conference on information warfare and security, Princess Anne, MD, 15–16 Mar. pp 173–181

Rowe N, Garfinkel S, Beverly R, Yannakogeorgos P (2011) Challenges in monitoring cyberarms compliance. International. J Cyber Warfare Terrorism 1(1):11–14

Seife C (2015) Virtual unreality: the new era of digital deception. Penguin, New York

Spafford E (1992) Are computer hacker break-ins ethical? J Syst Softw 17:41–47

Chapter 6
Delays

© Springer International Publishing Switzerland 2016
N.C. Rowe, J. Rrushi, *Introduction to Cyberdeception*,
DOI 10.1007/978-3-319-41187-3_6

Delaying tactics are often useful when you don't trust someone, or perhaps don't trust them yet. So they are useful for cybersystems when they are suspicious of the circumstances. Bureaucracies often do it, either deliberately or inadvertently (Wilson 2000). Often deception is involved in delaying because, for the delay to be most effective, the delayer should not tell the delayee why, but either avoid or evade the question if asked. Delaying works well with cybersystems because unexplained delays occur naturally from time to time when, for instance, network connections go down and a cybersystem is waiting for them, or when a cybersystem decides to do occasional housekeeping tasks.

6.1 Why Delay Defensively?

We can identify several situations where delaying is an appropriate tactic in defending computer systems and networks.

- If we are under a denial-of-service attack, we will get many related or similar commands. Since their purpose is to slow down our systems, deliberate delays make it appear that the denial of service is succeeding (Somayaji and Forrest 2000). At the same time, deliberate delays would help protect our system from actually being slowed down since they could greatly slow the attack.
- If we are cyberattacked during cyberwar, delaying can give us time to analyze the attack, marshal our forces, and institute countermeasures. This is particularly important during cyberwar because surprise is important to military success.
- If the attacker is impatient, delaying could cause them to abandon their attack. This could occur in time-critical cyberwar where an attacker could have goals that they must meet by a certain time.
- If the attacker's system monitors connections, it might notice a long delay and abort the connection automatically, causing additional trouble for the attacker. Many network protocols do this because it is insecure to leave an inactive network connection open.
- If a command is especially suspicious (as if it contains a known virus), a delay could signal to the attacker that an intrusion-detection system has recognized their threat and is dealing with it. This could scare the attacker away.
- If we are not certain we are under attack but have seen some suspicious behavior, delaying could give us time to see if the suspicious behavior continues. So delays permit a graduated response to attacks, something not possible with defensive methods like access controls.

In all these cases the defender needs to infer (at least to some probability) that they are under attack. Methods discussed in Chap. 11 can do this. Many cases will be unambiguous, however, as when we recognize a malware signature in input sent to us.

A simple implementation of automatic delaying is the "Labrea Tarpit" (labrea. sourceforge.net) that delays whenever it receives many requests for nonexistent addresses within a site during a short time period. Such requests are typical of foot-printing, the initial stages of attacks, and unlikely to be accidents. Labrea then slows the attacks down by responding very slowly to requests for further information, thereby burdening an attacker or attack script with considerable waiting. An icy surface could be another useful metaphor.

Is delaying necessarily deceptive? No, but it is often more effective when it is. If an adversary does not know that you are deliberately delaying them, they will persist longer in attempts that waste time. If they do know, they will figure they need measures to counter your countermeasures, and this is more work for them.

Delaying can be noticed by an alert deceivee. It can be noticed by network traffic analysis (Alt et al. 2014) and obviously delaying sites may get blacklisted so they are avoided by attackers. So delaying is not a very stealthy tactic unlike those in the subsequent chapters.

6.2   Delaying Tactics

There are many ways to accomplish a delay. Most programming languages have a process-suspension command, often called "sleep", that will pause execution of a program, allowing other ongoing programs to take that time for their own purposes. Delays accomplished this way are good against denial-of-service attacks because they dilute the effect of time-consuming activities intended to slow down systems. However, not all waiting mechanisms in programming languages will suffice, because some involve repeated checking of a flag or buffer which may less successfully dilute the effect of an attack.

Another delaying tactic is simulating a slower algorithm instead of an expected faster algorithm. This can be convincing because large variations in algorithm efficiency can be seen in the diversity of software today. Slower algorithms are often easier to implement, after all.

Delays can be constructed to be blamed on networks. For instance, a victim can be deliberately redirected to slower facilities as well as to honeypots (Qassrawi and Hongli 2010). A more elegant way to accomplish a delay is to involve the victim themselves, since humans operate much more slowly than computer technology. The delayer can repeatedly ask them or their attack script for unnecessary information such as a confirmation, their user name, their password, or a default directory. Excuses can be offered that the system needs to be careful. Questions like these can function like the "patter" or talking by a magician to distract people from the deception that is occurring (Schneider 2011).

Figure 6.1 shows an example window that we could pop up to cause the delayee some trouble; this could have the additional advantage of allowing us to steal information if they enter something. For instance, under Microsoft Internet Explorer, a user must repeatedly confirm downloading when the site is set to prompt for confirmation, even for the same download done many times before. This is annoying. If the attack is automated, unexpected requests may have the additional benefit of causing the attack script to fail.

Fig. 6.1 Example prompt window

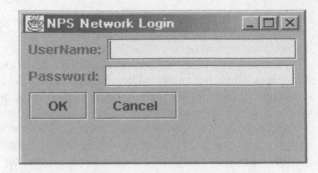

A related idea is to give the delayee a large amount of data to read or digest. This could mean much text on the screen or a complex screen design. This can be coupled to requests like Fig. 6.1 that require that they have read the text. A related idea is to use inconsistency in the user interface such as frequently changing the default directory, to further tax the delayee. We can also delay a user by deliberately choosing a wrong way to accomplish a task. For instance, if asked to look up a file name in a top-level directory, the system can deliberately "misunderstand" and search for the file name in every subdirectory too.

A related idea is to give faulty instructions for accomplishing something. We all know how frustrating it is to follow directions that do not work, something increasingly common with complex software like operating systems. Attackers can be given faulty instructions on how to retrieve or install something, resulting in legitimate error messages. This can be done with any piece of software that could sound appealing to the attacker, or with instructions for accessing sites with apparently enticing resources. The nice thing about faulty instructions is that attackers often try variations on them again and again in the hope they made some small error, wasting plenty of time.

Finally, delays can be accomplished by repeated evasion of a request: We can give false excuses why we do not want to do something. Chapter 9 talks more about false excuses.

6.3   How Much to Delay

Once we have decided to delay, a next question is how much. If we delay too little, we will be ineffective. If we delay too much, the deceivee may infer deception if they are paying attention. Even automated attacks are usually monitored to some extent by the attacker. To make matters more difficult for the delayer, a convincing delay should vary with the task requested.

Several strategies can be followed by the delayer. We could delay on any sufficiently suspicious command or on any command likely to be part of an attack plan. However, the delayee could then become suspicious themselves if this occurred

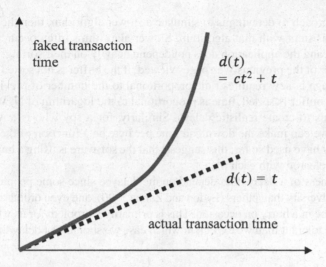

Fig. 6.2 Actual transaction time versus fake time for delaying tactics

Table 6.1 Sample numbers for the processing delay for $c = 1$

Processing time	0	1	2	3	10	30	100
Time including delay	0	2	5	10	110	930	10100

every time they did something they knew to be suspicious and never otherwise. An alternative is the "slow computer" where every action on a computer or network is slowed to a fraction of its normal speed whenever they are suspicious of a user. We may be able to restrict this to a subset of actions like those using the network, since networks are not as reliable as individual computers.

In general, the amount of delay should try to be a smooth function of the actual time required. Figure 6.2 shows the kind of function we need. It needs to be what mathematicians call "continuous" or have no sudden jumps in value, since these would seem artificial and suspicious. It also needs to be always-increasing ("monotonic"), since more work should always require a longer duration. Also its slope should be monotonically increasing too in a denial-of-service situation because we need to delay more the greater the attempt to slow us down. The simplest mathematical function that will satisfy these constraints is $d(t) = ct^2 + t$, where c is a delay-acceleration constant. For $c = 1$ and times measured in seconds, Table 6.1 gives some representative values. Note that the upward curve of the function is important with a honeypot where we want the attacker to continue to interact. If we just delay them equally on everything they want to do, they may decide our system is too much trouble to attack. But if we delay them only a little at first, and then progressively delay them more, they will feel more invested in the outcome, and will tend to keep trying.

If our approach to delaying is to simulate a slower algorithm, then the delay can be made consistent with that algorithm. Slower algorithms often occur when data are unsorted and the application does not depend heavily on their sorting. An example is a buffer of the previous Web pages viewed; if the buffer is not sorted, checking whether a page is new requires time proportional to the number of previous pages N, but if the buffer is sorted, time is proportional to the logarithm of N. We can use ideas like this to create realistic delays. Similarly, for a spy who is downloading many files, we can make the download time per byte be a function of the square of the time they have used so far; this suggests that the software is using a buffer which is not being cleared with each file.

Effectiveness of a delay does depend on the delayee since some people are more tolerant of adversity than others (Lydon and Zanna 1990), and even ordinarily tolerant people may be in a hurry on occasion. This is primarily a problem for us when delayees are more tolerant than we expect, in which case we should just delay them more.

6.4   Example: Delays in a Web Portal

We developed a delaying Web interface to an image library that used a keyword-input front end (Julian et al. 2003) based on the Java-servlet framework (Hall and Brown, 2003). It is shown in Appendix A. Figure 6.3 shows sample input and Fig. 6.4 shows

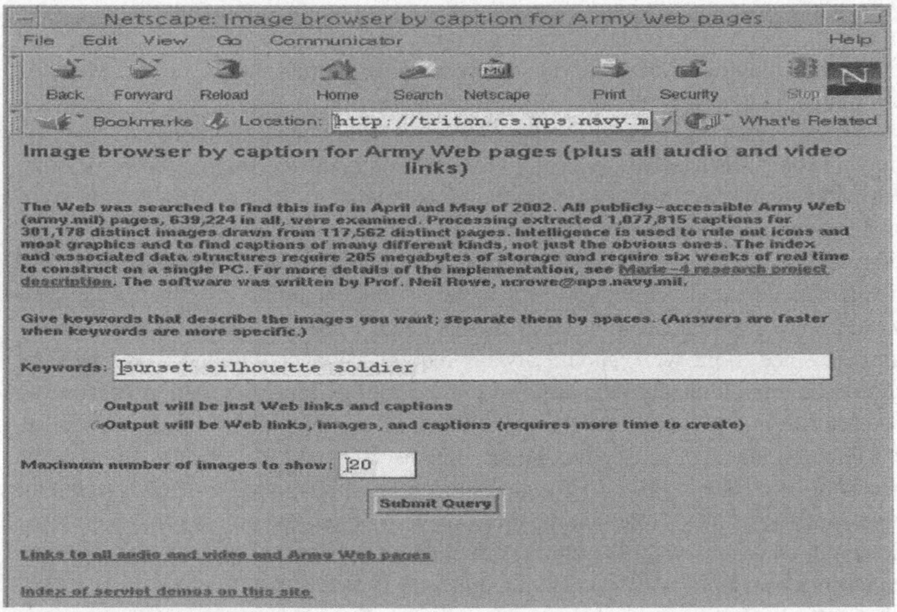

Fig. 6.3 Example image-portal input page

The above picture is from http://tradoc.monroe.army.mil/historian//pubs/1994/DefauR.htm
Caption of weight 0.574: " silhouette image of soldiers"

The above picture is from http://www.mvp.usace.army.mil/navigation/man_study/
Caption of weight 0.555: " Photo of Sunset on Mississippi River"

Fig. 6.4   Example image-portal output

output for it. Normally this functions as an image-retrieval portal. The user types some keywords and we find images whose captions match the keywords. But if what the user types looks like computer code such as HTML or Java, we conclude the user is attempting a code-injection attack, and delay them. A quick way to guess that the input is computer code is whether there are any punctuation marks other than commas, semicolons, plus signs, or spaces.

The standard way to implement a keyword lookup is hash each keyword to a list of all items mentioning the keyword, then intersect the lists. (Hashing is a classic technique in computer science to quickly map an input string to a location, by computing some pseudo-random mathematical function of the string.) Retrieving the lists requires time proportional to the length of each, and doing the intersection requires a number of operations equal to the total size of all the lists, provided they are kept sorted. This suggests that the time to answer a keyword query should be proportional to the total size of the keywords lists (which will be longer for more-common words). Thus for a realistic delay in responding to a keyword query, we should multiply this expected time by a constant, and the larger the constant, the more we are delaying. This is what we did in our implementation. However, if we need more of a delay, there is no need to imitate the standard algorithm. We could assume that the lists are not sorted, in which case the intersection operations will take time roughly the sum of the squares of the lengths of the lists. This would give us a delay curve similar to that in Fig. 6.2.

6.5   Unpredictable Delays

An alternative strategy is to delay unpredictably so that the delayee is kept guessing about how long an operation will take and will find it hard to plan. For defensive purposes, this only makes sense when the attacker is using resources (using the term of Sect. 4.5) with which they are not familiar, for otherwise they could be suspicious about something familiar. And it only makes sense if we mention the resources to the user. So we could say "Checking with cx37.mgt.com" or "Backing up CKG drivers" and take 30 min to respond. Unpredictability need not mean inconsistency, however; "Backing up CKG drivers" should delay a similar amount of time each time to avoid seeming suspicious. Chapter 7 will show ways to generate random names that would be difficult or impossible for users to confirm are real resources. In the meantime, we have a convincing excuse for a delay.

Inconsistency in the duration of execution does have some advantages. If sometimes downloading a file takes 1 s and sometimes 10 min, the delayee will be puzzled and may become suspicious. This is actually good if you want to create suspicion to scare the delayee away. Inconsistency tends to increase the analysis time for the attacker, and can tax them mentally if they start to look for reasons when there are none.

A variant on this is the "You broke it" claim where delays suddenly increase after a sufficiently unusual action has occurred. For instance, rootkits are stored in large files, so after an attacker downloads a large rootkit onto a victim machine, the victim could start delaying all subsequent commands by a factor of 10. A possible explanation could be that the download has depleted secondary storage, and finding free storage requires putting many fragments together. Operating systems rarely bother to explain their reasons for delays, so it is hard for the attacker to know what happened. Chapter 9 discusses this and other similar excuses.

6.6   Cascading Delays

Delaying provides a nice feature against attackers compared to legitimate users: Its effects multiply when operations in a chain each contribute their own delays (Fig. 6.5). This can occur when an attacker arrives at a target machine through a chain of compromised machines in an attempt to conceal their origin, a common tactic. If each machine and router can individually decide that the attacker is suspicious (as by noting many identical commands in the attacker's traffic), each can independently delay the attacker to achieve a cumulative larger delay. Similar advantages accrue when an attacker uses multiple software tools simultaneously.

Fig. 6.5 Effects of cascading delays

Fig. 6.6 The spectrum of delaying behavior

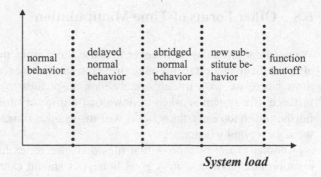

6.7   **The Spectrum of Delays**

It is desirable to provide a range of responses to cyberattacks (Caltagirone and Frincke 2005). One appealing aspect of delaying tactics is that they can vary smoothly with the degree of suspiciousness since a delay is quantifiable. Figure 6.6 shows a possible spectrum of responses for denial-of-service attacks as a function of their seriousness measured as the system load. A good application of this might be to management of a Web server. As the load on the server increases beyond the normal range, it will necessarily take longer to respond to page requests, and we could exaggerate these increased times in the form of process-suspension time if we are suspicious of the increased load. But if the load continues to increase, as could occur in a distributed denial-of-service attack, the overhead of maintaining large numbers of processes might be too difficult for the system even if many of those processes were suspended. So we might need to simplify or shorten the system response to new requests. For a keyword Web portal like our image portal, an abridged response could mean looking up only records for the first keyword (since users don't expect perfect accuracy in keyword-based retrieval anyway); for requests for different Web pages, we might respond with a single default Web page. Or we could respond with cached information if we have any, rather than calculating new information.

If an attack continues to increase in scope (as if the attackers have targeted us with a botnet), we may need to substitute a new kind of response for even the abridged response to forestall overloading of our system. An example would be returning a warning page stating that our system is not allowing connections, even if that is not quite true. Precomputed responses are a good strategy at this level of attack. For instance, we can play graphics or video, generate a fake file system to examine (as will be discussed in Chap. 7), or provide decoys appropriate for what the attacker has done, such as dumps of data to make it look like the attacker has broken through to the operating system.

Finally, if system load reaches a critical level despite all these countermeasures, we will need to terminate processes in one way or another, such as by killing time-consuming processes, refusing connections from certain nodes, or disconnecting from the Internet (though for most sites this should only be a last resort).

6.8   Other Forms of Time Manipulation

We need not just delay an attacker to cause them problems. Responding too early after a difficult request seems quite suspicious and is an excellent strategy for deceptions where we wish to deliberately look suspicious to scare people away. For instance, if a system is asked to download a directory from the hacker's site and finishes much too early, the attacker will suspect that something went wrong even if we say everything is fine.

Another aspect of time is that files and directories have associated times of creation and modification. A good honeypot should carefully craft these, as we shall address in the next chapter.

6.9   Conclusions

Delaying is an excellent way to handle suspicious people since it gives you time to muster defenses: time to probe them for more information to confirm your suspicions, time to assemble your own countermeasures, and time to await reinforcements. At the same time, delays may not be especially suspicious to the delayee because unexpected delays occur all the time with human interactions, and they occur even more often with cybersystems, which can be notorious for unreasonable delays.

6.10   Exercises

1. What clues are there that an attacker is in a hurry and would be hurt by delaying them significantly? Discuss clues in type of commands issued and in the resources identified in those commands.
2. Suppose a suspicious user is downloading many files from the Internet. For certain kinds of users, why could it be useful to delay them a widely varying amount rather than use the curve in Fig. 6.2? Describe also the kinds of users.
3. Suggest a plan by which a user hunting for passwords by keyword search through files on a computer could be kept busy for quite a while trying to find them, with the goal of still keeping them interested and hopeful of obtaining them.
4. The time to transfer a file across the Internet is not roughly proportional to its size when files are large. Discuss how the use of block transfers could increase the time significantly on large files. Give a reasonable delay formula based on simulating a block-transfer algorithm.
5. Cascading of delays requires that intermediate nodes identify suspicious behavior passing through them, and that is not easy. Suppose traffic seen by a router is encrypted except for the destination. What attacks could we still detect and be able to delay?

6. Suppose we are getting spammed with millions of identical email messages to users on our site. What strategies can we use to prevent them from slowing our systems significantly without just refusing the emails?
7. Give a series of possible "evasions" to a user that you wish to delay when they are querying the size of a file representing a download. An evasion differs from an outright delay in giving a reason why things are taking so long, but it needs different reasons as time progresses.

References

Alt L, Beverly R, Dainotti A (2014) Uncovering network tarpits with Degreaser. In: Proceedings of annual computer security applications conference, 9–12 Dec, 2014, New Orleans, LA. pp 156–165

Caltagirone S, Frincke D (2005) The response continuum. In: Proceedings of the IEEE workshop on information assurance and security, United States Military Academy, 15–17 Jun, 2005, West Point, NY

Hall M, Brown L (2003) Core servlets and JavaServer pages, vol 1, 2nd edn, Core technologies. Prentice-Hall, Upper Saddle River, NJ

Julian D, Rowe N, Michael J (2003) Experiments with deceptive software responses to buffer-based attacks. In: Proceedings of the IEEE-SMC workshop on information assurance, West Point, New York, 18–20 Jun, 2003. pp 43–44

Lydon J, Zanna M (1990) Commitment in the face of adversity: a value-affirmation approach. J Pers Soc Psychol 58(6):1040–1047

Qassrawi M, Hongli Z (2010) Deception methodology in virtual honeypots. In: Proceedings of the second international conference on networks security, wireless communications, and trusted computing, Wuhan, China, 24–25 Apr 2010. pp 462–467

Schneider A (2011) The theory and practice of magic deception. CreateSpace, North Charleston, SC

Somayaji A, Forrest S (2000) Automated response using system-call delays. In: Proceedings of the 9th Usenix security symposium, Denver, CO, 14–17 Aug, 2000. pp 185–198

Wilson J (2000) Bureaucracy, new edn. Basic Books, New York

Chapter 7

Fakes

Text and images are classic ways to do deception because they seem more permanent and believable than direct human interaction. We will call deception in constructed text and media "fakes". Fake documents and images have played important roles in history. "Operation Mincemeat" of World War II planted fake documents, including things like letters from home and theater tickets as well as some official letters, all suggesting that the British were planning to invade southern Europe rather than Normandy, and the deceptions were effective (Latimer 2003). Fake documents are also important for counterintelligence; if one makes the false information distinctive, it is easy to tell if an adversary has used it.

Fake information can be considered a manipulation of the information in a communications channel, so that it appears to communicate normally, but is actually sending less information than expected. The trick with designing a fake is to make

© Springer International Publishing Switzerland 2016
N.C. Rowe, J. Rrushi, *Introduction to Cyberdeception*,
DOI 10.1007/978-3-319-41187-3_7

it close to a normal communication so the difference is not noted. This is easiest when the real information is simple, as with many kinds of log files, or cryptic, as with binary data such as executables. Picture fakes can be easy to make with the many tools can construct them from copies or pieces (Amore 2015). Natural-language text is harder to fake since people can notice subtle changes to sentences. Sensitive methods are now available for detecting faked authorship of prose (Afroz et al. 2012), but someone needs to be suspicious in the first place to run them.

7.1 Other Possible Cyber-Fakes

In cyberspace, many things can be faked successfully beside text and images since cyberspace is a virtual world missing corroborative details present in the real world. Possible opportunities for fakes are:

- Error messages
- Other operating-system messages
- System files like configuration and log files
- Encrypted files
- Documents
- Source code
- Executables
- Operating systems (as with a honeypot)
- Cybersystems as a whole (as with a honeypot)
- Network packets
- Networks (as by pretended network connections)
- Attached devices
- Electronic emanations
- Hardware

Fakes are often easy to make for formatted information such as messages from an operating system. This includes error messages, file-directory listings, and process-status information. This information is technical and unfriendly so the user has trouble understanding it. Also good for fakes are information that the user is unlikely to compare for consistency to other information like log files. Another good opportunity is information appearing to be random such as compressed or encrypted files, which can be faked by generating bytes with a random number generator.

For convincing fakes with the other kinds of artifacts, it may be necessary to craft them at several levels of detail. For instance, it is not sufficient to use typical words of English for a fake document, but one must choose typical sequences of words too. Methods for detection of fake documents often rely on analysis of the sequences (Kaza et al. 2003).

7.2   A Grammar for Random Error Messages

A systematic way to create varied fake text is to provide a grammar for it, a program in a restricted formal language. Grammars output strings according to a set of grammar rules. There are several kinds of grammars, but for purposes of deception, "context-free grammars" are sufficiently powerful while still being easy to use. For fakes we need to generate strings randomly from a grammar, what is called a "stochastic grammar", so we need to specify probabilities for the rules too.

Appendix B gives Java code to implement such "stochastic grammars". You need to write them in a text file, giving rules with a left side and right side separated by the symbol "=". The left side represents a single symbol that can be replaced with the sequence of symbols on the right side. To generate strings from the grammar, the code starts with a string consisting of just a designated starting symbol. Then it repeatedly replaces symbols by their right sides given in the grammar rules until no more replacements can be made. Probabilities attached to each rule with the same left side give the likelihood that the rule should be chosen with a random choice. For instance, if the symbol "errormessage" can be replaced with either "Operation illegal at" or "Segmentation error at" followed by either the word "front" or "end", and the choices are equally likely, we could write these grammar rules:

```
0.5 errormessage = operation illegal at place
0.5 errormessage = segmentation error at place
0.5 place = front
0.5 place = end
```

Here is a larger grammar for some false error messages. As discussed in Chap. 9, alse error messages are an excellent way to deceive. These consist of a category name like "port error", a location, and additional details. The first and last can be randomly chosen from a set of options. The location information can use a random number of either 7, 8, or 9 digits. You run this grammar by giving it the starting symbol "start". The "~" is our special reserved symbol telling the grammar to insert a space in the string output.

```
0.4 start = "Fatal error at" ~ bignumber ":" ~ errortype
0.3 start = "Error at" ~ bignumber ":" ~ errortype
0.3 start = "Port error at" ~ bignumber ":" ~ errortype
0.333 bignumber = digit digit digit digit digit digit digit digit
digit
0.333 bignumber = digit digit digit digit digit digit digit digit
0.333 bignumber = digit digit digit digit digit digit digit
0.14 digit = 0
0.13 digit = 1
0.12 digit = 2
```

```
0.11 digit = 3
0.10 digit = 4
0.09 digit = 5
0.08 digit = 6
0.07 digit = 7
0.06 digit = 8
0.05 digit = 9
0.125 errortype = "Segmentation fault"
0.125 errortype = "Illegal type coercion"
0.125 errortype = "Syntax error"
0.125 errortype = "Attempt to access protected memory"
0.125 errortype = "Process limit reached"
0.125 errortype = "Not enough main memory"
0.125 errortype = "Stack inconsistent"
0.125 errortype = "Attempted privilege escalation"
```

Here are sample strings generated by this grammar from a starting string of "start":

Port error at 916827320: Process limit reached
Fatal error at 4950426: Illegal type coercion
Fatal error at 25812486: Segmentation fault
Error at 0055092: Attempted privilege escalation
Port error at 218013526: Not enough main memory

The details can be made more realistic by elaborating the grammar. For instance, we should limit the numbers to the range of the main memory of the computer. We may also want to use the numbers of the part of main memory in which the operating system resides, since many (but not all) errors occur in the operating-system portion of memory. Or we may try to associate the error types with the related places in the operating system. But it really depends on how convincing we want our deception to be; if most attackers won't notice subtle details as discussed in Sect. 3.1.2, they would be a waste of time.

7.3   A Stochastic Grammar for Directories

Consider the task of creating fake directory listings. This is useful to combat spies searching for information, as we can entice them deeper and deeper into an endless series of fake files. It is also useful on honeypots to give the impression that a system is being used by legitimate users without having to actually create a large number of convincing files. The deceiver must determine what to do if the attacker tries to use any of these files; we will discuss some options in Sect. 7.7.

Here is a stochastic grammar to generate MS-DOS style listings (what you get if you type "dir" for "Command Prompt" on a Windows system). Here the special symbol "$" is printed as a carriage return, which enables the output to be multiline. The numbers in front of the rules with the same left side do not necessarily sum to

1; these numbers are divided by their sum to get probabilities before the grammar is run, to make it easier to write rules.

```
1.0 start = intro dirlines totallines
1.0 intro = "Volume in drive C has no label." $ "Volume Serial
Number is 005B-52C0." $ $
0.2 dirlines = dirline $
0.8 dirlines = dirline $ dirlines
0.92 dirline = fulldate ~ ~ time ~ ~ ~ ~ ~ ~ ~ ~ ~ spacedfilesize ~
filename
0.08 dirline = fulldate ~ ~ time ~ ~ ~ "<DIR>" ~ ~ ~ ~ ~ ~ ~ ~ ~ ~ ~
~ ~ filename2
1.0 totallines = $ totallines1 $ totallines2 $ $
1.0 totallines1 = "100 Files        " bignumber ~ bytes
1.0 totallines2 = "1 Dir(s)         " bignumber ~ bytes
0.2 filename = filename2 extension
0.05 filename = filename2 digit extension
0.03 filename = filename2 digit digit extension
0.03 filename = filename2 digit digit digit extension
0.3 filename2 = syllable
0.2 filename2 = syllable nonalphchar filename2
1.0 filename2 = syllable filename2
0.1 filename2 = char char char
0.1 filename2 = char char char char
0.1 filename2 = char char char char char
0.2 syllable = consonant vowel
0.2 syllable = consonant vowel consonant
0.2 syllable = vowel vowel
0.05 syllable = consonant consonant
0.7 letter = consonant
0.3 letter = vowel
0.3 extension = ".doc"
0.2 extension = ".txt"
0.1 extension = ".cfg"
0.1 extension = ".ppt"
0.3 extension = ".exe"
0.1 extension = ".bin"
0.1 extension = ".sys"
0.1 extension = ".dat"
0.1 extension = ".dll"
1.0 fulldate = month "/" day "/" year
0.416 time = 0 digit ":" zerofive digit
0.416 time = 1 digit ":" zerofive digit
0.168 time = 2 zerothree ":" zerofive digit
0.5 year = 0 zerotwo
0.5 year = 9 digit
```

```
0.1 month = 01
0.1 month = 02  .
0.1 month = 03
0.1 month = 04
0.1 month = 05
0.1 month = 06
0.1 month = 07
0.1 month = 08
0.1 month = 09
0.1 month = 10
0.1 month = 11
0.1 month = 12
0.94 day = zerotwo digit
0.03 day = 30
0.03 day = 31
0.1 zerotwo = 0
0.1 zerotwo = 1
0.1 zerotwo = 2
0.1 zerothree = 0
0.1 zerothree = 1
0.1 zerothree = 2
0.1 zerothree = 3
0.1 zerofour = 0
0.1 zerofour = 1
0.1 zerofour = 2
0.1 zerofour = 3
0.1 zerofive = 0
0.1 zerofive = 1
0.1 zerofive = 2
0.1 zerofive = 3
0.1 zerofive = 4
0.1 zerofive = 5
0.5 zeroninedigit = 0
0.5 zeroninedigit = 9
0.05 filesize = 0
0.2 digitstring = digit
0.8 digitstring = digit digitstring
0.1 spacedfilesize = frontdigit digit digit ~ ~ ~ ~ ~ ~ ~
0.1 spacedfilesize = frontdigit digit digit digit ~ ~ ~ ~ ~ ~
0.1 spacedfilesize = frontdigit digit digit digit digit ~ ~ ~ ~ ~
0.1 spacedfilesize = frontdigit digit digit digit digit digit ~ ~ ~
~
0.1 spacedfilesize = frontdigit digit digit digit digit digit digit
~ ~ ~
0.1 spacedfilesize = frontdigit digit digit digit digit digit digit
digit ~ ~
```

```
0.5 mediumnumber = digit digit digit digit digit digit
0.5 mediumnumber = digit digit digit digit digit
0.5 mediumnumber = digit digit digit digit
0.5 bignumber = digit digit digit digit digit digit digit digit
digit
0.5 bignumber = digit digit digit digit digit digit digit digit
0.5 bignumber = digit digit digit digit digit digit digit
0.1 digit = 0
0.1 digit = 1
0.1 digit = 2
0.1 digit = 3
0.1 digit = 4
0.1 digit = 5
0.1 digit = 6
0.1 digit = 7
0.1 digit = 8
0.1 digit = 9
0.5 frontdigit = 1
0.25 frontdigit = 2
0.17 frontdigit = 3
0.125 frontdigit = 4
0.10 frontdigit = 5
0.082 frontdigit = 6
0.071 frontdigit = 7
0.062 frontdigit = 8
0.055 frontdigit = 9
0.075 vowel = "a"
0.140 vowel = "e"
0.067 vowel = "i"
0.074 vowel = "o"
0.030 vowel = "u"
0.003 vowel = "y"
0.013 consonant = "b"
0.035 consonant = "c"
0.036 consonant = "d"
0.022 consonant = "f"
0.017 consonant = "g"
0.042 consonant = "h"
0.003 consonant = "j"
0.005 consonant = "k"
0.036 consonant = "l"
0.034 consonant = "m"
0.067 consonant = "n"
0.024 consonant = "p"
0.003 consonant = "q"
0.061 consonant = "r"
```

```
0.067 consonant = "s"
0.099 consonant = "t"
0.017 consonant = "w"
0.003 consonant = "x"
0.013 consonant = "y"
0.001 consonant = "z"
0.05 char = "a"
0.05 char = "e"
0.05 char = "i"
0.05 char = "o"
0.05 char = "u"
0.05 char = "y"
0.05 char = "b"
0.05 char = "c"
0.05 char = "d"
0.05 char = "f"
0.05 char = "g"
0.05 char = "h"
0.05 char = "j"
0.05 char = "k"
0.05 char = "l"
0.05 char = "m"
0.05 char = "n"
0.05 char = "p"
0.05 char = "q"
0.05 char = "r"
0.05 char = "s"
0.05 char = "t"
0.05 char = "v"
0.05 char = "w"
0.05 char = "x"
0.05 char = "y"
0.05 char = "z"
0.15 char = digit
0.05 char = nonalphchar
0.05 nonalphchar = "-"
0.05 nonalphchar = "_"
0.03 nonalphchar = "+"
0.02 nonalphchar = "%"
0.02 nonalphchar = "?"
0.02 nonalphchar = ".
```

Here is example output from this directory grammar.

```
canis> java CFGen Directory.gram
Volume in drive C has no label.
Volume Serial Number is 005B-52C0.
```

```
10/29/90   13:18        43180      ea-sin23.exe
06/07/02   12:08        44739898   yrz35.doc
12/10/98   02:34        1899       0gm.doc
11/21/98   12:31        55461      eoso8.doc
05/12/94   22:08        1157665    ae.exe
12/14/99   10:01        620125     uottr.doc
07/20/90   13:00        173        oab.ppt
07/21/01   18:59        95832163   ppjh.sys
11/20/02   20:52        1752       nen.exe
10/24/00   19:27        5437406    ved.eaoehudiaeelpio662.exe
12/29/92   21:22        558139     yoyd4.dll
11/10/00   22:15        6684313    eareterie.doc
07/06/01   20:18        6508922    ni387.bin
04/27/95   07:57        33476      oorasix%eapirehal.sys
12/29/96   23:47        1973072    ttwehtisii.sys


100 Files 05148304 bytes
1 Dir(s) 446543464 bytes
```

Here the file sizes are not generated with equiprobable random digits, since file sizes tend to be evenly distributed on a logarithmic scale up to some limit. So the first digit "frontdigit" of a size string is chosen with a bias towards smaller digits (a tendency called "Benford's Law"). We also use two kinds of file names (not counting the characters after the last period, the file extension): totally random strings of evenly distributed characters, and (more commonly) syllable-based names. The syllable names try to imitate abbreviations of English words and their concatenations. They are made of random syllables where the characters in each syllable model English letter frequencies (so, say, "z" is unlikely). The probability of each character is based on the character distribution of English.

7.4   Building a Stochastic Grammar

How does one get the rules for a stochastic grammar? It is good to have plenty of examples of what the grammar should generate. This is called a "corpus". This can be done by manually writing down all the examples that we can think of. But it is better if we can get samples of the desired strings, as from a collection of real directory listings when one is writing a directory grammar.

Then you must "parse" the examples, or build trees that group the related parts of the example together. It helps to first focus on identifiable subparts of strings. For example, given time examples "1250AM", "403PM", "830AM", "0900PM", and "1122PM", we can guess that their format is three or four digits followed by "AM" or "PM". We can make a first attempt to summarize this by:

```
1.0 date = minutes meridian
0.5 meridian = AM
0.5 meridian = PM
0.5 minutes = digit digit digit
0.5 minutes = digit digit digit digit
```

We can refine these rules by running them with the program in Appendix B and looking for incorrect strings that are generated, then applying fixes to prevent them. For instance, the above rules will generate "8363AM" which has too large a number. This requires additional restrictions on the first three digits:

```
1.0 date = minutes meridian
0.5 meridian = AM
0.5 meridian = PM
0.5 minutes = digit digit06 digit
0.5 minutes = frontdigitpair digit06 digit
0.25 frontdigitpair = 0 digit
0.25 frontdigitpair = "10"
0.25 frontdigitpair = "11"
0.25 frontdigitpair = "12"
0.16 digit06 = 0
0.16 digit06 = 1
0.16 digit06 = 2
0.16 digit06 = 3
0.16 digit06 = 4
0.16 digit06 = 5
0.1 digit = 0
0.1 digit = 1
0.1 digit = 2
0.1 digit = 3
0.1 digit = 4
0.1 digit = 5
0.1 digit = 6
0.1 digit = 7
0.1 digit = 8
0.1 digit = 9
```

Recursion can be used in rules to permit arbitrarily-long strings. The simplest form is "tail recursion", where the last thing on the right side of a rule is the same thing on the left side. This sets up a form of indefinite looping, as for:

```
0.5 digitstring = digit
0.5 digitstring = digit digitstring
```

This gives a one-digit string 50 % of the time, a two-digit string 25 % of the time, a three-digit string 12.5 % of the time, a four-digit string 6.25 % of the time, and so on. A random choice of the first rule will prevent this from going on forever.

7.5   Detail-Changing Tactics

Another simple strategy for making fakes is to just change a few details in an existing example like its times and locations. This is helpful for finding spies as mentioned in Sect. 3.1.3. To accomplish this, we can define systematic transformations on text using the regular-expression facility in most programming languages. Dates and times are in a limited number of forms and are easy to find. Locations are more complicated, but there are latitude-longitude coordinates and word lists of geographical names, and location expressions often occur in specific places in the formatted messages. Similar easily-modifiable details are code numbers and email addresses. Consider this original message:

> From: ReviewersPHOOEY14@confinf.org
> Sent: Friday, June 11, 2014 12:38 PM
> To: Pompous, Professor
> Subject: EVALUATIONS...
> Dear Dr Professor Pompous:
> Thank you very much for reviewing the paper titled "Atavistic Obfuscation in Academic Discourse." Your evaluation has been received successfully. As we informed you before, your name will be included among the additional reviewers list, in the hard copies and in the CDs of the Conference Proceedings of PHOOEY 2014.
> Sincerely,
> Harry D. Chairperson

We can use this as a basis for a fake email by changing the times and dates in the header and in the body. We can identify these with the two digits before the "@" in the first line, the second line after the first word, and the last word of the paragraph. Then the new times can be defined as an evenly distributed in the interval of 0800 to 1700, and the new dates can be distributed randomly through the weekdays of the year. The title of the paper can be generated by a special set of grammar rules. Here's a possible transformation of the example message:

> From: ReviewersHUMBUG04@confinf.org
> Sent: Wednesday, October 4, 2015 09:21 AM
> To: Pompous, Professor
> Subject: EVALUATIONS...
> Dear Dr Professor Pompous:
> Thank you very much for reviewing the paper titled "Aspects of Massive Information Acquisition." Your evaluation has been received successfully. As we informed you before, your name will be included among the additional reviewers list, in the hard copies and in the CDs of the Conference Proceedings of HUMBUG 2015.
> Sincerely,
> Harry D. Chairperson

An alternative to using a grammar to model low-level details is to use it for higher-level details and make its bottom-level symbols represents blocks of text. Then the grammar can permit us to combine existing documents in random ways to make fake documents. Examples of useful blocks of codes can be extracted from the common kinds of messages and files on a cybersystem.

For instance, sentences of text can be extracted from routine jargon-laden messages. These can then be combined in random orders to make interesting fake messages. Header lines can also be extracted randomly from messages. With this approach, each sentence appears to make sense by itself, even if the combination does not make sense. This will not be suspicious if we limit the number of total sentences to a small number, or we embed sentences in a standard formatted structure. A good example of this is SCIGEN, a generator for fake computer-science technical papers (pdos.cscail.mit.edu/archive/scigen) that is good enough to fool some conference committees into accepting its output for conferences. Here an example paragraph generated by SCIGEN:

Motivated by the need for the development of the World Wide Web, we now present an architecture for showing that the well-known authenticated algorithm for the refinement of DHTs [23] is NP-complete. While statisticians often postulate the exact opposite, Inflow depends on this property for correct behavior. Rather than learning lambda calculus, our algorithm chooses to construct adaptive methodologies [2]. On a similar note, our heuristic does not require such a key allowance to run correctly, but it doesn't hurt. Rather than learning massive multiplayer online role-playing games, our approach chooses to harness certifiable modalities. Despite the results by W. Bhabha, we can show that sensor networks [4] can be made embedded, client-server, and autonomous. This is a robust property of Inflow. Consider the early framework by Sun et al.; our architecture is similar, but will actually realize this objective. Despite the fact that theorists largely assume the exact opposite, our heuristic depends on this property for correct behavior.

It should be noted that there are word clues to deception that a deceiver should try to avoid. Pennebaker et al. (2001) found four kinds in the frequency of words used: (1) decreased frequency of first-person pronouns like "I", (2) decreased frequency of words indicating exceptions like "but", (3) increased frequency of words indicating negative emotions like "hate", and (4) increased frequency of verbs of action like "run". These clues indicate a desire to camouflage information. So artificially generated fakes need to be checked to see if they are avoiding these clues.

7.6   Fighting Spam and Phishing with Fakes

Fakes are also useful in fighting misuse of the Internet in the form of spam and phishing in email. Many of these emails direct you to a Web site where you are persuaded to give up your money (for spam) or identity (for phishing (Jakobsson and Myers 2006)). This is often done by having you fill out Web forms. So a useful deception is to create some fake forms to counterattack these sites, confusing the attackers and filling their sites with useless data, in a kind of defensive denial-of-service.

For instance, consider a phishing email claiming to be from a bank, asking you to go to their Web site and confirm your account information. A program could extract the contents of that Web site, infer the form that needs to be submitted, and send a million copies with random data entries to the destination site. To tip off the bank being impersonated, fill the form with invalid data, e.g. account numbers with too many digits, user names consisting entirely of punctuation marks, or forms with blank required information. But you don't want to be too obviously wrong, because you want the phisher to send the information to the bank. The more they send in, the easier it is for the bank to trace them, and the more you will help human phishing victims.

7.7 Fake Software

Another useful type of fake file is fake software. Files that look like executables can be made by generating random characters with distributions similar to that of executable code. Then they will likely not hurt anything if executed. Deceptive executables that must be run (such as those implementing monitoring in a honeypot) require different methods. Concealment of the modification of executables in particular can be increased by making the code less understandable. This is known as "code obfuscation" (Heiderich et al. 2010; Dang et al. 2014), and a variety of techniques are practiced by writers of malware. For defense, this is only necessary for a few key routines, like a honeypot's forwarding of monitoring data. But for offense, obfuscation needs to be used routinely.

Fake exploit code (code that is claimed to enable attacks but which doesn't) can be posted or offered for sale at attacker sites. But since this will hurt the reputation of the poster, impersonation is necessary.

Fake software is helpful in detecting theft of software. Stolfo (2012) proposed generating Java source code that deceptively appears as valuable proprietary software. The deception target was an attacker trying to steal software that implements intellectual-property rights. Various beacons were inserted into the deceptive software to connect to a server operated by the defender and thus report the time and location of where the software was run. Beacons were implemented by inserting crafted Javascript code into PDF and HTML files which are made to appear as the documentation that accompanies the proprietary software. When those files were opened by the attacker, the Javascript code calls home. Another form of beacon was inserted into the deceptive Java source code itself in the form of a library dependency. When the source code was compiled, the user was notified that a library is required for the code to compile, and that that library can be downloaded from a remote server. The remote server logs the time and address of all connections that are made to it. Furthermore, upon compilation of the deceptive software files, the inserted blocks of code produce bytecode that can open a network socket and call home.

7.8 Fake File Systems

Using fake files, we could build an entire fake file system. This could be a good way to improve the credibility of a honeypot. Many operating-system files can be faked by copying and modifying legitimate files from a similar but busy machine.

Then we can do detail-shifting as in Sect. 7.5 to make copying less obvious. While most operating systems are reluctant to let you copy their files, techniques from digital forensics (Altheide and Carvey 2011) can circumvent the operating system to make copies of the contents of secondary-storage devices.

One easy way to implement this is through a fake Web interface, a Web program that creates files while pretending to show existing files. An open-source platform for doing this is the Honeyd software from the Honeynet Project (www.honeynet.org). We also built our own program to do this as a "honeypot for spies", designed to entice spies into seeing false connections between unrelated activities. The code in Appendix A does this in addition to delaying suspicious users as mentioned before. The code creates HTML for Web pages dynamically. It then generates a screen display, creating names of fake files for directories, and caches key information in a table to ensure consistency between return visits to this file or directory by this or other users. Figure 7.1 shows a sample screen from our program.

A few file names were generated at random, but most were real names of public Web files and directories at NPS, though not usually assigned to their original directories. Each of the files and directories on the screen can be clicked upon. Those that are supposed to be files show some appropriate data. Those that are supposed to be subdirectories cause a subdirectory listing to appear on the screen, with a new set of files and subdirectories generated in a similar manner to the original directory. In principle the directory structure is infinite, but the rate of inclusion of subdirectories is designed to decrease as the user descends in the structure, as with real directory structures.

Fig. 7.1 Example fake directory listing

Directory of /root

```
12/11/96 07:08 <DIR>
09/11/96 23:07 40        ArmedForcesAtNPS.htm
09/23/91 01:44 <DIR>     CMDC
06/29/02 12:43 <DIR>     Chapel
10/25/98 23:18 <DIR>     Club
03/07/98 04:24 <DIR>     Docs
08/23/97 15:07 <DIR>     Faculty
01/24/96 01:11 <DIR>     GSOIS
02/28/94 12:19 2635      HN.syc
03/12/98 01:07 <DIR>     ICON
01/06/02 12:54 <DIR>     Leisure_Serv
04/09/97 11:46 <DIR>     Nemesis
06/21/01 18:23 <DIR>     RSL
01/18/98 10:02 <DIR>     ResAdmin
03/20/96 16:26 130       SEAprogram.htm
06/29/96 10:56 <DIR>     Travel
10/14/00 20:11 2858      Tutorials.rzp
05/26/90 20:22 228558    WindmillsOct2002_files.cry
06/11/95 08:30 <DIR>     admin
07/20/98 08:22 415       announcement_april_01_2002_picture.html
07/02/02 14:20 65        announcement_april_02_2002_picture02.html
02/18/01 21:57 <DIR>     bugs
```

We designed a number of possible results of clicking on a file, to enhance believability of the system. An easy thing to increase attacker frustration is to give error messages. When a user tries to open any of the displayed files, sometimes at random they get a page saying that they do not have authorization to view the file; this can increase the interest for a spy because it suggests there are secrets here. The particular error message a user gets is generated by a pseudo-random process whose "seed" or originating number is the size of the file in the original directory listing, so a user will consistently get the same error message for the same file at any time. Other error messages we generate provide other kinds of access denial, like the excuse that a very large file is too big to load.

Otherwise if a random error message is not triggered, we try to show the user some plausible data when they attempt to open a file. Fake files with extensions "exe" and "bin" model executable files, "cry" and "rzp" model encrypted and compressed files, "gcc" and "syc" model some specialized file formats, and "htm" and "html" model traditional HTML files. All but the HTML files should appear to the user as mostly randomly generated strings as in Fig. 7.2, which shows randomly generated bytes (Unicode values 0–255) as viewed by a Web browser. Different kinds of randomness can give the impression of different kinds of content, as for instance using only the Ascii character set (Unicode values 0–127) is appropriate for text files, and using only base-16 or base-64 digits is appropriate for certain kinds of encoded files.

Fig. 7.2   Contents of fake file "WinmillsOct2002 files.cry"

The HTML files were created from actual images and captions at our school, as found by a Web "crawler" that retrieved pages and followed links. The only deception with these files is in the paths alleged to them, which involve a certain degree of random association. For instance, Fig. 7.3 shows the file provided for path "/root/Docs/redux1_files/ snort2xml/loops/op2.html". Since "Snort" is the name of a computer intrusion-detection system, it would interest a spy for it to be associated with a picture of satellite communication.

Another example is shown in Fig. 7.4, of file "root/Docs/4thofJuly1_files/modeling/teampics/hofler/brclr.htm". Its caption claims this to be a beer cooler, but all that electronics is hardly necessary to cool beer; a spy would likely infer a more sinister purpose. They would also wonder what this could have to do with modeling or the fourth of July, two terms randomly inserted in the path to the page. Given enough examples, there are bound to be a few juxtapositions like this that will intrigue a spy since the human brain is very good at seeing patterns where none exist.

7.9   Distribution of Fake Documents

Tools have been developed to generate, distribute, and monitor large numbers of fake documents. Bowen et al. (2009) developed the Decoy Document Distributor System, and (Voris et al. 2013) developed the Decoy Distributor Tool. These try to

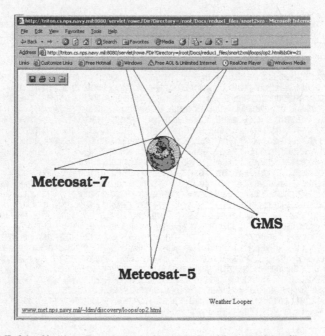

Fig. 7.3 HTML fake file "/root/Docs/redux1_files/snort2xml/loops/op2.html"

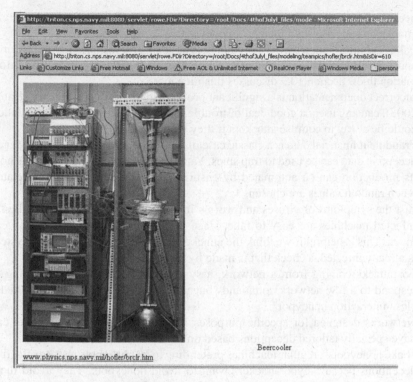

Fig. 7.4 Fake file "root/Docs/4thofJuly1_files/modeling/teampics/hofler/brclr.htm"

identify desirable traits of a decoy document, such as believability, enticingness, conspicuousness, and detectability, features that Chap. 11 will try to quantify. They then developed code that applies those traits to decoy documents. Next, they identified file-system locations that are most likely to be accessed by a malicious insider. The decoy documents were then placed in those locations, either integrated with genuine and existing documents or in a separate directory. Other tricks can be used too. For instance, decoy documents can be written in a foreign language (Voris et al. 2012), which makes it easy for legitimate users to tell which documents are decoys, and minimizes the interference of decoy documents with their work. An attacker may need to exfiltrate (copy) the document to translate it, which increases the detectability of the malicious activity.

7.10 Other Useful Fakes

Fakes can be useful for deception in several other ways:

- A few fake files can be stored within an otherwise normal file system to see if spies are collecting information from it (Whitham 2013). Then we would not need an entire fake file system. But it is more difficult to detect and analyze attacks on such a system than on a honeypot.

- Fake user information can be stored in files as "bait", for instance fake passwords and keys. Then the use of such information alerts you to the presence of an information thief. Section 10.3 discusses this idea more.
- Incorrect documentation is a significant problem in the software industry (Kaner 2003), causing users a good deal of trouble. So deliberately fake documentation could be a way to confuse attackers if they read it.
- Fraudulent financial data is a classic case of deception, and deliberately designed deceptive data can be used to trap spies. Yang and Mannino (2012) suggests how its production can be automated by ensuring that key numbers are correlated when random values are chosen.
- Just the symptoms of viruses and worms in a cybersystem can be faked. Badly infected machines are easy to fake, since the system doesn't need to do very much. This is helpful if we think the attacker will go away if they think a system is already infected, a check that is made by some sophisticated malware.
- For attacks coming from a network, a system can be faked by pretending to respond to a few network commands but not permitting login. This is called a "low-interaction honeypot".
- Networks designed for specific purposes like industrial control networks can have specially tailored deceptions based on simulations (see Sect. 15.3).
- "Fake honeypots", regular machines pretending to be honeypots, can be effective deceptions because cyberattackers want to avoid honeypots. They avoid them because honeypots collect data on attackers and discover attacker secrets, and honeypots are generally tough to subvert although they seem easy at first. So we could build a file system that looks like a honeypot, containing what seems to be monitoring software, in the hopes of scaring some attackers away. The attackers we scare away will be the smarter ones, so this type of fake has the rare advantage of working best against smarter adversaries.
- Computer hardware produces electromagnetic signals which can be picked up by electronic eavesdroppers under the right circumstances with the right equipment. This is particularly a problem for displays, but can also be a problem with keyboards, printers, modems, and wireless devices since they use slow signals. If eavesdropping is possible, fake signals can be generated to mislead the attacker.
- Computer hardware itself could be fake, looking like the real thing but actually containing malicious capabilities. A scare in 2008 about counterfeit Cisco routers created quite a stir, though no malicious capabilities were found (Lawson and McMillan 2008). Such fakes would be poorly cost-effective, however, because once discovered they would lose value quickly and be very difficult to use again.

7.11 Dynamic Fakes with Packet Manipulation

A weakness of most of the aforementioned fakes is that they are static or fixed. An alternative is to create fakes when needed as with the random-data files in our fake Web site of Appendix A. More elaborate fakes can be constructed by manipulating the attacker's communications directly to change slightly the information returning to them, enough to upset their plans. For instance, if we change the addresses or file sizes in operating-system data we may be able to stop buffer-overflow attempts based on it. Section 13.3 reports experiments with Snort Inline, a tool for modifying bits in packets to achieve deceptions.

7.12 Inducing Paranoia

Since most attackers know what they are doing is illegal and wrong, it is not difficult to encourage some paranoia in them about being monitored for criminal prosecution or counterattack. Many hackers in particular have a high sense of self-worth, and it may seem plausible to them that big organizations would spend countless hours watching their every move. Deception aimed at encouraging these fantasies may cause attackers to waste time on fruitless searches and might even scare them away from some systems. It is hard to predict exactly what paranoid attackers might do because this will vary with their personalities. However, most of the possible responses will be desirable for defenders because we are disrupting attacker plans.

A simple way to encourage paranoia is to leave clues semi-randomly for them to find. These can be in error messages, log files, process names, names of files, or text within files. Good clues are anything related to the name, session, or files of the attacker, and any words suggestive of monitoring, recording, or logging. For instance, if a hacker is logged in as "crakker57", the error message "Error at 038529483: log_crakker57.dmp overflow" could cause them to worry. Also suspicious would be a file in the operating system temporary directories called "log_crakker57.dmp" in the rare event that the attacker would look there; you might need to put similar files in many places through the file system to guarantee an effect. What could you put within those files? Random bits would be fine since they would suggest encryption.

Even better for encouraging paranoia would be direct messages to the attacker. These could even be designed to be clumsily obvious if the goal is to scare the attacker away. For instance, you could send the attacker periodic messages saying "We are watching your attack—Don't think you can get away with it." This could be appended to packets sent back to the attacker, sent in UDP messages to their IP address, or even emailed to them if their email address is known. Bear in mind, however, that different attackers will react differently to the same message, and some may just redouble their efforts. A more subtle approach could be to create files with names related to the attacker and which grow in proportion to what the attacker does.

A related idea is to degrade target files so attackers cannot get what they want, encouraging frustration as well as paranoia. This is the idea behind "decoy" music files that certain music-industry companies have inserted onto peer-to-peer networks under the same names as real music files (Kushner 2003). The decoys consist of noise or other forms of useless audio, and are placed with the idea of discouraging illegal downloads. Something similar can be done with files that are intelligence targets. Discovering such files does tell the attacker that they have been detected, which can be either good or bad depending on defender goals.

7.13   Conclusions

Fakes are a useful tool in deception, and are especially useful for defense where they can be used to manipulate cyberattackers. By giving them wrong information on what they need to exploit us, we can waste their time and get them confused. Fakes can be easy to construct by modifying existing documents and data, and we can measure their degree of plausibility to be more scientific. We can minimize problems with deceiving legitimate users by putting our fakes in places where only attackers will look.

7.14   Exercises

1. Create a stochastic grammar for fake system error-log entries, including time and date, command executed, and type of error generated. Such files could make a system look more "used", and they don't need to be in traditional places to be effective.
2. Create a stochastic grammar for plausible names of government organizations, e.g. "Office of Long-Term Strategic Planning", and their acronyms. These can be scattered in fake documents to make them look "official".
3. Write a stochastic grammar for the delay messages described in Sect. 6.2, that attribute the delay to some kind of nonexistent resource.
4. Suppose our strategy to make honeypots more convincing is to copy their disk contents from a single existing legitimate cybersystem. But attackers will notice things that are identical on every system they see. What things in the operating-system files should be highest priority to change on each honeypot to reduce the chances that attackers will be suspicious?
5. Suppose to fool foreign-government attackers of an intelligence network we construct a "fake network" to serve as a decoy. It will have collections of documents that appear to be related to secret intelligence activities.

   (a) How could we arrange it so that attackers would be more likely to find the decoy network rather than the real network?

(b) Why is it important to limit the size and scope of the network? Suggest a good way to do so.

(c) What kinds of files should we put on the decoy network to help convince attackers that it is the real network?

(d) Propose a way to keep the nodes of the network supplied with convincing fake data, while at the same time minimizing the revelation of true secret data.

(e) How should we modify those files over time to make them more convincing? Give some examples.

(f) What other kinds of clues should we put on the decoy network to help convince attackers that it is the real network?

(g) You want to allow spies onto this network, but what sort of activities do you want to prevent them from doing? How do you prevent these activities while minimizing their realization that they are being manipulated?

6. Fake honeypots benefit from having file systems that look obviously fake. What directories and characteristics of their files should be best to focus on to make it appear obviously fake? What should we do with them to make the fakery more noticeable?

7. An idea recently gaining popularity is to have deliberate differences between cybersystems so that any attack won't work on very many of them. One form of this is to have many different versions of operating systems, and lots of differences in the software running on those systems. This would seem to help, but what problems does this cause for creating good fake cybersystems? How much uniformity is necessary for useful fake cybersystems?

References

Afroz S, Brennan M, Greenstadt R (2012) Detecting hoaxes, frauds, and deception in online writing style. In: Proceedings of IEEE symposium on security and privacy, Oakland, CA, pp 461–475

Altheide C, Carvey H (2011) Digital forensics with open source tools. Syngress, Waltham MA, US

Amore A (2015) The art of the con: the most notorious fakes, frauds, and forgeries in the art world. St. Martin's, New York

Bowen B, Hershkop S, Keromytis A, Stolfo SJ (2009) Baiting inside attackers using decoy documents. Proceedings of the ICST conference on security and privacy in communication networks Athens, Greece, September, paper 19

Dang B, Gazet A, Bachaalany E, Josse S (2014) Practical reverse engineering: x86, x64, ARM, Windows kernel, reversing tools, and obfuscation. Wiley, New York

Heiderich M, Nava E, Heyes G, Lindsay D (2010) Web application obfuscation: '-/WAFs... Evasion.Filters//alert/Obfuscation/-'. Syngress, Rockland, MA

Jakobsson M, Myers S (eds) (2006) Phishing and countermeasures: understanding the increasing problem of electronic identity theft. Wiley-Interscience, New York

Kaner C (2003) Liability for defective documentation. In: Proceedings of SIGDOC 2003 conference, San Francisco, CA, US, 12–15 October 2003, pp. 192–197.

Kaza S, Murthy S, Hu G (2003) Identification of deliberately doctored 'text documents using frequent keyword chain (FKC) model. In: Proceedings of the IEEE international conference on information reuse and integration, Las Vegas, NV. pp 398–405

Kushner D (2003) Digital decoys. IEEE Spectrum 40(5):27

Latimer J (2003) Deception in war; the art of the bluff, the value of deceit, and the most thrilling episodes of cunning in military history, from the Trojan Horse to the Gulf War. The Overlook, New York

Lawson S, McMillan R (2008) FBI worried as DoD sold counterfeit Cisco gear. InfoWorld, May 12

Pennebaker J, Francis M, Booth R (2001) Linguistic inquiry and word count (LIWC). Lawrence Erlbaum, New York

Stolfo S (2012) Software decoys for insider threat. Proceedings of the 7th ACM symposium on information, computer, and communications security, Seoul, Korea, May 2012

Voris J, Boggs N, Stolfo S J (2012) Lost in translation: Improving decoy documents via automated translation. Proceedings of the workshop on research for insider threats, May

Voris J, Jermyn J, Keromytis A D, Stolfo S J (2013) Bait and snitch: defending computer systems with decoys. Proceedings of the cyber infrastructure protection conference, Strategic Studies Institute, September

Whitham B (2013) Canary files: Generating fake files to detect critical data loss from complex computer networks. Proceedings of the 2nd international conference on cyber security, cyber peacefare, and digital forensics, Malaysia, 2013

Yang Y, Mannino M (2012) An experimental comparison of a document deception detection policy using real and artificial deception. ACM Journal of Data and Information Quality 3 (3): 6:1–6:25s

Chapter 8
Defensive Camouflage

Camouflage, or concealment of something real, is a common technique of offensive cyberdeception (Ford and Howard 2007). It can be used for defense to hide valuable data and programs. Also, since it can also be used to conceal the perpetrators of an attack (Nunes et al. 2015), it can similarly conceal defenders. The techniques of Chap. 7 can aid camouflage, but there are others.

8.1 Hiding a Honeypot

The goal for most serious cyberattackers is to take control of your systems with rootkits. These are modified operating systems that, while seeming normal, permit the attacker the powers they want to do anything they want on your system. Naturally an attacker wants to conceal this because otherwise you could reinstall the operating

© Springer International Publishing Switzerland 2016

N.C. Rowe, J. Rrushi, *Introduction to Cyberdeception*,

DOI 10.1007/978-3-319-41187-3_8

system and destroy their rootkit. So most attackers have detailed methods to conceal their rootkits and their installation.

Defenders can also make use of rootkit ideas when they have something important to hide. An example is a honeypot: Attackers want to avoid honeypots, so designers of true honeypots should conceal the evidence of it in the code that collects data on the attacker. While many systems collect audit records, a honeypot collects more extensive data on the user, often including their actual commands ("keystrokes") much like the keyloggers used by cyberattackers. That means several things need to be hidden on a good honeypot:

- Running honeypot processes should be concealed if possible. One way is by modifying the process-listing code to explicitly ignore them (Holz and Raynal 2005). This trick is common with rootkits, since most rootkits need to run continuously to prevent anti-rootkit measures.
- Some of what an attacker does is logged automatically with the operating system (such as by Event Viewer on Windows systems), and those logs are easy for an attacker to check, and with sufficient privileges, modify. But honeypots need to keep their own more detailed logs which should be concealed to avoid detection and modification. This could be done by modifying the directory-listing and file-listing utilities of the operating system to avoid reporting those files in particular, an idea used first in the Sebek tool of the Honeynet Project (The Honeynet Project 2004) and its successors like Qebek.
- The more detailed logs needed by a honeypot require additional output commands which could be suspicious. One way to help conceal them is to modify the system "write" command, which echoes commands on the screen, to also send its data elsewhere, as with Sebek. To prevent an attacker from finding this modification, code obfuscation tricks can be used (Heiderich et al. 2010; Dang et al. 2014), or the key code can be deliberately concealed by the operating system if a user tries to list it.
- The data recorded by the honeypot needs to be encrypted quickly, since unencrypted data could alert the attacker that they are being monitored. Public-key encrypted data cannot be deciphered, although the user might get some clue that encrypted data represents monitoring from its steadily increasingly size.
- Usually honeypots occur in sets called "honeynets". Then it makes sense to aggregate data over the honeynet in a collection site. This site needs to be carefully concealed since its activities are quite different from normal machines and are suspicious to an attacker, and therefore will be a good attack target itself for a determined attacker. Two clever approaches will help (The Honeynet Project 2004):

  - Put the data-collection connections on a separate subnetwork unconnected to the regular network for the machines. This would require a second network card for each machine that connects to the data-collection subnetwork. This requires some hardware and setup time, but is quite secure.

- Let the data-collection machine eavesdrop on the network via its electromagnetic emissions. For instance, put a "bug" or electronic pickup on an easily recognized cable and send packets through it. This has the advantage of no obvious external transmission of packets.

- Even though honeypots are designed to be attacked, honeynet installations need to be "good citizens" and not attack other machines. This can be done with a "honeywall", an extra node limiting attack traffic from the honeypots, which has no equivalent on ordinary systems. Attackers may be able to infer a honeywall by studying the time-to-live values in packets, which normally are decremented with each node they traverse. Sebek addresses this by violating standard protocols by failing to decrement the time-to-live value for its packets passing through the honeywall, a useful trick.

- Honeypots need not only be passive. While taking advantage of their concealment, they can initiate traceback to find where attackers are coming from (Tian et al. 2007).

8.2 Disguising the Operating Systems and Networks

Another useful thing to conceal is the version of the operating system or application that is running on the defender's machine. Knowing the version saves the attacker time because many attacks are specific to particular versions. If we can fool them in the initial or "footprinting" phase of an attack, they may figure they cannot attack us and go away.

Most footprinting techniques for operating systems working by sending special packets to a system to see how it responds. There are some small differences between versions of operating systems in these responses because of different implementations of the protocols. Classic techniques involve sending unusual packets not anticipated by the protocol designers because these are more likely to be handled inconsistently, and sending packets to insufficiently tested protocols. More sophisticated techniques time the responses, but this is subject to network fluctuations with traffic and can require repeated tries.

How do we exploit this for deception? We get our operating system to fake characteristics of a different operating-system version so that it will attract higher numbers of ineffective attacks. For instance, a Windows operating system can pretend to be a Linux operating system. This can be done with the packet manipulations to be discussed in Chap. 13 using low-interaction honeypots like Honeyd. For now, note that we need either a modified protocol for each kind of attack or a special-purpose toolkit for manipulating a range of packets, like a more aggressive firewall. We can find how to manipulate the packets by checking the many references to footprinting online and in books. Or we can experiment with the attacker to learn what they respond to.

A way to camouflage a network is to randomly shuffle the addresses of systems and machines (Yegneswaran et al. 2007). IP addresses are essential to locating machines on the Internet. If we change the address of a machine every day, it will repeatedly invalidate footprinting that has been done on that machine. It would also make it difficult for a bot controller to maintain contact with a machine under their control. For this to work, we need to avoid confusing our own networks too. One way is to have "translation" hardware on our local networks that maps addresses to their daily assignment.

8.3 Concealing Patches

Bugs are being found in software all the time, requiring patches (fixes) by the vendor. The patches themselves are good intelligence information for attackers, because attackers can reverse-engineer them to figure out the vulnerabilities they are addressing, then attack the machines that have not updated yet. Why does that matter? Because it may take a long time for patches to reach all of a user community, particularly for vendors with few resources. Attackers often have a long window of opportunity between the first dissemination of a patch and successful patching by all users.

For defensive purposes, it may help to distribute patches clandestinely (Bashar et al. 1997). If attackers don't know that a patch is going out, they can't target its vulnerability immediately. Distribution could be done under the cover of normal communications on the Internet, and could use steganography (see below). It will help to change other files in the operating system at the same time so that it is harder for the attacker to discover which files contain a patch. These other files could be modified in trivial nonfunctional ways to further confuse an attacker.

8.4 Covert Channels and Steganography

Covert channels are ways to secretly move information on cybersystems. They are ways of not only keeping the information secret, but of keeping its very existence secret (or the acts of creating or transferring it). They differ from cryptography which just keeps its information secret. An encrypted file if often easy to recognize from its file extension and its byte distribution.

Steganography is the best-known covert-channel technique (Fridich 2009). It conceals data in the small details of innocent-looking data. Pictures are a good place because they require a large number of bits. When digitized as a set of pixel brightnesses, the least-significant bits have virtually invisible effects, so we can use those bits to hold a message. Similarly, we could hide a honeypot's monitoring data in the times of what appears to be routine log data within the recorded fractions of seconds at which events occurred; the fractions could code the command that an attacker used.

There are many ways to do steganography, some of them quite subtle, and people from which you wish to conceal something can't find them all. A classic case is a text file that encodes secret information in the pattern of spaces on the end of each line; few people will think to count the spaces, so the text file appears normal. Another example is using the first letter of each sentence to send a message. With binary data, a message can be hidden in a pattern of widely-spaced bits known only to the receiver. Steganography can even be done with computer programs by having the arrangement of interchangeable instructions represent the secret information. So steganography can be effective by the same reason as deceptions in general in Chaps. 4 and 5 in that the diversity of its forms makes detection very difficult.

To hide data even better, covert channels can use the times of actions to encode data. For instance, a defender could send a byte of all zeros to a data-collection site on occasion. Even though the data does not vary, the time at which it is sent provides information. A gap between data of more than 10 ms could denote a "1", and a gap of less than 10 ms could denote a "0". Using this scheme, you could send 100 bits per second while appearing to just send useless traffic, a data transfer rate sufficient to encode the names of the commands an attacker is using on a honeypot. To send more bits, we can signal something different with a gap of 9–10 ms, 10–11 ms, and so on. This is an example of a "timing convert channel". An attacker might be able to find the signaling machinery, however, and might figure out what it does by reverse engineering.

The general method for detecting steganography is to take many kinds of statistics on the data to see if anything is anomalous. For instance, we can compute the distribution of the last character in each word to see if it is similar to the distribution of typical files. We can do this for every steganographic technique we know. For instance, we should count the number of spaces on the end of every line in a text file, the distribution of first letters of every word in a text file, the histogram of bytes in the file, the order of pairs of successive instructions in a program, and the binned histogram of time intervals between successively transmitted messages. There are many things to check, and deceivees won't have the time to check them all. So steganography can be a quite effective communications tool.

Anderson et al. (2015) suggests some clever ways to conceal what the user of a digital device is doing with the device. This is useful for situations such as when someone wishes to read their email during a meeting but wishes to appear polite and not to appear to read it. The same techniques may be quite useful for spies or anyone who wants to appear uninteresting.

8.5   Other Anti-Forensics Techniques

Camouflage is an instance of the more general concept of "anti-forensics" which means attempts to thwart intelligence gathering by forensic techniques. Forensic techniques examine the contents of a cybersystem in a systematic way to find everything important there. Chinese hackers appear to be doing a considerable amount of forensic investigation in their espionage, so anti-forensics is particularly useful against them. Anti-forensics is rare since most users have little need to hide anything besides passwords, so it can surprise attackers.

Jahankhani and Beqiri (2010) enumerates categories of anti-forensic techniques. Of these, the most useful ones for defensive deception which we have not discussed before are:

- Planting large numbers of dummy files to confuse intelligence gathering: This can slow down analysis, but is obvious.
- Falsification of metadata on files: This can slow down analysis and also could hurt routine operations.
- Renaming of files: This requires modification of all references to the files, which could be a good deal of work.
- Hiding files in space marked as unusable on a disk or memory ("slack space" or "unallocated space") or in other odd places in the file system (Huebner et al. 2006): This requires circumventing the operating system and thus using special techniques to retrieve the data.
- Hiding data within main memory: This requires considerable setup time, and main-memory forensic tools can circumvent it.
- Systematic anonymization of data: This could be useful against data-gathering attacks. It can be done with Internet data as well to concealed Internet connections.

8.6 Conclusions

Camouflage in cyberspace is difficult against a determined attacker because automated tools can search thoroughly most ways in which data could be stored. Nonetheless, attackers do not have time to inspect most of the huge amounts of data on cybersystems and networks today, and this provides opportunities to hide things.

8.7 Exercises

1. Animals that live in forests often have spots on their skins to enable better camouflage since forests have considerable variation in brightness. Give a good analogy to this for cyberspace.
2. In changing IP addresses periodically on a local-area network to foil footprinting, it may be best to use addresses that are predictable according to an algorithm so that our network nodes can change without needing to communicate with one

another. Suggest a good algorithm that does not require much computation time but is difficult for an attacker to guess.

3. Early versions of the Microsoft Windows operating system stored the basic operating system in the same locations in the front of main memory for every machine. This made it easy for attackers to craft malware that would work on every machine. So later versions put the operating system in varied locations.

   (a) How can the operating system prevent attackers from just retrieving the table of the locations used by the operating system on a particular machine?
   (b) Relocation requires modifying the addresses in branch instructions in the code of each executable. How can this be done with registers without slowing down the execution speed?
   (c) Discuss the obstacles to making this dynamic, so that every time a machine reboots it would put the pieces of the operating system in different places in main memory.

4. (a) The following message is concealing steganographically some of a well-known number. What is the number?
      "Yes. I hate a brash complaint as anyone could now after betrayal."
   (b) The following message is concealing a well-known slogan steganographically. What is the slogan?
      "Let it be every regular time you are not doing just user sessions. Take it carefully except for overt recklessness and libelous links."
   (c) This following table from a database is concealing a message from a spy. What is it?

   Office Code MKTNG EYANHE PERSTR3 XQMARV TELECMA CYWPTO DEVUP1 QBSMXI SUPPRD AEVOKL SUPEPR NBWLLI PLANT2 OCUCGL ECOM1 ANWFFT MCOMN DIVWOP ADMO SLEZNP

5. Suppose a user is concealing data using steganography distributed over several files on a cybersystem. Steganography means hiding information by scattering it in small pieces over unnoticeable details of the files.

   (a) How could cryptographic hash codes on the files help give you candidate files to check? Cryptographic hash codes are complex functions computed on files using encryption methods to provide a generally unique number for each file.
   (b) How in some cases could you guess that files are being used for this purpose by analysis of their file creation, modification, and access times?
   (c) Suppose we also have hashes on the 4096-byte blocks of each file. How could this make it easier to detect such steganography than having hashes on the entire files?

References

Anderson F, Grossman T, Wigdor D, Fitzmaurice G (2015) Supporting subtlety with deceptive devices and illusory interactions. In: Proceedings of CHI 2015, Seoul, South Korea, 18–23 Apr 2015

Bashar M, Krishnan G, Kuhn, M, Spafford, E, Wagstaff, S (1997) Low-threat security patches and tools. In: Proceedings of the international conference on software maintenance, Bari, IT, 1-3 Oct, 1997. pp 306–313

Dang B, Gazet A, Bachaalany E, Josse S (2014) Practical reverse engineering: x86, x64, ARM, Windows kernel, reversing tools, and obfuscation. Wiley, New York

Ford R, Howard M (2007) How not to be seen. IEEE Security and Privacy 5(1):67–69

Fridich J (2009) Steganography in digital media: principles, algorithms, and applications. Cambridge University Press, Cambridge, UK

Heiderich M, Nava E, Heyes G, Lindsay D (2010) Web application obfuscation: '-/WAFs… Evasion..Filters//alert/Obfuscation/-'. Syngress, Rockland, MA

Holz T, Raynal F (2005) Detecting honeypots and other suspicious environments. In: Proceedings of the 6th IEEE-SMC information assurance workshop, West Point, NY, 15–17 June, 2005. pp 29–36

Huebner E, Bem D, Wee C (2006) Data hiding in the NTFS file system. Digital Invest 3(4): 211–226

Jahankhani H, Beqiri E (2010) Digital evidence manipulation using anti-forensic tools and techniques. In: Handbook of electronic security and digital forensics. World Scientific, Singapore, pp 411–425

Nunes E, Kulkarni N, Shakarian P, Ruef A, Little J (2015) Cyber-deception and attribution in capture-the-flag exercises. In: Proceedings of the IEEE/ACM international conference on advanced in social networks analysis and mining, Paris, France, 25–28 Aug, 2015. pp 962–965

The Honeynet Project (2004) Know your enemy, 2nd edn. Addison-Wesley, Boston, MA

Tian J, Li N, Wang Z (2007) A proactive defense scheme based on the cooperation of intrusion deception and traceback. In: Proceedings of the computational intelligence and security workshops, Harbin, China, 15–19 Dec, 2007. pp 502–505

Yegneswaran V, Alfeld C, Barford P, Cai J-Y (2007) Camouflaging honeynets. In: Proceedings of the IEEE global Internet symposium, May 2007. pp 49–54

Chapter 9
False Excuses

As bad children know, excuses are an excellent way to avoid doing something you do not want to do (Snyder et al. 1983). Excuses are also important for bureaucracies (Wilson 2000), and large software systems are like bureaucracies with many of the same problems. Cybersystems under attack are being asked to do things that they should not want to do, so excuses can be an excellent defensive tactic. Cybersystems already use plenty of excuses in the form of error messages during normal operations. (Carofiglio et al. 2001) provides a more general approach to verbal deception planning that includes excuses.

Excuses are familiar on cybersystems in error messages, and also with the people that run cybersystems (Foster 1999). Unfortunately, error messages are not always correct, and sometimes their falsity is obvious. If your execution of a process is aborted on a computer, data structures may not be cleaned up, and the system may

© Springer International Publishing Switzerland 2016
N.C. Rowe, J. Rrushi, *Introduction to Cyberdeception*,
DOI 10.1007/978-3-319-41187-3_9

tell you that certain processes are still ongoing when they are not. Misleading error messages may also occur when system designers try to be too nice, as when a system suggests that a Web page is not working when in fact you have misspelled its name. So users of cybersystems have seen plenty of false excuses.

Excuses are especially useful with fending off automated cyberattacks such as viruses and worms. If there is no human watching for suspicious behavior, the mechanisms of such attacks can be easily foiled by a few unexpected failures accompanied by excuses (Nazario 2004; Erbschloe 2005).

9.1   The Philosophy of Excuses

From one perspective, excuses are a polite way to refuse to do something. Rather than an outright refusal, the excuse-giver provides some reason or reasons that would logically entail the refusal, thereby making the excuser sympathetic to the refusee. The true reasons may make the deceivee unsympathetic or actually hurt the deceivee.

Another way to look at excuses is as "negative persuasion". People need to manipulate other people in all sorts of ways, to advance their own interests and make their lives happier. It is usually easier to not do something than it is to do something. Giving an excuse to not do something is an easy form of negative persuasion, and the excuse need not be true. It is particularly common when someone is requesting service (Dickson et al. 2005).

False excuses must be used sparingly, however. If there are too many, the odds of discovering the falsity of at least one can become significant. Discovery of deception can lead to overreaction by the deceivee, which is not generally good for the deceiver. The deceiver may be able to decrease the chance of discovery through a process of habituation. If the excuse represents a state of affairs that the deceivee has encountered frequently before, or thinks they have encountered before, they will be more willing to accept it. A classic example is "I'm busy then" in response to a dating (courting) request from one person to another. Deliberately increasing the rate of an excuse on a system can permit users to become accustomed to them. For instance, we can post messages about "System debugging this week" even if we are not debugging, so that we have a ready excuse if we need one for slow or buggy operations.

One argument is that false excuses need to be short since the longer ones can provide more clues to deception. Nonetheless, deception can be detected even in short "chat" messages (Derrick et al. 2013). But it can also be argued that multipart excuses distributed over time can be more effective since it makes the deceivee wait for the full effect. This is related to the claim that combinatorial messages like human language are biologically advantageous for mounting deceptions (Lachmann and Bergstrom 2004).

9.2 Types of False Excuses

Excuses have a rich taxonomy reflecting the full gamut of human ingenuity. We can distinguish two dimensions to excuses, the mechanism and the subject. When an excuse is rather general, we call it a "generic excuse". Generic excuses are desirable for defensive deception because they are sufficiently broad to enable a variety of defensive ploys that we may want to attempt.

In cyberspace, the best generic excuses relate to malfunctions of cybersystems. Some classic subjects of generic excuses ("resources") are:

- Networks. They have many hardware and software components, and it is easy for something to go wrong: networking software, authorization for use of the network, the physical connection to the network, a hub, a router, the network management, the intermediate destinations, the final destination, and the networking software for each protocol. Many of these failures are poorly identified by software, so in fact it may be sufficient to be vague and say "Network down" when we can. Since most cyberattacks, even insider attacks, exploit connections over some network, network malfunctions are a great excuse for stopping them.
- The operating systems of computers and devices. These are more reliable than networks, but still can have problems in both hardware and software. Components are the main memory, the secondary storage, the peripheral devices, the graphics processor, the file system, the "registry" of software, the ongoing processes, the paging mechanism, and so on.
- Programs. Everyone knows software can have bugs.
- Files, which can occasionally get damaged.
- Data being used such as passwords, keys, and access rights.

A generic excuse must specify a reason. There are many good reasons why something is not working:

- **Software updates**. New software and patches need to be installed from time to time, and systems and networks may stop working when this happens. The update may be perfectly fine, but it could be incompatible with other software or hardware that also needs to be updated, so things may stop working.
- **Debugging and testing**. New software and hardware may require a period of debugging during which unusual behavior occurs, including inconsistent responses to users.
- **Routine maintenance**. Some resources need cleanup actions or other kinds of system-administrator intervention periodically, which can prevent their use for a time. This is most common with shared resources such as databases and caches.
- **Features turned off**. Software changes all the time, and system administrators can reconfigure it even when the software is not changed. Complex resources like operating systems have many options that can be set. So the current settings may prevent software from working.

- **Incorrectly applied (or "sticky") defaults**. For instance, if a user downloads a file with a 100 megabyte buffer, all subsequent downloads could also use a 100 megabyte buffer, which may be insufficient for other programs.
- **Data or programs damaged in transit**. This works on network file transfers.
- **Environmental problems**. For instance, things slow down when system load is high, and may even stop working at very high loads.
- **An unexpected additional resource required**. This is a common ploy of bureaucracies attempting to delay people.
- **Authorization needed**. The user may need to supply a password or key to use some software, or may need an email confirmation from some important person.
- **Misunderstood data or instructions**. For instance, the wrong utility is used to open a file, or all the characters in message are converted to upper case when this matters.
- **Reversed action**. For instance, a file is transferred from the local to the remote site instead of vice versa, which could be blamed on incorrect syntax of a command.
- **Bugs**. Software has bugs all the time, and sometimes they are serious enough to prevent use.
- **"You broke it"**. The user disabled something in attempting to use a resource so that it and other related resources are now unavailable. For instance, an attacker attempted to download a large rootkit file, and appears to have damaged the storage buffer so no further file transfers can be done. This excuse has psychological advantages because it transfers blame to the user.
- **Cyberattack**. Denial-of-service attacks will slow things down, and all kinds of strange behavior are possible with other attacks. However, attacks are generally rare and thus not very good excuses why something is not working.
- **Practical joke on the user**. Though unlikely, its probability can be increased by the use of clever clues.

A special generic excuse is the "null excuse" where a computer refuses to do something but does not tell the user that it is refusing. For instance, if a user orders a download of a file, the system waits a while and then returns to ask for the next command without actually downloading the file. The user will find out the download was not done as soon as they try to use the file. This could be more disconcerting to a user than a false excuse because the user must do some extra work to determine it.

Null excuses occur all the time in software. For instance, if one attempts to save a file in Microsoft Word as of 2010 that has not been changed since its last save, the software will refuse to save it but will not tell the user that that is what it is doing. When a user issues a command, they expect it to be obeyed, and Word is ignoring a direct order. The software thinks that saving the file again will not make any difference, but sometimes it gets confused because of bugs and is wrong. Null excuses are common in software where designers think they are smarter than the user.

9.3 Ensuring Logically Consistent Excuses

The text of fake excuses is easy to generate with the grammar approach in Sect. 7.2. We can use a set of "excuse formats", filling in details from the abovementioned dimensions and from randomly generated strings where necessary to increase realism.

The challenge with excuses is to be consistent when you must give more than one, since inconsistency is a key clue to deception. (Inconsistency has been proposed as a defense (Neagoe and Bishop 2006), but it has little advantages over outright refusal of resources.) People have trouble being consistent, and police interrogators use this to detect lying as mentioned in Chap. 2. But cybersystems can track a large number of things and maintain consistency over them (Spalka 1994). So software could be very good at lying.

Ensuring consistency requires remembering both true statements and lies that you have given (Castelfranchi 2000; Jones and Trevino 2007; Rowe 2007). For instance, if we let an attacker modify one file in an operating-system directory, but then say they cannot modify another in the same directory with the same listed access privileges, we are being inconsistent, assuming that nothing relevant has changed in the meantime. Access rights do change from time to time. But if it has only been a few minutes, it is unlikely that one file can be opened but not the other. Section 9.4.2 will discuss this time issue more.

9.3.1 A Consistency Example

For now, assume that nothing significant changes over a period of interest on a computer system. Suppose that during this period:

1. A malicious user logs on to a system.
2. They list their home directory.
3. They download a small file.
4. They download a large suspicious file.
5. They log out.
6. Ten minutes later, the same user logs in again.
7. They download a large suspicious file.

It would be appealing to use the excuse of "network down" on step 4 once we see a suspicious file is involved. The problem is that we have previously allowed a download in step 3 and denial in step 4 could seem inconsistent. On the other hand, it is consistent to deny the download on step 7 if we deny the download on step 4 since that is a similar response.

We can be more precise about why if we list the resources needed for a download:

- A file to download at the remote site
- A directory we have access to at the remote site

- File-transfer software at the remote site
- A network connection between the remote site and our site
- A directory we have access to at our site
- File-transfer software at the remote site

When we downloaded the first file, we confirmed that these resources were sufficient. Recalling our discussion in Sect. 4.5, resources have six facets:

- Existence
- Authorization
- Readiness
- Operability
- Compatibility
- Moderation

If the network existed, was authorized for use by us, was ready to use, and was working for the first file, it should be working for the second file assuming that nothing major occurred in the short time interval. It could however be that the second file is of a type not compatible with the network (the "compatibility" facet), or exceeds the parameter limits such as size for the network (the "moderation" facet). So those are possible excuses. But we need to choose our wording carefully. "Network down" would be unconvincing because it is better suited to the first four facets. Better would be "File type not permitted for network transfer", "File type not permitted in target directory", "File too large for transfer", or "File too large to store".

Similarly on step 6, we can deny the second login only if we choose our excuse carefully. We cannot say that the system does not exist, is not authorized for use, is not ready to use, is not working, or is not compatible with our login name since those things would not change in a short period. But we could say that the login might exceed the number of allowed users since we could have been close to the threshold previously.

Null excuses are particularly tricky to make consistent because the user infers their own reasons. For instance, if we allow a download of a large file but then refuse to download an equally large file with a null excuse, that appears inconsistent with the inferred common reason for downloads that they are too large. Users are quick at inferring such plausible explanations of anomalous behavior. So null excuses are hard to make convincing; it is better to give a reason.

9.3.2 Generalizing Consistency Analysis

To be systematic about consistency, we need to know, for each command or action that a user could do, what resources it uses and what properties of those resources it confirms (Rowe 2007). This kind of problem is addressed in the subfield of automated planning in the field of artificial intelligence, which focuses primarily on logically necessary conditions like most resource-usage conditions. It will help to

Table 9.1 Resources associated with important user activities.

Command	Uses file system?	Uses operating system?	Uses applications software?	Uses local network?	Uses external network?	Uses access controls?
Login		Yes		Yes		Yes
List current directory name	Yes	Yes				
List directory contents	Yes	Yes				
Change current directory	Yes	Yes				
Edit file	Yes		Yes			Yes
Print file	Yes	Yes	Yes	Yes		
Modify database	Yes		Yes			
Download file	Yes	Yes		Yes	Yes	Yes
Decompress file	Yes		Yes			
Run Web browser			Yes		Yes	
Change access rights		Yes				Yes
Change auditing		Yes				Yes
Update operating system	Yes	Yes			Yes	Yes
Modify firewall		Yes	Yes	Yes		Yes
Logout		Yes				

make a list of possible user actions and a list of possible resources, and create a matrix with the actions as rows and resources as columns (Templeton and Levitt 2000). Table 9.1 is a start. Note that this table should represent the view of the user, not how things are actually implemented, since we want to fool the user. Then we need another table, Table 9.2, to relate excuses to the resources.

9.3.3 Inferences of Resource Facets

Determining the resources affected by commands can get further complicated by the fact that resources are hierarchical and interrelated. Hierarchical relationships occur because things have components. If the network is not working, it could be due to just one component of those mentioned in Sect. 9.2. In general:

- If we state a facet of a resource is valid, all its components have valid facets for that resource.

Table 9.2 Excuses for example resources.

Generic excuse type	Uses file system?	Uses operating system?	Uses applications software?	Uses local network?	Uses external network?	Uses access controls?
Software updates	Yes	Yes	Yes		Yes	Yes
Debugging and testing	Yes	Yes	Yes	Yes	Yes	Yes
Routine maintenance	Yes	Yes		Yes	Yes	
Feature turned off	Yes	Yes	Yes			
Sticky defaults	Yes	Yes	Yes		Yes	
Damaged in transit	Yes			Yes	Yes	
Environment wrong	Yes		Yes	Yes	Yes	
Additional resource needed	Yes	Yes	Yes		Yes	
Authorization needed	Yes	Yes	Yes			Yes
Command misunderstood		Yes	Yes		Yes	
Command reversed		Yes			Yes	
Bugs	Yes	Yes	Yes	Yes	Yes	Yes
Attack in progress	Yes	Yes	Yes	Yes	Yes	Yes
User broke something	Yes	Yes	Yes	Yes	Yes	Yes
System cyberattacked	Yes	Yes	Yes	Yes	Yes	Yes
Practical joker	Yes	Yes	Yes	Yes	Yes	Yes

- If we state that a facet of a resource is invalid, at least one (but possibly more) of its components is invalid in that facet.
- If we state that a facet of a resource is invalid, and the resource is a necessary component of some whole, then we can infer the whole has an invalid facet of that resource.

For instance, if the process-management methods of the operating system are not working, this implies that the operating system is not working. These classic inferences are forms of "part-whole inheritance", used in artificial intelligence and in programming languages.

Such inferences permit us more flexibility in designing excuses since we can engineer different excuses for similar resources in similar situations if we can isolate different components or properties of the two situations which we can blame. For instance, we can refuse a second download that is 100 kb after we accepted a first download that is 10 kb by inferring a size-limit excuse for a threshold between 10 and 100 kb. Similarly, we can refuse a second download of an "exe"-format file if we accepted a first download of a "txt"-format file by inferring a type prohibition on "exe"-format files. However, the more similar are two resources to which we want to give different treatment, the more difficult it is to construct an excuse.

Note that components of resources can be completely imaginary. For instance, an excuse might be "The network file buffer is full" when there is actually no network file buffer, because only developers would know that. However, cyberattackers like to think they know a lot, so we won't fool them for long if we often refer to imaginary things.

Type-subtype inheritance, the most common form of inheritance, is useful as well as part-whole inheritance. In general:

- If we state that a facet of a resource in invalid, then any supertype or generalization of that resource has that invalid facet.
- If we state that a facet of a resource is valid, then any subtype or instance has that valid facet.

An example would be if the user gets the excuse "network connections not working"; then an attempt to do file transfers across the network should get the same excuse.

Inheritances are just one form of inference possible. Other inferences relate the different facets:

- Authorization of a resource implies existence of that resource.
- Readiness of a resource implies authorization of that resource.
- Operability of a resource implies readiness of that resource.
- Compatibility of a resource implies operability of that resource.
- Moderation of a resource implies compatibility of that resource.

Each of these has a reverse with a negation which follows logically:

- Lack of existence of a resource implies lack of authorization for it.
- Lack of authorization of a resource implies lack of readiness for it.
- Lack of readiness of a resource implies lack of operability for it.
- Lack of operability of a resource implies lack of compatibility with related resources for it.
- Lack of compatibility of a resource implies lack of moderation for it.

However, the inferences are not bidirectional, e.g. existence of a resource does not imply authorization of the resource.

Special inferences can be made for actions closely connected to the attacker's goals. If we always give error messages at the most critical points in attacker's attack plans, they will become suspicious. Example critical points are the downloading of rootkits and their installation into an operating system, since those are the primary goals of most attacks. On the other hand, an error message about decompressing a rootkit after it has been downloaded will seem less suspicious even though it equally well blocks installation of the rootkit. So in general, we should avoid excuses on particularly suspicious actions that a cyberattacker wants to do, even though it is not logically necessary.

Other inferences can be made based on more detailed causal knowledge of how systems work. For instance, if we know that the file system is backed up periodically to another network site, then a possible reason for failure of the file storage commands could be that the backup system has crashed. But this requires detailed knowledge of which many attackers will not be aware.

9.3.4 *Implementing Excuse Checking*

Appendix C shows code to accomplish excuse consistency checking for a series of commands to an operating system. The commands and resources handled are just a start for purposes of illustration, and would need to be extended for practical applications.

This is written in the language Prolog, a language which implements automated backtracking on failure. This is particularly useful for this task because we need to collect a list of all resources status facts consistent with the statements made so far. So we just set up a set of constraints and let Prolog backtrack to find everything that satisfies the constraints.

To implement excuse consistency, the program takes as input a list of the commands issued so far from a user. Starting with an empty list, it adds the necessary resources for each command to the list. At each step we can generate a list of possible excuses consistent with the resources, and rank them using the methods described in the next section. For a demonstration, one can use the program of Appendix D that generates a rootkit-installation plan.

Brackets are used in Prolog to denote singly-linked lists, and periods are the command terminators. So the lines:

```
resource(download(P,F,S1,S2),
[site(S1), site(S2), file(F), located_at(F,S2), network(N),
network_of(S1,N), network_of(S2,N), logged_in(P,S1)],
[file(F)])
```

can be read as "The resources for person P downloading file F from site S1 to site S2 are S1, S2, and F, the network N that connects them, the fact that F is at S2, and the fact the P is logged into S1; this command creates a new resource of F which is a file."

9.4 Rating Excuses

The excuse-consistency program in Appendix C also rates possible excuses. This is helpful because there can be many possibilities, especially early in an interaction with a user, and we would prefer the most plausible ones. Also, implausibility builds through longer sequences, as will be analyzed in more detail in Chap. 11.

9.4.1 Prior Rate of an Excuse

One factor in the plausibility of an excuse is how likely its condition could occur based on historical data about it or similar problems. We can count the rate (frequency of events per unit time) of things that we might want to offer as excuses. For instance for systems with which the author is familiar, software updates occur daily on the average, the network goes down once a week, and the file system behaves improperly once a month. As another example, spammers know they can usually set up a mail proxy back to themselves with most mail servers but not with "spam honeypot" mail servers, so their inability to do so is rare and will be suspicious to them (Krawetz 2004).

The rate of a particular excuse can vary with the resources involved. For instance, the excuse that an executable is not working on a cybersystem is more plausible for untested and bigger executables than it is for well-tested and smaller executables. Fortunately, most digital resources behave similarly in most respects even if they are different sizes.

Created resources such as output files are more likely to cause errors because they have not been tested over time. For instance, editing software may save a new file in an incompatible format. So the rate of failure with new resources can plausibly be higher than for other resources.

Finally, another factor in the plausibility of an excuse is whether it was used in response to a suspicious action. When attackers do something they know is illegal, they like to think that the rest of the world is doing illegal things too, and they are more able to detect suspicious responses. So we need to lower the estimated excuse rate for excuses following a suspicious action so they seem less desirable.

9.4.2 Relaxing Consistency Over Time

Consistency deteriorates over time as random actions occur. That means that we can be increasingly inconsistent as time elapses. This could be important in a long session where otherwise increasingly fewer options would remain for new excuses as we commit ourselves by allowing access to resources.

We can quantify this. An event like a network going down can be modeled as a Poisson process with a certain "interarrival frequency" λ. That means that the average time between instances of the network going down is $1/\lambda$ though it could vary. Figure 9.1 shows a Poisson distribution of possible durations in multiples of λ between down times, $\lambda e^{-\lambda t}$.

Then the probability of the network going down in a time interval T is the area under this curve from 0 to T. This area is found from the integral of $\lambda e^{-\lambda t}$ which is $1 - \lambda e^{-\lambda T}$. For T=2 on Figure 9.1, that is 1-0.13=0.87. So if the network goes down once a week on the average, the chance that it has gone down in a two-week interval is 87%. We can do this calculation for any excuse for which we can estimate the average occurrence rate λ.

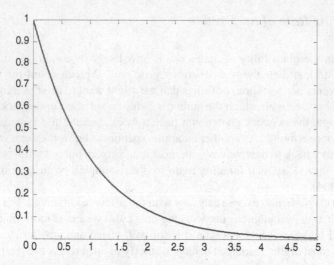

Figure 9.1 Poisson distribution of the probability of first occurrence of some event where the horizontal axis represents multiples of λ

For failure conditions, there is generally a reverse process that undoes the failure. For instance, when a system crashes, system administrators eventually bring it back to a working state. The reverse process can have its own rate based on properties of the repair methods. For restoring networks with which we are familiar, the λ is generally once per 2 h. So we need to calculate the probability of the network going back up if we have been previously told the user that it went down. For the above-mentioned rate, we can use the curve shape in Fig. 9.1 but where the numbers now represent units of 2 h rather than weeks (84 times less).

So for instance for a period of 2 weeks with a network that goes down once a week on the average, the probability it has gone down is 0.87, but the probability it is still down after two weeks is negligible unless it last went down in the last 12 h of the last day of the 2 weeks. If it went down an hour before the end of the day, the probability that it is still down 0.7; if it went down two hours before the end of the day, the probability that it was fixed is 0.4; and so on. That means the probability that it is currently down can be approximated as:

$$\left(\frac{1}{168}\right)\begin{bmatrix}0.607+0.368+0.223+0.135+0.082+0.050\\+0.030+0.018+0.011+0.007+0.004+0.002\end{bmatrix}=\frac{1.537}{168}=0.009$$

This theory gives us a better understanding of the observation that too many negative responses on different subjects are suspicious (Houston et al. 2013). If we ask every ten minutes whether a system is down, the answers should be correlated, and a repeated response that it is down is not particularly suspicious. But if we ask every week whether a system is down and it is always down, that is more suspicious because the time interval is long enough that the responses should be independent of one another.

9.4.3   Consistency Between Sessions

What if a cyberattacker logs out and then logs in again to try to fool us? We should remember what excuses we told before and try to maintain consistency, allowing for "time decay" as discussed. But a malicious user may fool us by logging in under a different name or from a different remote IP address. Thus it is useful to maintain consistency across a set of users if their numbers are small enough, even when we are not sure they are the same person. Otherwise, we can try to guess that two users at different times are the same user by looking for commonalities between their sessions such as resources used, a form of "guilt by association". This idea is frequently used by intelligence agencies in tracking suspicious people (Macskassy and Provost 2005).

9.4.4   Putting Together the Rating Factors

We can rate excuses by combining all these factors by multiplication:

$$r_i = f_i r_i \prod_{j=1}^{N} \left(1 - b_j e^{-\lambda_i \, t_{ij}}\right)$$

Here r_i is the relative likelihood that the resources involved would have this particular excuse applied to them, f_i is the prior frequency of the excuse, b_j is the likelihood that a user session j involves the same user and has a contradiction with this excuse, λ_i is the frequency at which the excuse occurs, Δt_{ij} is the duration since the last contradiction occurred with user j, and the big symbol means a product.

9.5   Conclusions

Excuses are versatile tactics for playing with attackers. They can be very useful tools for defense, particularly against smarter attackers who are paying attention even if they are using automated attack tools. There are many possible excuses, so we can provide attackers with plenty of variety. And if we plan carefully, we will be unlikely to run out of options.

9.6   Exercises

1. (a) Give a good excuse, based on the file type, for not downloading a file.
   (b) Give a good excuse, that refers to the printer attached to local-area network, for not downloading a file from the Internet.
   (c) Give a good excuse, that refers to an inserted USB flash drive, for not downloading a file.

2. How do we estimate the prior probability of a null excuse involving a file download? What information do we need to collect and how much information?
3. Consider the resource of the graphics coprocessor that is in most computers today.

   (a) What commands require this resource?
   (b) When would it be appropriate to give false excuses to a suspicious user regarding this resource?
   (c) What are some good excuses to give?

4. Give an inference rule that relates the properties of the secondary storage to the properties of a downloaded file.
5. Time of day affects certain excuses more than others. Give three examples where the probability is much higher at certain times of days than at others, and explain how the probabilities vary then.
6. Consider using deception on packets coming in over the network that do not have associated user names. Discuss how we could infer it likely that two packets sequences are likely from the same user even if they come from different IP addresses.
7. Assume the following is true:

   • If a module deceives, then any program it is a part of also deceives.
   • If a module deceives, then some module after it does not deceive.
   • Program p1 has modules m1 and m2.
   • Program p1 does not deceive.
   • Program p2 has modules m3 and m4.
   • Module m3 deceives.
   • Modules m4 and m5 are after m3.
   • Modules m4 and m5 are the only modules after m3.
   • Module m5 deceives.

   (a) Use the laws of logic to prove that m1 does not deceive. Justify each step.
   (b) Use the laws of logic to prove that m4 does not deceive. Justify each step.

References

Carofiglio V, de Rosis F, Grassano R, Castelfranchi C (2001) An interactive system for generating arguments in deceptive communication. Lecture notes in computer science, Vol. 2175, Proceedings of the 7th congress of the Italian association for artificial intelligence on advances in artificial intelligence, Springer, New York, pp 255–266

Castelfranchi C (2000) Artificial liars: why computers will (necessarily) deceive us and each other. Ethics Inform Technol 2(2):113–119

Derrick D, Meservy T, Jenkins J, Burgoon J, Nunamaker J (2013) Detecting deceptive chat-based communication using typing behavior and message cues. ACM Trans Manag Inform Syst 4(2):9.1–9.21

Dickson D, Ford R, Laval B (2005) The top ten excuses for bad service (and how to avoid needing them). Organ Dyn 34(2):168–184

Erbschloe M (2005) Trojans, worms, and spyware: a computer security professional's guide to malicious code. Elsevier, Amsterdam, Netherlands

Foster E (1999) Just when you thought you heard them all: Top 20 software support excuses. InfoWorld 1:89

Houston P, Floyd M, Carnicero S (2013) Spy the lie: Former CIA officers teach you how to detect deception. St.Martin's Griffin, New York

Jones J, Trevino P (2007) Automated high-level reasoning for deception detection: two scenarios demonstrated. In: Proceedings of the International Conference on Systems, Man, and Cybernetics. Montreal, Quebec. pp 338–342

Krawetz N (2004) Anti-honeypot technology. IEEE Secur Priv 2(1):76–79

Lachmann M, Bergstrom C (2004) The disadvantage of combinatorial communication. Proc R Soc Lond B 271:2337–2343

Macskassy S, Provost F (2005) Suspicion scoring based on guilt-by-association, collective inference, and focused data access. In: Proceedings of the intelligence analysis conference, McLean, VA, 2-4 May, 2005

Nazario J (2004) Defense and detection strategies against internet worms. Artech, Boston, MA

Neagoe V, Bishop M (2006) Inconsistency in deception for the defense. In: Proceedings of the new security paradigms workshop, Schloss Dagstuhl, Germany, 18–21 Sept 2006. pp 31–38

Rowe N (2007) Finding logically consistent resource-deception plans for defense in cyberspace. In: Proceedings of the 3rd international symposium on security in networks and distributed systems, Niagara Falls, ON, Canada, 21–23 May. pp 563–568

Snyder C, Higgins R, Stucky R (1983) Excuses: masquerades in search of grace. Wiley, New York

Spalka A (1994) Formal semantics of confidentiality in multilevel logic databases. In: Proceedings of the new security paradigms workshop, Little Neck, RI, 3–5 Aug, 1994. pp 64–73

Templeton S, Levitt K (2000) A requires/provides model for computer attacks. In: Proceedings of new security paradigms workshop, Cork, Ireland, 19–21 Sept, 2000. pp 31–38

Wilson J (2000) Bureaucracy: what government agencies do and why they do it. Basic Books, New York

Chapter 10
Defensive Social Engineering

The methods we have described in the last four chapters work within cyberspace and involve only an occasional human other than the attacker. But most human deception involves non-cyber interactions between people. There are plenty of semi-cyberdeception methods used by cyberattackers, for which the terms "social engineering" and "scams" are appropriate. Social media (Tsikerdekis and Zeadally 2014) are a particularly fertile ground for deception in social engineering. Untrained people are not particularly good at detecting deception, and this aids social engineering (Qin and Burgoon 2007).

Social engineering can be done against cyberattackers too. However, success is more difficult because attackers are smarter and there are fewer of them. When a phisher fails to fool a victim, they don't care because there are always plenty of victims. Nonetheless, attackers are not expecting to be fooled themselves and you may surprise them.

© Springer International Publishing Switzerland 2016
N.C. Rowe, J. Rrushi, *Introduction to Cyberdeception*,
DOI 10.1007/978-3-319-41187-3_10

10.1   Tactics and Plans for Social-Engineering Deceptions

Mitnick (2002) collects a variety of cases of social-engineering attacks on cybersystems, and an appendix provides a taxonomy of common social-engineering methods. Summarizing it and relating it to manipulation of attackers, the major methods we could use to deceive attackers are:

- Impersonation to gain access and privileges

  - Impersonation of authority figures like information-technology staff: Might scare some novice attackers away, but most attackers don't care if they are dealing with an authority figure.
  - Impersonation of vendors: Similarly not very useful.
  - Impersonation of other hackers: Might give you some credibility.
  - Impersonation of employees: Could make it easier to see what the attacker is after.
  - Impersonation of novices needing help: Might be helpful, though most hackers don't like novices.

- Camouflaging an object

  - Trojan horses in email: Not feasible since we rarely know attacker email addresses.
  - Trojan horses in media like memory devices: Not easy unless we can track down the attacker's computer.
  - Trojan horses in downloads: A good way to get them onto attacker's machines.
  - Popup windows requesting information: Could be useful in getting passwords and keys the attacker is using.
  - Changing the origin of an object (as in "transshipment"): Helpful in concealing your identity when interacting with a potential attacker.

- Eavesdropping

  - Overhearing people talking: Can be done with online chat among hackers.
  - Spyware: Great way to track attackers if you can get it onto their machines.

- Disinformation (usually via the Web)

  - Puffery: Claiming something is better than it really is. Web chat groups are an easy way (Seife 2015).
  - Denigration: Claiming something is worse than it really is. Can be used to discredit organizations or software.
  - Spreading false rumors: Good for planting new ideas.
  - Hoaxes: Spreading multipart coordinated lies.

Social engineering plans are then built from these tactics. For instance, phishing involves usually impersonation of a financial service with a camouflaged email, then impersonation of a financial-service Web site with a camouflaged Web site collecting data for identity theft. With person-to-person contacts, usually the plan has four main steps: Prepare groundwork, make contacts, build methods of manipulating the contacts, and manipulate the contacts to gain some key advantage. But the best scams involve more than one person to achieve an overall effect that no one victim can see. For instance, to track hackers with spyware:

1. Research current exploits.
2. Set up a hacker blog and download site (the "anonymous Web" accessed by anonymous browsers like Tor is a good place).

   (a) Set up secondary identities.
   (b) Get established on other hacker bulletin boards, and participate in the discussions.
   (c) Start your own bulletin board with paraphrased discussions from the others.
   (d) Get some exploits by paying for them.
   (e) Post the exploits on your bulletin board.

3. Make contacts with hackers on your site.

   (a) Give them or sell them some bait exploits.
   (b) Give them or sell them some exploits with spyware.

4. Close the bulletin board with a message giving good excuse (e.g., about you being arrested).
5. Let the spyware collect data on your hackers.

Note from the above that scams on the attacker can have other goals than discouraging them. Any information we can get that helps localize an attacker ("attribution") could be useful in tracking them down. We can try to fool attackers into telling us their email address, their home address, their phone number, and so on by offering them bait (Sect. 10.3). Criminal investigators and detectives know a wide range of tricks to track down people and some of these extend to cyberspace. For instance, it helps to know what dialect of English someone uses, what time of day they are online, what friends they seem to have in cyberspace, what the apparent speed of their modem is, and so on. Valuable such information can be obtained from social-networking sites if we can connect a suspect to one. This can narrow down a list of suspects, sometimes to the point where there are few enough that they can individually investigated in detail.

10.2   Techniques to Increase Likelihood of Accepting the Scam

Since we are dealing with people, the manner in which a scam is perpetrated is important to its success. Scam artists have developed a wide range of methods for intensifying the effectiveness of a scam:

- **In-group jargon**. Use the terms of the kind of person you are impersonating, like specialized acronyms. Hackers in particular use unnecessary jargon to keep outsiders out and build their own solidarity. Learning this jargon could be a major way to gain their confidence.

- **Appeals to authority**. In talking to an attacker, claim endorsements from other attackers or claim notorious accomplishments.
- **Appeals to friendship or sympathy**. Build up a relationship with the attacker so you can exploit it. Most hackers aren't particularly sociable, and you need to provide deeds rather than words to build their trust in you. This may mean pretending to accept their often-odd world views.
- **Appeals to reciprocity**. Give the attacker some exploits or passwords, and they may feel obligated to give you some of theirs. The challenge with this is what to give them in exchange. You should not want to help spread new attacks, so exploits would need to be "defanged" in some way, but attackers could figure that out and start to suspect you. You could give addresses of honeypots but attackers can figure out most honeypots pretty quickly.
- **Rewards and prizes**. Offer a prize in a contest for attacks but require contact information so you can locate the winners. Prizes can also be software with hidden Trojan horses.
- **Appeals to ego**. If you are unlikely to impress an attacker, it may be better to make them think instead that they are superior to you by doing stupid things, like exhibiting deceptions they can figure out. They may then be less likely to recognize a more sophisticated secondary deception that you use at the same time.
- **Appeals to urgency**. Put pressure on an attacker to cause them to make quick incorrect judgments. Most attacks are not time-critical, but an exception might be time-varying passwords.
- **Threats**. If carrots don't work, use a stick. Threaten to report the attacker to authorities, or pretend to be law enforcement like the FBI in the US. You can do this just with error messages to them. Many attackers will laugh this off, but it might make them think twice about what they are doing.

In addition to these ideas, there are general characteristics of attackers that we may be able to exploit. Hackers (amateur attackers) are generally young males (late teens or early twenties of age) with short attention spans and a desire for petty accomplishments. Professional attackers such as cyberwarfare specialists have longer attention spans and quite specific goals in mind for which they are persistent. Both groups like challenges, so making your system secure could seem a way to attract them. However in opposition to this is the natural desire of attackers to accomplish as many compromises as possible, so many attackers prefer attacking the easiest systems. This philosophy is apparent in botnets, which are constructed from large numbers of easily exploitable home and office computers.

Because of all these tactics that can be used against them, people are not always good at detecting social-engineering scams. Grazioli and Jarvenpaa (2000) reported worrisome levels of credence in online scams. Attackers could have similar weaknesses.

10.3 Bait

Several of methods mentioned offer "bait" to the attacker, some kind of information desirable to them, sometimes called "honeytokens" (Spitzner 2005). The bait can be something that will help trace the attacker or help harm them. Examples include:

- Files that spies want to steal like secret plans.
- Passwords for addresses to honeypots and honeynets, to encourage attackers to use them (Bojinov et al. 2010; Almeshekah et al. 2015). These can be posted in bulletin boards and blogs, or hidden on other honeypots.
- Decryption keys to disinformation. The very fact information is encrypted makes it more interesting.
- Fake credit-card and bank-account numbers, to encourage attackers to try using them. Then they can be caught if we monitor for use of these numbers with banks and credit-card companies.
- Database records containing sensitive information (Cenys et al. 2005).
- Files logging evidence of an attack since only attackers would try to change them (Yuill et al. 2004).
- Attack software ("exploits") since new exploits can be quite valuable for attackers. Spyware included in it can be used to locate the user when the exploit is run. It is probably a good idea to "defang" or limit the damage such an exploit can do, so that one is not just spreading malware, but it probably needs to do at least some minor damage to convince an attacker that the exploit is real.
- Decoy traffic on a wireless network containing what appear to be wireless-access credentials that attackers can steal (Gharabally et al. 2009; Bowen et al. 2010).

Bait can be either incorrect, partly incorrect, or correct for its intended purpose. If it is incorrect, as for instance an invalid password, it will prevent attacks and waste some attacker time. It helps to make incorrect bait at least a little difficult to confirm, however. For instance, the attacker need not be immediately refused access based on a bait password, but told the system is down.

Bait that is only partly incorrect for its intended purpose provides a way to track the attacker if the bait is unique. For instance, if a bank gets a false bank account number, they can let a user log in and watch what they do even if there is no such account. Banks can have a set of designated false numbers to make recognizing them easier. Similarly, bait in the form of malware can appear to work, but it could be defanged, and spyware within it could enable tracking.

Bait that is completely correct for its intended purpose can be useful for entrapment. Eventually the thief of a credit-card number may give a delivery address which the police can visit. Laws do limit the extent to which entrapment can be used (see Sect. 16.2.2).

Xiao and Benbasat (2007) postulates a number of principles for effectiveness of deception in electronic commerce that can be applied to enhance the appeal of bait, of which the most useful we judge to be:

- Whether it has a high perceived value to the deceivee, as with a rootkit claimed to be powerful (P1a, P8, P10);

- Whether the bait appears nondeceptive, as with apparent endorsements by authorities (P2);
- Whether the place it comes from appears nondeceptive, as for a site with a long track record (P5);
- Whether the bait offered is consistent with similar offerings, such as in a listing of many similar passwords (P12);
- Whether the bait is described in an accurate way, avoiding any similarity to phishing techniques (P21);
- Whether previous bait was taken and not detected (P22);
- Whether the deceivee does not think the source has a reason to be deceptive, as when they know honeypots could be at the source site (P23);
- Whether the deceivee has access to data on other people visiting the site (P27).

Bait is important in counterintelligence (see Sect. 3.1.3). It is good to have a few false secrets for spies to find. Bait and other forms of disinformation can be constructed somewhat systematically by following a few guidelines (Gerwehr et al. 1999).

Any social and political issues that motivate an attacker may be important in designing good bait. Most criminal cyberattackers could care less about who they are attacking. But North Korea has engaged in repeated pointless cyberattacks against South Korea since 2004, and they have not been random (Kshetri 2014). Usually they attack some organization that North Korea doesn't like, such as the South Korean military, anti-North-Korean newspapers, and banking organizations, and they usually do it on important anniversaries such as the start of the Korea War. So defenders have a pretty good idea of where they will attack and when, just not the methods. So these are good sites and times to operate honeypots. Such honeypots could deliberately encourage more attacks by using inflammatory language to describe themselves, or by using inflammatory bait such as criticisms of North Korea.

10.4   More About Spyware

We have mentioned spyware several times. Spyware is software used to eavesdrop on computer and device users without their knowledge (Thompson 2005). The eavesdropping can vary from just the sites they visit to everything they do. Spyware data can be collected for purposes of marketing, government or commercial espionage, or identity theft.

Spyware can be useful in defense against attacks. It can track what attackers are doing just as well as it can track innocents; it might give us early warning of an impending attack, or even clue us as to what exploits are being developed. Defenders won't likely get attackers to open email attachments or leave their operating system unpatched, the major ways that spyware arrives on civilian machines. But they may be willing to take bait as discussed in the last section. Spy agencies know additional methods to get spyware onto cybersystems. Spies are expert at getting bugs installed, and spyware is a kind of bug. But their favored technique is breaking and entering, which is illegal in most countries.

Once spyware is installed, it does need to be camouflaged to avoid being noticed. Rootkit (Kuhnhauser 2004) and botnet technology has pioneered in many effective ways to conceal itself. Noticeable slowing of a computer was an important clue to early spyware (Awad and Fitzgerald 2005). While most attackers are not looking for spyware, they may start looking if their systems behave sufficiently differently from normal. The Sebek honeypot did a good job by shipping out monitoring data to another site as quickly as it could, a site where most of the computation was done.

10.5 Reputation Scams

An interesting class of scams are those that try to persuade people by attacking reputations, by spreading lies or misleading information. The concept of "cognitive hacking" (Cybenko et al. 2002) is closely related. Since many sites such as EBay track reputations, targeting these can cause novel problems for a deceivee. Deceivers can try to influence opinion-collecting sites by flooding them with opinions (Mukherjee et al. 2013). This can work against cyberattackers too because the attacker and hacker communities are close-knit and depend on a certain level of trust. For instance, we can modify exploits posted for download to prevent them from working, or add noticeable spyware, with the goal of hurting the reputation of the author. We can slander attackers directly, but this isn't as effective as providing concrete evidence against them.

Second-order deceptions (Sect. 4.4) can make useful reputation scams. For instance, we could create a Web site with exploits full of obvious spyware, much like attempts to hurt music-sharing sites by posting faulty copies (see Sect. 7.12). Attackers will likely discover the spyware quickly, and start spreading the word. This could hurt attackers' own sites and dissemination methods because they might start to think twice about their trustworthiness, a second-order deception. The effects could be increased if our Web site deliberately copies features of attacker's own sites and their content in matters of terminology, presentation, and the nature of goods offered. With enough such sites, we are giving attackers one more thing to worry about even if the sites are not too convincing.

10.6 Hoaxes

Complex lies are called hoaxes (Boese 2006). Security hoaxes like fake virus alerts have been around for a long time, and usually are due to someone wanting to feel powerful, much like people who report false bomb threats. We can use hoaxes for defensive purposes in the form of fake file systems (Sect. 7.7), fake exploits (Sect. 10.3), fake vulnerabilities, fake news, and fake organizations. For instance, a hoax can falsely claim that an organization has a new hack-proof Web site, to scare away attackers or provide deterrence to attacks. Or they can claim that an organization can be attacked a particular way when it cannot, as a way to waste attackers' time and effort. Hoaxes will eventually be discovered, but they can be useful for time-critical defense.

Hoaxes generally exploit interpersonal communication to increase the power of their deception. However, a hoax is hard to control. Once it starts being disseminated broadly, it may fool friends as well as enemies. For instance, if we offer a new kind of security software that is just a hoax, friends and allies may want to buy it. Another problem is that as more people are exposed to a hoax, the more chance it will be discovered by someone, ending its usefulness. So if we start distributing software with a Trojan horse, and someone finds the Trojan horse, they can post this knowledge on security Web sites and ruin not just this hoax, but future attempts attributable to our organization. We will discuss the mathematics of this in Sect. 12.1. So hoaxes need to be narrowly targeted.

If they see enough hoaxes and other kinds of disinformation, victims may become paranoid about attempts to manipulate them. Section 7.12 touched on this. This actually may be good when hoaxing attackers because this may encourage them to either seek easier targets or waste time on unnecessary countermeasures against nonexistent obstacles on our systems. That is, we may be able to get clever attackers to outthink themselves. This seems ethical because attackers are criminals and we are under no obligation to be nice to them.

A cute example of this is to try to anger attackers by apparently deleting files as the attacker watches, making downloads take forever, and similar "dirty tricks" (Spafford 2011). Attackers spend much time downloading files, so they get irritated if they cannot get them. When a particular utility was run, the attacker would see the name of a file in a directory and a question mark. Regardless of what they typed, the system would say it was deleting the file. If the user tried to abort, it would say it was deleting the directory. It didn't actually delete the files or the directory, but this would be enough to worry and slow down most attackers.

10.7 Bureaucratic Games

Another social-engineering idea for cyberspace is "trolling", behavior designed to deliberately antagonize someone (Ravia 2004). For instance, a phishing victim that can find the phisher's email address could email them to ask stupid questions like "Do you enjoy this?" and "How do I fill out your form?" Automated responses like this could drive a phisher up the wall. Phishing often needs to use an Internet registry to obtain a new site for which they are required to provide a contact email address.

A class of social-engineering techniques involve manipulating a group of individuals. An example would be falsely reporting (suitably anonymized) to a security manager that an insider is stealing secrets on a system. Many managers will be forced to devote resources to an investigation, taking resources away from other activities. Similarly, you could claim a violation of the organization's laws or policies. With enough such tricks, one can sow so much suspicion in that organization that it is fighting itself rather than you. If the organization is bureaucratic, this could impede it significantly.

This could work against cybercriminal gangs or even government information-warfare units. In general, organizations can have their own weaknesses, independent of those of their members, that smart defenders can take advantage of. All organizations have a number of situations to which they overreact, and all have inherent delays which can be exploited.

10.8 Strategic Deception

So far we have talked about focused deceptions for particular focused goals we want to accomplish. Military organizations call these "tactics". But they also speak of "strategies", and for cyberdeception, strategies could mean elaborate hoaxes (Erdie and Michael 2005). These can have a big impact if done right. The D-Day invasion included a complex strategic deception in place and time (Sect. 3.1); the deception needed to be complex to match the operation.

Strategic deceptions can concern either capabilities or weaknesses. An example of a capability deception would be pretending to have a new technology for tracking attackers even when you don't. This might scare attackers away or make them take unnecessary countermeasures when attacking your systems. You could spread word of this through press releases and announcements on Web sites in a public-relations campaign. To support it, you could create fake news stories about how wonderful it is, and you could add visible features to your cybersystems like new security-related windows and new unnecessary passwords, what (Dunnigan and Nofi 2001) calls "displays".

An example of a weakness deception would be spreading word there is a flaw in some software on certain systems that can be exploited, when the true goal is to get attackers to reveal themselves by attacking the flaw. The flaw could be real but designed to do minimal harm and permit collecting data about attackers. Web servers are a good place to put it because they do provide some containment even when compromised. Or the flaw could be false but difficult to confirm; an example would be a flaw that requires careful timing or complex conditions to be set up.

Strategic deceptions have a serious disadvantage in requiring usually the cooperation of many people. Thus it is more difficult to keep the deception secret than with less elaborate hoaxes. Also, a broad scope of the deception provides many opportunities to analyze it. For instance with the fake new tracking technology, a person could ask their friends at the company offering it, a hacker could compromise a system with the alleged technology and discover no tracking was actually occurring, or someone could commit cybercrimes in view of the alleged monitoring and see if anyone noticed. And as with other hoaxes, revelation can do long-term damage to your reputation. Thus strategic deceptions are generally a poor investment except for time-critical D-Day-like events.

10.9 Conclusions

Social engineering is common and important as an offensive deception technique, with many powerful options. It can also be used against attackers because they are subject to human weaknesses too. Attackers rarely expect any kind of sophisticated defense against them, especially a social-engineering one, so they can be fooled.

10.10 Exercises

1. Discuss how the names of systems on the same subnetwork could be useful bait and why.
2. Suppose you know a particular attacker likes getting credit for exploits from their fellow hackers and has a weakness for contests. Design a scam that would be particularly effective against them.
3. Discuss how likely a hacker is to detect spyware placed on their computer. Don't they have better things to do, even if they are more adept at detecting spyware than the average user?
4. In what ways can the data about where someone went to school, as recorded on a social-networking site such as Facebook, be useful in tracking them down even if they went to school a long time ago?
5. Assess the effectiveness of each of these hoaxes in defending a network site N. Discuss both positive and negative factors.

   (a) "N has a new firewall that completely blocks attacks."
   (b) "N primarily contains honeypots."
   (c) "N is a 'drive-by download' site that secretly installs software on your computer."
   (d) "N is run by the US Central Intelligence Agency."
   (e) "N asks a lot more questions when you log in nowadays."

6. Consider a religion-based terrorist organization that is planning cyberattacks. What properties of that organization would be best to attack to impede the attack? How could deception be used to accomplish this?

References

Almeshekah M, Atallah M, Gutierrez C, Spafford E (2015) ErsatzPasswords: ending password cracking and detecting password leakage. In: Proceedings of annual computer security applications conference, Los Angeles, CA, 7–11 Dec, 2015. pp 311–320

Awad N, Fitzgerald K (2005) The deceptive behaviors that offend us most about spyware. Commun ACM 48(8):55–60

Boese A (2006) Hippo easts dwarf: a field guide to hoaxes and other bs. Harcourt, Orlando, FL

Bojinov H, Boneh D, Boyen X, Burszstein E (2010) Kamouflage: Loss-resistant password management. In: Proceedings of the 15th European conference on research in computer security. Springer, lecture notes in computer science 6345, pp 286–302

Bowen F, Kemerlis V, Prabhu, P, Keromytis A, Stolfo S (2010) Automating the injection of believable decoys to detect snooping. In: Proceedings of the 3rd ACM conference on wireless network security, Hoboken, NJ, 22–24 Mar. pp 81–86

Cenys A, Rainys D, Radvilavius L, Gotanin N (2005) Implementation of honeytoken module in DSMS Oracle 9iR2 Enterprise Edition for internal malicious activity detection. Proceedings of conference on detection of intrusions, malware, and vulnerability assessment, Vienna, Austria, Jul 2005

Cybenko G, Giani A, Thompson P (2002) Cognitive hacking: a battle for the mind. IEEE Comput 35(8):50–56

Dunnigan J, Nofi A (2001) Victory and deceit, second edition: deception and trickery in war. Writers Club Press, San Jose, CA

Erdie P, Michael J (2005) Network-centric strategic-level deception. In: Proceedings of the 10th International command and control research and technology symposium, McLean, VA

Gerwehr S, Rothenberg J, Anderson R (1999) An arsenal of deceptions for INFOSEC. Project Memorandum, National Defense Research Institute, Rand Corp., PM-1167-NSA, October

Gharabally N, El-Sayed N, Al-Mulla S, Ahmad I (2009) Wireless honeypots: survey and assessment. In: Proceedings of the International conference on information science, technology, and applications, Kuwait, Mar 20–22. pp 45–52

Grazioli S, Jarvenpaa S (2000) Perils of Internet fraud: An empirical investigation of deception and trust with experienced Internet consumers. IEEE Trans Syst Man Cybernetics A 30(4): 395–410

Kshetri N (2014) Cyberwarfare in the Korean Peninsula: asymmetries and strategic responses. East Asia 31:183–201

Kuhnhauser W (2004) Root kits: an operating systems viewpoint. ACM SIGOPS Operat Syst Rev 38(1):12–23

Mitnick K (2002) The art of deception. Cyber Age Books, New York

Mukherjee A, Kumar A, Liu B, Wang J, Hsu M, Castellaneos M, Ghosh R (2013) Spotting opinion spammers using behavioral footprints. In: Proceedings of the 19th ACM SIGKDD international conference on knowledge discovery and data mining, Chicago, IL, 11–14 Aug 2013. pp 632–640

Qin T, Burgoon J (2007) Judgment in detecting deception on potential implications in countering social engineering. IEEE International conference on intelligence and security informatics, New Brunswick, NJ, 23–24 May, 2007. pp 152-159

Ravia F (2004) Trolling lore. www.searchlores.org/trolls.htm. Accessed 23 Nov 2004

Seife C (2015) Virtual unreality: The new era of digital deception. Penguin, New York

Spafford E (2011) More than passive defense. www.cerias.purdue.edu/site/ blog/post/more_than_ passive-defense. Accessed 20 Jan, 2016

Spitzner L (2005) Honeytokens: the other honeypot. www.securityfocus.com/ infocus/1713. Accessed 30 May, 2005

Thompson R (2005) Why spyware poses multiple threats to security. Commun ACM 48(8):41–43

Tsikerdekis M, Zeadally S (2014) Online deception in social media. Commun ACM 57(9):72–80

Xiao B, Benbasat I (2007) Product-related deception in e-commerce: a theoretical perspective. MIS Q 35(1):169–195

Yuill J, Zappe M, Denning D, Feer F (2004) Honeyfiles: deceptive files for intrusion detection. In: Proceedings of the workshop on information assurance, West Point, NY, 10–11 Jun 2004

Chapter 11
Measuring Deception

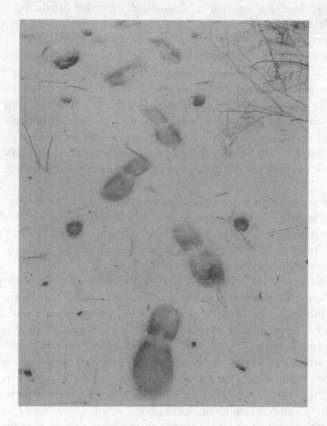

So far we have presented informally a wide range of deceptions for cybersystems. The remaining chapters will provide a more systematic approach. This chapter will explain how to measure the degree to which behavior or objects are suspicious, of either those of cyberattackers or cyberdefenders. Measuring those of cyberattackers will enable us to decide when we are under attack, and measuring those of cyberdefenders will enable us to design the most effective defensive deceptions. Chapter 12 will provide systematic methods for planning deceptions once we have decided to deceive, and Chap. 13 will discuss implementation options. Chapters 14–16 will describe implementations for some specific problems.

© Springer International Publishing Switzerland 2016
N.C. Rowe, J. Rrushi, *Introduction to Cyberdeception*,
DOI 10.1007/978-3-319-41187-3_11

11.1 Misuse Detection

Before we deceive, we must be reasonably confident we are under attack. (Sect. 12.1 will discuss the tradeoffs of collateral damage to non-attackers.) Fortunately, a variety of commercial and open-source products can recognize suspicious behavior of a user of a cybersystem. Such products are generally called "intrusion-detection systems" and "intrusion-prevention systems" (Rash et al. 2005; Trost 2009; Sanders and Smith 2013). There are two kinds, those detecting "misuse" (specific suspicious acts) and those detecting "anomalies" (statistically unusual situations).

Misuse detectors work by recognizing suspicious strings (both bit strings and character strings) in user-supplied data. These are called "signatures". For instance, many buffer overflows designed to seize control of cybersystems use precisely crafted long bit patterns that they write onto the program stack. These bit patterns cannot differ much between attacks without losing their effectiveness. Similarly, many attacks using "cross-site scripting" supply carefully tailored Web site addresses with special arguments that can be recognized. So intrusion-detection systems make up lists of these unusual strings and search for them in packets coming across their firewalls or, better yet, in commands supplied to a server. Exactly what signatures to seek can be found from security-information sites like www.cert. org.

Most of these systems examine packets transmitted to a cybersystem from outside. Here is an example packet that went to a honeypot run by us, as extracted by the TCPDump utility (Fig. 11.1). The left side shows the actual bytes of a 224-byte packet in 14 rows of 16 bytes per row, given in hexadecimal (base 16). The right transcribes any alphanumeric characters in the bytes.

You can see many "00" bytes (or "NOP"s), which are often used for padding in buffer overflows; the number of these in succession can be a signature. But more obvious are the suspicious "MARB" and "MEOW" strings which signal a particular kind of attack. The probability of either of these four-character strings occurring in any random four bytes is $256^{-4} = 2.33*10^{-10}$ since there are 256 possibilities for a byte. In the $16*14 = 224$ bytes shown above, there are 220 opportunities for such a four-character string. Hence the probability of it occurring in a random set of 224 bytes is roughly $220*2.33*10^{-10} = 5.13*10^{-8}$. That's a quite small number. But it also means there is an even smaller chance of $\left(5.13*10^{-8}\right)*\left(5.13*10^{-8}\right) = 2.63*10^{-15}$ of seeing both these four-character strings in the same packet, assuming they are independent as is generally true for signatures. Even though the Internet transmits large amounts of data, it will take a long time on the average before we see a random packet that accidentally contains these two strings.

The Snort open-source intrusion-detection system (from www.snort.org) is the most popular packet-based misuse-focused intrusion-detection product. Its standard configuration has a database of several thousand signatures. An example Snort rule is:

```
alert tcp $EXTERNAL_NET any ->$HOME_NET 139 (msg "DOS SMBdie
attack"; flags: A+; content:"|57724c65680042313342577a|";)
```

```
05 00 00 03 10 00 00 00 A8 06 00 00 E5 00 00 00    ................
90 06 00 00 01 00 04 00 05 00 06 00 01 00 00 00    ................
00 00 00 00 32 24 58 FD CC 45 64 49 B0 70 DD AE    ....2$X..EdI.p..
74 2C 96 D2 60 5E 0D 00 01 00 00 00 00 00 00 00    t,..`^..........
70 5E 0D 00 02 00 00 00 7C 5E 0D 00 00 00 00 00    p^......|^......
10 00 00 00 80 96 F1 F1 2A 4D CE 11 A6 6A 00 20    ........*M...j
AF 6E 72 F4 0C 00 00 00 4D 41 52 42 01 00 00 00    .nr.....MARB....
00 00 00 00 0D F0 AD BA 00 00 00 00 A8 F4 0B 00    ................
20 06 00 00 20 06 00 00 4D 45 4F 57 04 00 00 00      ..
...MEOW....
A2 01 00 00 00 00 00 00 C0 00 00 00 00 00 00 46    ...............F
38 03 00 00 00 00 00 00 C0 00 00 00 00 00 00 46    8..............F
00 00 00 00 F0 05 00 00 E8 05 00 00 00 00 00 00    ................
01 10 08 00 CC CC CC CC C8 00 00 00 4D 45 4F 57    ............MEOW
E8 05 00 00 D8 00 00 00 00 00 00 00 02 00 00 00    ................
```

Fig. 11.1 Example attack packet

Table 11.1 Probability of a signature of B bits triggering a false alarm

B	8	16	64
2^{-B}	0.004	0.0000153	0.0000000000000000000542

This says to send an alert message of a "DOS SMBdie attack" to the system administrator whenever packets of the TCP protocol incoming to port 139 have a particular binary string "57724c656580042313342577a", provided those packets have the "acknowledge" flag set. The Snort documentation explains the syntax.

If you pay the Snort organization some money you can get the most up-to-date version of the rules, otherwise you have to wait a few weeks. This matters because new attacks can appear quickly.

Snort can check for a variety of features of packets. But it has a rather low-level viewpoint. These packets are retrieved by the "libpcap" utility at level 2 from the bottom of the seven levels of the ISO/OSI protocol hierarchy, the "data link layer" just above the physical layer. This means that Snort can catch deliberately mal-formed packets and other tricks in individual packets involving format manipula-tion. But it means it is hard to correlate packets. Packets more than a minimum size are split into subpackets, and Snort may not be able to reassemble them when many packets are going by on a network. Sure, the packets will be reassembled by the operating system of the target computer eventually so they can be used, but Snort can't see that since it needs to be fast: It tries to check every packet going by to make sure it doesn't miss some obvious attack. Snort does have some "add-ons" that allow it to combine information from multiple packets, but these are necessarily limited by the low context-free level of detail at which Snort operates.

Misuse detection like that in Snort can have significant numbers of false posi-tives on short strings. If a signature is B bits long, it will occur accidentally with probability 2^{-B} in a random string of length B. Table 11.1 shows some example values. So on the Internet with millions or billions of packets going by, it is not hard to trigger a misuse rule accidentally for a short packet. Each time this happens, a human may be required to devote time to investigate.

Despite these problems, misuse detection by defenders can catch many kinds of attacks. It makes an attacker's job harder since it prevents them from using the easiest and best-known attacks. So it is an essential defensive tool.

Can misuse detection methods be used to detect defensive deception? Probably not, because this book has argued that such deceptions have a large number of options which can be exploited. Offensive deceptions tend to use the same methods repeatedly, so helpful signatures can be more easily constructed for them.

11.2   Anomaly Detection

An alternative to the all-or-nothing detection is a more statistical approach called anomaly detection. Most attacker activities look different from normal system activities. They use odd commands because they try to exploit a few scattered known flaws in software; they download large numbers of files onto the victim computer; and they try to modify key operating system files. All these things can occur with legitimate users too with less frequency, and it would be unfair to create signatures for them. Instead, we should count how often they occur, and raise an alert if many of these "suspiciousness" measures ("metrics") are especially high. Example metrics are system load, number of directories opened in the last hour, number of protection violations in the last hour (indicating attempts to open files that were not authorized), fraction of main memory used, and number of system files modified in the last hour. The more of these are high, the more suspicious the situation.

This problem has been addressed in hypothesis-testing from the field of statistics. We would like the average amount by which a set of metrics on activity of a cybersystem varies from their average values. However, some metrics vary considerably more than others, and it would be unfair to count their deviations from average as much. So the usual approach is to compute the normalized deviation, $(m_i - \mu_i)/\sigma_i$, where m_i is the value of the ith metric, μ_i is the mean of the ith metric over all observed systems, and σ_i is the standard deviation of the ith metric over all observed systems. We can then average this over all N metrics:

$$D = \sum_{i=1}^{N} (m_i - \mu_i)/N\sigma_i$$

This requires that we define our metrics so that large values indicate anomaly and small values indicate normality, as with the examples in the last paragraph.

By the Central Limit Theorem of statistics, the sum of many such "random variables" will tend to have a normal (Gaussian) distribution with mean of 0 and standard deviation of 1, since the "normalization" formula above adds N distributions which each have a mean of zero and a deviation of 1/N. We can then compute how

Table 11.2 The probability of a random value from a normal distribution

Number of standard deviations from the mean	Fraction of the distribution beyond that value
0.0	0.3969
0.2	0.3813
0.4	0.3520
0.6	0.3122
0.8	0.2261
1.0	0.2178
1.2	0.1714
1.4	0.1295
1.6	0.0940
1.8	0.0656
2.0	0.0440
2.2	0.0283
2.4	0.0175
2.6	0.0104
2.8	0.0060
3.0	0.0019

far D is from typical values on this distribution by comparing it to a table of the normal distribution like Table 11.2.

For instance, suppose we use three metrics:

- the load on the system
- the number of different directories viewed in the last hour
- the number of protection violations in the last hour

Assume:

- The average system load is 1 with a standard deviation of 1, and the current load is 2.
- Three directories are viewed in an hour on an average system, with a standard deviation of 3, and 4 directories were viewed in the last hour on this system.
- 0.5 protection violations occur in an hour on the average with a standard deviation of 0.5, and 1 protection violation occurred in the last hour.

Then:

$$D = \frac{(2-1)}{1} + \frac{(4-3)}{3} + \frac{1-0.5}{0.5} = 2.33$$

and by interpolating in the table, we can estimate the probability the situation is random as around 0.010 or 1 %.

Does that mean the probability that we are under attack is 99 %? No, because anomalousness can be caused by other things than a cyberattack such as a concurrent system backup. But if we choose enough metrics known to be correlated with cyberattacks, the odds of any other explanation applying to the particular kind of abnormal state we are seeing should be small.

While we can add any metrics that could suggest an attack, it is desirable to add "independent" ones as much as possible, metrics that do not correlate with one another. That is because we overestimate the total standard deviation when two metrics are positively correlated. Positive correlation means that when one indicates an attack, it is more likely that the other will indicate an attack. Positive correlation is more common than negative correlation with clues to attacks. Some examples:

- System load and number of directories visited are mostly independent because visiting a directory increases the system load very little.
- Number of directories visited and number of files opened are not independent because users who visit many directories are typically going to open many files in those directories.
- Number of protection violations in an hour and system load are mostly independent because system load is mostly due to computation and not file accesses.
- Number of protection violations in an hour and number of files viewed are not independent because the more files a user opens, the more the chance of a protection violation.
- Fraction of commands whose arguments were much longer than average and fraction of commands using unusual characters are not independent because buffer overflow attempts often feature both.

Anomaly detection can also be applied to detection of defensive deception by attackers. Examples of metrics they could use are:

- How much time a system takes to respond to a connection request
- How many more system files than user files are stored in a file system (high numbers may indicate a honeypot)
- How many times the system refused to open a file with some excuse
- How many passwords were found on the system (they may be bait)
- How many direct external connections the system has (high numbers may indicate a honeypot)

Even though attackers will not take the time to do a formal analysis using the above mathematics, they will still intuitively suspect something when several metrics are high.

11.2.1   Anomaly Detection of Insider Threats

A special challenge in information security is the "insider threat", or someone with malicious intentions within an organization, and having all the rights and privileges of any member of that organization (Capelli et al. 2012). Spies, both in business and government, are a classic example. But insider threats can be any disgruntled or desperate employees.

Insiders do not need to use malware so they will not trigger signature-based intrusion detection. But they could trigger anomaly-based detectors since to cause damage to an organization they need to do something out of the ordinary. A classic action is "exfiltration", or copying secrets of the organization to some external source. Typically this is copying of files to the Internet. Since businesses require Internet connections, exfiltration for corporate espionage is often easy.

To detect insiders, we need to compare rates of normal activities to those of a particular user. Rates need to be averaged over a good period of time to get accurate values for both normal users and for users to be monitored. Then actions like copying files can be modeled as Poisson processes (see Sect. 9.4.2) with an expected occurrence rate. However, much activity on cybersystems is "bursty" or exhibits wildly varying rates. File downloads are an example; often users download a lot one day, then nothing another day. Thus, a better model of an individual is often the distribution of the logarithm of the rate, and many of these approximate normal (Gaussian) distributions. Then we can measure the suspiciousness of some metric on a user by the number of standard deviations it is beyond the mean of the logarithm of the rate for the average user.

Since exfiltration is such a good clue to an insider threat, we would like to measure it for this approach. However, we cannot treat each exfiltrated document as an independent random variable because downloads are often bundled together. Probably we can only count the entire set of downloads in one day as a single event. This is why bait files (Sect. 10.3) are so valuable for detecting exfiltration, because they can be more easily engineered to be independent. We can do this by putting them in widely scattered locations and given them widely different contents. Then we can add the rate-anomaly metrics for each bait file exfiltrated to get a good total metric.

11.3 Bayesian Inference

An alternative to the statistical-distribution approach to anomaly detection is to do Bayesian inference (Korb and Nicholson 2004). This is a better mathematical framework when we have events that either occur or do not (that is, have Boolean values). But we can always set a threshold on a metric and turn it into a Boolean, as by saying a system load of 10 or more represents "high load".

Bayesian inference extends "Bayes' Rule" of probability theory: $p(H \mid E) = p(E \mid H) * p(H) / p(E)$

Read the "p" as "probability of" and the "|" as "given", so this says "The probability of H given E is the probability of E given H times the probability of H divided by the probability of E." This formula is useful when E is the occurrence of some piece of evidence and H is a "hypothesis" or explanation of that evidence. The two hypotheses in which we are most interested here are that our cybersystem is under attack (for which we will use the label A) and that an interaction is deceptive (for which we will use the label D). The p(H) and p(E) are called "prior probabilities" because they are your estimate when you have no additional conditions.

11.3.1   Naive Bayes Inference

Usually we need multiple clues to be sufficiently sure of a conclusion. Then it is often fair to estimate for two clues:

$$p\big(H \mid (E_1 \& E_2)\big) = p(E_1 \mid H)p(E_2 \mid H)p(H)/p(E_1 \& E_2)$$

and for three clues:

$$p\big(H \mid (E_1 \& E_2)\big) = p(E_1 \mid H)p(E_2 \mid H)p(E_3 \mid H)p(H)/p(E_1 \& E_2 \& E_3)$$

and so on for larger numbers of clues. These formulas are called "Naïve Bayes" because they blithely assume $p\big((E_1 \& E_2) \mid H\big) = p(E_1 \mid H)p(E_2 \mid H)$ and $p\big((E_1 \& E_2 \& E_3) \mid H\big) = p(E_1 \mid H)p(E_2 \mid H)p(E_3 \mid H)$, forms of conditional independence. Such independence is hard to guarantee, though assuming it seems to work fine in many situations.

It is easier to understand Naïve Bayes in the "odds form" created by some simple algebra on the formulas above. Odds o(X) are defined as

$$o(X) = p(X)/\big(1 - p(X)\big) \text{ so } (X) = o(X)/\big(1 + o(X)\big).$$ Using the odds we can divide $p(H \mid E)$ by $p(\sim H \mid E)$, and rewrite Naïve Bayes for m clues as:

$$o\big(H \mid (E_1 \& E_2 \& \ldots \& E_m)\big) = \left[\frac{o(H \mid E_1)}{o(H)}\right] * \left[\frac{o(H \mid E_2)}{o(H)}\right] * \ldots * \left[\frac{o(H \mid E_m)}{o(H)}\right] * o(H)$$

$$= o(H)\prod_{i=1}^{m}\big[o(H \mid E_i)/o(H)\big]$$

Here the "Π" symbol represents the product of terms from i = 1 to m. For the problem of detecting attackers, each term in brackets is a ratio of odds of an attack after the evidence to the odds of an attack before the evidence. If some evidence makes us more sure we are under attack (as is true with most evidence about attacks), the ratio will be greater than one; if some evidence makes us less sure we are under attack, it will be less than one. For instance, large numbers of protection violations support the notion of an attack since attackers often try to overwrite protected operating-system files; large numbers of documents created by the user suggest an ordinary user since most attacks do not involve documents. The product of all these ratios is multiplied by the initial odds of being under attack to get the cumulative odds of being under attack. Then if we prefer a probability, we can compute it from the odds with $p(X) = o(X)/\big(1 + o(X)\big)$.

Note the importance of o(H), the "prior odds" before we see any evidence at all. Since deception is rare, its o(H) will often tend to be low. This is the deeper explanation of "truth bias", the tendency of people to believe they are being told the truth.

The Naïve Bayes form given above treats each piece of evidence as independent. If we see an attacker doing a buffer overflow, that increases the probability that they will next try to gain administrator privileges, get a rootkit, and install it. If two pieces of evidence E_1 and E_2 are correlated, we can combine them into a single odds ratio with Naïve Bayes:

$$o\left(H \mid \left(E_1 \& E_2 \& \ldots \& E_m\right)\right)$$
$$= \left[\frac{o\left(H \mid \left(E_1 \& E_2\right)\right)}{o(H)}\right] * \left[\frac{o\left(H \mid E_3\right)}{o(H)}\right] * \ldots * \left[\frac{o\left(H \mid E_m\right)}{o(H)}\right] * o(H)$$

The disadvantage is that we have a more complex odds to estimate.

Even if we cannot estimate correlated probabilities well, Naïve Bayesian inference should work well for the two hypotheses in which we are particularly interested, the probability of attack and the probability of deception, because with these we only need to set a threshold for action, not compute an exact number. Even if the factors are not very independent and we are overestimating the probability of the hypotheses, we can compensate by setting the thresholds higher. Nonetheless, just as with the statistical methods of the last section, we should try to pick factors that are as independent as possible to get better estimates to start with.

11.3.2 Examples of Naïve Bayes Inference

As an example of inference of an attack, extend our example of Sect. 11.2:

- E1: the average system load is 1 with a standard deviation of 1, the current load is 2, and the probability of an attacker being present when the load is 2 is 0.2.
- E2: 3 directories are viewed in a hour on an average system, with a standard deviation of 3, 4 directories were viewed in the last hour, and the probability of an attacker being present when 4 directories are viewed is 0.1.
- E3: 0.2 protection violations occur in a hour on the average with a standard deviation of 0.2, 1 protection violation occurred in the last hour, and the probability of an attacker having one protection violation in an hour is 0.05.
- The probability of being under attack (A) at some random time is 0.01.

  Then:

- o(A)=0.01/(1-0.01)=0.0101
- o(A|E1)=0.2/(1-0.2)=0.25
- o(A|E2)=0.1/(1-0.1)=0.11
- o(A|E3)=0.05/(1-0.05)=0.05
- o(A|(E1&E2&E3))=(0.25/0.0101)   *   (0.11/0.0101)   *   (0.05/0.0101)   * 0.0101=1.34
- p(A|(E1&E2&E3))=1.34/(1+1.34)=0.57

So the attack probability is significantly increased from 0.01 to 0.57 with the three additional pieces of evidence when they are assumed to be independent.

As an example of inference of defensive deception, suppose an attacker uses a stolen password to log in to a system, and it takes longer than usual to respond. They then download the first file of their rootkit from the network. Then suppose they try to download the second file ten minutes later and they get the message "network maintenance ongoing". Deception does seem a possible explanation of such behavior. Assume:

- D: The initial (a priori) probability of deception (D) is small, say 0.01.
- E1: The initial probability of a login this slow is 0.2, and if deception were being practiced it could be 0.3.
- E2: The initial probability of network maintenance is 0.1, and if deception were being practiced it could be 0.2.
- Network maintenance termination is a Poisson process with average occurrence frequency of 8 h, so maintenance is unlikely to start within 10 min.

Then:

- $o(D) = 0.01/(1-0.01) = 0.0101$
- $o(D|E1) = 0.3/(1-0.3) = 0.42$
- $o(D|E2) = 0.2/(1-0.2) = 0.25$
- $o(D|(E1\&E2)) = (0.42/0.101) * (0.25/0.0101) * 0.0101 = 10.4$
- $p(D|(E1\&E2)) = 10.4/(1+10.4) = 0.91$

That is a significant increase in probability. Still, maintenance and pre-maintenance activities could also explain these observations. We should estimate their probabilities and compare them to this. More evidence of deception should also be sought now by the attacker. Defenders should track the odds of deception and make sure they are always less than a threshold, given as evidence all the things that an attacker has encountered.

11.3.3 Obtaining Necessary Probabilities

A challenge of Bayesian methods is obtaining the necessary prior and conditional probabilities. We could obtain them from statistics or by experts. Statistics require monitoring a representative set of systems over a period of time. Most systems do keep records of downtime and abnormal conditions, and we can use that for statistics. Unfortunately, many of the good clues to suspicious behavior are rare and monitoring is unlikely to provide enough data about them. So a Bayesian approach is often forced to use judgment of experts to estimate the necessary probabilities.

We at least need to estimate prior probabilities. Cyberattacks are statistically rare but do occur from time to time. Deception by the defender, except for honeypots, is even more rare. Excusable conditions such as "network down" can be counted on a random set of cybersystems over a time period. We can do better if we estimate these things for the particular context in which a machine is located, such as its network connections.

Conditional probabilities often lack adequate statistics, but there are principles that can be aid inference. For deception detection, the more implausibilities and the stronger they are, the more likely that deception is being employed (Whaley and Busby 2002). Implausibility can be in the properties of some object or its relationships to other objects. For instance:

- The excuse that the network is down is more plausible than the excuse that a virus has attacked a system because, in the experience of most users, the former is much more common than the latter.
- The excuse that the network is down, a minute after it was seen to be working fine, is implausible because things rarely change so quickly on a network.
- The excuse that the network file transfer utility is not working because the network is down is implausible if the remote shell utility is working fine.

These criteria can be turned into numerical estimates by experts.

Inconsistency (see Sect. 9.3) also affects these probability estimates. Inconsistent excuses trigger suspiciousness when over a threshold (Santos et al. 2005). If the network is working at one time, it is highly unlikely that it is not working one minute later. Similarly, if an attacker encounters an error message they have never seen before, that can be suspicious in itself. So we need special conditional probabilities to recognize the different kinds of inconsistency.

Another broad inference is that of conspiracy. If either an attacker or defender repeatedly encounters strange obstacles and curious coincidences preventing them from accomplishing their goals, they may hypothesize that some kind of conspiracy is at work. The conspiracy need not be deception, but the reactions are often similar. A conspiracy suggests that the deceivee should treat the cybersystem differently, as by checking error messages in independent ways, counterattacking, or leaving the system entirely. Defenders should want to prevent attackers from reaching a conclusion of conspiracy since most deceptions work better against unaware attackers. Fake honeypots, where we want to scare attackers away, are an exception.

11.3.4 Weighted Bayesian Inference

A problem with Naïve Bayes is that it rates all evidence the same. We usually have different degrees of confidence in different evidence, and these can be represented by weights w_i on each piece of evidence. The weights can be interpreted as the conditional probabilities of the conclusion given the strongest possible evidence of that type. For instance, if we have two clues to deception by a honeypot, its slow speed of response and the presence of known honeypot filenames, we can weight the second clue higher independent of its conditional probability because we trust better the reasoning behind it.

Taking a product in the Naive Bayes formula is equivalent to taking the antilogarithm of the sum of the logarithms of the factors. If you weight a sum of logarithms, you multiply each logarithm by a constant. That is equivalent to taking powers of the original probabilities. So assign positive weights w_i to the factors where $\sum_{i=1}^{m} w_i = 1$, representing the fractions of the total confidence in the conclusion due to each factor. Then the Naïve Bayes odds formula becomes:

$$o\big(H \mid (E_1 \,\&\, E_2 \,\&\,\ldots\&\, E_m)\big) = o(H) \prod_{i=1}^{m} \left[\frac{o(H \mid E_i)}{o(H)} \right]^{w_i} = \prod_{i=1}^{m} \big[o(H \mid E_i) \big]^{w_i}$$

since $\displaystyle\prod_{i=1}^{m} o(H)^{w_i} = o(H)^{w_1 + w_2 + \ldots + w_m} = \big(o(H) \big)^1 = o(H)$. As before, the Π means "product".

This applies to situations where we are monitoring evidence for a while, and we see new evidence, but we do not want to overweight it since we have already seen a good deal of evidence. We could use a formula like:

$$o\big(H \mid (E_{old} \,\&\, E_{new})\big) = \big(o(H \mid E_{old}) \big)^{0.99} \big(o(H \mid E_{new}) \big)^{0.01}$$

11.4   Coordinated Detection of Attackers

It can help if defenders do not need to wait to be attacked before starting defenses including deception. They can listen for reports of attacks on nearby sites. For instance, if a site starts seeing a large number of repeated ICMP messages with all the flags set, it could tell other sites so that they can start deceiving on any such messages right away rather than wait for a confirmed denial of service. Both misuse and anomaly detections can be broadcast to similar machines. Broadcast messages need not be large compared to other Internet traffic since observed misuse and anomaly types require only given code numbers and a few bytes of parameters to describe them, plus a count in the case of repeated instances.

How should we rate evidence from other sites in Bayesian reasoning? We should not weight it as heavily as evidence from our own site because we may never get attacked in the way the other site is being attacked. Other sites also may have features not shared by ours. such as different version numbers for the operating system and software, which could affect the success of an attack. So we need to weight evidence from other sites using the ideas of Sect. 11.3.4.

Averaging of distributed ratings is a popular approach in "reputation systems" for online sites like EBay. The idea is that the average rating of a vendor by multiple customers provides a more accurate and less subjective rating than rating by any individual customer. We can apply this idea to get the average rating of deceptiveness of a site from several attackers' attempts to interact with it. If we call the ratings p_{si}, taking their geometric mean (appropriate for quantities that tend to multiply) is equivalent to:

$$p_s = \left(\frac{1}{N}\right)\sum_{i=1}^{N} p_{si} = \sum_{i=1}^{N}\left(\log\left(e^{p_{si}}\right)/N\right) = \log\prod_{i=1}^{N} e^{p_{si}/N}.$$

Finding such consensus values for a probability has been explored in work on multiagent systems such as (Barber and Kim 2001; Yu and Singh 2003; Guha et al. 2004; Belmonte et al. 2006 Hu et al. 2007). The more sophisticated approaches distinguish your rating of a clue from the rating of the clue by others and from the rating of those others by you (Nurmi 2007). These approaches can run into problems if some of the clues are deceptive themselves (Johnson and Santos 2004), but rating sources can help.

11.5   More About Deception Detection

Sections 11.1 through 11.4 gave methods that apply to both detection of attacks and detection of deception. There are many products for the first but few for the second. So detection of deception deserves some additional discussion.

One important difference of offensive and defensive deceptions is that defensive deceptions can have more varied alternative hypotheses whose likelihoods we should assess too. Section 9.2 listed some alternative hypotheses useful as generic excuses that can also be used for other kinds of deceptions, as for instance:

- The system is new and has not been set up ("configured") properly.
- The system is undergoing maintenance and not all features are working.
- An abnormal abort left the system in an inconsistent state.
- Someone damaged something on the system, deliberately or inadvertently.
- The system has been attacked by a virus or worm.
- The system is being manipulated by a practical joker.

Each of these can have its own probability (albeit generally small) and its own odds calculation. Each of these explanations is inconsistent with deception, and each is inconsistent with the others. So the probabilities of these, plus the probability that none of them are true, should sum to 1. That means, to get a more accurate estimate, we should divide the final probability of deception by the sum of all the estimated probabilities of these other explanations.

The weighting of evidence discussed in Sect. 11.3.4 is particularly useful in modeling evidence of deception against an attacker because one good interpretation of a weight is the probability that an attacker notices. Unlike an automated intrusion-detection system, attackers are unlikely to be systematic in assessing whether they are being deceived. They will just make some observations from time to time, or if more active about it, they will only look for a few of their favorite clues. So the w_i in the equation can be our estimate of the probability that a piece of evidence i is noticed by the attacker when it appears. An example of evidence the attacker cannot ignore would be a failure of a command; an example the attacker will likely ignore would be the exact memory addresses given in system errors; and an example in between could be the details of a directory listing in a user account. But note that people are especially good at noticing inconsistencies (Sect. 2.5.2), so any clues related to these must be given extra weight.

The use of multiple deceptions can make a conclusion more convincing since deceivees (particularly attackers) rarely see a single deception, much less several at the same time. As we will discuss in Chap. 12, it is good to pick multiple deceptions that are either closely related or else highly independent of one another. Closely-related deceptions help support consistency; highly-independent deceptions make detection more difficult. One useful effect is that for many deceivees, once they have found the first deception, they will not look for further deceptions because they consider deception then a puzzle that they have "solved". This can be modeled by significantly decreased weights for the less-obvious deceptions after the first one. But not everyone behaves this way. A minority of attackers encountering a deception will react in the opposite way, namely become more determined to find other possible deceptions. This can occur when the deception hurt the attacker's self-esteem in some way, as when the deception was present for a long time before the attacker discovered it.

11.6   Active Deception Detection with Probing

So far we have assumed a deceivee who passively notices evidence of deception. Detection of deception is more effective, however, if the deceivee can ask questions or test the deceiver (Sect. 2.5.7). "Probing" is the term. A classic police interrogation technique is to ask carefully chosen interrelated questions of the suspect (Granhag et al. 2015). Inconsistencies and implausibilities in the answers will suggest deception that can be followed up. This can be used against spammers and phishers who can be contacted.

Analogously, an attacker who suspects an operating system or software is deceiving them could send carefully crafted commands and check for inconsistencies. For instance, when a file-transfer routine tells the user that the network is down, the attacker could try a Web browser or a software-update mechanism to see if they are down too. But there are three problems with this. Software, systems, and networks can be designed to be highly consistent because they are built on highly deterministic mechanisms, and the methods of Chap. 9 suggest additional ways to enhance consistency, all of which can be applied to maintain consistency of deceptions. Second, apparent inconsistencies could be blamed on inaccurate error descriptions by the software since error messages are not usually a high priority in programming; "Network down" may just be the software's lazy way to say something is wrong with the network connection. Third, probing behavior is unusual and easy to detect. It will likely involve unusual commands, unusual packets, or unusual timing, and once the defender sees them, they will know immediately that they are being probed, more easily than with most intrusion detection. The record of those probes is also valuable intelligence information, just what we need to build better intrusion-detection systems. So deception detection by probing is counterproductive.

11.7   The Asymmetry of Trust and Distrust

A phenomenon often noted is that trust does not work psychologically the same as distrust. Distrust tends to grow faster than trust grows. If Joe trusts salespeople by repeated exposure to them, and then gets cheated by a salesperson, it can take a long time for Joe to become trusting again despite all his previous experience. The Naïve Bayes model does not explain this very well because many instances of positive evidence for something will tend to overrule one piece of negative evidence.

This suggests the approach used by (Josang 2001) which is to treat distrust and trust as independent. This leads to a "three-value logic" where the sum of the probabilities of trust, distrust, and a "don't know" hypothesis is one. Then we can do separate Naïve Bayes calculations for evidence of trust t and evidence of distrust d. If we need an overall measure of belief, we can use $B = 0.5 * \left(1 + p_{trust} - p_{distrust}\right)$ which ranges between 0 and 1. If B is greater than a certain threshold, we can assume something is true. Variations in this approach can be used in reputation-based systems as an alternative to averaging (Sect. 11.4).

For instance, suppose three normal actions take place on a cybersystem, each with an associated odds ratio of 1.1 for the hypothesis N of "no deception on this cybersystem"; then one odd action with associated odds ratio of 10.0 for the hypothesis D of "deception on this cybersystem". Suppose a priori probability of a nondeceptive cybersystem is 0.99 and of a deceptive cybersystem is 0.01. Then the Naïve Bayes formulas compute:

$$o\left(N \,|\, E_1 \,\&\, E_2 \,\&\, E_3\right) = 1.1 * 1.1 * 1.1 * \left(\frac{0.99}{1 - 0.99}\right) = 131.8$$

$$p\left(N \,|\, E_1 \,\&\, E_2 \,\&\, E_3\right) = \frac{131.8}{1 + 131.8} = 0.992$$

$$p\left(D \,|\, E_1 \,\&\, E_2 \,\&\, E_3\right) = \frac{0.1010}{1 + 0.1010} = 0.092$$

$$B = 0.5\left(1 + 0.992 - 0.092\right) = 0.95$$

So 0.95 is our overall belief that the system is normal. Thus we have made a small but significant change in our trust by observing the one anomalous event.

11.8   More About Building Good Honeypots

Design of fake objects raises some additional issues beyond those discussed above. Detection of fake documents and images has been important historically (Rendell 1994). Design of fakes is important for honeypots because their effectiveness is enhanced by having a good fake file system. It is therefore desirable to evaluate fakes with quantitative criteria.

11.8.1 *Experiments with Detection of Manipulated Data*

We conducted experiments with human subjects to determine how much distortion they could detect in text (Rowe et al. 2006). The first experiment showed subjects pairs of text where one item of text was deliberately manipulated and one item was not. Text came from military-software requirements documents with which the subjects were not familiar. Manipulations were created by substitution for sequences of words that were used elsewhere in the documents with the same surrounding (or alternatively, preceding) words. We discarded manipulations that resulted in ungrammatical or accidentally correct sentences. An example fake sentence was "In the event of a network failure of electronic transmission failure, JMPS shall provide the capability to output graphics for printing in the error log." In a second experiment, we gave them pairs of file directory names where one of the pair was real and the other was built from names of real Web-page files and directories at our school by choosing names randomly.

In the first experiment, our subjects could detect text manipulations with an average of three modifications per example to a significant degree, but they were not perfect. We concluded that randomly modified sentences can be detected despite lack of familiarity with the subject matter, even though people have difficulty in general in detecting deception. We surmise that fake documents could be detected in our experiment by subtle inconsistencies created by substituting words. That suggests that good fake documents have minimal such substitutions. Since critical details of a document are often in the names, places, and times mentioned, those should be the targets for modification if possible to build a good fake. Online resources provide lists of names and places, and times can be changed systematically. However, plausible substitutions should replace items with equally-likely items—changing the name of a major city to a small town would be suspicious.

However in the second experiment, our subjects could not significantly detect the fake directories. Apparently context was sufficiently lacking, and context is a key resource in detecting deception. This is good news for honeypots with fake names for files and directories. Still, real attackers on real systems may do better because attackers spend more of their time looking at file directories. Dornsief et al. (2004) discusses general clues to honeypots, and Holz and Raynal (2005) discusses specific methods for detection of the Sebek honeypot from the Honeynet Project by examining a set of suspicious features. They obtained these clues from careful analysis of a running installation of Sebek, probing to find clues to its concealed operation. Such a manual approach requires extensive knowledge of an operating system. Many attackers of cybersystems do not have the knowledge or the time to use it. Thus hand-tailored honeypots may often suffice.

11.8.2 Building a Convincing Honeypot

To build a good honeypot we need to construct a good set of files and put them into a convincing structure. One good way is to model our fake on real systems. We could copy files from some real system to our honeypot. But this would not work well because too many coincidental similarities between two existing systems is suspicious if both can be accessed by the Internet. These could be similarities between the original and fake, but also similarities between two fakes if more than one honeypot is created from the same data.

Thus we need some variations in files to build a convincing honeypot. Not in the operating system and common software—those files, which are often the majority of files on a cybersystem, will be identical over many machines. Note that honeypots are most effective when deployed by the hundreds or thousands ("honeypot farms") (Vrable et al. 2005). Thus the variation needs to be displayed over the entire set of honeypots.

How do we copy most of the file system of a honeypot? Methods from digital forensics will help (Casey 2011). We can make a copy of the secondary storage of one computer using forensic tools (or at least the non-software files), then copy these bits to the secondary storage of the honeypot machine. The tools circumvent the operating system so they can copy everything on a machine including unused space and the operating system itself. Thus the copies will contain all the mundane details of a cybersystem that will make it convincing. We can also modify details like file times if we like during the copying.

11.8.3 Metadata of Typical File Systems

We have been studying a collection of 4265 drives containing 251.7 million files obtained from various sources around the world (Rowe 2016). The term "drive" means something intended for secondary storage, primarily magnetic disks and flash memories. Our collection (or "corpus") includes drives purchased as used equipment in 32 countries around the world, a selection of classroom and laboratory computers at NPS, and some miscellaneous contributions. This data provides the basis for a good model of a realistic honeypot.

Table 11.3 shows the percentages of file types for five sets from our 2015 data: The full set of files, the Windows computers after eliminating of common operating-system and software files, the mobile devices similarly reduced, the storage devices (like thumb drives) similarly reduced, and the drives having other operating systems (including Linux machines, Macintosh machines, digital cameras, auxiliary memory cards, and printers) similarly reduced. The reduction process eliminated common software files and involved nine different clues. There were a total of

Table 11.3 File-type distributions for drives in our corpus

File type	All files (%)	Windows drives after filtering (%)	Mobile drives after filtering (%)	Storage drives after filtering (%)	Other op. systems after filtering (%)
No extension	9.7	11.8	8.5	1.0	9.2
OS extension	6.1	2.0	7.9	0.0	1.2
Graphics extension	15.5	12.5	10.8	4.0	6.2
Photo extension	3.6	8.8	4.4	11.5	8.4
Temporary extension	0.9	3.2	0.4	0.1	1.4
Web extension	9.1	9.1	23.3	17.0	10.7
Document extension	2.9	5.8	4.5	53.2	8.3
Database extension	0.4	0.4	0.3	0.0	0.5
Mail extension	0.1	0.3	1.6	0.0	1.1
Link extension	0.5	1.6	0.0	0.0	0.3
Compressed extension	1.1	1.3	4.0	1.6	9.2
Help extension	0.5	0.3	0.0	0.0	0.1
Audio extension	1.4	2.9	1.3	0.6	2.4
Video extension	0.3	0.7	0.3	0.8	0.4
Program source extension	9.3	7.0	5.5	0.0	5.8
Executable extension	10.9	6.8	1.4	0.5	2.2
XML extension	3.0	2.5	1.4	3.6	1.7
Log extension	0.3	1.0	0.1	0.8	0.5
Geographic extension	0.1	0.4	0.0	0.1	0.0
Copy extension	0.2	0.4	0.3	0.0	0.3
Index extension	4.4	1.7	0.0	0.0	0.1
Configuration extension	2.9	2.6	4.7	0.1	2.6
Installation extension	1.5	0.6	0.8	0.3	5.3
Security extension	0.2	0.1	0.0	0.0	0.1
Game extension	1.5	1.0	0.2	0.0	0.5
Sci. and eng. extension	0.9	0.5	0.0	0.0	0.0
Multipurpose extension	9.7	11.5	16.0	1.5	15.7
Miscellaneous extension	0.8	1.4	2.1	1.7	3.6

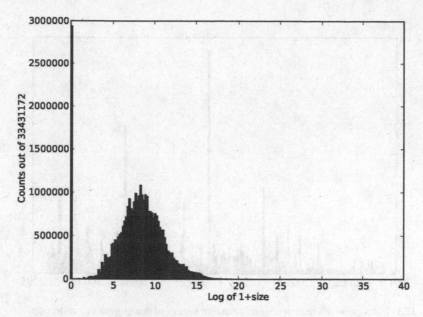

Fig. 11.2 Distribution of the logarithm of one plus the file size for a random sample of the files on our drives

251.7 million files for the first set, 58.8 million on 1819 drives for the Windows set, 6.5 million on 374 drives for the mobile-device set, 1.1 million on 350 drives for the storage-device set, and 0.5 million on 693 drives for the other-operating-system set. That meant the average Windows drive had 32,325 files, the average mobile device had 17,271 files, the average storage device had 3,267 files, and the average other operating system had 665 files. Note that useful honeypots can be mobile devices and storage devices too. This data gives guidelines for how to allocate files by type for a good honeypot. Surprisingly, there is not much published data of this type, though Douceur and Bolosky (1999) and Pang et al. (2004) are a start.

A honeypot should also have plausible directory information ("metadata") about the individual files. As we say, we shouldn't try to copy the same files repeatedly because that would be suspicious, but we could create files of similar characteristics like size in bytes. The logarithm of size plus one often forms a normal distribution, so we need to pick a set of files for a honeypot that fits this distribution. Figure 11.2 shows the distributions of the logarithms of one plus the size in bytes for the filtered sets used in Table 11.3. Note there are many zero-size files that do not follow the pattern of the rest of the distribution. Zero-size files are either initialized but unused files, or temporary files used for purposes not currently ongoing. They need to be included in proportionate numbers in honeypots we create.

Times associated with files (creation, modification, and access) also need to be convincing in a honeypot. If we copy files from another drive, we can systematically add a fixed amount to each time to make a consistent set with some forensic tools. Note that times are not evenly or normally distributed on most file systems because

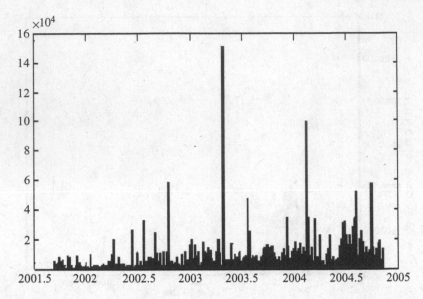

Fig. 11.3 Distribution of creation time on a random sample of drives from our collection

periodic updates affect a large number of files at once. To illustrate this, Fig. 11.3 shows the distribution of creation times for a subset of 1012 drives from our corpus. Sharp peaks represent major software updates.

Individual differences between drives are more clear if we look at a shorter time scale as in Figs. 11.4 and 11.5. The Chinese drive is used at more varied times than the Mexican drive. So in building a fake drive we need to be clear about what kind of drive we are imitating.

Note the daily ("diurnal") patterns and weekly patterns in these last two figures. If we are going to imitate a file system, we also need to duplicate these phenomena. That suggests that if we are to create creation, modification, and access times by adding a fixed number to the times on another drive, we should be careful to add an amount that is exactly a multiple of a week (or better yet, a year).

We are going to plant bait files on a honeypot, we should also ensure they have plausible names. For instance in Fig. 7.1, "Public Works", "Research", "Summer2002", and "Web Committee" are plausible names of directories for an academic institution. For this analysis, we should split words into subwords when we can; announcement_april_01_2002_picture.html is plausible because each of its six words and numbers is common. For non-English words like "cs" and "ctiw", we should use the likelihood of the category of the word if we can guess it; we can guess because of their length that "cs" and "ctiw" are acronyms, and acronyms are common on an organization's Web pages. As for the file extensions in the Figure, the "htm", and "html" are familiar, the invented extension "rzp" looks similar to the common "zip", and the invented extension "cry" suggests "cryptographic", a plausible adjective for a file containing secrets.

Fig. 11.4 Distribution of
creation times within the
week on a drive from
China

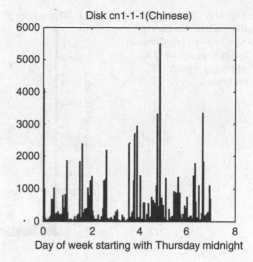

Fig. 11.5 Distribution of
creation times within the
week on a drive from
Mexico

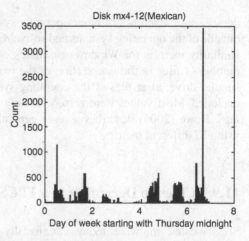

Statistics on directories vary less than statistics on files and thus more useful for assessing the reasonableness of a file system. For instance, the mean, standard deviation, smallest, and largest file sizes in a directory, the number of characters in a filename, or the date a file was last modified. We can take a weighted average of different metrics to get a cumulative metric with distribution closer to a normal distribution, and we can apply tests of significance to values obtained from this metric to assess to what degree a file system is suspicious. This could be important if we must create a large number of bait files and cannot just copy a file system from somewhere.

Another issue is interdrive differences. If we construct a honeypot "farm" we want to make sure that drives have plausible degrees of similarities to one another. We computed the number of files with identical contents (ignoring their names) on our reduced corpus, separately for Windows machines, mobile devices, storage

Fig. 11.6 Histogram of the fraction of common files between two drives in our corpus, ignoring the operating system and software

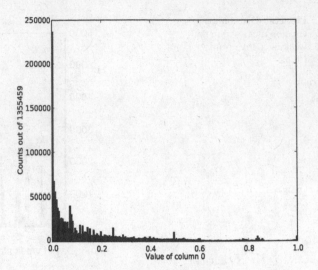

devices, and machines of other operating systems. We found few files in common outside of the operating systems and software. Figure 11.6 shows the distribution of similarity metrics for Windows machines, where the metric was the ratio of the number of files in the intersection of the two drives to the number of files in the smaller drive, after files of the operating system and common software had been excluded. Most values were zero, with only a few pairs showing significant overlaps. Rowe (2006) describes a more general way of comparing two file systems using 72 different metrics.

11.9 Clues to Deception in a File System

Sophisticated malware today can usually avoid triggering a misuse-analysis intrusion-detection system. So where does it tend to hide? We did a careful survey of existing malware in our corpus and tested a variety of clues, and found that malware was definitely distributed unevenly. Rowe (2016) reports the following clues were useful positive clues to malware, and likely to other kinds of deceptive files too.

- Files whose size had a natural logarithm of more than 15
- Files at the top level of the directory hierarchy
- Files where the file extension category was incompatible with its header category
- Files created at atypical creation times for their directory
- Files with hash values that occurred only once in the corpus
- Files with unusual characters in their paths like "#" and "l"
- Executables

- Files related to hardware
- Temporary files
- Files with extensions that occurred only once

This work also identified negative clues to malware, clues whose occurrence made it less likely that the file was malware:

- Files at depth 10 or more in the file hierarchy
- Double extensions, e.g. "foobar.exe.txt"
- Files with no extension
- Video extensions
- Engineering-related extensions
- Game top-level directories
- Operating-system immediate directories
- Backup immediate directories
- Data-related immediate directories

This analysis is necessarily limited, being confined to 398,949 files identified as malware in our corpus by at least one of five methods, out of a total of 262.7 million files. It was interesting that many classic clues like long names and files deep in the hierarchy were not confirmed.

This data can be used to rank files for potential for deception using a Bayesian evidence-combination approach. Rowe (2016) found that this significantly improved the accuracy of identifying malware files compared to just analysis of executables.

11.10   Conclusions

We have presented some tools to analyze both attacker and defender behavior for suspiciousness. Are they overkill? It depends on circumstances. When one needs to be careful about hurting normal users of a system, or when one needs to deceive sophisticated attackers as in cyberwar, or when one needs to automate a deception, the effort to carefully monitor the suspiciousness of users and ourselves can be worth it.

11.11   Exercises

1. Suppose you are clustering Snort alerts to reduce the amount of data transmit-ted in alerts. Suppose you get a new cluster involving copying a considerable number of files from one machine to another, where both machines are inside your firewall. This might be evidence of a spy or data theft.

   (a) What nonmalicious causes could account for the behavior? Suggest at least three.

(b) What steps do you take to find out if the behavior is malicious or not? List the factors you would investigate, and how you could recognize each of your three cases in (a).

2. The time-to-live (TTL) value in a packet indicates a packet-hop maximum for that packet. Typical starting values for Windows are 32 or 128, and these values are decremented at each hop between sites.

   (a) In general, what could suspicious values for the TTL be? What additional clues could you use to rule out false alarms?
   (b) How could the TTL values give you a clue you are being subjected to a reconnaissance phase by an attacker in which they are trying to map your network?
   (c) How could the TTL values give you a clue that you are seeing IP spoofing on the origins of packets (perhaps as part of a distributed denial-of-service attack)?
   (d) Suppose you are deceiving an attacker by manipulating their packets. What clues could they see in the TTL values of the packets you send them?

3. One type of attack on encryption of cookies used by a Web site is to send near-identical user names to the site and then inspect the cookies sent back. If we do an exclusive-or of the results, we can discover if the site (stupidly) is using the same one-time pad for every user with an exclusive-or. Describe precisely how a Snort-like intrusion-detection system could detect this kind of attack. What parts of Snort would you modify, and how could you implement this with a low computational load?

4. Suppose we have three metrics on a system at some time: system load (which is 1.5 standard deviations above the mean), ICMP traffic (which is 2.0 standard deviations above the mean), and number of protection violations (which is 0.5 standard deviations below the mean). Suppose these metrics have normal distributions. Suppose previous tests say that 40 % of the time on average, significantly abnormal metrics represent malicious activity. Estimate the probability of malicious activity at this time using the Naïve Bayes odds formula. Show your calculations and state any additional assumptions you need to make.

5. Suppose we are examining network flow data as a way to detect suspicious behavior. Flow data records the number and size of packets per source and destination. Anomalies can be more than excessive values of a parameter.

   (a) Why could an abnormally low rate of a type of flow signal an attack?
   (b) Why could having the same value for a type of flow on different days signal an attack?
   (c) Why could having a value that is a multiple of 60 for a day signal an attack? (We saw this once with a honeypot.)

6. Suppose you are an attacker and you notice three unusual things on a system you are attacking: It is quite slow, it keeps giving error messages about authorization, and it does not seem to have very many user files. Based on your experi-

ence, the probability of a honeypot given each of these three clues is 0.2, 0.5, and 0.6 respectively. Suppose you weight the three clues as 0.25, 0.25, and 0.5. What is the estimated probability this is a honeypot using the weighted Naive Bayes formula?

7. An increasing amount of traffic on the Internet is encrypted. From packets of such traffic we can only obtain a few things like packet size, time of transmission, alleged source, and destination. But we would still like to do intrusion detection as much as possible on such packets. Note that the mere use of encryption is a factor that should increase our suspicion about a packet.

   (a) How could you tell from a sequence of encrypted packets that a user is interacting with an operating system rather than sending a data file?
   (b) Encrypted data is generally transmitted in fixed-size blocks, where the last block is padded with blank or null characters to reach the block size. Suppose the average message is N blocks long and is transmitted in 128-byte packets, whereas the average encrypted message is sent in 4096-byte packets. What is the expected ratio in bytes between the encrypted form of a message and the unencrypted form of the same message?
   (c) Suppose a common malicious use would be to control a "zombie" or "bot" computer in a network used for launching denial-of-service or spamming attacks. What clues could an intrusion-detection system use to distinguish this kind of behavior in a sequence of encrypted packets from legitimate traffic involving use of a commercial Web site with sales capabilities?
   (d) Could the same clues you mentioned in (c) be used by an attacker to detect if responses to them are being programmed? What countermeasures could the deceiver take to make such clues less obvious?

8. Suppose an operating system is not trying to deceive anyone, and the probability of the result of a command being due to deception is 0.02 for all commands.

   (a) Suppose an attacker interacts with the system in ten commands. What is the probability of deception perceived by the attacker using the Naive Bayes odds formula?
   (b) Suppose an attacker interacts with the system in twenty commands. What is the corresponding probability?
   (c) It does not seem fair that the numbers are different. How would you fix the formula mathematically to give a more reasonable answer in this and similar situations?
   (d) Suppose instead we do separate computations of trust and distrust using the odds formula, with the probability of a command being not due to deception being 0.98 for all commands. We then subtract the two resulting probabilities. Will this solve the difficulty introduced above? Explain why or why not.

9. Some drives with plenty of files have size-logarithm distributions with sharp peaks at a narrow range of size values. What do the peaks represent? Why is it important to reproduce those for a convincing honeypot?

10. All drives have a period in which they were most intensively used, between when they were purchased and when they were sold or given away. Suppose you are creating a honeypot by copying a drive that was used for a period of three years, and you want to create a honeypot that appears to have been used for a period of six years. How do you handle the creation of the times for the files of the honeypot?

11. Suppose a spy is stealing secret files. Assume each file they steal provides a value to them of b. But there is an independent probability p that they will be caught stealing a file. Then assume if they are caught, there will be an investigation, their exfiltration site will be found and confiscated, and they will lose all the files they stole. Give a formula for the net benefit to the spy of stealing M files. Are there best values for them for some b and p?

References

Barber R, Kim J (2001) Belief revision process based on trust: agents evaluating reputation of information sources. In: Falcone R, Singh M, Tan Y-H (eds) Trust in cyber-societies, LNAI 2246. Springer, Berlin, pp 73–82

Belmonte M, Conejo R, Perez-De-La-Cruz J, Triguero F (2006) Experiments on robustness and deception in a coalition formation model. Concurrency and Computation: Practice and Experience 18(4):371–386

Capelli D, Moore A, Trzeciak R (2012) The CERT guide to insider threats: how to prevent, detect, and respond to information technology crimes (theft, sabotage, fraud). Addison-Wesley, Upper Saddle River, NJ

Casey E (ed) (2011) Digital evidence and computer crime: forensic science, computers, and the Internet. Academic, Waltham, MA

Dornsief M, Holz T, Klein C (2004) NoSEBrEaK – attacking honeynets. In: Proceedings of the fifth IEEE workshop on information assurance and security, West Point, NY, 10–11 June 2004. pp 123–129

Douceur J, Bolosky W (1999) A large-scale study of file-system contents. In: Proceedings of the ACM international conference on measurement and modeling of computer systems, Atlanta, GA. pp 59–70

Granhag P, Vrij A, Verschuere B (eds) (2015) Detecting deception: current challenges and cognitive approaches. Wiley-Blackwell, Chichester, UK

Guha R, Kumar R, Raghavan P, Tomkins A (2004) Propagation of trust and distrust, Proc. ACM conference on the World Wide Web. New York, NY, May 2004. pp 403–412

Holz T, Raynal F (2005) Detecting honeypots and other suspicious environments. In: Proceedings of the 6th IEEE-SMC information assurance workshop, West Point, NY, 15–17 June 2005. pp 29–36

Hu Y, Xiao Z, Panda B (2007) Modeling deceptive information dissemination using a holistic approach. In: Proceedings of the ACM symposium on applied computing, Seoul, Korea. pp 1591–1598

Johnson G, Santos E (2004) Detecting deception in intelligent systems I: activation of deception detection tactics. In: Proceedings of the 17th conference of the canadian society for computation studies of intelligence, London, ON, Canada, 17–19 May. pp 339–354

Josang A (2001) A logic for uncertain probabilities. Int J Uncertain Fuzz Knowledge-Based Syst 9(3):279–311

Korb K, Nicholson A (2004) Bayesian artificial intelligence. Chapman and Hall/CRC, Boca Raton, FL

Nurmi P (2007) Perseus – a personalized reputation system. In: Proceedings of the international conference on Web intelligence, Silicon Valley, CA, 2–5 Nov, 2007. pp 798–804

Pang R, Veqneswaran V, Barford P, Paxon V, Peterson L (2004) Characteristics of Internet background radiation. In: Proceedings of the 4th ACM SIGCOMM conference on internet measurement, Taormina, IT, 25–27 Oct 2004. pp 27–40

Rash M, Orebaugh G, Pinkard B, Babbin J (2005) Intrusion prevention and active response. Syngress, Rockland, MA

Rendell K (1994) Forging history: the detection of fake letters and documents. University of Oklahoma Press, Norman, OK

Rowe N (2006) Measuring the effectiveness of honeypot counter-counterdeception. In: Proceedings of the Hawaii international conference on systems sciences, Koloa, Hawaii, 4–7 Jan, 2006

Rowe N (2016) Identifying forensically uninteresting files in a large corpus. EAI Endorsed Transactions on Security and Safety (in press)

Rowe N, Duong B, Custy E (2006) Fake honeypots: a defensive tactic for cyberspace. In: Proceedings of the 7th IEEE workshop on information assurance, West Point, NY, 21–23 June 2006. pp 223–230

Sanders C, Smith J (2013) Applied network security monitoring: collecting, detection, and analysis. Syngress, Rockland, MA

Santos E, Zhao Q, Johnson G, Nguyen H, Thompson P (2005) A cognitive framework for information gathering with deception detection for intelligence analysis. In: Proceedings of the 2005 international conference on intelligence analysis, McClean, VA

Trost R (2009) Practical intrusion analysis: prevention and detection for the twenty-first century. Addison-Wesley, Upper Saddle River, NJ

Vrable M, Ma J, Chen J, Moore D, Vadekieft E, Snoeren A, Voelker G, Savage S (2005) Scalability, fidelity, and containment in the Potemkin virtual honeyfarm. In: Proceedings of the ACM symposium on operating system principles, Brighton UK, 23–26 Oct, 2005. pp 148–162

Whaley B, Busby J (2002) Detecting deception: practice, practitioners, and theory. In: Godson R, Wirtz J (eds) Strategic denial and deception. Transaction, New Brunswick, NJ, pp 181–219

Yu B, Singh M (2003) Detecting deception in reputation management. In: Proceedings of the conference on multi-agent systems, Melbourne, Australia, 14–18 July 2003. pp 73–80

Chapter 12
Planning Cyberspace Deception

With so many possible ways to deceive, we can be more effective if we plan systematically. Several methods can be used to plan deceptions ranging from informal to formal. Planning can be either strategic, broad in scope (Heckman et al. 2015), or tactical, focused in scope. We will focus on the latter here.

12.1 Cost-Benefit Analysis of Deception

We can decide if a deception in general is cost-effective by calculating its costs versus benefits. This can be used to analyze both whether we should deceive and what the attacker is likely to do. For this we can use ideas from "decision theory" and "game theory" (Osborne 2003), two branches of applied mathematics that analyze decision-making and competitive situations respectively. They can be used to recommend how decisions should be made, and how conflicts should be resolved for maximum benefit to one or both parties.

© Springer International Publishing Switzerland 2016
N.C. Rowe, J. Rrushi, *Introduction to Cyberdeception*,
DOI 10.1007/978-3-319-41187-3_12

We will show some examples below of this cost-benefit analysis. Much more can be made of this approach using decision theory (Greenberg 1982; Liu et al. 2005) and game theory (Garg and Grosu 2007; Chou and Zhou 2012). Games involve multiple moves and we can anticipate sequences of measure-countermeasure ploys with them. Specialized analysis can be done for deception in network communications (Alexander and Smith 2011; Chen et al. 2013). Some of this is occurring already with honeypots, as attackers try to discover them and defenders try to conceal themselves from new discovery techniques (McCarty 2003).

12.1.1 Analysis of a Single Defensive Deception

The most basic defensive case is the choice as to whether we should perform a single deception, like giving a false excuse to a user, to get them to leave our system (Rowe 2007). Here we have the choice to either deceive or not deceive, and the user can be either malicious or nonmalicious (legitimate). Based on our deception, the user may choose to log out with a certain probability. We need the following parameters:

- Let c_m be the cost of allowing a malicious user onto the system. This could include the cost of repairing damage they cause (like reinstalling the operating system if necessary) and steps to prevent them from attacking us again. This will be a positive number.
- Let c_l be the cost of hurting a nonmalicious user by our deception, by for instance causing them to waste time or log out. This will be a positive number too since it hurts us to hurt nonmalicious users. But it should usually be significantly smaller than c_m since attacks can have catastrophic effects on a system.
- Let p_m be the probability of a malicious user. Initially, this will be the fraction of the time a random user on the system is malicious, a small number except on honeypots. But if we accumulate more evidence that a user is suspicious using the techniques of Chap. 11 , we will increase this probability.
- Let p_{mr} be the probability that a malicious user will remain on the system after our deception. This measures the effectiveness of our deception, and can vary considerably with the user and the type of deception.
- Let p_{lr} be the probability that a nonmalicious (legitimate) user will remain on the system after our deception. For instance, if a legitimate user gets funny error messages, they may figure the system is not working and log out.

Figure 12.1 shows a cost-benefit tree for this general case of a single defensive deception. We can assess the expected cost/benefit of each leaf node of the tree by multiplying the probability of reaching that node by the sum of the costs/benefits incurred. Here we have assumed the probabilities are independent so we can multiply them to get an overall probability.

This tree can be used to decide whether it is to our benefit to deceive. We do this by comparing the sum of the expected costs for all the "deceive" branches to the

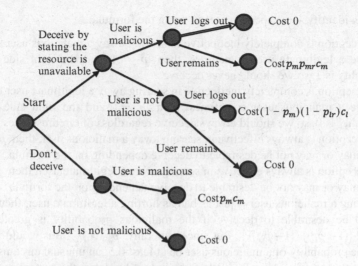

Fig. 12.1 Basic decision tree for defensive deception

sum for all the "don't deceive" branches. If the first sum is less than the second sum, then it is desirable to deceive. For this tree we should deceive if:

$$p_m p_{mr} c_m + (1 - p_m)(1 - p_{lr}) c_l > p_m c_m$$

We can factor out the p_m terms and rearrange this inequality to get an inequality for when it is desirable to deceive:

$$p_m > 1 / \left[1 + \left(\frac{c_m (1 - p_{mr})}{c_l (1 - p_{lr})} \right) \right]$$

For instance, if the cost of a malicious attack is 100 h to repair things, the cost to a legitimate user of our deceptions is 1 h, the probability of a malicious user remaining after the deception is 0.2, and the probability of legitimate user remaining after the deception is 0.05, the probability of a malicious user must be greater than:

$$\frac{1}{\left[1 + \dfrac{100 * (1 - 0.2)}{1 * (1 - 0.05)} \right]} = 0.012$$

So we only need to think there is at least a 1.2 % chance of the user being malicious before it is cost-effective to start deceiving.

We can identify some special cases in using the formula:

- If a deception is completely ineffective in scaring away a malicious user but can deceive a legitimate user sometimes, then $p_{mr} = 1$ and the right side of the inequality is 1, so we should never deceive.
- If a deception is completely ineffective in scaring away a legitimate user but can deceive a malicious user sometimes, then $p_{lr} = 1$ and the right side of the inequality is 0, so we should always deceive regardless of circumstances.
- If a deception is always effective in scaring away a malicious user, then $p_{mr} = 0$ but it may or may not be desirable to deceive depending on the formula.
- If a deception is always effective in scaring away a legitimate user, then $p_{lr} = 0$ but it may or may not be desirable to deceive depending on the formula.
- If hurting a malicious user is just as bad as hurting a legitimate user, then it still should be desirable to deceive if the malicious probability is greater than $1 / \left[1 + \left((1 - p_{mr}) / (1 - p_{lr}) \right) \right]$. But since generally $p_{mr} > p_{lr}$, this would require that the probability of a malicious user be at least 0.5, an unusual circumstance.
- If a legitimate user is equally likely to be induced to leave the system as a malicious user, then we should deceive if the malicious probability is greater than $c_l / (c_l + c_m)$. This is unexpected since it seems intuitive that one should not deceive then.

This model assumes that the user is completely blocked on attempting to access the resource. If the deception is not so obvious, we may be able to keep the user interested for a while. For instance, Zhao and Mannan (2013) suggests responding to password guessing by automatically connecting a user to honeypots in software (which they call "fake sessions") that would take a while to recognize. Then the user could run up considerable additional cost before they realize they are being deceived, increasing the net benefits of deception.

12.1.2 Analysis of Two-Stage Offensive Deception

Similar trees arise when analyzing the relative benefits of particular kinds of attacks for offense. Figure 12.2 shows a tree for guessing passwords. Even though user passwords are easier to guess, it is more cost-effective to try to guess an administrator password because then you can often grab the password file and decipher user passwords through brute force. Here assume:

- c_g is the cost to the attacker of guessing a password, assumed to be the same for administrator and user passwords.
- p_{ga} is the probability that the attacker can guess the administrator password, and p_{gu} is the probability the attacker can guess a user password. Typically $p_{ga} < p_{gu}$ significantly.
- b_{ea} is the benefit to the attacker of a successful exploit on the administrator (expressed as a positive number), and b_{eu} is the benefit to the attacker of a successful exploit on a user. Typically $b_{ea} > b_{eu}$ significantly.

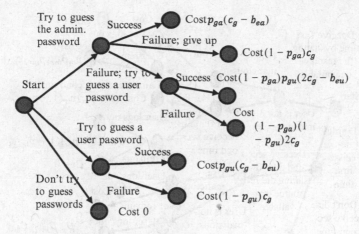

Fig. 12.2 Basic decision tree for password guessing

Then we can calculate the expected cost of each leaf node of the tree. Adding up these values for each of the four strategies, we get four numbers to compare. The cost of doing nothing is 0. The cost of guessing just the user password is:

$$p_{gu}\left(c_g - b_{eu}\right) + \left(1 - p_{gu}\right)c_g = c_g - p_{gu}b_{eu}$$

The cost of guessing just the administrator password is:

$$p_{ga}\left(c_g - b_{ea}\right) + \left(1 - p_{ga}\right)c_g = c_g - p_{ga}b_{ea}$$

The cost of guessing the administrator password and then the user password if necessary is:

$$p_{ga}\left(c_g - b_{ea}\right) + \left(1 - p_{ga}\right)p_{gu}\left(2c_g - b_{eu}\right) + \left(1 - p_{ga}\right)\left(1 - p_{gu}\right)2c_g$$

$$= c_g - p_{ga}b_{ea} + \left(1 - p_{ga}\right)\left(c_g - p_{gu}b_{eu}\right)$$

- The smallest of these four numbers corresponds to the best plan. For instance, suppose the probability of guessing an administrator password is 0.005, the probability of guessing a user password is 0.020, the cost of guessing a password is 60 min, the benefit of a successful administrator login is 1000 min, and the benefit of a successful user login is 100 min. Then the cost of doing nothing is 0, the cost of just guessing a user password is $60 - (0.020*100) = 58$, the cost of just guessing the administrator password is $60 - (0.005*1000) = 55$, and the cost of guessing the administrator password followed by the user password if necessary is $60 - (0.005*1000) + (0.995*(60 - (0.020*100))) = 60 - 5 + 58 = 113$. So just try-

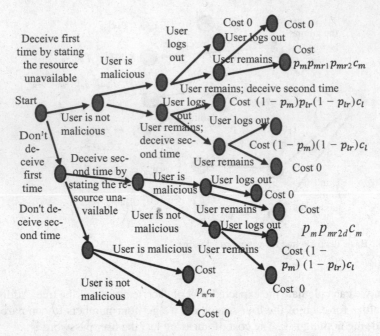

Fig. 12.3 A two-stage decision tree for defensive deception

ing to guess the administrator password and stopping on failure is the best because the administrator password is so much more valuable to guess.

12.1.3 Analysis of Two-Stage Defensive Deception

Defensive deception can also involve multiple stages. If the first deception does not deter an attacker, maybe a second or third one will (Yang and Wang 2008). This is an application of the military principle of multiple lines of defense.

Figure 12.3 shows a decision tree for the case where we deceive twice with different methods in an attempt to be more persuasive against a malicious user. If the methods are sufficiently different, what the user does for one will be probabilistically independent of what the user does for the other. We need additional parameters:

- Fig. 12.3 A two-stage decision tree for defensive deceptionLet p_{mr1} be the probability that a malicious user will remain on the system after our first deception is presented to them.
- Let p_{mr2d} be the probability that a malicious user will remain on the system after just the second deception is presented to them.

- Let p_{mr2} be the probability that a malicious user will remain on the system after both deceptions are presented to them.

We can evaluate the expected cost of three possible strategies, and choose the strategy that is the lowest cost:

- No deception: $p_m c_m$
- Deceive only at the second opportunity:

$$p_m p_{mr2d} c_m + (1 - p_m)(1 - p_{lr}) c_l$$

- Deceive at both opportunities:

$$p_m p_{mr1} p_{mr2} c_m + (1 - p_m)(1 - p_{lr}) c_l + (1 - p_m)(1 - p_{lr}) p_{lr} c_l$$

These trees are just a start at analyzing multistage deception problems. For instance, Axelrod (1979) considers the problem of measuring the benefits of postponing a surprise, which among other things could be a deception. If we wait with a deception until an opportune moment, we may be able to have considerably more effect than using it at the first opportunity. Adversaries may also start adjusting their attack methods if they recognize we are using deception on them (Dalvi et al. 2004), which we may be able to anticipate and proactively foil if their adjustments are easy to predict.

12.1.4 Analysis of a Fake Honeypot

"Fake honeypots" are cybersystems that try to look like honeypots to scare attackers away. An attacker usually gives up when it becomes clear that it will require significantly more effort to compromise a particular cybersystem than a random one. Most amateur attackers (hackers) and even some professional attackers treat all computers initially as equally valuable to compromise. That is because their most common goals are stealing money, building botnets to manipulate, or collecting salable intelligence about cybersystems and their configurations. They prefer the easiest targets they can find.

To analyze fake honeypots mathematically, assume:

- c_r is the average cost to an attacker to reconnoiter or "footprint" a randomly chosen system.
- c_c is the average cost to the attacker to subsequently compromise a randomly chosen system.
- c is the remaining cost to the attacker to compromise a randomly chosen system after reconnoitering it.
- b_c is the benefit to the attacker of compromising a machine.

- p_h is the attacker's estimate of the probability a system is a honeypot based what they have seen the system do and their prior probability.
- r_h is the attacker's estimated rate of damage (in terms of additional future cost) to them by an average honeypot due to its learning of the attacker's attack methods.
- v_h is the attacker's ratio of the value of compromise of a honeypot to the value of compromise of a non-honeypot. This should be less than 1 for most attackers, since honeypots try to prevent attacks from spreading and are thus less useful to an attacker, but this could be greater than 1 for "honeypot-hating" attackers. When the attacker is not sure a computer is a honeypot, the simplest model is to assume a linear weighting of $v = 1 - p_h(1 - v_h)$ where v is the relative value to the attacker of a machine that is uncertain to be a honeypot.

When an attacker recognizes clues to a honeypot, they must choose whether to continue trying to compromise it or try to attack another computer. If they choose the second option, they will then need to reconnoiter and incur the full cost of compromise on the other computer, but that could be a good tradeoff if they can avoid an obvious honeypot. Honeypots are currently rare, so the probability is high that a random second computer is not a honeypot.

Changing the attack target can be evaluated in terms of the rate of compromises per unit time; if the attacker compromises a machine of relative value v compared to a normal machine, they need to do $1/v$ of these to get the same benefit of compromising one normal machine. Hence the attacker should give up on a machine and try another random one if:

$$\frac{c + r_h p_h c}{v} > c_r + c_c$$

or with the simple model for v if:

$$c > \frac{\left(1 - p_h(1 - v_h)\right)\left(c_r + c_c\right)}{1 + r_h p_h}$$

- To illustrate the inequality, suppose a typical reconnaissance is 1 minute, the cost to compromise a typical cybersystem is 30 min, the attacker's perceived relative value of compromise of a honeypot is 0.2, and the rate of damage to an attacker by being on a honeypot is 0.03 per min (this factor does not affect the result much so it need not be precise). Then if an attacker thinks a machine is a honeypot with probability 0.5, the right side of the inequality becomes (1+30) * (1-0.5*0.8) / (1+0.03*0.5) = 18.6, so an attacker should go away from this machine if they have more than 18.6 minutes to go in the expected time of 31 min for the attack, else keep at it. This is encouraging for design of fake honeypots because it is not hard to design them so attackers will be more than half certain a machine is a honeypot after 60 % of their attack.

12.2 Analysis of Propagation of Deceptions

The effectiveness of a deception can be enhanced when it is reported from one person to another, and this is the key to hoaxes (Sect. 10.6), rumors, and fads. Assume there is a population of N people who have a probability p_h of having heard a deception, and p_b of believing it, who will tell an average of s people about something they believe, and these numbers are independent. Then if the population N is large, we expect Np_hp_b people to believe the deception from direct exposure, $Np_hp_b^2s$ from secondary exposure (assuming that people will only tell others about the deception if they believe it themselves), $Np_hp_b^3s^2$ from third-hand exposure, and so on. If p_b is small, the total number of people in the population who eventually believe the deception is a geometric series, for a total of

$$Np_hp_b \sum_{k=0}^{\infty} p_b^k s^k = \frac{Np_hp_b}{1-p_bs} \; provided \; p_bs < 1$$

So for instance, if 0.01 of a population hear about it, 0.3 are deceived, and they tell 2 other people on the average, 0.025 of the population eventually believes it.

If on the other hand $p_bs \geq 1$, then the deception spreads unbounded through the population until everyone is affected. The number of people to which a person can transmit the deception is roughly proportional to the fraction of the population that has not heard it already. Then the number of new people believing the deception starts to slow down after a certain point because the population is getting "saturated" with the belief. In general, the number of people in the population with the belief at time t will be:

$$N / \left[1 + \left(\left(\frac{1}{p_h} \right) - 1 \right) e^{-Nst} \right]$$

This will always increase over time, but tends to increase faster for some intermediate period. Its shape is called a "logistic" curve (Fig. 12.4).

The "population" involved in spreading a deception need not be large. If the deception involves something technical like security flaws, the population is only those who can understand the concepts. Then saturation of the population can occur quickly if they are well connected.

Disbelief in an attempted deception can also be propagated by the same mechanisms, if for instance someone tests the deception directly and discovers its falsity. So both belief and disbelief can propagate independently in the population when people hear only one of the two. But matters are more complex if someone hears both belief and disbelief and needs to combine them, perhaps using the methods of Sect. 11.7. They can weight the evidence on both sides using the criteria of Sztompka (1999), including the trustworthiness of the people they hear it from and the trustworthiness of the alleged original source of the information. Eventually people must decide whether to propagate the belief, disbelief, or neither, and to how many people.

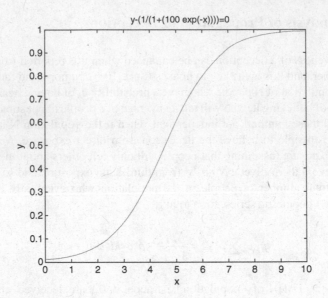

Fig. 12.4 A logistic curve

12.3   Quantifying Tactics from the Deception Taxonomies

Once we have decided to deceive, the next problem is to choose a deception.
Chapter 4 provides several useful taxonomies. We can then rate deception options
and choose the most promising ones. This is good when the deceptions we choose
are not likely to interact. De Rosis et al. (2003)) takes this approach. High precision
is not possible with the ratings since they are subjective anyway (e.g. the ratings in
Sects. 4.2 and 4.3) and a good deception plan should not be too predictable (as
mentioned in Sect. 3.1.2).

As an example, consider deception by false excuses. Table 12.1 combines each
case-grammar deception category in Sect. 4.3 with the best generic excuses mentioned in Sect. 9.2. The scale is 0–10 where 0 is unsuitable and 10 is highly suitable.

Table 12.2 then combines the generic excuses with a command to the operating
system to rate opportunities to deceive on those commands.

Each of these numbers is like an odds factor in a Naive Bayes model. So we can
multiply them to get an overall rating of a deception opportunity, as suitability
(deception,case) * suitability(deception,action) * suitability(case). The first number
comes from Table 12.1, the second from Table 12.2, and the third from Sect. 4.3.3.

For instance, consider the false excuse "the network is down" in response to a
file-transfer command by an attacker, an external-precondition deception. We would
rate it as 10 for external precondition, 10 on compatibility with the generic excuse

Table 12.1 Suitability of excuses to case-grammar deception methods

Grammar case	Net down	Test	Bugs	Comm. faulty	Policy change	Hacked	Joker	Deception
Object	0	3	3	0	6	8	8	10
Location-from	0	5	2	0	5	8	6	5
Location-to	0	7	5	0	5	8	8	10
Direction	0	0	3	0	0	8	5	5
Frequency	8	10	8	8	4	1	5	1
Time-at	0	8	2	2	0	8	2	5
Time-through	0	8	5	8	5	8	8	8
Cause	10	10	10	7	10	5	5	10
Purpose	0	0	0	0	10	0	8	10
Preconditions	10	7	10	0	8	0	10	10
Ability	10	5	5	5	2	1	10	1
Accompaniment	0	5	2	0	0	10	5	7
Content	0	2	5	7	2	10	8	7
Measure	0	5	2	0	5	2	3	7
Value	3	8	5	10	2	10	8	7
Effect	10	0	10	5	3	8	10	10

Table 12.2 Suitability of excuses with operating-system commands

Attacker action	Net-work down	Test	Bugs	Comm. faulty	Policy change	Hacked	Joker	Deception
Login	7	10	4	8	6	3	1	1
List directory	0	3	8	8	10	1	1	1
Scan ports	10	5	5	10	10	5	8	10
Connect at port	10	5	7	5	7	5	6	7
Buffer overflow	0	10	10	10	7	5	2	10
File transfer from another Site	10	5	5	5	10	7	8	7
Decompress file	0	7	5	0	5	5	5	5
Move file	0	7	5	2	8	5	5	7
Test operating system	2	10	10	2	7	10	8	10

of "network down", and 10 on compatibility with the file-transfer command, for a total of 1000. On the other hand, the false excuse of "system testing" on the same command would rate is 10*7*5 = 350 which is not as good.

12.4 Counterplanning Against Attacks with Deception

Once we have decided to deceive defensively and chosen a general method, we need to choose specific tactics to fight it.

12.4.1 Attack Plans

We can do better at selecting deceptions if we know more about what an attacker is trying to do. Although we could deceive in response to everything an attacker does, we will be more effective if we deceive only on the most critical parts of the attack. That is because the plausibility of our deceptions will be maximized with the minimum amount of total deception, following the analysis of Sect. 11.5 and the discussion of magicians in Sect. 3.2.4.

Modeling of attack plans (McClure et al. 2012) is useful for "red teaming" (deliberately attacking systems for purposes of testing them) and for developing more effective intrusion detection. At first glance there appears to be considerable variety in attack plans, judging by the diversity in targets and methods reported at attack-intelligence sites like www.cert.org. However, the underlying principles of attacks are usually the same. Most attacks try to gain access to the operating system of a computer by finding "holes" into it. Most commonly, this can include a variety of forms of social engineering (David et al. 2015), buffer overflows, and cross-site scripting. Then once access is gained, the remaining steps of an attack show little variety: Download attack tools, install them, simplify subsequent access, and cover one's tracks. So attacks are frequently characterized by considerable trial-and-error in a first phase, then little variety in the second phase. We can certainly foist deceptions during the first phase, particularly with automated software that can track myriads of variants. But the second phase is better because of its predictability. We can analyze the second phase thoroughly and carefully design some good deception plans for it.

Figure 12.5 shows a typical attack plan for mostly the second phase. This is displayed as a "hierarchical plan", a problem-decomposition tree used for planning in artificial intelligence by methods like "means-ends analysis". Hierarchical attack plans can be built several ways, including with grammars (Al-Mamory et al. 2008). Arrows indicate subparts of the plan; arrows below and to the left indicate handling of preconditions (things that are necessary for the action above), and arrows below and to the right indicate handling of postconditions (things that are necessary to "clean up" after the main action is completed). "Install rootkit" is the root of the tree because it is the main goal of the attacker. But we cannot install a rootkit unless we obtain administrative status; we cannot obtain administrative status unless we cause a buffer overflow or something similar; and we cannot cause a buffer overflow until we connect to the machine on some port. After we have obtained administrative status, we still cannot install the rootkit until we can download it. Then after we have installed the rootkit, it is important to install a backdoor to make remote control easier.

An alternative way to represent an attack plan is as an "attack graph" equivalent to a finite-state machine (Chu et al. 2010). This takes the tree and builds sequences of state transitions consistent with it. While this makes analysis easier, the attack graph usually has considerably more states than the corresponding hierarchical plan since every combination of goals must be considered in advance, whereas the

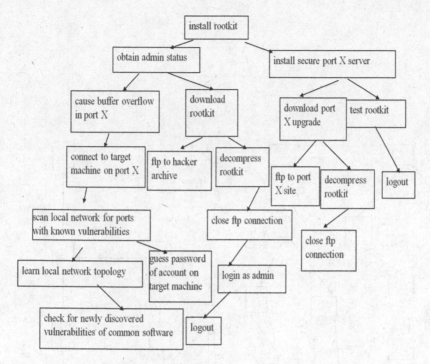

Fig. 12.5 Example attack plan in form of a tree

hierarchical plan can be modified dynamically. The reason for this is that hierarchical plans are equivalent to context-free grammars, whereas attack graphs are equivalent to less-powerful regular or finite-state grammars.

Figure 12.6 shows an attack graph corresponding to Fig. 12.5. Here the numbers in the boxes are state numbers for identification, the numbers next to them are the estimated times in seconds to the goal state, and the numbers beside the arrows are the probabilities of taking that branch. This particular diagram was created by running the tree model ten times with constrained random choices each time, so the probabilities are all fractions of at most ten events. If we run it more times we will get better probability estimates and additional states.

We can create trees and graphs like this by reading the literature carefully and trying to translate it into pictorial form. Many attack-graph projects do this by identifying "stepping stones" or intermediate goals that attackers are likely to use based on observation (Nicol and Mallapura 2014). However, there is a more systematic way to build attack graphs using artificial-intelligence planning techniques. This requires that you specify the logically necessary conditions associated with each action, specify some goals, and reason out a sequence of actions that will achieve the goals. The logically necessary conditions are preconditions on actions (facts that must be true before) and postconditions on actions (facts that become true and facts that become false after the action). The conditions on the "download" action could be specified this way:

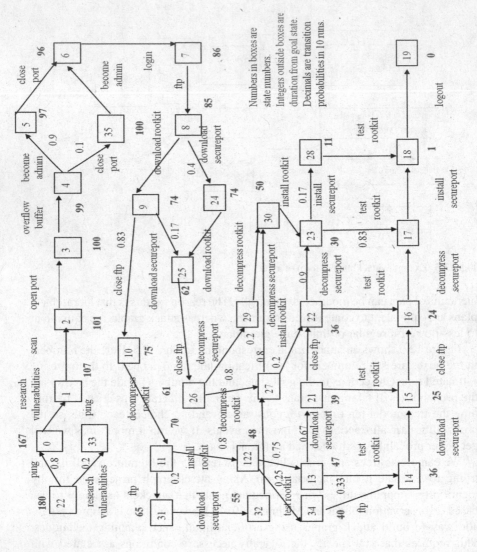

Fig. 12.6 Example attack graph created from the plan in Fig. 12.5

- Arguments: user U who wants to download, remote file name RF, remote directory name RD, remote site name RS, network N connection RS to current site, local directory LD to which to copy file RF, local site name LS.
- Preconditions: File RF exists in directory RD on site RS, user U has "copy" access rights to RF, network N is working, RF is permitted to be transferred across N, U has "write" access rights to directory LD on site LS, U is logged in on LS, U is authorized to use file-transfer software on LS.
- Postconditions: File RF is in directory LD on LS.
- Purpose: To get file RF on LS.

A logical specification like this provides reasons for actions. This enables us to find a sequence of actions that makes sense to accomplish our goals. We can use the means-ends analysis algorithm to find the plan tree and A* search (seeking multiple solutions) to find the plan graph. If we use A*, we use the times next to the states in Fig. 12.6 as the heuristic evaluation function, and we use the actual duration of the branches as the cost function.

Planning can take into account the costs and benefits of actions. For instance, for each action we can include:

- The average duration of the action.
- The standard deviation of the duration of the action.
- The average cost of the action to the user.
- The standard deviation of the cost of the action to the user.
- The average cost of the action to the system.
- The standard deviation of the cost of the action to the system.
- The average probability that the action succeeds once begun.
- The standard deviation of the probability that the action succeeds once begun.
- The average probability that the action will be detected by an intrusion-detection system.
- The standard deviation of the probability the action will be detected by an intrusion-detection system.

This information helps us both to rate plans of the attacker and to rate deceptive defenses. In analyzing an attack where speed is critical, such as an information-warfare attack, the attacker wants to minimize the time to achieve their objectives. We should then perform a search using expected durations of actions as their costs to figure what the attacker is likely to do. We should find multiple good solutions too, just in case the attacker does not make all the optimal choices. On the other hand, in analyzing a careful attack that wants to maximally conceal itself, we should take as cost the negative of the logarithm of one minus the probability of being detected. (Maximizing the product of numbers is mathematically equivalent to minimizing the negative of the sum of the logarithms of those numbers.) Similarly, in analyzing an attack that wants to have the best chance of success when methods are not completely certain, we should take cost as the negative of the logarithm of the probability of success.

Attackers may not be this systematic as they are prone to habits just like the rest of us. Thus they may perform unnecessary steps after planning conditions change as well as failing to perform necessary new steps. This is particularly true with cyberattacks because there are only a few attackers with good technical understanding of the attacks they are using because of the frequent reuse of attack code. So most attacks will contain unnecessary and missing steps compared to an ideal plan. We need then to ignore unnecessary steps for deceptions since their failure does not affect failure of the plan. Nonetheless, having the ideal plan to compare against gives us a good roadmap to what the attacker is trying to do.

12.4.2   Tracking Attack Plans

How do we track attackers as they follow a plan so we can know when to deceive? This can be hard if an action by the attacker could be used to achieve several different goals. This kind of problem has been studied in artificial intelligence under the name of "plan recognition" where "parsing" the observed sequence of actions is done to understand it. Recognizing attacks is often easier than the general plan recognition problem since there is less variety in most parts of attack plans than with other kinds of human behavior. It is not easy to attack systems, and even slight variations from a workable plan may fail. Examples of work that models attack plans are Cohen (1999), Steffan and Schumacher (2002), Julisch (2003), Liu et al. (2005). It is also helpful to generate normal-user plans to compare against, such as by the command-sequence generator of Chinchani et al. (2004).

We first need to index the actions in the possible plans. That is, for each type of action, we store what attack plan it occurs in and where it occurs in the plan. The index can include both general and specific information. For instance, it can keep an index of all places where a "decompress" action occurs, as a well as a shorter list of places where a "decompress" is done within an operating-system directory. Matching to a general kind of action requires variable bindings to the specifics of its setting.

Then when we see an attacker perform an action, we can look up possible attack plans it could belong to and plan locations. When we see the next action, we look up its locations too and use the constraint that the second action must follow the first in the plan to rule out possibilities. We keep a list of possible matches and prune it as we get more information; with enough observations of plan-relevant actions, we can be pretty sure what plan the attacker is executing and where we are in that plan. For instance for the plan in Fig. 12.6, if the attacker does a "decompress foo.gzp" action, it could match six places in the plan (26–29, 29–30, 26–27, 27–30, 22–23, and 16–17), binding the name of the file in each case to "foo.gzp". But if it is followed by what appears to be installing of the file and then testing of it, we must be following the sequence 26–27–22–16 in the middle of the diagram. Note that most attack graphs will have considerably more branches for each node than Fig. 12.6 because it was created from only ten runs, so there will be considerably more work in general to follow an attack plan.

A possible problem with plan recognition is extraneous actions in the user's plan. For instance, an attacker may stop to list a directory before proceeding, even though that is not necessary to their plan. So in matching actions to plans, it is important to note that specified action sequences just give a partial order of actions, and may be interrupted any number of times by additional actions.

12.4.3 Ploys for Counterplans

Now let us consider how to plan to stop ("foil") an attack. Planning to foil someone's plan is called counterplanning (Carbonell 1981; Christian and Young 2004). There has been work on automated analysis of attack plans, mostly for vulnerability assessment (Yang et al. 2010), but some on choosing the best countermeasures (Zhou et al. 2012; Santhanam et al. 2013; Fayyad and Meinel 2013; Durkota et al. 2015). Deception is a class of countermeasures not much previously considered.

To counterplan, we can try to prevent key attack steps from succeeding. If the attack is automated using a script, this will often cause the entire script to fail. If the script is more clever, or a human attacker is monitoring it, the attacker can try again or find another way to accomplish those plan steps. This could slow them down considerably. If we impose enough obstacles on the attacker, they may decide to stop and go attack something else, following the model of Sect. 12.1.1.

We can define a "ploy" as something unexpected that interferes with the success of an attack plan. A counterplan consists of a set of ploys. Many good ploys involve resource access as described in Sect. 4.5, and many involve false excuses as in Sect. 9.2. For instance, when an attacker tries to download their rootkit, a ploy could be to claim it is too big to transfer even if it is not. Ploys can identify a feature of a resource that the user needs, and claim that feature prevents usage. There can be more global ploys, such as warning a user their behavior is suspicious in an attempt to scare them away, or systematically misinterpreting commands as by deleting the first letter.

Chapter 9 provided a way to choose logically consistent false excuses. We can also rate the remaining possibilities and turn the problem into a heuristic search. If attack duration is the cost the attacker wants to minimize, then the best ploys are those that delay them the most. For instance for Fig. 12.6, it would be better to use the false-excuse ploy for "test rootkit" than for "download rootkit" because testing is later in the plan and will force the attacker to repeat more steps, wasting more of their time. If we do this in state 16, we will throw the attacker back into state 7, thereby costing them $86-20=66$ s. We can also incorporate a probability that our ploy is unsuccessful: We just multiply the cost of the replanning by the probability that we will convince the attacker to do it. So if we only fool a random attacker 60 % of the time that the test of their rootkit fails, the expected cost is $66*0.6=39.6$ s.

In general, each ploy does not change the attacker's state, but deceives them about the state. That requires the attacker to respond with a subplan to get to a state from which they can resume their original plan, what we will call a "fixplan". Then deception will impose additional cost on the attacker if:

$$c\left(s_{pp}, s_b\right) + c\left(s_b, s_g\right) > c\left(s_p, s_g\right)$$

where c(x,y) is the cost from state x to state y, s_{pp} is the state the attacker perceives due to the deception of the ploy, s_p is the actual state then, s_b is the last state of the fixplan (a state of the original attack plan that the attacker wants to get to), and s_g is the final goal state of the attack plan. Note that the ploy will only be desirable if the left side of the inequality is significantly larger than the right side, since there is no point deceiving someone unless the gains are large: Deception carries risks if it is discovered.

Since there are many possible deceptions and many places to do them, the search space for ploys is large. Thus it is helpful to recognize inheritance situations with fixplans. We can give two principles that will save us effort:

- (Rightward inheritance with respect to time) If F is a fixplan for ploy P at action A, then F is the fixplan for ploy P at any subsequent action B provided that none of the conditions affecting F change between A and B. For instance in Fig. 12.6, consider the ploy "rootkit malfunction" that can be applied to "test rootkit" for either the transition from state 22 to state 16 or the transition from state 23 to state 17. If they are paying attention, most attackers will conclude that something is wrong with the rootkit copy, and their fixplan will probably try to download it again by restarting the file-transfer protocol, transferring, and terminating the protocol. The only difference between states 22 and 23, the downloading of an additional file, does not affect the success or failure of this fixplan, so the fixplan inherits from 22–16 to 23–17.
- (Leftward inheritance with respect to time) If F is the fixplan for ploy P at action A, then F is the fixplan for ploy P at any previous action B provided that none of the conditions affecting F change between A and B. Similarly, the fixplan for state 23 in the previous example inherits to state 22.
- (Downward inheritance with respect to part-of): If F is the fixplan for ploy P in action sequence S, then F is the fixplan for any action A of S. For instance, if we have a general action "download F from S" that consists of three subactions "ftp to S", "get F from S", and "close ftp", the ploy "Say the file is too big" could apply to the general action. This ploy could have a fixplan of "login to S", "split F into two pieces", "logout of S", and "download the two pieces". This fixplan will inherit from the "download F from S" action to the "get F from S" action .
- (Downward inheritance with respect to specialization): If F is the fixplan for ploy P for a general action A, where F contains variables, then a specialization of F to F2 by making variable bindings is the fixplan for ploy P at action A2 which is a specialization of A created by making the same variable bindings. For instance, if the general action "download file F" has ploy "Say the network is down" with fixplan "wait an hour" and "try to download F again", then a specialized ploy and fixplan created by variable bindings will apply to "download foobar.exe" to result in "wait and hour, then try to download foobar.exe again".

12.4.4 Greedy Counterplanning

Since there are often many possible deception plans of considerably different effectiveness, it helps to have an efficient algorithm to find a good one. We want a set of ploys for a deception plan rather than a single ploy in case the deceivee is not fooled by just one. A first choice for similar problems is a "greedy algorithm" that in this case would rank all ploy options, then choose a set of the highest-ranking ones to use. Greedy algorithms do have the weakness that they can fail to find the best plan if there are interactions between the choices, as when deceptions are inconsistent with one another. Nonetheless, they can often give a reasonable plan. Appendix E gives a Prolog program implementing a greedy counterplanner. This version is tailored for rootkit-installation attack plans, so we also include compatible attack-planner code in Appendix D. Roy et al. (2012) represents an alternative approach where countermeasures (not necessarily deceptions) are integrated into the attack tree to provide single data structure for analysis.

Table 12.3 shows some top-rated ploys for Fig. 12.6, and to what state they could be applied, using some rough estimates of the time in minutes it takes to do each of the actions. The top-rated ones involve deletions of facts from a state, and a few involve changing a fact. The last column includes the probability that the ploy succeeds. Taking that into account seriously downgrades the first-listed ploy, which

Table 12.3 The top-rated ploys computed for Fig. 12.6

State number	Ploy deletion	Ploy addition	Delay due to ploy	Expected delay
1	Know recent vulnerabilities	None	60.4	3
33	Know recent vulnerabilities	None	60.4	3
14	Rootkit installed	None	31.3	24
15	Rootkit installed	None	31.3	24
16	Rootkit installed	None	31.3	24
...	...	...	...	...
18	Secure port installed	None	28.3	21
19	Secure port installed	None	28.3	21
28	Secure port installed	None	28.3	21
12	Rootkit installed	None	22.4	17
14	Rootkit tested	None	21.2	10
15	Rootkit tested	None	21.2	10
16	Rootkit tested	None	21.2	10
14	Secure port downloaded	None	20.3	15
15	Secure port downloaded	None	20.3	15
16	Secure port downloaded	None	20.3	15
17	Secure port downloaded	None	20.3	15
...	...	...	...	...
23	None	Secure port compressed	5.7	5
27	None	Secure port compressed	5.2	5

Table 12.4 The best deception plans computed for the data of Table 12.3

State number	Run number	Ploy deletion	Ploy addition	Weighted delay
18	1	Installed rootkit	none	313.5
18	2	Installed secure port	none	226.5
18	1	Tested rootkit	none	135.6
23	3	Secure port software obtained	none	55.0
18	2	Installed rootkit	none	38.5
7	1	Logged in as administrator	none	37.1
10	1	Rootkit software obtained	none	21.0
18	3	Secure port installed	none	14.3
18	2	Tested rootkit	none	10.7
1	1	Know recent vulnerabilities	none	10.1

amounts to trying to unconvince the attacker that they do not know a recent vulnerability.

Table 12.4 shows a deception plan built from the best-rated ploys in Table 12.3, using a greedy algorithm but taking into account the interactions of the ploys. The run number indicates which run of the plan the deception applies to, since each run encountered different states and thus could have different costs for the same ploy.

An alternative to a greedy algorithm is A* search, which can find the lowest-cost solution for these planning problems but requires more time. It requires we find a "heuristic evaluation function" consistent with our cost function, that calculates a cost to a goal state for any possible state. We can estimate it if we can observe a large number of counterplans and compute the average cost to a goal state for each state.

12.4.5 Planning Multiple Deceptions

Defensive counterplanning need not be as complex as it might seem. That is because once we choose a ploy at some time, we should try to be consistent in similar situations. So each deception choice usually entails effects in several places in the attack plan, and we do not need to choose very many distinct deceptions. In fact, a general deception like a "network down" excuse may foil all steps of an attack plan. The disadvantage is that attacks may more easily circumvent a single deception.

Nonetheless, using multiple deceptions can increase the chances of stopping an attack because only one may need to work. One approach is to choose related deceptions, as by false excuses claiming separately that the Web, file-transfer utilities, and chat utilities are down. This helps with consistency and increases the credibility of the deceptions. But if the deceivee becomes suspicious of one, they become suspicious of the others. Another approach is to choose deceptions that are as different as possible, "independent" deceptions. This would be good if we need to be maximize the chances of stopping an attack. This is similar to the theory of "outs" in stage magic, the idea of having a quite different alternative if one method fails (Nelms 1969).

Multiple independent deceptions also permit the "layering" of second-order deceptions, a technique which is often highly effective. Second-order deceptions (Sect. 4.4) use a more-obvious deception to conceal a less-obvious deception. For example:

- An outer deception could be the refusal to download a big file for a file transfer. The inner deception could be secretly modifying the file when it is transferred by another method, so that the file is faulty.
- An outer deception could be broadcasting warnings about new hacker tracking methods on certain sites, methods that are easy to circumvent. The inner deception could use well-camouflaged honeypots on those sites.
- An outer deception could be an encryption key in an easy-to-find location such as a Web site. The inner deception could be fake documents encrypted by the key.

More than two layers of deceptions can be done (Wang et al. 2012; Virvilis et al. 2014) to further increase the difficulty for attackers, something particularly important with sophisticated attacks. A three-layer deception could be where one password is needed to open a file containing another password, which is used to open a fake file. But many-layered deceptions have the disadvantage of requiring the attacker to follow several steps. If the attacker fails to notice the first deception, then other deceptions will not work.

12.4.6   Ploy Presentation

Use of ploys also requires some decisions as to how to present them to a victim, as mentioned in Sect. 4.6. For instance, the ploy "The network is not working" could be presented as one of the following:

- When the victim tries to establish a file-transfer connection, an error message says "We are sorry—the network does not appear to be working at this time".
- When the victim tries to establish a file-transfer connection, an error message says "A connection could not be established".
- When the victim tries to establish a file-transfer connection, an error message says "Network down".
- When the victim tries to establish a file-transfer connection, an error message says "14487: NWD".
- When the victim tries to establish a file-transfer connection, no response is ever received and the command never terminates.
- After the victim has apparently established a file-transfer connection, an error message "File does not exist on remote site" is given for any file transfer attempted.
- After the victim has apparently established a file-transfer connection, any file transfer attempt never finishes.

- After the victim has apparently established a file-transfer connection, any file transfer attempt appears to work, but the involved files never appear on the destination system.

All these deceptions could be effective, but there are several factors to weigh in choosing one. Deception should be consistent in similar situations as discussed in Sect. 9.3. Otherwise if politeness will help persuade the attacker, the first two tactics are good. If delaying the attacker is a high priority, the last four tactics are best.

12.4.7   *Entropy Measurement of Deceptions*

An interesting alternative approach to choosing deceptions is to use information theory and calculate the information content of the deception. Two approaches can be used: We can design deceptions to look a similar as possible to normal activities, or we can design deceptions to be maximally confusing.

For honeypots, Sect. 11.8 discussed some useful statistics that can be computed on file systems to define an average system, but there is a more general approach. That is to calculate entropy:

$$E = \sum_{i=1}^{N} - p_i \log(p_i)$$

This can be applied to any situation that has choices and a set of probabilities p for those choices. For a fake file, the probabilities could be the distribution of characters in the file, the distribution of words in the file, the distribution of the concepts conveyed by the sentences in the file, and so on. For a file system, the probabilities could be those of the type of file, the size of the file, and the times associated with the file. For network activities, the probabilities could be of particular messages such as "busy" alerts and of the distribution of delay times.

Entropy provides us a new way to conceptualize deceptions. One strategy is to send a deceptive message with the same apparent entropy as a legitimate message, but a decreased actual entropy. That is, we can try to design deceptions to seem like normal information that somehow is faulty in the end (Khasnabish 1989). An example is the British strategy in World War II of only sending secrets to Germany through its double agents that would not benefit Germany significantly, such as positions of British ships when no German ships were nearby (Dunnigan and Nofi 2001).

An alternative strategy is to increase the entropy as much as possible for the attacker to make things as confusing as possible, a kind of "dazzling" in the (Bell and Whaley 1991) model of Sect. 4.1. For instance, a honeynet can provide a large number of fake cybersystems, each with many fake files, so the attacker cannot find the real nodes and files (Cohen and Koike 2003). This approach makes no attempt to conceal the fact of a deception, but challenges the attacker to find their way.

This is only useful for time-critical attack targets since automated tools enable deceivees to systematically search through large amounts of data to eventually find the real information. It is a form of the notion of heterogeneity as a defensive strategy, which has been important in many military and crime-protection applications. Entropy measures heterogeneity.

12.5 Conclusions

Deceptions do not need to be simple to be effective. We can exploit the ability of cybersystems to handle complexity to come up with consistent and effective deception plans well beyond the limits of human planning abilities. That does not necessarily mean they are beyond the limits of human detectability, however. We still need the techniques of Chap. 11 to monitor our deceptiveness. However, automated planning may be just what we need in responding to sophisticated attacks such as polymorphic (time-varying) ones, and may in fact be the only effective defense against novel attacks.

12.6 Exercises

1. Consider the first decision-tree model of Sect. 12.1. Show your analysis of the situation where $c_m = 100, c_l = 10, p_m = 0.8, p_{mr} = 0.7, and\ p_{lr} = 0$. Draw the tree with expected costs on each node and say whether deception is worth it.
2. For the first decision-tree model of Sect. 12.1, explain under what circumstances c_l could be negative. Does this make any of the choices in the decision tree automatic? Show your mathematical analysis.
3. Using Tables 12.1 and 12.2, rate the suitability of deceptions involving:

   (a) lying that your system is being debugged when the victim tries to list a directory;
   (b) pretending to misunderstand the command when asked to decompress a file.

4. Referring to Fig. 12.5, suppose that it is necessary when installing a rootkit to change the protection status of the destination directory and delete old copies of EXE-format files there. How would the plan tree need to be modified to include these two actions and where?
5. Consider the transition from state 12 to state 34 in Fig. 12.6.

   (a) Give an example of a ploy there that is undesirable on the basis of cost.
   (b) Give an example of a ploy there that takes a victim to a state in the Figure that is desirable for the deceiver on the basis of time cost. Calculate the amount of cost it adds.

(c) Give an example of a ploy there that takes a victim to a state not in the Figure that is desirable for the deceiver on the basis of time cost. Calculate the fixplan, the cost it adds, and the total cost to the victim.

6. Give an efficient algorithm to determine whether a fixplan inherits to a later state. Describe carefully the data structures it needs.

7. Consider the list of example ploy presentation tactics in Sect. 12.4.6.

(a) Which are more appropriate for hackers (amateur attackers)? Why?
(b) Which are more appropriate during state-sponsored cyberwar? Why?
(c) Which are more appropriate for automated attacks? Why?

8. Suppose we are considering the installation of deception on our local-area network of 20 hosts. We can install a tool on either our network or our hosts. The network-based tool costs $50,000 and the host-based tool costs $5,000 but we need 20 copies for 20 hosts. On the network, it will see 1000 attacks a day, and the tool will scare away all but 20 attacks but also 50 legitimate users per day. On our hosts when used without the network tool, it sees 1000 attacks a day and scares away all but 10 of these but also 100 legitimate users. A failed deception of an attacker costs us $100 to deal with, and a scaring away of a legitimate user costs us $10 to deal with. The clues found by the network-based tool do not have much in common with the clues found by the host-based tool, so we can assume that the probability of finding an attack with one is independent of the probability of finding one with the other.

(a) Calculate the expected cost over D days of four things: (1) not installing either tool, (2) installing just the network tool, (3) installing just the host tool on each host, and (4) installing both the network tool and the host tool. Make reasonable assumptions as necessary and state what your assumptions are. Show your calculations.
(b) What is your recommendation to management about what should be implemented? What qualitative arguments would you add to strengthen your case?

9. Suppose an attacker uses deception against us, and we mount deceptions against them in response.

(a) How is a counter-counterdeception by the attacker different from a deception? Is a good counter-counterdeception just the same as a really good deception?
(b) Suppose both the attacker and the victim are automated. Describe how cycles of deception and counterdeception, counter-counterdeception and counter-counter-deception, etc., could go on indefinitely.
(c) What reasons, both theoretical and practical, could prevent such cycles from continuing forever?

10. Consider a game search for cyberattacks. The attacker has the following possible actions for a site:

- attack1: This costs 50 and adds a Trojan to the system. It can only be done if the system is not cut off, no Trojan is already on the system, and it has not been done before.
- attack2: This costs 40 and adds a Trojan to the system. It can only be done if the system is not cut off, no Trojan is already on the system, and it has not been done before.
- install_rootkit: This requires that some Trojan is on the system. It costs 45 for the attack1 Trojan and 60 for the attack2 Trojan.

The defender has the following actions:

- cutoff: Cut the Internet connection. This costs 20. Note that states that are cut off have no successors, but you cannot find that out until you visit them.
- search: Look for Trojans and rootkits and remove any you find. This costs 70.
- do_nothing. This costs 0.

The evaluation of a state is:

- 200 if a rootkit is installed in a state and the state is not cut off, 300 if a rootkit is installed and the state is cut off.
- Otherwise 100 if a Trojan is present on the system and the state is not cut off, 200 if a Trojan is present and the state is cut off.
- Otherwise 0 if the state is not cut off and 100 if it is cut off.

The total rating of a state is the evaluation plus the costs of a defender to get there minus the costs of an attacker to get there. The defender is trying to minimize the rating and the attacker is trying to maximize the rating.

(a) Draw the complete game tree for this situation down to the fourth level from the starting state (two moves for each player). Give the costs on the branches, evaluations of the leaf nodes, and the total ratings for every state using minimax search. You should have about 25 states. Minimax search computes the total ratings of all states four steps from the start, then uses those numbers to compute total ratings of all states three steps from the start, then uses those numbers to compute total ratings of all states two steps from the start, then uses those number to compute total ratings of all states one step from the start.

(b) Predict the game path if these are the only states that both parties consider and they choose their optimal branch at each opportunity.

11. Suppose an attacker's goals are to install their bot tools on a system. This has two preconditions, that they install their rootkit and they download their bot tools, not necessarily in that order. Installing a rootkit or bot tools requires downloading it. They cannot download anything until they add themselves to the access list and set their privileges. They cannot do either of those last two

things until they run an exploit to gain root privileges. That cannot do that until they find a vulnerable site, which has no preconditions. Suppose the attacker is named "joehacker".

Draw the problem-decomposition tree for this task showing precondition actions below and to the left of actions, and further "cleanup" actions below and to the right of actions. When you traverse your tree in "inorder" mode (first the left subtree, then the node, then the right subtree), you should obtain a correct order to accomplish the goals.

References

Alexander J, Smith J (2011) Disinformation: a taxonomy. IEEE Secur Priv 9(1):58–63

Al-Mamory S, Zhang H, Abbas A (2008) Modeling network attacks for scenario construction. In: Proceedings of the international joint conference on neural networks, Hong Kong, China, 1–8 June, 2008. pp 1495–1502

Axelrod R (1979) The rational timing of surprise. World Politics 31(2):228–246

Bell J, Whaley B (1991) Cheating. Transaction, New York

Carbonell J (1981) Counterplanning: a strategy-based model of adversary planning in real-world situations. Artif Intell 16:295–329

Chen PY, Shih IJ, Lin F (2013) Maximization of muti-round network survivability under considerations of the defenders' defensive messaging strategies. In: Proceedings of the international conference on mobile wireless middleware, operating systems, and applications, Bologna, Italy, 11–12 Nov, 2013. pp 148–155

Chinchani R, Muthukrishna A, Chandrasekaran M, Upadhyay S (2004) RACOON: rapidly generating user command data for anomaly detection from customizable templates. In: Proceedings of the twentieth annual computer security applications conference, Tucson, AZ, 6–10 Dec, 2004. pp 189–202

Chou HM, Zhou L (2012) A game theory approach to deception strategy in computer mediated communication. In: Proceedings of the conference on intelligence and security informatics, Washington DC, 11–14 June, 2012. pp 7–11

Christian D, Young R (2004) Strategic deception in agents. In: Proc. 3rd Intl. joint conference on autonomous agents and multiagent systems, New York, NY. pp 218–226

Chu M, Ingols K, Lippmann R, Webster S, Boyer S (2010) Visualizing attack graphs, reachability, and trust relationships with NAVIGATOR. In: Proceedings of the 7th international symposium on visualization for cyber security, Ottawa, ON, Canada, 14 Sept 2010. pp 22–33

Cohen F (1999) A mathematical structure of simple defensive network deceptions. all.net/journal/deception/mathdeception/mathdeception.html. Accessed 15 Jan, 2016

Cohen F, Koike D (2003) Leading attackers through attack graphs with deceptions. Comput Security 22(5):402–411

Dalvi N, Domingos P, Mausam, Sanghai S, Verma D (2004) Adversarial classification. In: Proceedings of the 10th ACM SIGMOD international conference on knowledge discovery and data mining, Seattle, WA, 22–25 Aug 2004

David F, David A, Hansen R, Larsen K, Legay A, Olesen M, Probst C (2015) Modeling social-technical attacks with timed automata. In: Proceedings of the international workshop on managing insider security threats, Denver CO, 16 Oct, 2015. pp 21–28

De Rosis F, Castelfranchi C, Carofiglio V, Grassano R (2003) Can computers deliberately deceive? A simulation tool and its application to Turing's imitation game. Comput Intell 19(3): 235–263

Dunnigan J, Nofi A (2001) Victory and deceit, second edition: deception and trickery in war. Writers Club, San Jose, CA

Durkota K, Lisy V, Kiekintveld C, Bosansky B (2015) Game-theoretic algorithms for optimal network security hardening using attack graphs. In: Proceedings of the 14th international conference on autonomous agents and multiagent systems, Istanbul, Turkey, 4–8 May, 2015. pp 1773–1774

Fayyad S, Meinel C (2013) New attack scenario prediction methodology. In: Proceedings of the 10th international conference on information technology: New generations, Las Vegas, NV, 15–17 Apr, 2013. pp 53–59

Garg N, Grosu D (2007) Deception in honeynets: A game-theoretic analysis. In: Proceedings of the 2007 IEEE workshop on information assurance, West Point, NY, 20–22 June 2007

Greenberg I (1982) The role of deception in decision theory. J Confl Resolut 26(1):139–156

Heckman K, Stech F, Thomas R, Schmoker B, Tsow A (2015) Cyber denial, deception, and counter deception: a framework for supporting active cyber defense. Springer, New York

Julisch K (2003) Clustering intrusion detection alarms to support root cause analysis. ACM Trans Inform Syst Security 6(4):443–471

Khasnabish B (1989) A bound of deception capability in multiuser computer networks. IEEE J Select Area Commun 7(4):590–594

Liu P, Zang W, Yu M (2005) Incentive-based modeling and inference of attacker intent, objectives, and strategies. ACM Trans Inform Syst Security 8(1):78–118

McCarty B (2003) The honeynet arms race. IEEE Secur Priv 1(6):79–82

McClure S, Scambray J, Kurtz G (2012) Hacking exposed 7: network security secrets and solutions, 7th edn. McGraw-Hill Education, New York

Nelms H (1969) Magic and showmanship: a handbook for conjurers. Dover, Mineola, NY

Nicol D, Mallapura V (2014) Modeling and analysis of stepping stone attacks. In: Proceedings of the winter simulation conference, Savannah, GA, 6–10 Dec, 2014. pp 3046–3057

Osborne M (2003) An introduction to game theory. Oxford University Press, Oxford, UK

Rowe N (2007) Planning cost-effective deceptive resource denial in defense to cyber-attacks. In: Proceedings of the 2nd international conference on information warfare, Monterey, CA, 8–9 Mar. pp 177–184

Roy A, Kim D, Trivedi K (2012) Attack countermeasure trees (ACT): towards unifying the constructs of attack and defense trees. Secur Commun Networks 5(8):929–943

Santhanam G, Oster Z, Basu S (2013) Identifying a preferred countermeasure strategy for attack graphs. In: Proceedings of the 8th annual cyber security and information intelligence research workshop, Oak Ridge, TN, US, January, paper 11

Steffan J, Schumacher M (2002) Collaborative attack modeling. In: Proceedings of the symposium on applied computing, Madrid, Spain, 10–14 Mar. pp 253–259

Sztompka P (1999) Trust. Cambridge University Press, London, UK

Virvilis N, Vanautgaerden B, Serrano R (2014) Changing the game: the art of deceiving sophisticated attackers. In: Proceedings of 6th international conference on cyber conflict. pp 87–97

Wang W, Bickford J, Murynets I, Subbaraman R, Forte A, Singaraju G (2012) Catching the wily hacker: A multilayer deception system. In: Proceedings of the 35th IEEE Sarnoff symposium, 21–22 May, 2012. pp 1–2

Yang L, Wang XM (2008) Study on the network active defense technology based on deception. Journal of the National University of Defense Technology (China), June: pp 65–69

Yang X, Shunhong S, Yuliang L (2010) Vulnerability ranking based on exploitation and defense graph. In: Proceedings of the international conference on information, networking, and automation, Kumming, China, 18–19 Oct, 2010. pp V1-163–V1-167

Zhao L, Mannan M (2013) Explicit authentication response considered harmful. In: Proceedings of the new security paradigms workshop, Banff, AB, Canada, 8–12 Sept, 2013. pp 77–85

Zhou Y, Kantacioglu M, Thuraisingham B (2012) Adversarial support vector machine learning. In: Proceedings of the conference on knowledge discovery and data mining, Beijing, China, 12–16 Aug, 2012. pp 1059–1067

Chapter 13
Software Engineering of Deceptive Software and Systems

This chapter considers further details in how to implement the deceptions described in this book. For readers interested in still more details, Heckman et al. (2015) provides a top-down view of deception planning, and Bodmer et al. (2012) offers useful alternative approaches to operationalizing deception. Heckman et al. (2015) situates cyberdeception in the context of military operations planning, and Bodmer et al. (2012) is a good resource for people on the front lines of cyberattacks.

© Springer International Publishing Switzerland 2016
N.C. Rowe, J. Rrushi, *Introduction to Cyberdeception*,
DOI 10.1007/978-3-319-41187-3_13

13.1 Experimental deception

We encourage readers interested in deception tactics to actually build deception architectures and try them on networks. Circumstances vary widely so every site can provide unique data. The more experiments we have, the better prepared are we for the future. Most of the ideas presented in this book are legal, not dangerous to the deceiver, and unlikely to result in retaliation.

Of course, deceivees are not cooperative experimental subjects. They are unlikely to be predictable, and may experience strong emotions when they suspect or discover they are being deceived. Nonetheless, deception experiments are quite doable provided we are patient enough to collect a good deal of data where evanescent phenomena can average out.

13.2 Deception architectures

A key decision with cyberdeception is on what machines or devices to do it. Figure 13.1 illustrates six major options: On the attacker's computer, on the attacker's local-area network, on an Internet network router or hub, on the defender's local-area network, on a honeypot, and on the defender's machine. All six can be sites of either offensive or defensive deception.

Let us consider the sites for defensive deception:

- Deception on the attacker's computer would be the most effective way to deceive them and the safest method for the defender, since it is before the attackers reach the defenders or the Internet. It could be something in the operating system that pretends to connect to the Internet but does not, or something that systematically changes their attack commands to make them harmless. However, most methods of implementing such deceptions are illegal, such as by installing Trojan horses or by breaking into their house in the middle of the night (Yost 1985). Modifying someone's cybersystem without their authorization is hacking, and is illegal in most countries. This doesn't stop spy agencies from trying, however.
- Deception on the attacker's local-area network has similar problems of illegality. However, it could be easier to implement since firewalls are a precedent and they

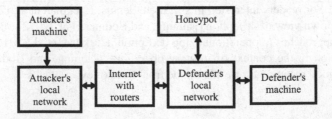

Fig. 13.1 Deployment options for deceptions

control outgoing as well as incoming traffic (Noonan and Dubrawsky 2006). We could modify the policies of a firewall to stop certain kinds of destination connections using certain protocols.

- Deception on the routers or hubs of the Internet is possible but difficult because packets are fragmented and hard to assemble, and in some cases encrypted. Router protocols are standardized and the pace of innovation is slow, so introducing a new kind of router software would be difficult. If it were accomplished only on some routers, attack traffic could learn to bypass it. Nonetheless, some intrusion detection can be done in routers (Chang et al. 2001), which suggests that some deception can be done there too.
- Deception on the defender's local-area network can be done similarly to deception on the attacker's network. Defensive deception here has the advantages that it can stop attackers before they are more dangerous, just a few installations can protect an entire network, efficient algorithms can run them fast enough so they provide little slowdown to the network, and updating is straightforward since they use simple filtering rules. A disadvantage is that packets still need to be reassembled. This approach is related to honeynet deployment (Provos and Holz 2008).
- Deception can be done on honeypots attached to the defender's local-area network using many of the methods described in this book. Specialized deceptions can be accomplished with dedicated machines focusing on limited classes of traffic like spam and SSH (secure-shell) traffic.
- Deception on the defender's machine can be accomplished in a variety of ways in different parts of the operating system and applications software. However, as with full-access honeypots, defensive deception here allows attackers onto the target system where they may find ways around the deceptions. Such deceptions also are harder to set up because of many necessary decisions, and thus are also difficult to update.

We can also use the sites for offensive deceptions:

- Offensive deception on the attacker's computer can be in the forms of attack plans and mechanisms for concealment.
- Offensive deception on the attacker's local-area network can be in the form of impersonation.
- Offensive deception on the routers and hubs of the Internet can be in spoofing of addresses.
- Offensive deception on the defender's local-rea network can be in the form of impersonation.
- Offensive deception on honeypots is difficult.
- Offensive deception on the defender's machine can use a large array of concealment tricks such as impersonation, hidden processes, hidden memory locations, etc.

The most natural place to implement a wide range of defensive deceptions is on victim (host) machines and devices. That is because we can see the attacks more

clearly on their intended victims, and we can exploit a wider range of resources'
there to foil them. It is also the best place for offensive deceptions because subvert-
ing the operating system makes everything else easy, which is why rootkits are the
goal of most serious attackers. Defensive deceptions in an operating system with
legitimate users too can however fool them too, so we should either put deceptions
in things a legitimate user is not likely to encounter, or else use honeypots.

It is also desirable for a deceiving machine to use "self-deception" since humans
find this quite useful (Smith 2007). Self-deception means trying to push the details
of the deception out of consciousness. For cybersystems, this means hiding the
deception machinery as deep as possible to prevent detection.

13.3   Defensive Deceptive Firewalls

Deception at the level of the local-area network could filter packets (decide whether
to let them through or not) using deception principles, or modify packets in transit.
The technology is similar to that of firewalls. A number of firewall vendors offer
products that add "active response" features. Usually this just means terminating
connections from suspicious users, either locally or by sending commands like the
"reset" command for TCP packets back to the user's site. But a number of sources
offer more creative methods in the direction of honeypots. The "honeypot server" of
Hernacki et al. (2004) is an example.

Snort Inline (from www.snort.org) is a simple open-source tool for building
deceptive firewalls. The user writes rules in the style of the regular Snort intrusion-
detection system, but the rules can include packet deletion (dropping) and modification in addition to the usual logging and alerting options. For instance, this rule says
to change the 20th byte of the incoming data portion (payload) of a TCP-protocol
packet to an upper-case "X" when the packet contains two zero bytes.

```
alert tcp $EXTERNAL_NET any -> $HONEYNET any (msg:"Exp2-TCP-
offset-50";      content:"|00|";      offset:20;      flags:      P+;
replace:"X";classtype:exp2; priority:10; sid:9002001;rev:1;)
```

How does one choose the modifications? One can study a class of attacks and
craft responses for each of them. For instance, one can find the key strings for buffer
overflows to change them slightly to make them ineffective. (Usually the end of a
buffer-overflow constant is the most critical.) But a good deal of useful harassment
can be obtained just by making changes at random with simple rules like that above.
Since most changes made by this rule to command packets will cause the command
to fail, it will have some denial-of-service effect. In fact, running Snort Inline with
the above rule for 2 days on a honeypot caused the number of ICMP Ping and
NETBIOS alert messages on our test system to increase 20 %, a significant amount.

Packet modifications can be done systematically to see what causes the attacker
the most trouble. We can set up honeypots specifically for this kind of experimentation

(Rowe and Goh 2007; Frederick et al. 2012). Trouble can be measured by the amount of additional duration the attacker takes compared to a normal attack, as with the counterplanning in Sect. 12.4.4. This extra duration could be in repeated attempts with the same command, attempts to find ways around it, or even thinking time if the attacker is a live human being. In any event, we are creating obstacles for the attacker that will slow their attack.

So we can turn defense of cyberspace into an experimental science by trying a variety of deceptions and seeing which work the best at impeding attackers over a large number of attacks. (The attackers we test ourselves against need not be live ones: We can use a set of known attacks such as those of Metasploit, which permits more controllable testing, although those are dated.) If we find something that seems to work well, we can try modifications of it to see if they work any better. For instance if the above rule works well, we could try next:

- the same modification at the 21st byte;
- the same modification at the 19th byte;
- simultaneous modifications to both the 20th and 21st bytes;
- modification by a "Y" instead of an "X";
- modification for messages containing "000" instead of "00";
- modification for messages containing "01" instead of "00";
- the same modification on outgoing packets from our system.

Making random modifications to try to improve something is the idea behind "genetic algorithms". These are search methods that try to mimic biological evolution by having random "mutations" and random "crossings" or combinings. The bulleted items above are mutations. Crossings could be when we take two independent modifications that both seem to fool attackers well and combine them in the hope of finding something that fools attackers even better; crossings help prevent search for a better deception from being too localized. Genetic algorithms are exciting because they could allow us to discover truly new methods to deceive attackers rather than choosing from preplanned methods. And there is plenty of Internet data to analyze. Automated machine learning methods for new attacks as in Wuu and Chen (2003) can be used as to automatically implement new deceptions.

Genetic algorithms require a metric for assessing performance. We can measure the extra duration or the increased number of alerts, but both of these have a large standard deviation. For instance, Table 13.1 shows counts of alerts (warnings about suspicious behavior) from running five experiments with small modifications of packets. Each experiment lasted two days and experiments were conducted on successive days on the same honeypot. (It would be better to run each experiment simultaneously on a different honeypot since there are trends in attacks that vary over time.) The control experiment had no packet modifications and the other experiments changed the packets at one designated byte; the last two experiments changed the bytes to "W" rather than "X"; and the last experiment last ignored the flags.

There is more variability than one would expect considering the small modifications. For instance, experiment 3 saw a repeated FTP attack that the other experiments did not. Thus it is important to run such genetic algorithms for a long time.

Table 13.1 Snort alert counts by category under five deceptive packet manipulations

	Control (no change)	Exp. 1 (offset 10)	Exp. 2 (offset 20)	Exp. 3 (offset 100)	Exp. 4 (offset 20)	Exp. 5 (offset 20)
FTP	0	0	0	68794	0	3735
ICMP Ping	155	162	198	239	194	186
MS-SQL	48	32	34	50	44	30
NETBIOS	76	19	15	96	22	173
POLICY	0	2	1	0	0	1
SHELLCODE	74	57	33	38	65	148
WEB	0	0	0	1	35	0

Both large counts and small counts on attacks can be interesting. Large counts indicate we found a way to tie up attackers, and thus represent good delaying tactics. Small counts indicate we found a way to discourage attackers, and thus represent good tactics for scaring them away.

Another useful deception on packets is to modify the "time to live" (TTL) values. Normally when a packet is sent through a firewall, the packet's TTL value is decremented to indicate that it was processed by the firewall. The idea behind the TTL values is to prevent infinite loops and other routing inefficiencies, since the packet is dropped if its TTL value reaches zero. So the Sebek tool from The Honeynet Project fails to decrement the TTL values of packets passing through its "Honeywall" firewall with the goal of concealing it. However, firewalls are common and discovery of an intervening machine like a firewall is not unusual on ordinary cybersystems anyway.

13.4 Low-Interaction Honeypots

The easiest honeypots to run are "low-interaction" honeypots that permit only a limited set of attacker actions. These can be installed either on a local-area network as a kind of firewall or on the host system itself. Usually they simulate the first steps of network protocols, but do not allow an attacker to log in to the real machines, and are thus much safer than regular honeypots. Cohen (1999) pioneered this approach. A number of low-interaction honeypot products are available including Honeyd, the Google Hack Honeypot, HoneyBOT, honeytrap, KFSensor, Multipot, and Nepenthes (ShadowServer 2007). These can be a good way to collect data on the first steps of new attacks.

13.4.1 Overview

Low-interaction honeypots are not difficult to construct, since details of protocols are published and easily available. The honeypots simulate the first steps of the protocol and look for an exploit. If they see one, they can refuse it with an access-related deception, such as denying that the user has presented proper credentials. They could also usually simulate further steps since many low-interaction honeypots like Honeyd permit scripting of responses with arbitrary programs.

A low-interaction honeypot can act as a router and can control access to a set of machines. This permits existence deceptions where you pretend that many more machines exist than really do (Cohen and Koike 2003). Attacks on nonexistent machines are desirable because they are safe. Sure, attackers discover the machines are nonexistent quickly, but if fake machines outnumber the real ones, the attackers can waste much effort trying to find them. If the probability of finding a real machine is p, the number of tries to find a real machine is approximately $1/2p$; so if $p=0.01$, the expected number of tries is 50.

Another useful idea in building low-interaction honeypots is to have them try to respond positively in some way to everything an attacker wants to do, although sometimes with deception. This idea has been called "ubiquitous redirection" (Bakos and Bratus 2005) and is the opposite of false excuses for not doing something. For instance, when asked to download a file, we can download the wrong one. Attackers are less likely to give up if they are getting some kind of result, so always-positive responses can useful for helping honeypots collect data or delay attacks on other sites. Low-interaction honeypots are good for ubiquitous redirection since we can specify responses to inputs in advance.

Low-interaction honeypots may display suspicious timing behavior since they are not really running protocols, just pretending to. They may respond too quickly or too slowly to commands, and an attacker observing response delays can notice this. So it is helpful to the effectiveness of the honeypot to measure timing behavior of real systems, and then simulate it on the honeypot with delays and some randomness added for realism (Fu et al. 2006).

We describe next three implementations we have done of low-interaction honeypots. These should convey some of the things that can be done and describe some of the necessary infrastructure.

13.4.2   Case Study: The Honeyd Honeypot Tool

Honeyd (www.honeyd.org) is a relatively simple tool for deploying low-interaction honeypots. It allows a user to create virtual hosts to mimic several different types of servers and network configurations, providing opportunities for deception. Services can be simulated by scripts or can be forwarded to real servers for execution. The virtual hosts also support a virtual network topology including support for route-tracing, simulation of latencies, and simulation of packet losses. Honeyd logs both network packet-level traffic and system activity for later analysis.

We experimented on a small network at our school NPS that was outside the school firewall (Frederick et al. 2012). We used a Windows XP machine as host; it also ran as "guests" first a Fedora 14 virtual machine and later a Security Onion machine, both using VMware virtual-machine software. We used seven IP addresses for virtual honeypots. We used a hub to connect to the network which also connected to a Windows machine running Snort, configured to log and create Tcpdump files for the alerts which could be read with Wireshark. On the Fedora virtual machine we installed Honeyd, which generated its own packet and system logs.

Between every run, the machines were updated and patched to harden them against possible attacks. Antivirus software and Snort were also updated whenever possible. Undoubtedly we would see more interesting traffic if we did not update, but that would require more frequent monitoring of our machines which we did not have time to do. Honeyd can be detected in several ways, but we saw no evidence of attackers doing so in our experiments.

We ran a different configuration of the virtual honeypots every week. Our goal was to maximize the number, variety, and duration of attacks. We discarded configurations that were unsuccessful judged by the amount of traffic and number and variety of alerts. The experimental plan by week was:

- In week 1 we ran only the host computer as a control experiment using Fedora 14.
- In week 2 we ran Honeyd in the guest virtual machine. It claimed all 32 addresses of the network from other users, as Honeyd is aggressive in capturing IP addresses. This was antisocial, so the Ethernet connection was closed by our information-technology department.
- In week 3, we ran Honeyd on the guest virtual machine simulating three Windows hosts and two Linux hosts. Each host had two open ports for the operating system.
- In week 4 we configured several TCP and UDP open ports, and emulated services like SMTP, HTTP, FTP, SSH, telnet, NetBIOS, POP3, IMAP. We also used the proxy function of Honeyd to redirect some attacks to their source.
- Week 5 was the same as Week 4 except without one virtual machine.
- In week 6, the IP address of the virtual-machine host was switched with that of one of the honeypots, and the host was changed to Security Onion because it promised better monitoring capabilities.
- Week 7 was the same as Week 6.
- In week 8, we replaced the Linux virtual machines with Windows virtual machines to increase attacks. Analysis of results also showed that some emulated services were worse than simulated open ports, so we set only open ports with no services running.
- In week 9 we used only the four most successful scripts.
- In week 10 we ran another control experiment.
- Week 11 was like week 10 except even without the guest virtual machine.
- Week 12 was the same as week 9.
- In week 13 we added a Perl script with a fake Telnet server in port 23 and simulated Windows Server 2008 and Windows XP Service Pack 3.
- Week 14 was the same as week 11.
- In week 15 we replaced the fake Telnet server with a fake internal Web server in maintenance status, and we had one honeypot send back to the source everything it received on port 445. Also, we switched the IP addresses of four honeypots.

Table 13.2 Statistics on a low-interaction honeynet

Week	Number of packets	Number of alerts	Different alerts	ICMP alerts	TCP alerts	UDP alerts
1	438661	388	4	388	0	0
3	1191410	8589	24	8366	2185	5
4	1313693	259776	36	255744	4016	16
5	701771	2525	12	1940	584	1
6	906893	2823	17	2176	647	0
7	740769	6686	11	2990	3696	0
8	897552	3386	14	2144	1242	0
9	951556	2957	19	2651	306	0
10	618723	1325	13	757	568	0
11	541740	756	16	476	270	10
12	995235	2526	10	2270	256	0
13	807712	3711	15	3445	266	0
14	518659	488	5	488	0	0
15	1066743	4694	14	3082	1612	0

Table 13.2 shows aggregate results with the deceptive honeypots. The number of packets in the network increased 40 % when Honeyd was running, which is good news for honeypot designers. Though not shown, network flows showed similar trends. Both the total number of alerts and the number of different alerts increased. Note that what we did in weeks 5–8 substantially discouraged attacks, so it would be useful for a fake honeypot.

Some honeypots had more variation in traffic than others; for instance, in week 4, honeypots 73, 74, 77, and 79 had 99, 121, 371, and 94 ICMP packets respectively; in week 6, they had 5, 68, 0, and 118 respectively. This illustrates a degree of randomness in attack targets.

The most common Snort alerts during the experiment were NetBIOS, and they appeared in bursts and not every week. Shellcode NOOP alerts occurred more regularly and were associated with several Snort identification numbers. Other common alerts were on attempts to connect to the hosts with the remote desktop protocol and on constructed bit-string heap corruption. The most frequently probed and attacked ports less than 1024 were 445, 80, 135, 139, 53 and 22. Port 445, Microsoft-DS Active Directory, had 95.3 % of the TCP protocol alerts with many repetitions. Next were port 80 (HTTP) with 3.3 %, 135 (Microsoft End Point Mapper) with 0.84 %, and 139 (NetBIOS Session Service) with 0.34 %.

Scripts simulating services varied in their effectiveness due to two factors. One was the novelty effect of a new service, similar to the novelty of a new host, which tends to attract attacks. This was clearly seen by the increased traffic in week 4. Within a short time, between one and two weeks depending on the script, this novelty effect was lost, as we can see in weeks 5 and 6. We will show similar results for full honeypots in Fig. 13.3. We conclude that a deception script will have significantly less success if continued past a few weeks. Secondly, services that were old, had errors, or were not logical according to the host's configuration were quickly recognized by attackers who then avoided the honeypot, as is seen in week 6 where the same configuration was running for 3 weeks. Identification took less time than the novelty effect. Hence it was better to keep the port open instead of running a uncredible script, as is seen in weeks 8 and 9 (weeks with a small number of scripts but many ports open), for both attack-encouraging and attack-discouraging purposes.

We also compared the alerts on production hosts (normal users of the local network on which the honeypot resides) with the alerts on the honeypots. In week 4 we saw 92.7 % of the alerts on the production hosts; in week 5 this decreased to 10.2 %, and remained under 16.0 % for the remaining experiments. Week 15 showed a typical distribution of 4.6 % on the host machine, 49.9 % on the guest machines, 40.0 % on the Honeyd honeypots, and 5.7 % on the production hosts. So the many new sites in week 4 acted as attack encouragement on the unchanged production hosts, but this quickly faded and most targets quickly centered on the honeypots and the guest machines enclosing them.

13.4.3 Case Study: A Deceptive Web Server with Honeyd

We received many HTTP attacks in the previous experiment even though we were not trying to run a Web server. It makes sense to give attackers of honeypots what they want. So we adapted a Web service script supplied with Honyed. It was important before these experiments to reduce protection violations, a key difficulty in using Honeyd, which required manual modification of directory properties.

We developed a dynamic homepage for the honeypot to keep intruders interested. It had links to resources and a frame to show downloaded content. We generated a variety of errors to the HTTP request, hoping to frustrate attackers. This is done by adding a shell script that ran concurrently with Honeyd and selected error codes from a list. As before, we ran Snort on Windows XP to capture attack packets and IDS alerts, and we ran Honeyd on Ubuntu. We used honeyd15.conf and modified the configuration file in the simulated Windows Web server to run the script on port 80. Traffic averaged around 10,000 hits with a minimum of 7,668 and a maximum of 15,412 for the server volume.

Table 13.3 compares the results over time. In December, we established a connection with one Web page; in January, we added Web pages; and in February, we sent back various HTTP error messages part of the time. The table shows that the error messages in February definitely increased both the rate of interaction with the honeypot and the rate of attacks on it. This was a surprise since it was an attempted discouragement. On the other hand, the overall rate of Web interactions decreased in February due to the increased error messages. Altogether, Web page requests were 3.3 % of the total traffic in the last 5 days, so most attacks had other targets than the Web pages, but Web attacks may be especially interesting in indicating attacker intentions.

Table 13.3 Rates per day for the uncooperative Web server

	December	January	February
Number of days running	12	21	9
Rate of all Honeyd log entries	3389	3913	5695
Rate of Snort alerts	176	208	1069
Rate of all Web log entries	16.1	74.1	30.9
Rate of GET commands	5.7	34.9	10.2
Rate of OPTIONS commands	8.9	35.9	18.7
Rate of HEAD commands	1.4	2.2	1.1

The most common string arguments received in Web page requests in these experiments were "yes" and "no" with 717 and 492 occurrences respectively; other common arguments were "admin", "test", "info", "david", "michael", "mike", and "richard". This method of collecting strings should provide excellent data for scripted responses, since attackers will be more responsive if we give them what they ask for. The most common electronic-mail user names on the honeypot that were received were "test", "info", "admin", "sales", "web", "contact", and "postmaster", and they should provide an excellent basis for email responses.

13.4.4   Case Study: A Deceptive Web Server with Glastopf

Glastopf (www.honeynet.org) is another open-source Web-server honeypot; Zarras (2014) offers an alternative. It responds to requests to draw attackers' attention and trigger more interactions with the honeypot. It can detect attacks like SQL injection, remote-file injection, and local-file injection. When the attacker sends a malicious request, Glastopf processes uses a vulnerability emulator to respond in a way that suggests that vulnerability exists in the Web server. Glastopf uses two main deception principles, dorks and attack surfaces. A dork is a vulnerable path on an application. The attack surface is a Web page that contains many dorks that the search engine adds to its index. Glastopf can dynamically generate the attack surface from predefined dorks based on requests coming to the honeypot. Its providing of features attractive to both attackers and crawlers, however, means it sees traffic from both.

We deployed Glastopf on the same commercial Internet connections described in Sect. 13.4.2, on a connection outside the school firewall to get unfiltered traffic (Yahyaoui and Rowe 2015). We tested two methods of deployment: direct installation on a Linux machine and installation on a virtual machine. To assess the attacks, we ran the Snort intrusion-detection system and the Wireshark network-traffic analysis tool. We configured Snort with two network cards; one card had no IP address, which reduced the possibility of compromise from an external machine. The other card had a private IP address and was connected to the same network as an administrative machine. The latest public Snort rule set was downloaded.

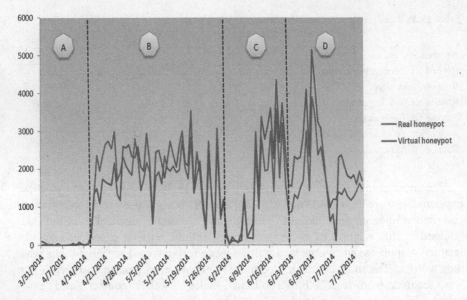

Fig. 13.2 Attack events over time for the real and virtual Web honeypots

We used three computers, one desktop and two laptops. The desktop was used for the intrusion-detection system; one laptop was the real honeypot; and one laptop held the virtual honeypot. All computers were connected to a hub with an external Internet connection. We obtained IP addresses, a gateway address, and a DNS server address. We indexed the gateway in the Google search engine. We installed the Ubuntu Linux operating system on the real honeypot and used it for the intrusion-detection system. For the virtual honeypot, we installed Microsoft Windows 7 Service Pack 1 since it received a higher rate of attack than a Linux system. We installed the Glastopf v3 Web honeypot directly on the real honeypot. We installed them on two virtual machines running Ubuntu on the virtual honeypot. Judging by their source URLs, 3 % of the data for the NPS real Web honeypot was for Web crawlers, and 6 % of the data for the NPS virtual Web honeypot, so indexing by crawlers was rare.

We observed four distinct time periods, labeled A, B, C and D in Fig. 13.2. In period A, the two honeypots started with low rates during the first few weeks despite a small peak during the first days of indexing them. This was probably because the honeypots, after being indexed, took a few days to be examined by crawlers, and only then started receiving malicious requests. In the beginning of phase B, the real honeypot had higher rates of attack than the virtual honeypots; after that, the virtual Web honeypots received higher rates.

To introduce deceptions, we added links at the end of period B in the main Web page for both honeypots that redirected traffic to our own Web server. The server ran in a virtual machine within the real Web honeypot. The Web site had a sign-up page where users could enter information like username, password, email address, phone number and address. It also had a MySQL database running in the background for

Table 13.4 Top ten URL requests for the real and virtual honeypots

Honeypot	Rank	Requested URL	Count
Real	1	/comments	6849
Real	2	/cgi-bin/comments	4578
Real	3	/pivotx/includes/timthumb.php	3271
Real	4	/board/board/include/pivotx/includes/wp-content/pivotx/includes/timthumb.php	3022
Real	5	/sqlmanager/setup.php	2954
Real	6	/irekani/browse	2869
Real	7	/bb_lib/comments	2845
Real	8	/plugins/content/plugin_googlemap2_proxmy.php	2831
Real	9	/phpMyAdmin-2.6.3-pl1/scripts/setup.php	2813
Real	10	/cgi-bin/standard.php	2585
Virtual	1	/comments	7874
Virtual	2	/cgi-bin/comments	7576
Virtual	3	/dbadmin/comments	4116
Virtual	4	/.br/comments	3191
Virtual	5	/server-status	2845
Virtual	6	/cgi-bin/newsletter/admin/home.php	2639
Virtual	7	/cgi-bin/enter.php	2399
Virtual	8	/wp-phpmyadmin/phpmyadmin/setup.php	2395
Virtual	9	/admin.php	2377
Virtual	10	/phpMyAdmin-2.6.0-alpha/scripts/setup.php	2374

storing information. This redirection increased the amount of malicious traffic significantly in period C for both honeypots. Although we did not get many sign-up attempts because most of the malicious traffic was automatic and could not handle interaction, putting links to another Web site resulted in still more malicious traffic coming to both honeypots. At the end of period C, the traffic decreased again, apparently because the Web honeypots started losing the attention of attackers after a certain period of time.

In period D we added new deceptions in the form of static Web pages to the index page for the honeypots. This again stimulated the traffic received, and we saw a peak in the middle of period D. Eventually toward the end of period D, the novelty was gone and the traffic decreased again. It is clear that defenders can do a number of things to stimulate traffic on a honeypot, but each stimulus only has effect for a limited amount of time.

Table 13.4 shows the top 10 URLs requested for the real and virtual Web honeypots. Clearly there is some randomness in these because of the differences between the real and virtual honeypots, though everyone wants to see the comments files. These lists provide useful data for planning deceptions because if these are the pages that attackers want, we can create fake pages for these to keep them busy.

13.5   Implementing Simple Deceptions in Full-Interaction Honeypots

We can also set up full-interaction honeypots that allow attackers to log in and do most of the things they want to do. Such honeypots give further opportunities for deception. We can modify the software, and even in some cases the operating system, to see how attackers react. But we need to monitor such honeypots carefully to prevent attacks from spreading.

Figure 13.3 shows the results of time and packet-property clustering on the first 46 weeks of running a full-interaction honeypot (Rowe and Goh 2007). Counts of two kinds of alert clusters are shown, those within a 10-min time period from the same Internet address (solid line), and those with the same protocol and alert category (dotted line). The two methods show different things: Time clustering shows the degree of determination of attackers, and property clustering shows the variety of attack methods they are throwing at us. Attackers tried many attack methods when the machine was first connected to the Internet, but stopped experimenting after a while when they found they couldn't exploit it. Meanwhile a steady background of just a few kinds of attacks continued. This suggests that a genetic algorithm for defense methods should use a weighted average of both time and property clusters to measure success.

Experiments like these can provide other insights. For instance, we see in Fig. 13.3 that the two times the honeypot was turned off (weeks 7–12 and 28), attack volume and especially attack variety were at an increased rate when the honeypot

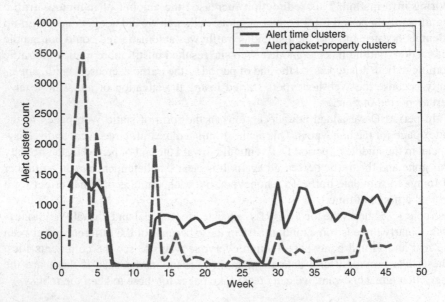

Fig. 13.3 Total alert clusters in the first 45 weeks of running a full-interaction honeypot

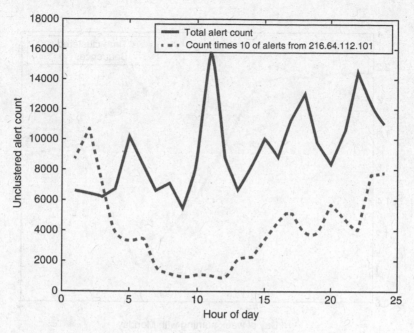

Fig. 13.4 Effect of time of day on count of Snort alert clusters

came back online. That suggests that going offline periodically is a good way to increase attacks on a honeypot. We can also plot attacks as a function of time of day (Fig. 13.4) and day of the week (Fig. 13.5). These suggest that we should put honeypots online on weekends in the middle of the night for increased traffic. Note if we focus on a particular attacker, we can do even better at predicting their attack times. By tabulating characteristics of each attacker, we can tailor deceptions to each of them.

Variability in metrics over time is a common problem in measuring the Internet. While there is a certain amount of steady activity, the "background radiation" of the Internet (Pang et al. 2004), most attacks are not random because they can surprise better if they are sudden and massive. It helps to cluster Internet data and count the clusters instead of individual data as we did for Fig. 13.5, combining events within the same 10-min interval for the upper curve, and combining known sequences for the lower curve. In general, we can cluster all events originating from the same IP address, or all events within a certain period of time, or cluster packets that are similar. Using this reduces the variability of attack counts significantly, as is seen in Table 13.5 for two 3-week time periods on a honeypot we ran. The first number in each entry is the first time period and the second number is the second time period. We averaged 500 alerts per day on this honeypot, so clustering on 3-min or 30-min windows was reasonable, but a busier honeypot may need a shorter time-clustering interval.

In a related experiment, Cohen et al. (2001) put "red teams" or groups of designated attackers in one room and victim computers in the other. Attackers were given

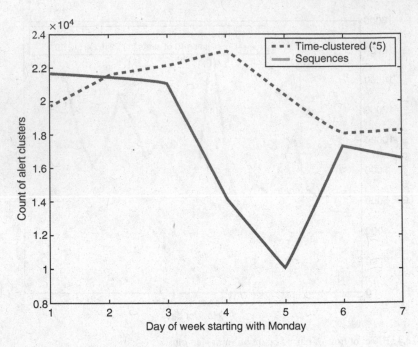

Fig. 13.5 Effect of day of week on count of Snort alert clusters

Table 13.5 Snort alerts for two 21-day periods on a honeypot (separated by slashes), raw and clustered three ways

Snort alert class	Raw count	Time-clustered count, 3 min window	Time-clustered count, 30 min window	Remote-IP clustered count
NETBIOS	46078/29484	927/899	661/480	2302/4895
BAD-TRAFFIC	3230/946	708/370	550/287	729/383
MS-SQL	2310/2214	2115/2013	1032/1014	2058/2034
INFO	2720/37	11/25	11/17	13/27
SHELLCODE	1875/1448	708/583	452/313	321/258
ICMP	1382/656	195/234	188/214	359/352
WEB-PHP	202/351	23/44	21/40	23/44
WEB-CGI	152/99	43/24	37/21	51/29
WEB-IIS	148/18	22/11	21/10	22/11
WEB-ATTACKS	30/0	9/0	9/0	9/0
WEB-FRONTPAGE	4/1	4/1	2/1	2/1
WEB-MISC	15/41	9/16	7/13	7/23
SCAN	32/89	30/68	26/47	25/53
POLICY	30/24	27/18	27/17	27/17
EXPLOIT	22/1	7/1	5/1	5/1
SNMP	12/30	6/6	6/6	6/6
ATTACK-RESPONSES	1/0	1/0	1/0	1/0

specific plans to accomplish, which gave a higher yield of interesting behavior than experiments with random attacks. The experimenters systematically varied the deceptions to see how they affected the time attackers spent on the systems, and they saw results similar to those above. Unfortunately the deceptions used have been only vaguely described, making it difficult to duplicate the results. Another interesting experiment with red teaming was that of Heckman et al. (2013), where they tested a honeypot architecture with denial and deception in each honeypot. Though red teaming was able to get through the first line of defense, they were fooled by false information in the second line of defense, an example of a second-order deception. So the experiment was a qualified success for deception.

13.6 Server and Spam Honeypots

A variety of specialized honeypots are available for implementing particular kinds of deceptions. The Honeynet Project provides a good start with its open-source tools (www.honeynet.org/project).

One kind is a honeyclient, is a honeypot for malicious network utilities (for example, Honeyc from the Honeynet Project). Most commonly they try to find malicious Web sites, but they can also test other network resources. They crawl the Web automatically, trying to find sites that will attack them. They know they have been attacked when they find downloaded files afterwards they did not request. These could be links to malicious sites, configuration files to enable easier exploits on their systems, nonstandard cookies, or executable code. Not much deception is required other than eagerness to sample all the features of a Web site. Once a malicious site is found, it can be blacklisted.

Another kind of honeypot is a sever honeypot that runs an Internet site and looks for attacks on it (for example, Glastopf and Honeytrap from the Honeynet Project). It can look for attempts to inject code and break into the operating system through the server. Deception along the lines of Sect. 7.7 can help make it look convincing.

A spam honeypot is a honeypot designed to collect spam. It provides a mail server with only fake users. Fake email addresses for this server can be disseminated by Web pages making deceptive statements about them. Then any mail that comes to the honeypot is suspicious, and repeated messages are likely to be spam. This enables identification of source addresses used for spamming, and these can be blacklisted.

13.7 Honeypots Attacking Other Machines

Zou and Cunningham (2006) points out a key weakness of honeypots: They should be configured to avoid attacking other machines if possible, since their safety is necessary to justify their use. So attackers could detect a honeypot by giving it some malicious mischief to do against another machine, then check whether it does it. This checking could efficiently be done by a botnet.

To address this, we could allow attacks on other honeypots, giving them good early warning about the type of attack. For all other machines, we could just simulate the effects of the attack. Alternatively, we could "defang" the attacks by modifying them to include well-known malware signatures for which most machines already have defenses, triggering alerts so the attack will do little harm.

13.8   Strategies for Deception Implementation

13.8.1   Hand-Coded Deceptions

If we have only a few deceptions to implement, we may be able to build a modified application program or even modify an operating system by hand. Most rootkits are hand-tailored. The Sebek tool for implementing better-concealed honeypots modifies the operating system in just a few key locations to hide code and processes. Rootkits similarly often modify the file-listing and process-listing utilities of the operating system to prevent listing suspicious files and processes. Even main-memory access can be controlled by a good rootkit. Many of the things that must be modified are in the "security kernel" of the operating system, a relatively small block of code. Nonetheless, hand-coding of deceptions can get complex because there can be many interactions between components.

13.8.2   Software Instrumentation with Wrappers

A general way to implement deceptions is to insert deception code systematically in the operating system and applications software, as "software wrappers" (Michael et al. 2002) on regular code (Fig. 13.6). The deception code can be placed before and/or after the normal execution code. It should check to see if conditions are sufficiently suspicious using the methods of Chap. 11 and intrusion-detection systems. It could use a threshold on average suspiciousness of all events, maximum suspiciousness, total suspiciousness, or some combination of all three. If suspiciousness does not exceed the threshold, the regular execution is done. Otherwise, deception actions are done before either aborting or resuming execution.

Wrappers in general are an important technique in software engineering, "instrumentation" of code (Kempf et al. 2009). Often software engineers need to measure execution of code by such metrics as execution time and the size of data structures. Inserting wrappers around code blocks is a good way to make such measurements (e.g., the Trace class in the Microsoft .NET framework). Instrumentation is also helpful in debugging of code, since wrappers make it easier to pause execution at break points and to query variables (e.g., the Debug class in the Microsoft .NET framework). Instrumentation can be automated by tools that operate on code to produce augmented code with wrappers according to specifications.

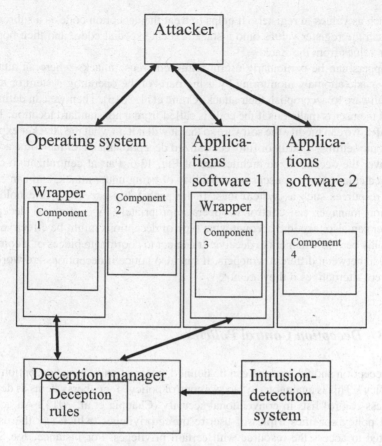

Fig. 13.6 Software-wrapper architecture for deceptions

Deception wrappers need only implement the deceptions appropriate for their software module, so each could be considerably simpler than a centralized deception manager. For instance a wrapper on a Web site could only delay suspicious pages, whereas a wrapper on a directory-listing command in the operating system could only create false directory information. A localized deception architecture can be better tuned to the specific software in a system, and can be more efficient. Wrappers need not be elaborate to be effective; Rinard et al. (2004) proposes instrumenting executables to just return a default value for out-of-bounds memory references that appear to be buffer overflows. Similar tactics can involve returning default Web pages in response to script attacks on Web sites.

Wrappers can be put around source code, partly-compiled code such as Java class files, and executables. Each has advantages and disadvantages. Wrapping of source code is the easiest but source code is not often available. Instrumentation of executable code can be done systematically with some defined code transformations, but it cannot access variable and subroutine names and many other things which make programming easier; it also must be careful not to change the execution state such as values in registers. It helps to treat the deception code as a subroutine call: Push the register values onto a stack, execute special code, and then pop the register values from the stack.

Wrappers can be particularly useful with code-reuse attacks where an attacker tries to evade anomaly monitoring by using parts of the operating system or legitimate software to accomplish their attack (Crane et al. 2013). Then we can definitely tell that the user is malicious if the code is called from a nonstandard location. To be even safer, we can modify the software so that it will not do what the attacker expects.

In some settings a partly or fully centralized deception manager has some advantages over the decentralized architecture of Fig. 13.6. Partial centralization could enable calculation of a consensus probability of being under attack, and can check global resources such as system logs. If the probability exceeds a threshold, the deception manager can control wrappers appropriately. A centralized deception manager can also take into account what type of deceptions might be effective, and direct only certain wrappers to deceive. It can act to coordinate pieces of a complex deception between different wrappers. It can also notice if deceptions are working, and direct alternatives if they are not.

13.8.3 Deception Control Policies

How deception should be done can be defined systematically by a "deception control policy". This is analogous to "access control policy" for cybersystems as defined by access-control lists in conventional security (Chapple et al. 2013). An access-control policy specifies triples of user-resource-privileges, which say the user is permitted to access the resource with certain privileges. For instance, Joe Smith could be allowed access to the directory "foobar" on a shared drive with read-only privileges. Inheritance allows access-control policies to be specified just once for classes of users and classes of resources.

A deception-control policy can similarly specify quadruples: a minimum level of suspiciousness, a resource or location in the operating system, an action applied to the resource or location, and the deceptions that should be applied. But much more variety is possible with deceptions than with just the allow/deny options used by access-control lists, as this book has suggested. There can also be random choices among deceptions. Just as with access-control policy, inheritance can occur for classes of resources and locations in the operating system as well as for actions.

Table 13.6 shows an example deception-control list, where "*" is the wild card character that matches anything. We can use the table by considering the rows top down until we find a row that matches in the first three columns, and then we implement the deceptive action listed in the fourth column, or a random choice if more than one action is listed. Note that normal (nondeceptive) responses can be included too.

Deception-control lists like this could be implemented in a centralized location like the deception manager shown in Fig. 13.6. An alternative is to treat them just

Table 13.6 Example deception-control list

Minimum maliciousness probability	Resource or location	User command	Deceptive action
0.5	/bin/*	write	Only pretend to do it
0.3	/bin/*	read	Lie that user not authorized
0.2	/sys/*	write	Delay five minutes
0.3	*	delete	Give null excuse
0.5	*/usr/secret	list	Disallow
0.2	*/usr/secret	list	List a different nonsecret directory
0.2	printer	*	Lie that printer is broken
*	*	*	Do nothing

like access control and put them in the security-critical code of the operating system, the "security kernel". This has the advantage of protecting the code well because operating systems implement special protections for their security kernels. The disadvantage is that the kernel is the primary target of many rootkits.

One advantage of deception-control policies over access-control policies is that they need not be consistent from machine to machine, or even consistent on the same machine at different times. Deceptions that are based on errors or faults could be expected to be idiosyncratic. However, it makes sense that if a certain level of deception is good on one machine, roughly the same level is appropriate on a similar machine. So for instance if we gave a false excuse to prevent access to the "bin" directory on one machine, we should give a similar but not necessarily identical false excuse on a similar machine.

13.8.4   Virtualization and Redirection

A technique increasingly used for both software development and analysis of malicious code is "virtualization" or implementing a virtual machine inside a real machine. Operating systems can be virtualized and these have been called "hypervisors" (Ford and Howard 2007). Hypervisors can store multiple versions of an operating system so that if one is attacked, an earlier "safe" version can be restored. This is important for full-interaction honeypots since they may need to be restored frequently. Attackers are starting to look for clues to the most common hypervisor products, so installing a hypervisor is now a good start towards a fake honeypot that will scare sophisticated attackers away. Hypervisors are also good for defensive deceptions because not all deceptions work.

Honeynets (collections of honeypots) frequently exploit redirection of attack traffic. This can be done to exhibit many more network nodes than there really are, to selectively redirect suspicious traffic while leaving legitimate traffic untouched, and to simplify defensive management (Shiue and Kao 2008). Redirection permits putting attackers into a different environment than the one they originally reconnoitered where they may be better controlled. This can be done at level 3 of network protocols (the network layer) but is better at level 2 (the data-link layer).

13.8.5   Deceptions in Hardware

Since cyberattackers have so many ways to subvert software, no software deception can ever be guaranteed tamperproof. An improvement could be to put deception in hardware, or at least in firmware (programmable hardware), where it could be much more difficult to discover and neutralize. This would be the ultimate goal of many defenders.

One place this could be done is in the disk controller, the code that controls access to a magnetic disk. Normally this is an obedient servant to the commands of the operating system. But it could be programmed to retrieve or store blank pages of data instead, or give error messages, under suspicious circumstances. The trigger could be an intrusion-detection system run by the operating system. A more basic trigger for "anti-forensics" behavior would be high numbers of requests for disk addresses ("inodes") in sequence, which suggests trying to copy the disk, as for instance any request for over a million consecutive inodes.

More elaborate deceptions are possible with the disk controller where, under suspicious circumstances, disk addresses are modified to access an entire fake file system, extending the ideas of Sect. 7.8. A fake file system could be constructed along with the real file system on the disk, including software, and a flag from the operating system could control which version is used.

The lower levels of network protocols (like the "data-link layer") are often accomplished in hardware, and represent another opportunity for deception. Suspicious signatures can be searched for and blank data provided when they are found. Since network connections vary considerably in speed, it may be difficult for a user to tell if this kind of deception is being practiced on them.

Deception could also be incorporated into other hardware that supports an operating system such as the hardwired boot instructions. This has been a worry of the U.S. government since so much of their hardware is manufactured abroad. However, such deception is generally not cost-effective because if it is discovered it cannot be easily replaced. If an attacker sends you some malware in software and you discover it, they can just send you some other malware in software. But hardware is not generally replaced once someone buys a product, and firmware is only replaced under carefully controlled circumstances. So hardware deception will need to be very subtle to avoid being discovered, while still not being so subtle that it has no real effect. This is difficult.

13.9   Conclusions

A wide range of tools can implement deceptions. Some of them derived from familiar attacker technology such as rootkits, some are derived from software engineering, and some are unique. While simple deceptions can be effective as well as easy
to implement, we need more sophisticated deceptions to fool the smarter attackers,
and we need automated help in designing them. It is useful to think of a deception
policy as driving this implementation, and such a policy can be translated systematically and even automatically into executable code.

13.10   Exercises

1. Even if an attack were encrypted, how might a router recognize an attack was
   going through it? What deceptions could be implemented against such attacks?
2. Snort Inline does not permit changing the size of a packet, though it does permit
   deletion (dropping) of packets. Why did the designers probably choose to
   impose this restriction when they permitted a number of other manipulations?
3. Suppose you are getting a large number of attacks with similar packets. So you
   try changing individual digits that you see in the packets when you see Ascii
   digits rather than characters. Some changes make a bigger difference to the
   attack than others. What possible explanations are there? What metrics on the
   attack could you use in a genetic algorithm to find effective modifications?
4. The results in Sect. 13.4.3 show there is a time lag between changes made to the
   honeypot configuration and responses by attackers, but then there is a quick
   increase in traffic. What accounts for this? Surely attackers are not communicating with one another.
5. Suppose we have a set of "canned" exploits like Metasploit. How do we systematically test our defensive deceptions against it to find the best ones? And
   how can you define "best" quantitatively?
6. A potential problem with wrappers would occur if the wrapper were encountered while the code was waiting for a slow process to terminate such as reading
   a block of data from a disk. Discuss how wrappers on executables should handle such ongoing processes.
7. Spam honeypots can receive more spam by automatically filling out Web forms
   on some Web sites. How could they automatically find good candidates for such
   sites, and what information should they enter in the forms to be reasonably
   convincing?
8. Consider a honeypot for spam botnets. These are botnets that take over control
   of computers so they can spam from them, by modifying the mail services to
   download spam and address lists, and then send the spam to everyone on the
   address list. They do this by implementing a rootkit that hides their processes.

(a) Why could it be useful to implement a honeypot for this kind of threat?
(b) What deceptive methods could you use to make it more likely that a honeypot would be taken over for a botnet?
(c) What clues could a rootkit use to guess you are running a honeypot? What secondary deceptions could you use to prevent this?
(d) You don't want your honeypot to successfully send spam, but you want the bot controller to think so. What deceptions can you do to fool it into thinking spam is either successfully delivered or refused through no fault of the honeypot?

9. An option not considered in Sect. 13.6 is to put deception into a database server. For what purposes would this be useful? Discuss the advantages and disadvantages of putting the deception there rather than somewhere else to accomplish similar goals.
10. How could recording the messages sent to and from botnet nodes be helpful in constructing a deception for the botnet?

References

Bakos G, Bratus S (2005) Ubiquitous redirection as access control response. In: Proceedings of the 3rd annual conference on privacy, security and trust, New Brunswick, Canada, 12–14 Oct, 2005

Bodmer S, Kilger A, Carpenter G, Jones J (2012) Reverse deception: organized cyber threat counter-exploitation. McGraw-Hill Education, New York

Chang H-Y, Wu S, Jou Y (2001) Real-time protocol analysis for detecting link-state routing protocol attacks. ACM Trans Inf Syst Secur 4(1):1–36

Chapple M, Ballad B, Ballad T, Banks E (2013) Access control, authentication, and public key infrastructure, 2nd edn. Jones and Bartlett, New York

Cohen F (1999) A mathematical structure of simple defensive network deceptions. all.net/journal/deception/mathdeception/mathdeception.html. Accessed 15 Jan 2016

Cohen F, Koike D (2003) Leading attackers through attack graphs with deceptions. Comput Security 22(5):402–411

Cohen F, Marin I, Sappington J, Stewart C, Thomas E (2001) Red teaming experiments with deceptions technologies. all.net/journal/deception/ RedTeamingExperiments.pdf. Accessed 15 Jan, 2016

Crane S, Larsen P, Brunthaler S, Franz M (2013) Booby trapping software. In: Proceedings of the new security paradigms workshop, Banff, AB, Canada, 9–12 Sept, 2013. pp 95–105

Ford R, Howard M (2007) How not to be seen. IEEE Secur Priv 5(1):67–69

Frederick E, Rowe N, Wong A (2012) Testing deception tactics in response to cyberattacks. National symposium on moving target research, Annapolis, MD, 11 June, 2102

Fu X, Yu W, Cheng D, Tan X, Streff K, Graham S (2006) On recognizing virtual honeypots and countermeasures. In: Proceedings of the 2nd IEEE international symposium on dependable, autonomic, and secure computing, Indianapolis, IN. pp 211–218

Heckman K, Walsh M, Stech F, O'Boyle T, DiCato S, Herber A (2013) Active cyber defense with denial and deception: a cyber-wargame experiment. Comput Security 37:72–77

Heckman K, Stech F, Thomas R, Schmoker B, Tsow A (2015) Cyber denial, deception, and counter deception: a framework for supporting active cyber defense. Springer, New York

Hernacki B, Bennett J, Lofgran T (2004) Symantec deception server: experience with a commercial deception system. In: Proceedings of the seventh international symposium in resent advances in intrusion detection, Sophia Antipolis, France, 15–17 Sept, 2004. pp 188–202

Kempf T, Karuri K, Gao L (2009) Software instrumentation. In: Wah B (ed) Wiley encyclopedia of computer science and engineering 1 (11). Wiley-Interscience, New York

Michael J, Auguston M, Rowe N, Riehle R (2002) Software decoys: intrusion detection and countermeasures. In: Proceedings of the IEEE-SMC workshop on information assurance, West Point, New York, 17–19 June, 2002. pp 130–138

Noonan W, Dubrawsky I (2006) Firewall fundamentals. Cisco, Indianapolis, IN

Pang R, Veqneswaran V, Barford P, Paxon V, Peterson L (2004) Characteristics of Internet background radiation. In: Proceedings of the 4th ACM SIGCOMM conference on internet measurement, Taormina, IT, 25–27 Oct, 2004. pp 27–40

Provos N, Holz T (2008) Virtual honeypots: from botnet tracking to intrusion detection. Addison-Wesley, Upper Saddle River, NJ

Rinard M, Cadar C, Dumitran D, Roy D, Leu T (2004) A dynamic technique for eliminating buffer overflow vulnerabilities (and other memory errors). In: Proceedings of the 20th annual computer security applications conference, Tucson, AZ, 6–10 Dec, 2004. pp 82–90

Rowe N, Goh H (2007) Thwarting cyber-attack reconnaissance with inconsistency and deception. In: Proceedings of the 8th IEEE information assurance workshop, West Point, NY, 20–22 June, 2007. pp 151–158

ShadowServer (2007) What is a honeypot? www.shadowserver.org/wiki/ pmkiki. php?n=Information.Honeypots. Accessed 22 July, 2008

Shiue LM, Kao SJ (2008) Countermeasure for detection of honeypot deployment. In: Proceedings of the international conference on computer and communication engineering, Kuala Lumpur, Malaysia, 13–15 May, 2008. pp 595–599

Smith D (2007) Why we lie: the evolutionary roots of deception and the unconscious mind. St. Martin's Griffin, New York

Wuu L-C, Chen, S-F (2003) Building intrusion pattern miner for Snort network intrusion detection system. In: Proceedings of the 37th IEEE Carnahan conference on security technology, 14–16 Oct 2003. pp 477–484

Yahyaoui A, Rowe N (2015) Testing simple deceptive honeypot tools. In: Proceedings of SPIE defense and security, Baltimore MD, 20–24 April, 2015. Paper 9458-2

Yost G (1985) Spy-tech. Facts on File, New York

Zarras A (2014) The art of false alarms in the game of deception: Leveraging fake honeypots for enhanced security. In: Proceedings of the Carnahan conference on security technology, Rome, Italy, 13–16 Oct 2014. pp 1–6

Zou C, Cunningham R (2006) Honeypot-aware advanced botnet construction and maintenance. In: Proceedings of the international conference on dependable systems and networks, Philadelphia, PA, 25–28 June, 2006. pp 199–208

Chapter 14
Decoy I/O Devices

Decoy or fake I/O devices can thwart malware attacks by incorporating diversity, misdirection, and confusion into an operating system, while preserving system usability and manageability. The idea is to display on a computer system evidence of the decoy I/O devices following Chap. 7 ideas. Their projection would make them appear as valid targets of interception and malicious modification, or as means of propagation to target machines.

- Storage devices such as disks and USB flash drives.
- Transmission devices such as network cards and modems.
- Human interface devices such as keyboards, mice, monitors, and webcams.

Decoy I/O devices work best on a legitimate target machine, not a honeypot, and require support at the hardware level. These devices will need to be dynamic to maintain a consistent resemblance to their real counterparts. Their dynamics should be

© Springer International Publishing Switzerland 2016
N.C. Rowe, J. Rrushi, *Introduction to Cyberdeception*,
DOI 10.1007/978-3-319-41187-3_14

supported by safe modifications of kernel data structures to display the existence of user-mode processes along with kernel threads which appear to interact with those decoy I/O devices.

14.1   Motivation

Decoy I/O devices could detect and remove malware that has never been encountered before by the mere fact the malware has tried to access a nonexistent device. This approach has advantages over static code analysis for signatures of malware (Szor 2005) or dynamic code analyses of such things as disk access patterns, sequences of system calls, and behavior graphs because both require prior training on known instances of malware.

Emulation of the dynamics of decoy I/O devices overcomes the main limitation of honeyfiles, decoy documents, decoy database records, and decoy software, namely the absence of records of normal access to those resources. Decoy I/O devices can run alongside the native components of the operating system, as users do their work on the computer. This is an advance over honeypots, which cannot coexist with production functions and need to occupy the entire machine. Decoy I/O devices could also be useful against insider threats since they catch low-level activity and are not usually required to enforce access rights.

Much malware targets I/O devices. Keyloggers, for example, operate to intercept key scan codes, the codes of the keys pressed and released by a user on a keyboard. This permits keyloggers to read commands, messages, and passwords. Computer monitors are an obvious target for interception by malware. In addition to I/O ports, a graphics controller has a large buffer in memory that stores monitor contents. Intercepting that data enables malware to learn a good deal about what is happening on a machine, including commands, files, pictures, and graphical user interface content in general.

Powerful data interception tools are sold on the hackers' black market. These cyber-spying tools are called remote access tools (RATs) or remote-control systems (RCSs). An example RAT is DarkComet (Kujawa 2012) which can intercept the webcam video on a compromised machine. Disk or file system interceptors are a common module of advanced malware writers for capturing file traffic to I/O storage devices. Disk encryption is ineffective against such interceptors since the attack code instruments the kernel to access I/O request packets before encryption.

14.2   Design Issues for Fake I/O Devices

To implement decoy I/O devices we need:

- A kernel-level capability in the operating system to display the existence and operation of the decoy devices. These phantom devices should be indistinguishable from real I/O devices on the machine, and serve the purpose of entrapping malware. They can be fake hard disks, flash memory, webcams, keyboards, network interface controllers, and monitors. But a user logged into a cybersystem must be told which devices are real and which are fake.

- Emulation of I/O device dynamics to make decoy I/O devices appear to be operating normally. This includes creation and emulation of decoy processes, kernel threads, and instrumentation of kernel data structures. Those instrumentations can be done through device-driver programming (Reeves 2010).
- Measures to enable the coexistence of decoy I/O devices and related data structures with real I/O devices and the operating system at large.
- Hardware support for decoy I/O devices to thwart reconnaissance probes by advanced malware. These can be mounted directly on hardware buses.
- A capability for pinpointing malware based on its interactions with decoy I/O devices. The capability will locate the malware code in memory, and could even try to remove it.

14.2.1   Design Details

Attack code is assumed to have access to the kernel of the operating system and may also have modules that run in user space. But we assume that the device details including which I/O devices are real are known only to the defender.

Hardware support for a phantom I/O device must be positioned in a randomly selected order relative to the existing I/O devices on the machine. The order is changed at random after the machine reboots. An attempt to disable a phantom I/O device should result in detectable activity. All external memory accesses to the driver stack of the phantom I/O device should be reported to the defender as indications of attack. Each driver creates data structures called device objects and driver objects.

Decoy I/O devices need to be handled by the I/O subsystem of the operating system, as what we call "I/O projectors". They should require only a low overhead on the CPU and memory and the overall functioning of the computer. An I/O projector could run alongside the native components of the operating system as a user works on the computer. The I/O projector should not interfere with legitimate users, since they have no reason to access the fake I/O devices. But malware looking for secrets might find the projected devices quite interesting.

As an example (Fig. 14.1), consider an I/O projector displaying a webcam. Whenever the user is not using the real webcam, the projector displays fake cam data of its own, making those data appear as if originating from the Peripheral Component Interconnect (PCI) bus. If malware intercepts this fake video traffic, the interception would be noted by the kernel and allow for tracking down of the interception software. This would be effective against the BlackShades RAT which targets webcams.

Decoy I/O devices can be deployed as low-level drivers in the kernel, more specifically as miniport drivers. For example, for a phantom NIC (network information card) on a Microsoft Windows machine, the miniport driver should be coupled with

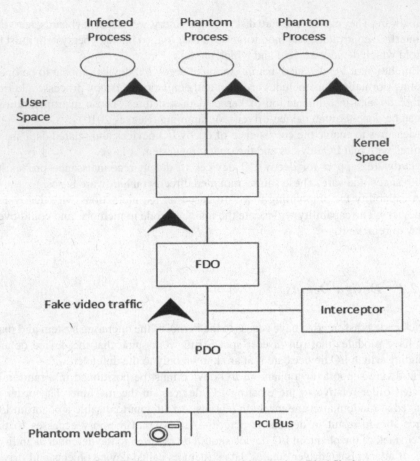

Fig. 14.1 Scheme of a decoy webcam to neutralize malware such as BlackShades

the network driver interface specification (NDIS) library. Each miniport driver can be stacked on top of a kernel driver that manages the hardware bus for the corresponding I/O device. The miniport driver attaches its device object to that of the kernel driver that manages the underlying hardware bus. That prevents inspection of the stack of device objects that are associated with the phantom I/O device.

When malware attempts to access the phantom I/O device, its I/O request packets traverse the device stack of that phantom device to reach the device object of our miniport driver. The I/O manager follows the pointer from the device object of our miniport driver to the driver object associated with it. The I/O manager inspects the major function code of each of those I/O request packets, and uses that code to index the dispatch table in the driver object at hand. The dispatch table of the driver object contains pointers to driver routines. That reference yields a pointer to one of the functions implemented in the miniport driver.

In the case of the device stack of an existing I/O device, the miniport driver sends the I/O request packet down to the device object associated with the kernel driver that

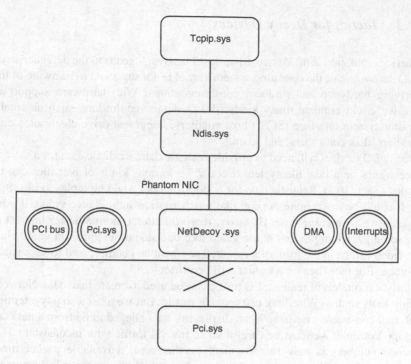

Fig. 14.2 Deceptive I/O device emulation

manages the underlying hardware bus. The hardware bus here is a PCI, and hence the driver is Pci.sys. The miniport driver emulates the behavior of Pci.sys and, to some degree, that of the PCI bus. The miniport driver then returns the I/O request packet up through the device stack of our phantom NIC as if the communication with Pci.sys, and the transmission or reception through the PCI bus, took place. The miniport driver's intervention is transparent to the caller that sent the original I/O request packet.

An example of functionality that can be emulated by the miniport drivers is that of handling interrupts. In the case of the device stack of an existing I/O device, the regular miniport driver does not receive interrupts from that I/O device. Pci.sys is the kernel driver to receive interrupts when data that are intended for the miniport driver arrive on the PCI bus. Pci.sys then notifies the regular miniport driver. In the case of the device stack of a phantom I/O device, the miniport driver does not interact or react to Pci.sys at all. The miniport driver emulates the arrival of network packets on a queue that simulates the PCI bus, and thus mimics the handling of those interrupts. The miniport driver then constructs device requests that carry the emulated data, and returns those I/O requests to kernel drivers at higher levels.

A miniport driver can emulate most of the operation of the phantom I/O devices, making them appear as real I/O devices with bus-master Direct Memory Access (DMA), as shown in Fig. 14.2. Each of the miniport drivers can emulate the DMA controller of the respective phantom I/O device to manage the transfer of emulated data between the imaginary physical media and host memory.

14.2.2   Tactics for Decoy Devices

I/O device emulation at the device driver level is advantageous to the defender since the I/O subsystem of the operating system kernel is not supposed to be aware of the underlying hardware and protocol communications. With hardware support in place, we could emulate many kinds of I/O device controllers, such as small-computer-system interface (SCSI) host adapters, integrated drive electronics disk controllers, disk controllers, and so on.

Decoy I/O devices will need to provide realistic data. Realistic data for a storage device would be a fake file system (Sect. 7.7). Various kinds of bait files can be included (Sect. 10.3). Realistic data for a video camera could be replayed information. It could be made quite boring, like much routine surveillance video, if your goal is to waste attacker time. However, it would attract more attacker interest to stage some interesting events in the video like one side of an apparent video chat. Fake video can be in the form of a repeated segment and compressed to save space in storage. But fake data for a toaster will be difficult.

Statistical models of realistic I/O traffic can be used to create fake data. Network sniffing tools such as Wireshark can provide traffic. But we must also pay attention to internal consistency of data. When displaying data alleged to be from a network card, for example, we must be careful since invalid traffic with inconsistent TCP sequence numbers is easy to recognize. Furthermore, reasonable packet times require modeling of the latency of the network to which the machine is connected, and reasonable secondary-storage retrievals require modeling of the disk controller. In general, realistic times are important to a convincing cyberdeception for all decoy I/O devices, and they may need to be emulated by implementation of scheduling algorithms.

The fake-device management should also modify kernel data structures to display user-mode processes and threads along with kernel threads that issue I/O requests to, and receive responses from, phantom I/O devices. For example, we could instrument the system-wide open file table in the operating-system kernel to display the existence of open files which appear to be residing on disks. Similarly, we could display a per-process open-file table to associate those fake entries of the system-wide open-file table with specific processes.

At boot time, an operating system probes the hardware buses to determine which I/O devices are present. Instead of trusting our deceptive device drivers, the malware could do the same, by executing special I/O instructions to probe the hardware buses. If no valid responses are returned, the attacker can conclude that the displayed I/O devices do not exist. However, fake devices are so rare that it would be an exceptional malware that would waste time trying this.

In fact, the possible presence of I/O projectors need not be secret. The attacker's awareness of that helps make adversarial reconnaissance more complex and less likely to succeed. The attacker may be able to intercept a real I/O device, but may decide not to proceed with the interception out of concern that the target I/O device is a decoy.

14.2.3 Hardware Support for Decoy Devices

The defender can also rewrite the microcode of I/O device hardware to facilitate fake devices. Signatures or even covert authentication mechanisms based on applied steganography can enable the microcode to differentiate between calls issued in normal usage and those issued by malware. An alternative on a multiprocessor machine is to use one processor as a "deception coprocessor" to implement for device management the wrappers described in Sect. 13.8.2. This is easiest to do for USB ports since the protocols are versatile and can accommodate a wide variety of real devices. If a graphics coprocessor is not being used much, it could be repurposed. A coprocessor could put data on the buses that suggests a phantom I/O device that the main processor needs to attend to.

A possible architecture is shown in Fig. 14.3. It depicts a deception coprocessor responding to queries for disks, keyboards, and webcams on the PCI bus. In addition to displaying phantom I/O devices at the hardware bus level, the deception coprocessor could support and collaborate with drivers and other data structures to project phantom I/O devices in the kernel of the operating system and all the way to processes in user space.

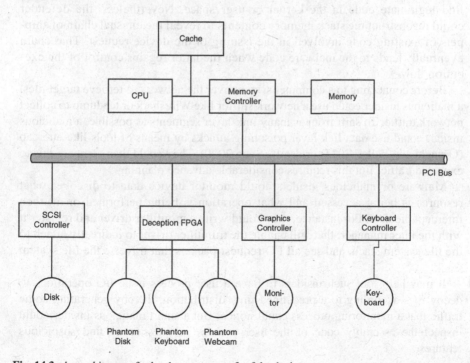

Fig. 14.3 An architecture for hardware support for fake devices

14.2.4   Tracking Down Malicious Activity

When a phantom I/O device is accessed, the goal will be to track down malware by locating the code that initiated the access to it. Any interaction with the phantom I/O device will require the caller to create device requests either directly or by system calls. Those requests will then be sent to the driver stack of the phantom I/O device, which includes our low-level deceptive driver. Since there is no actual hardware bus that sends and receives data through the phantom I/O device, the low-level deceptive driver must entirely emulate the interaction with the kernel driver that manages the underlying hardware bus.

The low-level deceptive driver can access data structures maintained by the memory manager of the operating system to maintain full awareness of the base memory location and size of each module loaded in the kernel. Upon reception of a device request, it can log the details of the origin, and perhaps perform a precise removal of the malware by removing perhaps just a few lines of code.

A possible complication is that the malware may use return-oriented programming to conceal itself by attributing a device-related call to existing legitimate code. Return-oriented programming pushes return addresses onto the stack to cause the execution of snippets of existing legitimate code to fill the device buffers and subsequently send a device request. Tracking the caller will then find legitimate code in the kernel or user space. Nevertheless, the defender could reconstruct the stack memory contents to reveal the unusual chain of snippets of existing code involved in the issuing of the device request. That chain eventually leads to the malware code when the latter regains control of the execution flow.

Before connecting to a computer system over the network to retrieve target files, a malicious insider could use a network sniffer like Wireshark or tcpdump to collect network traffic. To sniff from as many link-layer segments as possible, a malicious insider could use data-link layer poisoning attacks by means of tools like ettercap (Ornaghi and Valleri 2015) or dsniff (Song 2000). They could then compare this to expected traffic. But this requires considerable advance planning.

Malware or malicious insiders could monitor device data to discover what resource is being accessed and what operation is being performed on it, then intercept the data. For instance, they could write a minifilter driver and register it with the filter manager; that will enable the minifilter driver to indirectly attach to the file system stack, and see all I/O request packets that traverse the file system stack.

It may help fool such insiders to have a user process issue I/O operations to decoy files according to a predefined time distribution, thereby generating some traffic that a monitoring process could notice. But a smart malicious insider could inspect the assembly code of the user process in question to find suspicious features.

14.3 Case Study: Decoy Network Interface Controller

We experimented with the implementation of a low-level network driver for the Windows operating system (Rrushi 2016). This driver emulated the operation of a NIC (network interface controller), and reported to higher-level drivers in the device stack as if the decoy NIC were existent, fully functional, and had access to a computer network. The testbed consisted of a network of Windows machines equipped with the decoy NIC. Those machines were deliberately infected with over one hundred malware samples. Most of the samples were worms and Trojans, but there were also a few email viruses. Most of those malware samples were known, and thus represented a certain malware base to test against, while others were picked up through nonselective drive-by-downloads in which we visited malicious Web sites and collected what files they left on our computer.

14.3.1 Anti-Malware Testing

The miniport driver was loaded into the Windows kernel prior to the controlled malware infections. The miniport driver implemented two functions to attribute I/O request packets to actual code:

- It recorded the base memory location and size of each module loaded into the Windows kernel at the time of its load, namely in its DriverEntry() routine. This was done also to identify kernel code that builds custom device requests without any involvement of user-space code.
- It interoperated with the Windows kernel to obtain the identifiers of the processes that issued system calls, which in turn built the device requests and sent them to the device stack of the phantom NIC.

As the malware samples installed their files and thus sought to infect other machines on the network, the phantom NIC began to receive device requests from those malware samples at irregular times. The miniport driver responded with device requests that were the result of its emulation of a real NIC. The phantom NIC could follow up on malware connections up to the first few packet exchanges. Current malware has mechanisms to detect virtualized execution environments such as VMware, virtual boxes, Qemu, and the presence of a debugger. Nevertheless, we found that the malware samples that we ran were unprepared for an NIC to be a decoy, and no mechanisms were observed to probe the NIC before actual data transmission.

14.3.2   Results of Testing

The main network activities of malware that were detected by the phantom NIC were:

- Mounting network and port scans to search for other target machines on the network.
- Launching network exploits against those target machines in order to infect them.
- Contacting remote command-and-control servers, or searching for other infected machines on the network that are part of a peer-to-peer botnet.

Conficker is an example of malware that was detected by its attempts to exploit other machines on the network. It made numerous network connections over the phantom NIC, searching for machines with open network shares, weak passwords, and specific buffer-overflow vulnerabilities. Other malware samples that we observed performing similar activities included Changeup, Cridex, Extrat, Fixflo, and Picazburt.

A series of typical network traffic bursts exhibited by the malware samples over the phantom NIC are shown in Fig. 14.4. The upper curve represents the network traffic generated by malware, and the lower curve represents the traffic emulated by the phantom NIC in response. The data are for a 60-s time window; bursts of malicious network traffic do not continue long beyond the time window shown since the phantom NIC does not emulate complete services. Nevertheless, the initial network traffic bursts coming from malware suffice to detect and thus prepare for their removal. The malware would notice the abrupt interruption of network communication with what appears as its target service, peer-to-peer node, or command-and-control server. However it would be too late for the malware to conceal itself.

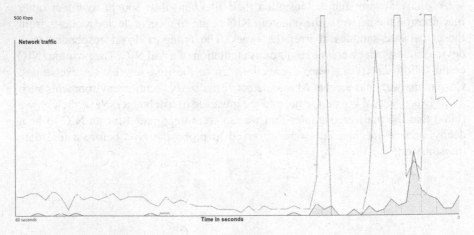

Fig. 14.4 A plot of network traffic bursts generated by malware over the phantom NIC

Our phantom NIC did receive legitimate device-request traffic. Some network services are configured to listen for connections on all NICs that are present in the system. Legitimate network services that invoked functions like socket(), bind(), and accept() resulted in requests. Nevertheless, none of that traffic actually transmits data, so it cannot carry payloads that exploit and infect other computers. The phantom NIC also caused no adverse effects on those legitimate network services. When socket() was invoked, the phantom NIC created a socket object structure, and thus returned the pointer to that structure in the original device request. The phantom NIC then bound that socket to a local transport address per the application's request. From that point on, the remaining device requests were queued at the driver, as if awaiting an incoming connection. This is the same behavior that a network service encounters when interacting with a real NIC.

Malware can create server sockets as well to receive command-and-control data from an attacker along with software updates. Nevertheless, malware first needs to call home to report the IP addresses of the compromised machine. Without that report, remote attacker-controlled machines cannot connect to the server socket on the compromised machine to gain access to it over the network. The phantom NIC makes external addresses appear as reachable over it. If the report to the remote attacker-controlled machines is made over the phantom NIC, the malware is detected immediately.

The backdoor malware Poison was detected this way. The machine infected by Poison sought to communicate with a proxy server over the phantom NIC, apparently to conceal the IP address of the final command-and-control server. Another example was the Terminator malware. The infected machine made a HTTP request over the phantom NIC to an external command-and-control server on port 80. The purpose of that network communication was to serve as a beacon that signals the command-and-control server of the infection of our machine, and to receive from the command-and-control server an executable that mounts tailored malware operations. The malware sample included one whose main method of infection was file sharing through removable media, such as Golroted, Ippedo, and Plagent. Those malware samples were detected due to their subsequent network-wide activity, mostly calling home. Although the propagation vector involves no network communications, the exfiltration of sensitive data harvested from a compromised machine must take place over the network.

Malware was not the only code that attempted to send network packets over the phantom NIC in our experiments. One of the Windows machines modeled a work computer in our department and had software and network services of a typical work environment. Table 14.1 shows some of the network protocols used for legitimate purposes by this machine over the phantom NIC, though their usage was low. Though we did not see it in these experiments, security software such as anti-malware products and network security scanners actively scans all of the networks of the machine on which they run. However, only the defender can run such tools, and only when their code has been properly audited and validated. So the defender could temporarily disable a phantom NIC when running any of those tools, or alternatively choose to validate the generator of each device request on a phantom NIC and thus permit the CPU utilization spikes.

Table 14.1 Protocols of
legitimate network traffic
over the phantom NIC

Protocol	Frequency
ARP	Average
NTP	Sporadic
NBNS	Average
TCP	Sporadic
UDP	Sporadic
BROWSER	Sporadic
LLDP	Sporadic

A phantom NIC should be visible to all network visualization and administration tools. An insider threat's use of a phantom NIC either directly through system commands would help identify them since legitimate users would not need to get that deep into a system. But note that a curious but honest computer user is a challenge to the I/O decoy approach. A phantom NIC cannot validate human intentions in trying to use its services.

The miniport driver, which is the foundation of a phantom NIC, is relatively compact and simple. Access to the phantom NIC by legitimate applications typically shows CPU utilization below 1 % incurred only at the time of access. The CPU utilization was observed to rise up to 14 % when malware performed network operations over the phantom NIC. The overhead, however, does not interfere with the functions of the machine since it occurs only when a piece of malware generates device requests that traverse the device stack of the phantom NIC, and thus would incur overhead with a legitimate NIC.

All the malware samples were observed to use all active NICs on the compromised machine, real and phantom. Many called the GetIpForwardTable() function to retrieve the IPv4 routing table, which displayed fake entries associated with phantom NICs, and many called the GetIpInterfaceEntry() function to retrieve IP information for a NIC, and then scan its subnet for reachable machines. Of the malware samples that did not use the network for propagation, only 13 % used all NICs on the machine including phantom ones. These accessed only a real NIC to communicate with command-and-control servers and would escape detection by the phantom NIC. Nevertheless, those malware samples could be detected when the machine is placed in a deliberate malware search mode.

14.3.3   More About Coexistence with Real NICs

The order of a phantom NIC relative to the existing NICs on a machine can be easily changed after an attack is detected. Reactivation of a phantom NIC should require a change of the media access control (MAC) addresses assigned to real NICs and phantom NICs.

A phantom NIC that displays an internal network should not share the destination IP address space with any real NICs. The separation of the IP addresses to which the real and phantom NICs connect allows for the least interference with legitimate communications, and the most accurate detection of attack. Malware connects to internal networks to exploit other machines, or search for already infected machines to form peer-to-peer botnets.

With the deployment of various levels of security perimeters enforced by firewalls, confidential data are often stored on servers that reside in internal networks. Data and services for public access, such as a company's Web site, are typically placed in the demilitarized zone facing the Internet. Malware wants to jump from the demilitarized zone to the internal network, and access high-value servers on the internal networks. Insider threats are also interested in internal resources so they can obtain confidential data that they are not authorized to access. Both external and internal threats can be caught by a phantom NIC on a server.

A phantom NIC that provides fake access to Internet shares the destination IP address space with a real NIC. Here we differentiate between the actual contents of the routing table, and the contents that are displayed to system administration tools when those are launched by anyone other than the defender. All requests for connection to an IP address on the Internet by code executing in user space are serviced with reference to the actual contents of the routing table. The phantom NIC should not affect the servicing of those requests to protect legitimate applications from disruption of their networking. In consequence, malware and insider threats running in user space that connect only to an IP address on the Internet will go undetected.

The routing table that is displayed in user space to users other than the defender will contain entries associated with phantom NICs. In our implementation, those entries are placed in a random order. The display of this routing masks the local index value for the NIC that is actually used to communicate with the Internet at large. The attacker could try to send network packets from user space to the Internet, and then at the kernel level check the device requests that travel through the driver stack of each NIC. That, however, requires access to the driver stack of the phantom NIC, which is what is manipulated in our design to detect and pinpoint the attack. Of course, the attacker may be lucky and access the driver stack of a real NIC first, but may also be unlucky and access the driver stack of a phantom NIC first and therefore fall into a trap. Furthermore, all accesses to the routing table in kernel mode by modules other than the routing-table manager are reported to the defender.

A phantom NIC that provides fake access to Internet at large also has a chance to detect malware in these cases:

- When malware accesses all NICs on the machine. An example is the Havex (Sect. 15.5) which issues Wnet calls to discover all the servers that are reachable.
- When malware sends network packets from within the kernel by creating device requests directly to avoid detection, then sending those requests through the

driver stack of a NIC. Usually this is done by invoking the IoCallDriver() routine. Once the request goes through the driver stack of a phantom NIC, the intrusion is immediately detected.

To limit the escape of malware through the main real NIC that provides connectivity to Internet at large, the defender can use a second-line defensive strategy. Traditional anti-malware systems allocate a dedicated period of time from a few minutes to 1 or more hours to run the system intensively during which the machine is in "maintenance" and not very available. A phantom NIC approach can use a full period of time like that. It can disable the real NIC, and replace it with an identical phantom NIC which has the characteristics and local index value of the original real NIC. Thus, all NICs would be fake at that point, and we can run the system looking for malware device requests. We refer to this as a temporary malware search mode of the machine. The mode can be further enhanced by creating fake processes which appear to communicate with IP addresses in Internet over the phantom NIC. All client applications can also be disabled and replaced with fake processes. An example is a Web browser which is replaced with a fake browser process that appears to view pages from a Web site on the Internet. At the end of a limited period of time, the real NIC is enabled, the fake processes and related data structures are removed, and the machine is brought back into production.

14.4   Conclusions

Decoy I/O devices are not difficult to implement by adding fake drivers to an operating system. They are particularly useful for network interface controller, but can be used for all kinds of I/O devices.

14.5   Exercises

1. Suggest deceptions that would be useful in the camera function of a mobile smartphone carried by a malicious person attacking your computer systems.
2. Would hardware support be needed for a phantom I/O device when countering only user-space malware?
3. Why emulate the dynamics of an I/O device in order to support its phantom counterpart? Wouldn't a passive phantom I/O device be effective anyway?
4. What determines the usability of a phantom I/O device on a machine in production?
5. How can the legitimate user of a computer system be encouraged to use only the legitimate NIC rather than the decoy ones?

References

Kujawa A (2012) DarkComet. Available at blog.malwarebytes.org/intelligence/2012/06/you-dirty-rat-part-1-darkcomet

Ornaghi A, Valleri M (2015) Ettercap., Available at ettercap.github.io/ettercap/ index.html

Reeves R (2010) Windows 7 device driver. Addison-Wesley Professional, Upper Saddle River, NJ

Rrushi J (2016) NIC displays to thwart malware attacks mounted from within the OS. Computers & Security 61:59–71

Song D (2000) Dsniff., Available online at, www.monkey.org/~dugsong/dsniff

Szor P (2005) The art of computer virus research and defense. Addison Wesley, North Saddle River, NJ

Chapter 15
Deception for the Electrical Power Industry

"Mirage" is a defensive deception approach to disrupt and investigate cyberattacks on critical infrastructure and industrial control systems in particular. The main thrust is to create a decoy ("mirage") system that cyberattacks can target harmlessly. The idea is to adapt the concept of decoy data (honeytokens) to an industrial-control context. The honeytokens represent dynamics, configuration, operation, and location of systems that attackers want to manipulate. The decoy data resides in phantom I/O devices like those in Chap. 14 and on computers that perform control-systems tasks.

Cyberattacks on the industrial control systems can involve espionage, extortion, or sabotage. Motivation can be monetary or political. Because it is hard to update, much software for industrial control systems is based on long-obsolete operating systems and software with many known vulnerabilities, and systems generally have backdoors to the Internet, so they are easy to attack (Carr and Rowe 2015).

© Springer International Publishing Switzerland 2016
N.C. Rowe, J. Rrushi, *Introduction to Cyberdeception*,
DOI 10.1007/978-3-319-41187-3_15

15.1 Simulating Electrical Power Plants

This chapter will use the example of an electrical power plant. Physical components include physical equipment and processes such as large water pumps, mechanical machines, and fuel reactions. Power plants also use many programmable logic controllers. Those are industrial computers that can interface directly with physical equipment and processes. In a real power plant, the controllers are attached to physical equipment; in a simulated power plant, the controllers are attached to simulated physical equipment.

Simulation of a power plant is aided by the commercial simulation tools for power-plant engineering. These tools use reactor theory along with power-plant engineering models to create virtual reactor models (Jain et al. 2010). The models are typically implemented in three-dimensional computer-aided design (CAD) formats and then imported into a virtual environment. Special methods they use are drawn from computational fluid dynamics, control theory, porous media approximation, nodal integral methods, and lattice Boltzmann models. Simulations also use virtual control rooms that permit interactivity with objects such as control panels and touchscreen monitors (Markidis and Uddin 2006).

Simulation can be concealed through a stealth controller module which places a barrier on the cyber intrusion. An attack-redirection capability based on the phantom I/O devices of the last chapter can project credible decoy plant data generated with power plant expertise.

Traditional honeypots (The Honeynet Project 2004) are of limited value for attacks on power plants since plant software and data is quite specialized. Plants are constantly in action, reading from sensors, processing data, reporting to operators, and writing to actuators. We must create records of that activity to fool attackers. Furthermore, data reflects physical laws, so it cannot be arbitrary; for instance, many processes report a smoothly varying number at evenly spaced time intervals. Hence we need a full simulation of a plant if we are to fool attackers.

The goal of a mirage power plant is to trap and reverse-engineer most attempts at cyber intrusions. It increases the defender's understanding of the vulnerabilities that were exploited and the attack techniques that were applied. It enables the defender to pinpoint and eradicate malware, and to better protect targets as yet unattacked. It also enables the defender to perform an informed analysis of cyberattack methods, and helps discover who the attackers are.

15.2 Building a Power-Plant Simulator

We have developed a research testbed that integrates power-plant simulation with real industrial controllers (Rrushi 2011); similar work is that of An et al. (2013). We built continuous simulation models of an alternating-current induction motor that drives a water pump, common equipment in a power plant. We ran those models on a cluster of personal computers to perform a deceptive simulation of the induction motor and water pump. We instrumented analog-to-digital and digital-to-analog modules to connect the deceptive simulation cluster to a programmable logic controller. The converter modules emulated sensors and actuators.

We asked a team of students to distinguish between the mirage induction motor and a real one through an analysis of the network traffic that involved the corresponding controllers. As a further challenge, some of the data we gave them was "noise" data randomly generated. The tests indicated that a real induction motor was indistinguishable from its simulated counterpart. This confirmed our approach for a critical component.

Uddin and his reseach group have implemented a power plant simulator in LabVIEW, a simulation tool. Their simulator is based on the 1000 MWe Westinghouse pressurized-water reactor design. It allows real-time monitoring of the state of the reactor, and allows an operator to control a limited number of parameters. The simulation includes a Triple-Modular Redundant controller and a signal transmitter. The front LabVIEW panel in the simulator represents a digital control room where operators can monitor the state of the reactor. It also has knobs and switches to allow control. The simulator code is dynamically linked with the parameter values controlled by the operators.

15.3 Mirage Architecture

Attempted malicious activity on an industrial control system is not difficult to recognize. Since there is so much predictable routine activity, any activity involving unusual data flows, unusual data values, and unusual protocols stands out easily (Carr and Rowe 2015). However, the networks of industrial control systems are so heavily distributed that it is difficult to monitor everything. Resilience to attack based on deception could be a better strategy.

Once an attacker or malware launches exploits against a mirage power plant, tools can intercept details of the attacker's activity. Details include the network traffic they generated, executables and code uploaded, file-system reads and writes, and data written. Plant dynamics and related code, data, and configurations are some of the first elements to be checked by malware prior to target selection. So they would be a high priority to simulate well and monitor in a mirage architecture. It requires some expertise in power-plant operation for the engineered decoy data to be consistent and technically correct for a knowledgeable attacker. One way of providing it would be honeyfiles on fake disks. Another way would be the emulation of industrial network communications through phantom network-interface controllers. Other ways of projecting decoy plant data would be fake keyboards, monitors, and webcams.

System interception mechanisms could be implemented in hardware at the programmable-logic-controller level. Hardware solutions are important for similar areas of information security such as making a system copy-resistant and

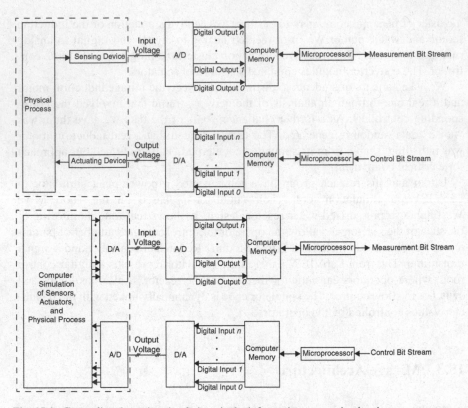

Fig. 15.1 Concealing deceptive simulation via the information conversion barrier

tamper-resistant (Lie et al. 2000) and certifying program execution (Lie et al. 2000). Implementing mirage functions in hardware is desirable because interception mechanisms should operate assuming of a full system compromise given the history of malware takeovers of industrial control systems. Interception mechanisms can be implemented in a hardware chip attached to the main circuit board of a controller. The interception chip, which can be a field programmable gate array (FPGA), should access to the main peripheral component interconnect (PCI) bus as well as to the memory bus so it can monitor all activity on the operating system, especially the network packets sent or received by the controller. It could be best to attach it to the backplane, the bridge that connects the microprocessor module, networking module, and I/O modules in a controller (Zonouz et al. 2014).

An alternative for implementing mirages are the analog-to-digital and digital-to-analog converter modules in a programmable logic controller that implement the interface between digital and physical equipment in a power plant (Fig. 15.1). Intruders cannot see beyond the information conversion layer and cannot know whether the electrical signals are real or simulated. Modifications require specialized hardware design, however.

The mirage approach does not require secrecy of the active redirection capability since knowledge of this could scare away attackers. By advertising that a mirage power plant exists somewhere in the power grid, the defender increases paranoia in the attacker about their movements and target selection.

15.4   Defense of Electrical Substations

An electrical substation in a power plant serves as an interface between power generators and the electric power grid. It uses step-up transformers to elevate the voltage generated by the power plant. Electrical substations have several computers that are programmed to monitor and control its physical parameters and equipment, most commonly intelligent electronic devices (IEDs). In addition, a substation typically includes a local control center comprised of one or more computers that receive and send data from and to the IEDs. The control functions that are performed by IEDs include protection of physical equipment from various kinds of faults. When a fault is detected, the IEDs perform computations on power data and also communicate with each other over the computer network to determine the best action to take along with its location, and may subsequently trip one or more circuit breakers. The typical computer network in an electrical substation is based on Ethernet buses, and has a bandwidth of 10 or 100 Mbps. A substation network is considered to be workable only if it can transmit fast enough to enable a final response by IEDs within hard real-time thresholds, typically within 4 milliseconds. Electrical substations also communicate with each other via network protocols.

Malware has targeted electrical substations. A recent case caused a power failure that left hundreds of thousands of homes without power in Ukraine (Goodin 2016). The intrusion into the electrical substations was done by the malware BlackEnergy which infected multiple Ukrainian power utility companies. Unfortunately, the private networks of utility companies are often connected to the computer networks of the electrical substation networks that they own or operate, and are possible entry points for cyberattacks. Furthermore, IEDs typically provide engineering access through dial-in modems, another entry point for malicious activity.

15.4.1   Defensive Deception for Electrical Substations

A possible defensive deception is to advertise to malware and attackers some network traffic patterns associated with a fake substation. Those patterns can be designed to have specific characteristics which can be recognized through time-series analysis (Box et al. 2015). A mirage electrical substation can be developed with the help of a real-time digital power-system simulator (RTDS Technologies 2016). The defensive goal would be to encourage intruders to mount a mimicry attack by sending network packets that exhibit the advertised patterns of the fake substation. Since no legitimate service would use these patterns, we can quickly identify an intruder. To create convincing data, monitoring of real substations can estimate the probabilities of occurrence of the directional-overpower, directional-comparison, and distance-protection functions in a given time window on an IED in a substation. The probabilities of occurrence of those functions help the defender set the frequency of activation of decoy IEC 61850 logical nodes.

A key technique that intruders use to sabotage an electrical substation is to trip or close electrical circuits to cut power to customers. They may also initiate physical damage to equipment such as power transformers or power generators in the substation. For this reason the defender gains particular advantage by deploying decoys of logical nodes in the switchgear group, especially circuit breaker (XCBR) logical nodes and virtual circuit switch (XSWI) logical nodes. In addition to probabilities of occurrence, analysis of legitimate system data can identify the logical devices and hence the IEDs that are optimal for hosting decoy logical nodes. It helps to have a good map of the entire electrical network.

15.5 Deception Engineering for a Real Example of Malware

An example of malware targeting industrial control systems is Havex (Wilhoit 2014; Hentunen and Tikkanen 2014). This section discusses the reverse engineering and analysis of the Havex malware plugin. We found that despite its notoriety in the media, Havex uses a plain and unsophisticated target-selection process. That permits targeted deception mechanisms to neutralize Havex and similar malware.

15.5.1 Operation of Havex

FireEye, F-Secure, and Microsoft identify Havex as Backdoor:W32/Havex.A. Havex uses three ways to infect its targets: (1) direct exploitation of network services and phishing emails, (2) malicious links to Web browsers, and (3) execution of Trojanized installers. The Havex code drops and executes mbcheck.dll. That executable connects to command-and-control servers over the network, awaiting instructions to download and run malware plugins. One Havex plugin targets industrial control systems. More specifically, it searches for Object Linking and Embedding for Process Control (OPC) servers (OPC Foundation 2003; Mahnke et al. 2009). Reverse engineering has discovered a number of command-and-control servers on the Internet which communicated with Havex plugins.

We reverse-engineered with IDA Pro (Hex-Rays 2015) the machine code of the main Havex DL and its industrial-control-system plugin. The plugin relies on Windows networking (WNet) to discover servers including OPC ones. Havex imports MPR.dll so that its Wnet calls are forwarded to provider executables which handle network connections and data transfers. OPC servers are discovered when the MPR executable has a registered network-provider executable for OPC when Havex issues the WNet calls. Havex then enumerates the network resources on the compromised machine. It is interested in all network resources, their types and usage. Havex starts with the topmost container in the tree of network resources and then explores the paths down to the leaves.

Havex checks each OPC server for Microsoft's Component Object Model (COM) interfaces (Rogerson 1997). It attempts to create over the network an instance of the OPC Server Browser class on each of the servers in question. If it can, it receives an array of structures. One of those structures includes a pointer to the interface identifier, along with a pointer that can be used to invoke functions on the object. Knowledge of the class identifier of an OPC server object enables the Havex plugin to issue calls through its standard interface, which permits reading the attributes associated with an item of interest. It can also read the data tags of each OPC server that references memory locations in a controller and can store a physical parameter related to the process monitored or controlled. These tags can be used to identify the physical process behind the controller, a step toward ability to program the controller to damage that physical process.

The generation of fake OPC tags to be given to the Havex plugin is straightforward. They could be randomly generated values, or at least values correlated according to known formulas under ideal conditions. Havex's inability to check whether tags represent true target industrial control systems enables a defender to provide large amounts of fake data to confuse it. If Havex decides to attack those systems, it will just provide us with details of its attack methods without causing any harm.

15.5.2   Experiments with Havex

We conducted a number of experiments with Havex to test its ability to recognize valid targets. Similar experiments are important with any kind of fake resources to test if the resources are convincing.

A Windows machine was infected by Havex in a physically isolated network and had access to real servers on that network. Havex discovered the servers on the network correctly in most of these tests, though in a few cases the MPR executable could not find a network-provider executable or Havex encountered various WNet errors. We also conducted "noise" tests where the Windows machine infected by Havex had no access to any servers over the networks but ran deceptive network drivers that emulated the operation of the network interface controller on that machine. These deceptive network drivers were paired with real network-provider executables. The setting was similar to that of Wilhoit (2014)). In most of those noise trials, Havex pursued the phantom servers as valid targets.

We also conducted tests in which servers hosted true COM objects and interfaces. Havex created an instance of the OPC Server Browser class on each of those servers. Thus, those were all valid targets for the Havex plugin. Havex pursued those servers as valid targets in most cases, but missed a few due to classes not in the registration database and a few errors with interfaces. "Noise" tests were also done in which none of the servers hosted COM objects and interfaces but each generated a fake response when queried for COM objects and interfaces, acting like a honeypot. The Havex plugin accepted most of those servers as valid targets.

A final set of "noise" tests had servers that supported COM but did not host any OPC server objects. Those servers, however, acted like honeypots by returning lists of OPC server objects that did not exist. The Havex plugin did follow up by attempting to read attributes from those nonexistent OPC server objects, and did accept several of those as valid targets. But we could not follow up on this due to the difficulty of simulating a complete OPC interaction.

These results should not seem too surprising because malware has plenty of other threats to worry about such as getting trapped for forensic analysis and losing its surprise value (Chen et al. 2008). Fixing a low rate of propagation is not usually a priority because the amenability of environments varies considerably. This suggests that deception in targets can be very effective, and will continue to be effective for some time.

15.6   Conclusions

Industrial control systems are particularly vulnerable to cyberattacks. Deception can play an important part of their defense. We have used an example of electrical power systems, an important part of critical infrastructure.

15.7   Exercises

1. Power plants are big and complex. Why is it possible to think we have a reasonable chance of simulating one for purposes of deceiving attackers?
2. How could a system simulation capability take into account adversarial models rather than be entirely preprogrammed?
3. Why is speed of the computer simulating a power plant an important factor in the success a redirection deception?
4. If a malicious person tries to turn off an electrical substation that is a decoy, they may be able to see that it did not work by noting whether the power goes off in the area served by the substation. How can we make it more difficult for them to remotely tell if the power went off?
5. Why did the writers of Havex use a software plugin for industrial control systems? How can this be a basis for deception?
6. The Stuxnet malware that targeted Iranian nuclear facilities used several kinds of deception. There is quite a bit of documentation about it. Research its deception methods and assess how effective they were.

References

An Y, Uddin R, Sanders W, Sollima C (2013) Digital I&C and cyber security in nuclear power plants. Trans Am Nucl Soc 109: November

Box G, Jenkins G, Reinsel G, Ljung G (2015) Time series analysis: forecasting and control, 5th edn. Wiley, New York

Carr N, Rowe N (2015) A prototype forensic toolkit for industrial-control-systems incident response. Proceedings of the 2015 SPIE Defense + Security Conference, Baltimore, MD, April

Chen B, Morris R (2003) Certifying program execution with secure processors. Proceedings of the usenix workshop on hot topics in operating systems, Lihue, Hawaii, May

Chen X, Anderson J, Mao ZM, Bailey M, Nazario J (2008) Towards an understanding of anti-virtualization and anti-debugging behavior in modern malware. Depend Syst Networks, June. pp 177–186

OPC Foundation (2003) OPC data access custom interface specification. Available at www.matrikonopc.com/downloads/147/specifications/index.aspx

Goodin D (2016), First known hacker-caused power outage signals troubling escalation. Available at arstechnica.com/security/2016/01/first-known-hacker-caused-power-outage-signals-troubling-escalation

Hentunen D, Tikkanen A (2014) Havex hunts for ICS/SCADA systems. Available at www.f-secure.com/weblog/archives/00002718.html

Hex-Rays (2015) Interactive disassembler. Available at www.hex-rays.com/products/ida/

The Honeynet Project (2004) Know your enemy, 2nd edition. Addison-Wesley, Boston, MA, US

Jain P, Popov E, Yoder G, Uddin R (2010) Parallel simulation of 2D/3D flows using lattice Boltzmann models. Transactions of the American Nuclear Society, Las Vegas, NV, Nov 2010

Lie D, Thekkath C, Mitchell M, Lincoln P, Boneh D, Mitchell J, Horowitz M (2000) Architectural support for copy and tamper resistant software. Proceedings of architectural support for programming languages and operating systems. pp 168–177

Mahnke W, Leitner S, Damm M (2009) OPC unified architecture. Springer, New York, March

Markidis S, Uddin R (2006) A virtual control room with an embedded interactive nuclear reactor simulator. In Proceedings of the 5th international topical meeting on nuclear plant instrumentation controls, and human machine interface technology, Albuquerque, NM, Nov. pp 675–679

Rogerson D (1997) Inside COM. Microsoft, Redmond, WA

Rrushi J (2011) An exploration of defensive deception in industrial communication networks. Int J Critic Infrastruct Protect 4(1):66–75, August

RTDS Technologies (2016) Real time digital power system simulator. Available at www.rtds.com

Wilhoit K (2014) Havex, it's down with OPC. Available at www.fireeye.com/blog/threat-research/2014/07/havex-its-down-with-opc.html

Zonouz S, Rrushi J, McLaughlin S (2014) Automated PLC code analytics for detection of industrial control malware. IEEE Security & Privacy, 12(6): November/December

Chapter 16
Law and Ethics for Software Deception

We have discussed many ways in which deception can be used with cybersystems, both for offense and defense. Many of these can be highly effective. However, deception is not always permitted by laws, policies, and ethical principles. We need to consider these limits. We first examine ethics, the theory of under what circumstances some deception is acceptable, and then the legal problems that can be posed by cyberdeception.

16.1 Applying Ethics to Cyberspace

Deception is a technique for persuading or manipulating people by causing them to have incorrect knowledge of the state of the world. Most ethical theories proscribe many forms of deception while permitting a few kinds (Bok 1978). Deception

© Springer International Publishing Switzerland 2016
N.C. Rowe, J. Rrushi, *Introduction to Cyberdeception*,
DOI 10.1007/978-3-319-41187-3_16

smooths social interactions, controls malicious people, and enables doing something for someone's unrecognized benefit (Scheibe 1980; Nyberg 1993). The harms of deception can be the failure to accomplish desired goals and damage to the trust necessary to sustain social relationships without which much human activity could not be accomplished.

Quinn (2006) categorizes ethical theories applicable to computer technology. He distinguishes subjective and cultural relativism, divine-command theory, Kantian rule-based ethics, social-contract theory, and act and rule utilitarianism. Subjective relativism, cultural relativism, and divine-command theory do not apply well to cyberspace because cyberspace is a shared social resource that spans diverse cultures with diverse opinions, and it needs cooperation to work properly. Kantian rule-based ethics is difficult to apply in general, though it helps resolve specific issues. Social-contract theory has uses but does not provide specific enough guidance to resolve most ethical dilemmas in cyberspace. Alternative formulations of cyberethics such as the "disclosive" approach of Brey (2000) can also be explored, but they are relatively new.

That leaves utilitarianism, which attempts to decide ethical questions by assessing the net benefit to society of a particular act or ethical rule. So we have followed a utilitarian approach in this book, and rule utilitarianism in particular. We will argue that a particular policy of deception is ethical if its net benefits minus costs exceeds that of not deceiving, considering benefits and costs to a society in the long term (Artz 1994). This is what we followed in Sect. 12.1. Benefits include achieving the goals of the deceiver and the value of those goals. Costs include the direct damage caused by the deception as when it destroys or damages something, direct costs of the deception being discovered such as retaliation, and indirect costs of discovery such as increased distrust of the parties making it more difficult to cooperate to their mutual benefit in the future. If someone attacks a computer, a deception that could make them go away could be justified if the cost of a successful attack on the computer in the hours of work to reinstall the operating system and damaged files, whereas the cost to the defender of a lie that makes the attacker go away is much less. As in Sect. 12.1, both benefits and costs must be multiplied by probabilities to obtain expected values when they are uncertain due to such factors as whether the deception will succeed or whether it will be discovered.

It is important to note that deception can be primarily benevolent (Adar et al. 2013) and thus have negative costs. Misleading the user can reduce their stress, as by offering buttons in a display that do not do anything but give the user an illusion of a small amount of control.

Software itself can deceive, as its deception methods can be programmed. The ethical responsibility with such software lies with the programmer, since the software acts as their agent. However, new developments in artificial intelligence are continuing to increase the human-like characteristics of software, and we can now conceive of automated agents with their own ethics (Belloni et al. 2015).

The two main professional societies for information-technology professionals, the ACM and the IEEE Computer Society, have a joint policy on ethics (ACM/

IEEE-CS 1999). But it does not address many key issues raised here. For instance, it proscribes deception in speaking to the public about software, but says nothing about writing deliberately deceptive software or foisting malicious deceptive cyber-attacks. So we need further ethical principles for cyberspace.

16.1.1   Ethical-Climate Issues

A concern can be raised that the use of deception tends to create a climate of general distrust. Every time a cybersystem deceives, it tends to lessen the trust the users have in all cybersystems. Sztompka (1999) points out the far-reaching consequences of distrust in organizations since this affects their operations at many levels, and trust issues have been important in recent years in management science.

One response is that cybersystems are not organizations, and we do not have a social contract with them as we do with other people. They are, after all, tools without feelings that are not attempting to maintain relationships with us, and they cannot commit perjury because they cannot swear oaths. Everyone is familiar with tools that do not work properly.

It is true that frequent cyberdeception will make users more cautious and less able to accomplish things there. But this is happening already with Web sites: People are becoming increasingly aware of scams like phishing and less likely to be fooled by grand claims that come via email. People realize that scams are the price we pay for ease of commercial transactions on the Web. So people may come to be accepting of defensive deceptions as well.

16.1.2   Escalation of Distrust

Another concern about deception is that it might encourage more deception by deceivees, which might lead to more deception by the original deceiver, and so on in further escalation. But this should not be much of a danger because the deception that cybersystems do is difficult for users to repay in kind. If a computer lies that the network is down, it does no good for an attacker to lie that their own network is down, whereas it might make sense that you would lie to a neighbor that they cannot borrow your lawnmower if they have lied to you previously that you could not borrow their lawnmower.

Furthermore, cybersystems do not have feelings of anger that would encourage escalation of conflicts. If they are attacked more, they should continue with the same defenses as long as they are effective. They should only try new deceptive defenses if the old defenses are failing. But that is independent of whether the attack is escalating or not.

16.1.3 Ensuring Minimal Harms

Deception can cause harms. If used offensively, the harm must be justified by some greater good such as stopping an attack by a counterattack. If used defensively, the harm of side effects to legitimate users must be less than the harm to attackers. Our argument has been that most defensive deceptions proposed in the book provide little harm to the legitimate user. Deceptions with honeypots are a good example because legitimate users should not encounter a honeypot. Delays and excuses also tend to cause less harm to legitimate users, since attackers are in more of a hurry.

Could defensive deceptive tactics get "out of control" and cause more damage than they intend? If we must modify an operating system, we might make mistakes and cause it to fail and to harm legitimate user activities in wide-ranging ways. These issues are the same issues with any kind of buggy software, but can arise more often with deception because it often deliberately seeks to prevent actions from occurring. Our goal should then be to make minimal changes to software to implement our deceptions. Many tactics discussed like delays and fakes are simple to implement and limited in their effects, and this should help.

Lengthy persistence of effects could turn a mild deception into something more serious. So ethical deceptions should have time limits, especially after the deceivee has disappeared. For instance, if we delayed an attacker, we should not continue delaying everyone else for a long time just in case the attacker comes back. It will help to choose deceptions randomly under similar circumstances, so if we hurt legitimate users one way we will less likely to hurt them again, since legitimate users are unlikely to use many of the resources that an attacker uses.

Users of cybersystems in organizations must consent to a wide range of security measures even without deception. Thus there is an implicit acceptance by many legitimate users of security measures which make their lives more difficult. This acceptance could well be expanded to include deception.

16.1.4 Privacy

A frequent concern of cyberethics is the danger to privacy of the individual (Spinello 2013). Privacy of the attacker is not an issue with the defensive deceptions of this book because most attackers will be anonymous when they can engage in illegal activities. So they try very hard to avoid giving any personal information.

Privacy of defenders, however, is a concern. Ethical deceptions should be designed so defenders do not inadvertently reveal their personal information. This could happen if they encounter a fake login prompt, defensive phishing, or some of the social-engineering techniques of Chap. 10. Then we should ensure that the private information is encrypted or deleted as soon as it is confirmed to be from a legitimate user.

16.1.5   Entrapment

Entrapment is an ethical issue because it amounts to encouraging people to do bad things. Of the tactics we have discussed, bait (Sect. 10.3) raises the most concerns about entrapment. Good bait might induce someone to commence an attack they would not have tried otherwise, or might encourage them to try to similar attacks with data they steal elsewhere. However, it can be argued that bait is always passive, and the user of it takes an active role that is always ethically questionable. It is hard to see most other deceptions like delays or false excuses as entrapment because they are discouraging the attacker, not encouraging them.

16.1.6   Trespassing

More active kinds of deceptions, such as tracing an attacker back to their computer and planting spyware there, raise ethical issues about trespassing (Himma 2004) since many of the techniques are the same as those used by attackers. So we must be careful with such techniques. An argument needs to be given that such trespassing was for a legitimate suspicion and the goals could not be accomplished by any other means.

16.1.7   Strategic Deception

Strategic cyberdeception (Sect. 10.8) can be considerably broader than most of the deceptions considered in this book. For this reason, it raises serious ethical problems because broad-scale deception affects many people, and there are more ways for someone to be hurt. For instance in the case of a fake but advertised cyberdefense, contractors may waste time trying to sell software to the organization in support of the fake defense, or the public may assume the organization with the fake defense is impregnable and underestimate risks associated with it. It is also difficult to maintain a secret involving many people, so many such deceptions will be revealed early, wasting the resources used for their planning and implementation which could have been spent more effectively on other kinds of defenses.

16.2   Legal Issues in Deception

There are laws against many kinds of deception in all countries. So it is important to consider whether the methods proposed in this book could encounter any legal objections. Intergovernmental legal cooperation is increasing in cyberspace (Berman 2002), so crime crossing international boundaries can increasingly be prosecuted.

16.2.1   Fraud

Fraud can be punished in both criminal and civil courts and can be punished by fines and prison terms (Ramage 2009). U.S. tort law defines fraud as "calculated efforts to use misrepresentation or other deceptive efforts to induce the innocent or unwary to give up some tangible interest." The methods of this book are certainly calculated and deceptive. Defenders can certainly be innocent and unwary because they have more important things to do than check constantly for attacks. So many offensive deceptions would be considered fraud by U.S. law, though not necessarily in other countries. Are attackers "innocent or unwary"? Probably not, because they are attacking defenders against their desires, and know that defenders would want to stop them if they could.

"Tangible interest" is a key phrase here. It is usually interpreted to mean money or property in fraud cases. Is use of your computer a "tangible interest"? Probably, because people pay money for computer time and resources. Just because your computer is attached to the Internet does not give intruders the right to break in, any more than they could break into your house because it is on a public street. But systems that offer services to outsiders, like Web and file systems, could be argued to have an implicit contract with users to provide them with services, particularly if users are paying for it. Even then only some of the deceptions described in this book could be considered violations of contracts—delays and excuses are common in cyberspace so their use by a defender could not be considered fraud.

Fraud by software is also hard to prove because software is rarely guaranteed. In the U.S., software is not subject to the "implied merchantability" laws that apply to other commercial products. So if you buy a software product, you're just lucky if it works like it is supposed to, because you have no legal recourse if it does not. Software license agreements that purchasers are often forced to sign to use the product try to ensure this. This is a good argument to justify both offensive and defensive deceptions in cyberspace, and there are already plenty of them (Seife 2015).

U.S. fraud law does say that the "victim's nature or acts are irrelevant" and that fraud need only be "reasonably calculated to deceive persons of ordinary prudence and competence". This is useful in prosecuting offensive deception. However for defensive deception, it would be hard for an attacker to prove damages in being impeded from performing an illegal action. Even if they could prove damages, it would be hard to prove legal responsibility since a defender could have been fed faulty information by some other software that caused the apparent deception.

16.2.2   Entrapment

Entrapment (see Sect. 16.1.5) can have legal as well as ethical implications. Evidence obtained by entrapment as defined in the law in the U.S. is not admissible in court. For instance, U.S. police cannot offer illegal drugs for sale and then arrest the buyers. But the definition is not always clear. U.S. police can legally run "sting" operations on the Internet where they pretend to be underage girls to attract propositions from sexual predators. So it is not usually considered entrapment solely to gather information, as when bait with spyware is used to locate a hacker in another country.

Offensive entrapment, surprisingly, can be legal in many cases if performed with a good justification. It can be analogous to police doing raids to catch people doing illegal things.

In cases in which a defensive deception does legally meet the definition of entrapment, it only means that you cannot prosecute attackers you catch. You may still be able to manipulate attackers with the deception, which is usually its primary purpose.

16.2.3 Retaliation

Retaliation is the idea of responding to an attack in "kind" or in the same way as the attack. Defensive retaliation is legal in warfare according to the laws of armed conflict as a counterattack. But it is not legal between individuals or groups within a society, such as with a business counterattacking a hacker, since anti-hacking laws generally apply equally well to attacks and counterattacks.

For defense, law generally limits the degree to which a person can retaliate for a harm done to them. It needs to be an immediate response that contributes to stopping an attack, such as shutting down a site that is running a denial of service against us. Retaliation is often not justified in cyberspace because good defense can seek many other goals such as increasing the attacker's required level of effort, confusing them, wasting their time, or frightening them. In fact, harming the attacker often is counterproductive, since harms can be good incentives for them to keep fighting us or to escalate a conflict.

16.2.4 International Law on Cyberattacks

We have pointed out several times that the laws on cyberattacks are different when one country attacks another than when individuals attack one another. Such attacks can constitute a form of "armed aggression", and if broad enough, can be called "cyberwar". The international laws of armed conflict should apply, both the laws about starting a war ("jus ad bellum") and conducting a war ("jus in bello") (Byers 2007). There are many disagreements about applicability of specific laws to cyberwarfare (Ohlin and Govern 2015). Nonetheless, it is generally agreed that wars can take place entirely in cyberspace and there can be aggressors and defenders. Generally, the victim of an attack is allowed to use a wide range of defensive measures. Defensive deception fits in this range. It is almost always a tactic commensurate with attack and thus does not raise issues of proportionality or over-reaction (Gardam 2004). Even if a deception is legal, it still must be a "measured response" proportionate to the attack; Michael et al. (2003) provide some guidelines.

Possible exceptions could be deceptions that involve masquerading as neutral parties, what is known as "perfidy" (Rowe 2013). In traditional warfare, an example of perfidy would be soldiers masquerading as Red Cross workers. It seems unlikely that most of the defensive deceptions proposed here would qualify since most are not identity deceptions, and those that are do not imitate neutral parties, and certainly not for purposes of aggression. But offensive deceptions could definitely be perfidious. For example, inserting a deceptive operating system onto an adversary's computer is like impersonation of neutral software and would be illegal by international law as well as tort law in the victim country.

Another important part of the laws of armed conflict is the admonition to avoid attacks that disproportionately target civilians ("collateral damage"). Defensive deceptions will rarely risk this since their targeting is generally limited to the attacker. But offensive deceptions could definitely hurt third parties. For instance, if a deception convinces a system-administrator victim that a resource shared with the public like a network is malfunctioning, they may shut it down, hurting the public. A defense to responsibility for collateral damage is that the damage was unintended. This can be the case when key information about targets is kept secret. For instance, if an attacking government tries to keep the functions of its network nodes secret from the rest of the world, it cannot complain too much when deceptions or even counterattacks hit them accidentally.

16.3   Conclusions

People tend to assume that all deliberate deceptions are all unethical and illegal, despite the frequent unacknowledged use of deception in many areas of human activity. But actually, few legal issues are raised by defensive deception, and the ethical issues raised are not often serious. Offensive deceptions are another story. We need to be careful how we conduct these since they are a form of aggression and there are many laws controlling aggression.

16.4   Exercises

1. Suppose you have read this book, but decide that these techniques aren't for you. You want to build a cybersystem that never lies to anyone. What problems would you encounter in truly ensuring that it never lies to anyone? How would this affect its usability?

2. Camouflage is often considered ethically neutral. But give some examples where defensive camouflage by the designers of an operating system could raise ethical problems.
3. Suppose you deceive a suspicious user by modifying an executable file they have downloaded to your system, by changing a few bits here and there. Explain how the harm of doing so could propagate to other systems and their functions.
4. A defense to trespassing is that you were invited. How could this be used a valid excuse for offensive deceptions?
5. Does the use of deception make an illegal defense more illegal? Why or why not?
6. You caught a hacker attacking your network, and have taken them to court. Their defense attorney argues that the existence of honeypots on your network is a form of entrapment, since those honeypots are not necessary to operation of your network and are just there to trick innocent people like their client. How would you rebut this argument?

References

ACM/IEEE-CS Joint Task Force on Software Engineering Ethics and Professional Practices (1999) Software engineering code of ethics and professional practice. www.acm.org/service/code.htm. Accessed 15 April 2007

Adar E, Tan D, Teevan J (2013) Benevolent deception in human computer interaction. In: Proceedings of the CHI conference on human factors in computing systems, Paris, France, 27 April–2 May 2013. pp 1863–1872

Artz J (1994) Virtue versus utility: alternative foundations for computer ethics. In: Proceedings of the conference on ethics in the computer age, Gatlinburg, TN. pp 16–21

Belloni A, Berger A, Boissier O, Bonnet G, Bonnet G, Bourgne G, Chardel P-A, Cotton J-P, Evreux N, Ganasscia J-G, Jaillon P, Mermet B, Picard G, Rever B, Simon G, de Swarte T, Tessier C, Vexler F, Voyer R, Zimmerman A (2015) Dealing with ethical conflicts in autonomous agents and multi-agent systems. In: Proceedings of the 2015 AAAI workshop on artificial intelligence and ethics. pp 21–27

Berman P (2002) The globalization of jurisdiction. University of Pennsylvania Law Review 151(2):311–545

Bok S (1978) Lying: moral choice in public and private life. Pantheon, New York

Brey P (2000) Disclosive computer ethics: the exposure and evaluation of embedded normativity in computer technology. Comput Soc 30(4):10–16

Byers M (2007) War law: understanding international law and armed conflict. Grove, New York

Gardam J (2004) Necessity, proportionality, and the use of force by states. Cambridge University Press, Cambridge, UK

Himma K (2004) The ethics of tracing hacker attacks through the machines of innocent persons. Int J Inform Ethics 2(11):1–13

Michael J, Wingfield T, Wijiksera D (2003) Measured responses to cyber attacks using Schmitt analysis: a case study of attack scenarios for a software-intensive system. In: Proceedings of the 27th IEEE computer software and applications conference, Dallas, TX, 3–6 Nov, 2003. pp 622–626

Nyberg D (1993) The varnished truth: truth telling and deceiving in ordinary life. University of Chicago Press, Chicago, IL

Ohlin J, Govern K (eds) (2015) Cyber war: law and ethics for virtual conflicts. Oxford University Press, Oxford, UK

Quinn M (2006) Ethics for the information age. Pearson Addison-Wesley, Boston, MA, US

Ramage S (2009) Fraud investigation: criminal procedure and investigation. iUniverse, Bloomington, IN

Rowe N (2013) Friend or foe? Perfidy in cyberwarfare. In: Allhoff F, Evans N, Henschke A (eds) The Routledge handbook of war and ethics: just war theory in the twenty-first century. Routledge, New York, pp 394–404

Scheibe K (1980) In defense of lying: on the moral neutrality of misrepresentation. Berkshire Rev 15:15–24

Seife C (2015) Virtual unreality: the new era of digital deception. Penguin, New York

Spinello R (2013) Cyberethics: morality and law in cyberspace, 5th edn. Jones and Bartlett, Sudbury, MA

Sztompka P (1999) Trust. Cambridge University Press, London, UK

Chapter Photographs

All photographs were taken by Neil Rowe.

Chapter 1: Yellowstone National Park, Wyoming, US
Chapter 2: Kruger National Park, South Africa
Chapter 3: Mackinac Island, Michigan, US
Chapter 4: San Francisco, California, US
Chapter 5: Kruger National Park, South Africa
Chapter 6: Jungfrau, Switzerland
Chapter 7: Cape Breton Highlands National Park, Nova Scotia, Canada
Chapter 7: Kruger National Park, South Africa
Chapter 9: Ingonish, Nova Scotia, Canada
Chapter 10: Channel Islands National Park, California, US
Chapter 11: Washington, California, US
Chapter 12: Carson Pass, California, US
Chapter 13: Monterey, California, US
Chapter 14: Monterey, California, US
Chapter 15: Moss Landing, California, US
Chapter 16: Thessaloniki, Greece
Appendix A: Grass Valley, California, US
Appendix B: San Rafael, California, US
Appendix C: Monterey, California, US
Appendix D: Las Cruces, New Mexico, US
Appendix E: Palm Springs, California, US

© Springer International Publishing Switzerland 2016
N.C. Rowe, J. Rrushi, *Introduction to Cyberdeception*,
DOI 10.1007/978-3-319-41187-3

Appendix A: Fake Directory Generator

This Java program generates Web pages that look like file directories but are fake. It is written in Java and uses the "servlet" classes to create and display Web pages This requires you set up a Web server and give it access to this code. The program is mentioned first in Sect. 6.4 and also uses ideas described in Chaps. 7 and 9.

This requires four text files, edr.out, hedr.out, edrindex.out and hedrindex.out. Example files (from our school's Web site) are loadable at the book's Web site. The format of edr.out is a set of lines, one for each directory. Each line contains a name of the directory, followed by "||", followed by the names of files and subdirectories each separated by "|". Subdirectories are assumed to be any name without an extension (e.g. ".html"). The format of edrindex.out is one line per line of edr.out, giving the starting number of the character of the line in edr.out, followed by a "|" and the name of the subdirectory on that line in edr.out. For instance, edr.out could begin:

© Springer International Publishing Switzerland 2016
N.C. Rowe, J. Rrushi, *Introduction to Cyberdeception*,
DOI 10.1007/978-3-319-41187-3

```
VisualizingAUVOperations_files||slide0001.htm|v3_slide0009.htm|
v3_slide0018.htm|v3_slide0027.htm|slide0007.htm|slide0009.
htm|slide0018.htm|slide0019.htm|slide0027.htm|slide0003.
htm|slide0012.htm|slide0013.htm|slide0014.htm|slide0025.
htm|~britten||oc4220.html|main.html| prog02||2002DistinguishedSpe
aker.htm|OverallProgram2002.htm|
```

and then edrindex would begin:

```
0|VisualizingAUVOperations_files
239|~britten
273|prog02
```

The file hedr.out is in the form of HTML code describing image-caption pairs, one per line. The format can be any HTML code that will do both the image and the caption, as for example the following. This which gives the image reference using the "img" tag, followed by centered text giving the caption and then a clickable link to the page in which the image was found.

```
<img    src="http://www.nps.navy.mil/PAO/50_Years_Slideshow/    50%20
year%20panels/50%20year%20panel%201.gif"><center>New Page 1</center>
<a href="www.nps.navy.mil/PAO/50_Years_Slideshow/ 50%20year%20panels/
NPShistorypanel1.htm">www.nps.navy.mil/PAO/ 50_Years_Slideshow/50%20
year%20panels/NPShistorypanel1.htm</a><img src="http://www.nps.navy.
mil/PAO/Internal/ships-2.gif">          <center>Alumni in the News</
center><a  href="www.nps.navy.mil/  PAO/Internal/Index_alumni.htm">
www.nps.navy.mil/PAO/Internal/ Index_alumni.htm</a>
```

```
<img src="http://www.nps.navy.mil/nps/images/NPSJournalTiny.gif">
<center>NPS   Journal  -  The   Joint   Vision   of   NPS</center>
<a href="www.nps.navy.mil/nps/pao.htm"> www.nps.navy.mil/nps/pao.
htm</a>
```

File hedrindex.out provides a similar byte-oriented index to this file, e.g.:

```
NPShistorypanel1.htm|0
Index_alumni.htm|305
pao.htm|509
```

The files edr.out and hedr.outs can be created by a wide range of methods. One way is to use a Web crawler to extract directory-subdirectory and image-caption relationships from Web pages.

Here is the program that uses this data.

```
// Servlet that generates a random fake directory structure. */
// Author: Neil C. Rowe
import java.util.*;
import java.io.*;
import java.text.*;
import java.awt.*;
import javax.servlet.*;
import javax.servlet.http.*;
public class NFDir extends HttpServlet {
    /* For probabilities of rules with same left side */
    static double ruleweights[] = new double[10000];
    /* For word index of left side, start of right side in rule-
    terms, */
    /* and end of right side in ruleterms. */
    static int rules[][] = new int[10000][3];
    static int numrules = 0;
    /* For indexes of words on right side of a rule */
    static int ruleterms[] = new int[10000];
    static int numruleterms = 0;
    /* For storing all the words and symbols in the rules */
    static String wordIndex[] = new String[10000];
    static int wordIndexCount = 0;
    static Random R = new Random();
    String Dir [][] = new String[10000][2];
    int nextDirLine = 0;
    HashMap dirhm = new HashMap(1000000);
    HashMap htmlhm = new HashMap(100000);
    int Dirscount = 0;
    int htmlcount = 0;
    long Dirptrs [] = new long[700000];

    // Initialize the servlet by loading main data structures
    public void init () {
      loadGrammar("/work/rowe/myjava/SDirectory.gram");
       /* Change the following file name for your implementation */
      try {FileReader fri = new FileReader("/work/rowe/myjava/
            edrindex.out");
      BufferedReader bri = new BufferedReader(fri);
      String Inputline, Key, SDirptr, Ptr;
      long Dirptr, IPtr;
      int k1, M, htmlcount, IKey;
      while ((Inputline = bri.readLine()) != null) {
```

```
        M = Inputline.length();
        k1 = Inputline.indexOf('|');
        SDirptr = Inputline.substring(0,k1);
        Key = Inputline.substring(k1+1,M);
        /* Put regular directory entries in dirhm */
        if ((Dirscount < 500000) & ((Key.indexOf(".htm")) == -1)) {
            Dirptr = (Long.valueOf(SDirptr)).longValue();
            Dirptrs[Dirscount] = Dirptr;
            dirhm.put(Key, new Integer(Dirscount));
            Dirscount++; } }
    fri.close();
    /* Change this file name for your implementation   */
    FileReader frx = new FileReader("/work/rowe/myjava/hedrin-
    dex.out");
    BufferedReader brx = new BufferedReader(frx);
    htmlcount = 0;
    while (((Inputline = brx.readLine()) != null) & (html-
    count<50000)){
        M = Inputline.length();
        k1 = Inputline.indexOf('|');
        Key = Inputline.substring(0,k1);
        Ptr = Inputline.substring(k1+1,M);
        IPtr = (Long.valueOf(Ptr)).longValue();
        /* Put index pointers to html text entries in htmlhm */
        htmlhm.put(Key, new Long(IPtr));
        htmlcount++; }
    frx.close();
    System.out.println(Dirscount + " directories stored and " +
            htmlcount + " simple HTML pages stored."); }
    catch (IOException e)
    {System.out.println("edrindex.out file could not be read");} }


    /* Create a fake directory listing, store in Dir array, and
display */
  public void doGet(HttpServletRequest request, HttpServletResponse
response)
    throws ServletException, IOException {
    int i, j, k1, k2, RI, RI2, Maxnumrows, Dirdepth, Numnewrows;
    long Dirindex, HTMLPtr;
    Long OHTMLPtr;
    char CI, inchar;
    boolean dupflag;
    double FI, FI2, FI3, Filechoiceprob, Dirchoiceprob;
    String Fulldate, Time, Filesize, Filename, XFilename, Filenames,
        RLine, NSDirflag, ShortDirname, tempstring, OldXFilename,
```

```
        Readchars, Extension, tmpstring;
String tempdir[] = new String[1000];
int Numrows= 0;
/* Open the two data files for random accesses. */
/* Change the file names for your implementation. */
File af = new File("/work/rowe/myjava/edr.out");
RandomAccessFile raf = new RandomAccessFile(af,"r");
File haf = new File("/work/rowe/myjava/hedr.out");
RandomAccessFile hraf = new RandomAccessFile(haf,"r");
String dirchoices[] = new String[10000];
String filechoices[] = new String[10000];
int numdirchoices = 0;
int numfilechoices = 0;
/* Set up servlet response */
response.setContentType("text/html");
PrintWriter pw = response.getWriter();
/* Extract the inputs from the front Web end page, SearchCaps.
html */
String Dirname = request.getParameter("Directory");
String SDirflag = request.getParameter("IsDir");
        System.out.println("doGet called with SDirflag " +
        SDirflag +
                    " and Dirname " + Dirname);
if (SDirflag == null) SDirflag = "14872";
k1 = Dirname.lastIndexOf('/');
if (k1 == -1) ShortDirname = Dirname;
else ShortDirname = Dirname.substring(k1+1,Dirname.length());
/* If this is a file not a directory (IsDir>0), several options
are possible. */
if (!(SDirflag.equals("0"))) {
    k1 = Dirname.indexOf('.');
    if (k1 > -1) Extension = Dirname.substring(k1+1,Dirname.
    length());
    else Extension = "";
    RI = R.nextInt(10);
    /* Deny authorization to all gcc files */
    if (Extension.equals("gcc")) response.sendError(401);
    /* Give authorization errors randomly part of the time */
    else if (RI == 0) response.sendError(403);
    /* For HTML files, display the image-caption code stored in
    the */
    /* hash table (actually, just one image and caption from
    page). */
    elseif((Extension.equals("htm"))|(Extension.equals("html")))
    {
```

```
        if (htmlhm.containsKey(ShortDirname)) {
            OHTMLPtr = (Long) htmlhm.get(ShortDirname);
            HTMLPtr = OHTMLPtr.longValue();
            hraf.seek(HTMLPtr);
            Readchars = hraf.readLine();
            pw.println(Readchars); }
        else {
            response.sendError(403);
            System.out.println(ShortDirname + " missing in hash "
            ); } }
        /* Treat .exe and .bin files as executables that are missing
        software */
        else       if       (Extension.equals("exe"))       response.
        sendError(405);
        else       if       (Extension.equals("bin"))       response.
        sendError(503);
        /* Otherwise, display random characters in Ascii code 0-127
        */
        /* (32-127 for cry, 64-127 for rzp files) but give error if
        file too big */
        else {
        int IFilesize = (Integer.valueOf(SDirflag)).intValue();
        Random R2 = new Random((long)IFilesize);
        {try {Thread.sleep(IFilesize/10);}
        catch (ExceptionExc) {System.out.println("Sleepaborted");}
        }
        if (SDirflag.length() > 6) response.sendError(413);
        else if (Extension.equals("rzp")) {
            for (i=0; i<IFilesize; i++) {
            CI = (char) (64+(R2.nextInt(64)));
            pw.print(CI); } }
        else if (Extension.equals("cry")) {
            for (i=0; i<IFilesize; i++) {
            CI = (char) (32+(R2.nextInt(96)));
            pw.print(CI); } }
        else {
            for (i=0; i<IFilesize; i++) {
                CI = (char) (R2.nextInt(128));
                pw.print(CI); } } } }
/* Otherwise display some directory info */
else {
    int foundloc = -1;
    /* For consistency, check if directory has been displayed
    before, and */
    /* give same info if so. */
```

```
      for (j=0; ((j<nextDirLine)&&(foundloc == -1)); j++)
      if (Dirname.equals(Dir[j][0])) foundloc = j;
      if (foundloc > -1) {
    pw.println("<title>Index of " + Dirname + "</title><br>");
    pw.println("<h1>Index of " + Dirname + "</h1><br>");
    pw.println("<table>");        pw.println("<tr><td><ul>Name</
    td><td>Date</td><td>
        Time</td><td>Size</td></tr></ul><br>");
    pw.println("<hr><br>");
    i = foundloc;
   while ((i<nextDirLine) && ((Dir[i][0]).equals(Dirname))) {
        pw.println(Dir[i][1]);
        i++; }
    pw.println("</table></body></html>"); }
    /* Otherwise generate random directory lines from known
    names. */
    else {
    /* Load the known files and subdirectories of this */
    /* directory, store in arrays dirchoices and filechoices.
    */
    if (dirhm.containsKey(ShortDirname))
    Dirindex  =  Dirptrs[((Integer)dirhm.get(ShortDirname)).
intValue()];
    else Dirindex = Dirptrs[R.nextInt(Dirscount)];
    raf.seek(Dirindex);
    boolean startflag = true;
    Readchars = "";
    Readchars = raf.readLine();
    k1 = Readchars.indexOf('|');
    ShortDirname = Readchars.substring(0,k1);
    Readchars = Readchars.substring(k1+2,Readchars.length());
    k2 = -1;
    k1 = 0;
     while ((k2 = Readchars.indexOf('|',k1)) > -1) {
        tmpstring = Readchars.substring(k1,k2);
        if ((tmpstring.indexOf('.') > -1) &
        (okListing(tmpstring,Dirname,false))) {
         filechoices[numfilechoices] = tmpstring;
         numfilechoices++; }
      else if (okListing(tmpstring,Dirname,true)) {
         dirchoices[numdirchoices] = tmpstring;
         numdirchoices++; }
        k1 = k2+1; }
    Dirdepth = countup(Dirname,'/');
    FI2 = (R.nextInt(1000)/1000.0);
```

```
FI3 = (R.nextInt(1000)/1000.0);
Dirchoiceprob = (0.7*FI2) + (5.0/(3.0+Dirdepth)) - 0.5;
Filechoiceprob = (0.5*FI3) +
(5.0/(3.0+Math.sqrt(Dirdepth))) - 0.15;
/* Choose directories randomly from the possibilities */
for (i=0; i<numdirchoices; i++) {
    FI = (R.nextInt(1000))/1000.0;
    if (FI < Dirchoiceprob) {
        NSDirflag = "0";
        Filesize = "&lt;DIR&gt;";
        Filename = fixSpecialChars(dirchoices[i]);
        add_dir_line(tempdir,Dirname,Filesize,Filename,
NSDirflag,Numrows);
        Numrows++; } }
/* If too few directories, pick randomly from the hash table
*/
if (Numrows == 0) {
    Numnewrows = (int)(R.nextInt(10)/Dirdepth);
    System.out.println("Numnewrows " + Numnewrows);
    for (i=0; i<Numnewrows; i++) {
    Filesize = "&lt;DIR&gt;";
    Filename = "";
    while (Filename.equals("")) {
        Dirindex = Dirptrs[R.nextInt(Dirscount)];
        raf.seek(Dirindex);
        Readchars = "";
        while ((inchar = (char)raf.read()) != '|')
        Readchars = Readchars + inchar;
        Filename = Readchars; }
    NSDirflag = "0";
    if (okListing(Filename,Dirname,true))
add_dir_line(tempdir,Dirname,Filesize,
Filename,NSDirflag,Numrows);
    Numrows++; } }
/* Choose files randomly from the possibilities */
for (i=0; i<numfilechoices; i++) {
    FI = (R.nextInt(1000))/1000.0;
    if (FI < Filechoiceprob) {
    Filename = fixSpecialChars(filechoices[i]);
    if ((Filename.indexOf(".htm")) > -1)
        Filesize = generateString("htmlfilesize");
    else Filesize = generateString("shortfilesize");
    NSDirflag = Filesize;
add_dir_line(tempdir,Dirname,Filesize,
Filename,NSDirflag,Numrows);
```

```
                    Numrows++; } }
        /* Add a few random files to the directory */
        Numnewrows = 1+(int)(R.nextInt(10)/Dirdepth);
        System.out.println("Numnewrows " + Numnewrows);
        for (i=0; i<Numnewrows; i++) {
            Filesize = generateString("shortfilesize");
            Dirindex = Dirptrs[R.nextInt(Dirscount)];
            raf.seek(Dirindex);
            Readchars = "";
            while ((inchar = (char)raf.read()) != '|')
            Readchars = Readchars + inchar;
            Filename = Readchars + generateString("extension");
            NSDirflag = Filesize;
    add_dir_line(tempdir,Dirname,Filesize,Filename,
NSDirflag,Numrows);
            Numrows++; }
    /* Sort the random directory lines by file name; create dynamic
    */
    /* Web page for them, then delete header on front used for
    sorting */
    Arrays.sort(tempdir,0,Numrows);
    pw.println("<title>Index of " + Dirname + "</title><br>");
    pw.println("<h1>Index of " + Dirname + "</h1><br>");
    pw.println("<table>");                                    pw.
    print("<tr><td><ul>Name</td><td>Date</td><td>");
    pw.println("Time</td><td>Size</td></tr></ul><br>");
    pw.println("<hr><br>");
    for (i=0; i<Numrows; i++) {
            pw.println(tempdir[i]);
            Dir[nextDirLine][0] = Dirname;
            Dir[nextDirLine][1] = tempdir[i];
            if (nextDirLine < 10000) nextDirLine++; }
    pw.println("</table></body></html>"); } }
    pw.close();
    raf.close();
    hraf.close();
    /* Store session data in "nfdirscript.out" for later analysis
    */
    Date date = new Date();
    String sessiondata = date + " " + Dirname + "\n";
    byte buffer[] = sessiondata.getBytes();
    OutputStream so = new FileOutputStream("nfdirscript.out",
    true);
    for (j=0; j<buffer.length; j++) so.write(buffer[j]);
    so.close();   }
```

```
    /* Treat POST requests just like GET requests */
  public void doPost(HttpServletRequest request, HttpServletResponse
response)
    throws ServletException, IOException {
    doGet(request,response); }


    // String generator from a context-free grammar using random
    choices.
    // Grammar in the form of <prob> <sym> = <sym1> <sym2> …
    // where everything is separated by spaces, <prob> is a decimal
    number,
    // and <sym>s are any alphanumeric strings.
    // The <prob> represents the likelihood of choosing that rule
    among all
    // rules with the same left side (and these are automatically
    normalized).
    // A linefeed should terminate each grammar rule (and no
    linefeeds
    // are allowed within the rule).
    // The only special symbols allowed on right side are " around
    strings,
    // ~ to denote spaces, and $ to denote linefeeds.


    /* Initialize the data structures with grammar loaded from a
    file */
    static void loadGrammar (String Infile) {
    String Inputline, Word;
    int i, j;
    try {
        FileReader fr = new FileReader(Infile);
        BufferedReader br = new BufferedReader(fr);
        while ((Inputline = br.readLine()) != null) {
        StringTokenizer st = new StringTokenizer(Inputline,"
        \t\n");
        /* Store an individual grammar rule in the rules array */
        if (st.hasMoreTokens()) {
            Word = st.nextToken();
            while (Word.length()==0) Word = st.nextToken();
            ruleweights[numrules] =
(Double.valueOf(Word)).doubleValue();
            if (st.hasMoreTokens()) {
            Word = st.nextToken();
            while (Word.length()==0) Word = st.nextToken();
            rules[numrules][0] = lookupWordIndex(Word);
```

```
                    rules[numrules][1] = numruleterms;
                    if (st.hasMoreTokens()) {
                        Word = st.nextToken();
                        while (Word.length()==0) Word = st.nextToken();
                        if (Word.equals("=")) {
                        while (st.hasMoreTokens()) {
                            Word = st.nextToken();
                            while (Word.length()==0)
Word = st.nextToken();
                            /* Assemble quoted strings */
                            if (Word.charAt(0)=='"')
                            while ((st.hasMoreTokens()) &&
                                    (Word.indexOf('"',1)!=
            (Word.length()-1)) )
Word = Word +
" " + st.nextToken();
                            ruleterms[numruleterms] =
lookupWordIndex(Word);
                            numruleterms++; }
                        rules[numrules][2] = numruleterms-1;
                        numrules++;  } } } } }
        fr.close(); }
    catch (IOException e) {System.out.println("Grammar reading
error");}
    /* Normalize weights for same left side, assuming rules con-
tiguous */
    int lastleft = rules[0][0];
    int lastleftindex = 0;
    double totalprob = ruleweights[0];
    for (i=1; i<numrules; i++) {
        if (rules[i][0] != lastleft) {
        for (j=lastleftindex; j<i; j++)
            ruleweights[j] = ruleweights[j]/totalprob;
        totalprob = 0.0;
        lastleft = rules[i][0];
        lastleftindex = i; }
        totalprob = totalprob + ruleweights[i]; }
    for (j=lastleftindex; j<i; j++)
        ruleweights[j] = ruleweights[j]/totalprob; }

    /* Find index of Word in wordIndex if there, else fill next empty
    entry */
    static int lookupWordIndex (String Word) {
    int j = 0;
    String XWord = removequotes(Word);
```

```
    while ((j<wordIndexCount) && (!wordIndex[j].equals(XWord)))
    j++;
    if (j==wordIndexCount) {
        wordIndex[j] = XWord;
        wordIndexCount++; }
    return j; }


    /* Generates a random string using the grammar and its proba-
    bilities */
    static String generateString (String Sym) {
    int i;
    String XSym = removequotes(Sym);
    for (i=0; ((i<wordIndexCount)&&(!wordIndex[i].equals(XSym)));
    i++)
{};
    if (i==wordIndexCount) {
        System.out.println("Starting symbol " + Sym + " not
        recognized.");
        return ""; }
    else    return    ((generateStringRec(i)).replace('~',' ')).
    replace('$','\n'); }


    /* Recursively generate a string starting from a given leftside
    index */
    static String generateStringRec (int index) {
    double rand;
    int i;
    for (i=0; ((i<numrules)&&(rules[i][0]!=index)); i++) {};
    if (i==numrules) return wordIndex[index];
    else {
        rand = R.nextDouble()-0.00001;
        while (rand > ruleweights[i]) {
        rand = rand-ruleweights[i];
        i++; }
        return generateStringRecList(i); } }


    /* Generate a string for a given rightside index */
    static String generateStringRecList (int index) {
    String Out = "";
    for (int i=rules[index][1]; i<=rules[index][2]; i++) {
        Out = Out + generateStringRec(ruleterms[i]); }
    return Out; }



    /* Run some checks on proposed file and directory names to rule
    */
    /*out strangeness */
```

```
static boolean okListing(String Filename, String Dirname, bool-
ean isDir) {
int N = Filename.length();
if (N == 0) return false;
String XFilename = "/" + Filename;
if (Dirname.indexOf(XFilename) > -1) return false;
if (Filename.indexOf(".org") == (N-4)) return false;
if (isDir) {
    if (Dirname.indexOf("_files") == (N-6)) return false;
    if (Dirname.indexOf("_images") == (N-7)) return false; }
if (!isDir) {
    if (Filename.charAt(0) == '~') return false; }
return true; }


/* Substitute for the reserved characters of HTML and make
table row */
static String fixSpecialChars (String In) {
String Out = In;
int i;
while ((i=(Out.indexOf('<'))) > -1)
    Out = Out.substring(0,i) + "&lt;" + Out.substring(i+1,Out.
    length());
while ((i=(Out.indexOf('>'))) > -1)
    Out = Out.substring(0,i) + "&gt;" + Out.substring(i+1,Out.
    length());
while ((i=(Out.indexOf('&'))) > -1)
    Out = Out.substring(0,i) + "&" + Out.substring(i+1,Out.
    length());
while ((i=(Out.indexOf('"'))) > -1)
    Out = Out.substring(0,i) + "&quot;" + Out.substring(i+1,Out.
    length());
while ((i=(Out.indexOf(' '))) > -1)
    Out = Out.substring(0,i) + " " + Out.substring(i+1,Out.
    length());
return Out; }


/* Removes quotation marks around a string before storage */
static String removequotes (String In) {
String Out = In;
if ((In.charAt(0)=='"')&(In.charAt(In.length()-1)=='"'))
    Out = In.substring(1,In.length()-1);
return Out; }


/* Given list of options separate by bar symbols, picks a ran-
dom one */
static String randomFileChoice (String In) {
```

```
    String Out, Choice;
    int N = 0;
    int i, RI, k, k2;
    String choices [] = new String[1000];
    int numchoices = 0;
    i=0;
    k2 = 0;
    while (((k = In.indexOf('|',k2)) > -1) & (numchoices < 1000)) {
        Choice = In.substring(k2,k);
        if (Choice.indexOf('.') > -1) {
        choices[numchoices] = Choice;
        numchoices++; }
        k2 = k+1; }
    k2 = 0;
    if (numchoices == 0) {
        while (((k = In.indexOf('|',k2)) > -1) & (numchoices <
        1000)) {
        choices[numchoices] = In.substring(k2,k) + ".dcc";
        numchoices++; }
        k2 = k+1; }
    if (numchoices == 0) Out = generateString("filename");
    else {
        RI = R.nextInt(numchoices);
        Out = choices[RI]; }
    return Out; }

    /* Counts the number of occurrences of a symbol in a string */
    static int countup (String In, char C) {
    int k = 0;
    int N = In.length();
    for (int i=0; i<N; i++) if ((In.charAt(i)) == C) k++;
    return k; }

    static void add_dir_line(String tempdir[], String Dirname,
    String Filesize,
                String Filename, String NSDirflag, int Numrows) {
    String Fulldate, Time, XFilename, RLine;
    Fulldate = generateString("fulldate");
    Time = generateString("time");
    XFilename = "<a  href=\"http://triton.cs.nps.navy.mil:8080/
    servlet"
        + "/rowe.NFDir?Directory=\"" + Dirname + "/" + Filename
        + "\"&IsDir=" + NSDirflag + "\">" + Filename + "</a>";
    RLine = "<tr><td>" + XFilename + "</td><td>" + Fulldate +
            "</td><td>" + Time + "</td><td>" + Filesize + "</td></tr>";
    tempdir[Numrows] = RLine; }
}
```

Appendix B: Stochastic String Generator

This Java program generates random strings according to a context-free grammar with rule probabilities, as described in *Sect.* 7.2. This program is written in the language Java. It is run from the command line; you start a command window and type in "java CFGen" followed by a space and the name of your grammar-defining file. Currently it generates 10 example strings; change the assignment to "numstrings" if you want to modify this. Further details are provided in the comments.

```
// String generator from a context-free grammar using random
choices.
// Grammar in the form of <prob> <sym> = <sym1> <sym2> ...
// where everything is separated by spaces, <prob> is a decimal
number,
// and <sym>s are any alphanumeric strings.
// The <prob> represents the likelihood of choosing that rule among
all
```

© Springer International Publishing Switzerland 2016
N.C. Rowe, J. Rrushi, *Introduction to Cyberdeception*,
DOI 10.1007/978-3-319-41187-3

```
// rules with the same left side (and these are automatically
normalized
// to sum to 1). A carriage return should terminate each grammar
rule
// (and no carriage returns are allowed within the rule).
// The only special symbols allowed on right side are double quotes
// around strings, ~ to denote spaces, and $ to denote carriage
returns.
// The top-level grammar symbol must be "start".
// Author: Neil C. Rowe.

import java.io.*;
import java.util.*;
import java.text.*;


class CFGen {
  /* For probabilities of rules with same left side */
  static double ruleweights[] = new double[10000];
  /* For word index of left side, start of right side in ruleterms,
  */
  /* and end of right side in ruleterms. */
  static int rules[][] = new int[10000][3];
  static int numrules = 0;
  /* For indexes of words on right side of a rule */
  static int ruleterms[] = new int[10000];
  static int numruleterms = 0;
  /* For storing all the words and symbols in the rules */
  static String wordIndex[] = new String[10000];
  static int wordIndexCount = 0;
  static Random R = new Random();


  public static void main (String args[]) throws IOException {
    String Out;
    loadGrammar(args[0]);
    int numstrings = 10;
    for (int i=0; i<numstrings; i++) {
      Out = generateString("start");
      System.out.println(Out); } }


  /* Initialize the data structures with grammar loaded from a file */
  static void loadGrammar (String Infile) throws IOException {
    String Inputline, Word;
    int i, j;
```

```
FileReader fr = new FileReader(Infile);
BufferedReader br = new BufferedReader(fr);
while ((Inputline = br.readLine()) != null) {
  StringTokenizer st = new StringTokenizer(Inputline," \t\n");
   /* Store an individual grammar rule in the rules array */
   if (st.hasMoreTokens()) {
Word = st.nextToken();
while (Word.length()==0) Word = st.nextToken();
ruleweights[numrules] = (Double.valueOf(Word)).doubleValue();
if (st.hasMoreTokens()) {
  Word = st.nextToken();
  while (Word.length()==0) Word = st.nextToken();
  rules[numrules][0] = lookupWordIndex(Word);
  rules[numrules][1] = numruleterms;
  if (st.hasMoreTokens()) {
    Word = st.nextToken();
    while (Word.length()==0) Word = st.nextToken();
    if (Word.equals("=")) {
      while (st.hasMoreTokens()) {
    Word = st.nextToken();
    while (Word.length()==0) Word = st.nextToken();
    /* Assemble quoted strings */
    if (Word.charAt(0)=='"')
      while ((st.hasMoreTokens()) &&
        (Word.indexOf('"',1)!=(Word.length()-1)) )
        Word = Word + " " + st.nextToken();
    ruleterms[numruleterms] = lookupWordIndex(Word);
    numruleterms++; }
      rules[numrules][2] = numruleterms-1;
      numrules++;  } } } } }
for (i=0; i<numrules; i++)
   /* Normalize weights for same left side, assuming rules
   contiguous */
   int lastleft = rules[0][0];
   int lastleftindex = 0;
   double totalprob = ruleweights[0];
   for (i=1; i<numrules; i++) {
   if (rules[i][0] != lastleft) {
for (j=lastleftindex; j<i; j++)
  ruleweights[j] = ruleweights[j]/totalprob;
totalprob = 0.0;
lastleft = rules[i][0];
lastleftindex = i; }
  totalprob = totalprob + ruleweights[i]; }
for (j=lastleftindex; j<i; j++)
  ruleweights[j] = ruleweights[j]/totalprob;
}
```

```
/* Finds index of Word in wordIndex if there, else fill next empty
entry */
static int lookupWordIndex (String Word) {
  int j = 0;
  String XWord = removequotes(Word);
  while ((j<wordIndexCount) && (!wordIndex[j].equals(XWord)))
  j++;
  if (j==wordIndexCount) {
    wordIndex[j] = XWord;
    wordIndexCount++; }
  return j; }



/* Generates a random string using the grammar and its probabili-
ties */
static String generateString (String Sym) {
  int i;
  String XSym = removequotes(Sym);
  for (i=0; ((i<wordIndexCount)&&(!wordIndex[i].equals(XSym))));
  i++) {};
  if (i==wordIndexCount) {
    System.out.println("Starting symbol not recognized.");
    return ""; }
  else    return    ((generateStringRec(i)).replace('~',' ')).
  replace('$','\n'); }



/* Recursively generate a string starting from a given leftside
index */
static String generateStringRec (int index) {
  double rand;
  int i;
  /* System.out.println("Generating string for " + index); */
  for (i=0; ((i<numrules)&&(rules[i][0]!=index)); i++) {};
  if (i==numrules) return wordIndex[index];
  else {
    rand = R.nextDouble()-0.00001;
    while (rand > ruleweights[i]) {
    rand = rand-ruleweights[i];
    i++; }
    return generateStringRecList(i); } }
```

```
/* Generate a string for a given rightside index */
static String generateStringRecList (int index) {
  String Out = "";
  for (int i=rules[index][1]; i<=rules[index][2]; i++) {
    Out = Out + generateStringRec(ruleterms[i]); }
  return Out; }


/* Removes quotation marks around a string before storage */
static String removequotes (String In) {
  String Out = In;
  if ((In.charAt(0)=='"')&(In.charAt(In.length()-1)=='"'))
    Out = In.substring(1,In.length()-1);
  return Out; } }
```

Here is an example grammar file that can be run with this program.

```
0.4 start = "Fatal error at" ~ bignumber ":" ~ errortype
0.3 start = "Error at" ~ bignumber ":" ~ errortype
0.3 start = "Port error at" ~ bignumber ":" ~ errortype
0.5 bignumber = digit digit digit digit digit digit digit digit
digit
0.5 bignumber = digit digit digit digit digit digit digit digit
0.5 bignumber = digit digit digit digit digit digit digit
0.1 digit = 0
0.1 digit = 1
0.1 digit = 2
0.1 digit = 3
0.1 digit = 4
0.1 digit = 5
0.1 digit = 6
0.1 digit = 7
0.1 digit = 8
0.1 digit = 9
1.0 errortype = "Segmentation fault"
1.0 errortype = "Illegal type coercion"
1.0 errortype = "Syntax error"
1.0 errortype = "Attempt to access protected memory"
1.0 errortype = "Process limit reached"
1.0 errortype = "Not enough main memory"
1.0 errortype = "Stack inconsistent"
1.0 errortype = "Attempted privilege escalation"
```

Appendix C: Resource-Deception Consistency Checker

This Prolog program suggests possible deceptions in a sequence of operating-system commands as discussed in Sect. 9.3. Part 1 takes a list of commands in a text file, one per line, and puts them into a list; it requires the "goruns.pl" file created by the progrma in Appendix D or by some similar program. Part 2 analyzes this list and produces a set of possible deceptions that will not violate consistency of resources status. This requires a "ld1.outl" file created either manually or by the program in Appendix D, that specifies the plan followed by the attacker in the form of a

© Springer International Publishing Switzerland 2016
N.C. Rowe, J. Rrushi, *Introduction to Cyberdeception*,
DOI 10.1007/978-3-319-41187-3

*bracketed list and using Prolog predicate notation for the actions. Type "p1" to the
Prolog interpreter to run part 1, and p2 to run part 2.*

```
   /* PART 1 */
/* Author: Neil C. Rowe, 3/07. */
/* Find resources requirement for a command sequence. */
p1 :- run_conclusions.
run_conclusions :- open('goruns.pl',read,SR), read(SR,_),
  open('ld1.out',write,SW), run_conclusions2(SR,SW,1), close(SR),
close(SW).
run_conclusions2(SR,SW,K) :- get_commands(SR,XCommands,TGCL),
  make_last_command_first(XCommands,Commands),
 \+length(Commands,0),write(SW,c(K,Commands,TGCL)),write(SW,'.'),
 nl(SW), Kp1 is K+1, !, run_conclusions2(SR,SW,Kp1).
run_conclusions2(_,_,_).
get_commands(SR,Commands,TGCL) :- read(SR,PE),
  ((PE=end_of_file, Commands = [], TGCL=[]);
   (PE=run(_), Commands=[], TGCL=[]);

( P E = s ( _ , C o m m a n d , _ , _ , S t a t e 1 , S t a t e 2 ) ,
get_commands(SR,Commands2,TGCL2),
    Commands=[Command|Commands2],
 ((goal_condition_achieved(Command,State1,State2),
 TGCL=[Command|TGCL2]); TGCL=TGCL2) );
(write('Command not recognized: '), write(PE), nl, Commands=[],
TGCL=[]) ), !.
/* Routine to check if a transition between a pair of states
achieves top-level */
/* goals, since that's a reason to avoid doing deception for it
(too obvious). */
goal_condition_achieved(_,State1,State2) :-
   deleteitems(State1,State2,APL),      deleteitems(State2,State1,
   DPL),
   goal(hacker,GL), member(G,GL),
   (member(G,APL); (G=not(NG), member(NG,DPL));
    (G=reported(PE), member(PE,APL));
    (G=reported(not(PE)), member(PE,DPL));
    (G=reported(PE,_,_), member(PE,APL));
    (G=reported(not(PE),_,_), member(PE,DPL)) ), !.
make_last_command_first(XCommands,Commands) :-
   append(XCommands1,[F],XCommands),
   append([F],XCommands1,Commands), !.
```

```
/* PART 2 */
/* Find deceptions logically consistent at each step in a command
*/
/* sequence; uses boolean suspiciousness to rule out deception. */


p2 :- p2('ld1.out').
p2(Infile) :- consult(Infile),
  open('ld2.out',write,SW), p2b(SW), close(SW),
  consult('ld2.out'),open('ld2b.out',write,SW2),pq(SW2),
  close(SW2).
p2b(_) :- abolish(df/3), c(_,FullCommands,Topgoalcommands),
    first_suspicious_command(FullCommands,FirstSusp),
    append(PrevCommands,[Command|_],FullCommands),
    member(FirstSusp,[Command|PrevCommands]),
    \+ member(Command,Topgoalcommands),
    previously_created_resources(PrevCommands,CRL),
    setof(D,possible_deception_p2(PrevCommands,Command,CRL,D)
    ,DL),
    member(Decep,DL),
    resfailprob(Decep,Command,[Command|PrevCommands],PD),
    assertz(df(Command,Decep,PD)), fail.
p2b(SW) :- bagof(PD,df(Command,Decep,PD),PDL), mean(PDL,APD),
    write(d(Command,Decep,APD)),
    write('.'), nl,
    write(SW,d(Command,Decep,APD)), write(SW,'.'), nl(SW), fail.
p2b(_).
p2bonce(_) :- abolish(df/3), c_once(FullCommands,Topgoalcomma
nds),
    first_suspicious_command(FullCommands,FirstSusp),
    append(PrevCommands,[Command|_],FullCommands),
    member(FirstSusp,[Command|PrevCommands]),
    \+ member(Command,Topgoalcommands),
    previously_created_resources(PrevCommands,CRL),
    setof(D,possible_deception_p2(PrevCommands,Command,CRL,D)
    ,DL),
    member(Decep,DL), resfailprob(Decep,Command,[Command|PrevComm
    ands],PD),
    assertz(df(Command,Decep,PD)), fail.
p2bonce(SW) :- bagof(PD,df(Command,Decep,PD),PDL), mean(PDL,APD),
    write(d(Command,Decep,APD)), write('.'), nl,
    write(SW,d(Command,Decep,APD)), write(SW,'.'), nl(SW), fail.
p2bonce(_).
c_once(RC,TGC) :- c(RC,TGC), !.
```

```
pq(SW) :-bagof(P,C^D^d(C,D,P),XPL), sort(XPL,RPL), reverse(RPL,PL),
member(PD,PL), d(Command,Decep,PD), realize(SW,Command,Decep,PD),
fail.
pq(_).
first_suspicious_command([C|_],C) :- suspicious_command(C), !.
first_suspicious_command([_|CL],C) :-first_suspicious_command(CL,C).


/* Main subroutine enumerating possible deceptions at a command */
possible_deception_p2(PrevCommands,Command,CRL,PE) :-
  Command =.. [_|_],
  resources(Command,RL), member(R,RL), \+ unchangeable(R),
  \+ previously_used_resource(PrevCommands,R),
  possible_deception_type(R,RL,CRL,Command,PE).
possible_deception_type(R,_,CRL,Command,exists(R))              :-
member(R,CRL),
  \+ resource_created_by(Command, R).
possible_deception_type(R,_,_,_,authorized(R)).
possible_deception_type(R,_,_,_,password(R)).
possible_deception_type(R,_,_,_,working(R)).
possible_deception_type(executable(R),_,_,_,terminates(executabl
e(R))).
possible_deception_type(R,_,CRL,Command,initialized(R,Command)) :-
  member(R,CRL).
/* Define incompatibility of resources using a problem-dependent
definition,*/
/* but also exclude resources that are created by the command. */
possible_deception_type(R,RL,CRL,Command,compatible(R,R2)) :-
  \+     resource_created_by(Command,R),     append(_,[R|R2L],RL),
  member(R2,R2L),
  \+ incompatible_pe(R,R2), \+ incompatible_pe(R2,R),
  \+ resource_created_by(Command,R2).
possible_deception_type(R,RL,CRL,Command,max(R,Type,M)) :-
  find_resource_max(R,Command,Type,M).
/* We deceive only on resources that haven't been successfully used
before; */
/* note this excludes resources that appear only as outputs of com-
mands. */
previously_used_resource(PrevCommands,R) :- member(Command,
PrevCommands),
  resource3(Command,RL,_), member(R,RL), !.
previously_created_resources(Commands,CRL) :-
  nice_setof(CR,previously_created(Commands,CR),CRL).
previously_created(Commands,CR)          :-          member(C,Commands),
resource3(C,_,CRL2),
```

```
member(CR,CRL2).


/* Enumerate all possible resources */
resources(Op,RL) :- setof(R,resource2(Op,R),RL), !.
resources(Op,[]) :- write('Could not find any resources for '),
write(Op),
   nl, !.
resource2(Op,R) :- resource3(Op,RL,_), member(R,RL).
/* Executables for system commands are resources too */
r e s o u r c e 2 ( O p , e x e c u t a b l e ( O ) )
:- Op=..[O|_], nonsystem_commands(NCL),
   \+ member(O,NCL), !.
/* Allow for optional extra (agent) argument in resource facts */
resource3(Op,RL,NL) :- resource(Op,RL,NL).
resource3(Op,RL,NL) :- \+ resource(Op,RL,_), Op=..[Pred|AL],
   XOp=..[Pred,_|AL], resource(XOp,RL,NL).


/* Problem-dependent definitions of resources and their properties
*/
/* First arg is name of command (with first arg generally the
agent); */
/* second arg is list of resources; third arg is list of resources
*/
/* specifically created by this command. */
resource(ping(_,N),[network(N)],[]).
resource(scan(_,hacker,sites),[network(homenetwork)],[]).
resource(scan_for_vulnerability(S),RL,CL) :-
   resource(scan_for_vulnerability(user,S,_),RL,CL).
resource(scan_for_vulnerability(_,S,N),
   [site(S),network_of(S,N),network(N)],[]).
resource(connect_at_port(_,T,S),

[port(T),site(S),network(N),network_of(S,N),open(T)],[open(T)]).
resource(overflow(buffer,T,S),
   [buffer(T),buffer_of(S,T),port(T),system(S)],[]).
resource(get(P,C,status,S),
   [status(P,S,C),system(S)],[status(P,S,C)]).
resource(close_port(P,T,S),RL,CL) :- resource(close(P,T,S),RL,CL).
resource(close(_,T,S),[port(T),site(S),network(_)],[]).
resource(login(P,S),RL,CL) :- resource(login(P,S,_),RL,CL).
resource(login(P,S,F),[site(S),file_system(S,F),logged_in(P,S)],
   [logged_in(P,S)]).
resource(ftp(P,S1,S2),
   [site(S1),site(S2),network(N),network_of(S1,N),
```

```
          network_of(S2,N),logged_in(P,S1)],[]).
resource(download(P,F,S1,S2),
   [site(S1),site(S2),file(F),located_at(F,S2),

network(N),network_of(S1,N),network_of(S2,N),logged_
in(P,S1)],[file(F)]).
resource(close_ftp(_,S1,S2),
   [site(S1),site(S2),network(N),network_of(S1,N),
    network_of(S2,N)],[]).
resource(decompress(P,F,S),
   [file(F),logged_in(P,S),site(S),located_at(F,S),uncompressed(F)]
   ,[file(F)]).
resource(install(_,F,S),[file(F),site(S),located_at(F,S)],[]).
resource(test(_,F,S),[file(F),located_at(F,home),
     installed(F,S)],[installed(F,S)]).
resource(logout(P,S),[site(S),logged_in(P,S)],[]).
resource(cd(P,D,S),
   [site(S),logged_in(P,S),file_system(S),directory_of(D,FS)],[]).
resource(edit(P,F,S),
   [site(S),logged_in(P,S),file_system(S),file_of(F,S)],[]).


/* Miscellaneous problem-dependent specifications */
incompatible_pe(R,R2) :- R=executable(_),
     (R2=site(_); R2=network(_); R2=file_system(_); R2=buffer(_)).
nonsystem_commands([ping,scan,scan_for_vulnerability,
connect_at_port,overflow, get,close_port,close]).
complex_resource_pred(Pred) :- member(Pred,[logged_in,status,file_
system]).
unchangeable(R) :- R=..[Pred|_],
member(Pred,[file_of,directory_of,network_of,located_at,password_
of]).
find_resource_max(site(_),_,users,15).
find_resource_max(file(_),_,size,100000).
find_resource_max(file_system(_,_),_,size,500000).
find_resource_max(file_system(_,_),_,users,100).
find_resource_max(network(_),_,bandwidth,100000).
find_resource_max(network(_),_,users,64).
find_resource_max(port(_),_,users,1).
find_resource_max(password(_,_),_,usage,100).
find_resource_max(logged_in(_,_),_,count,6).


resfailprob(C,Op,PrevCommands,P) :- C=..[Facet|Args],
     facetfailprob(Facet,P1), O1 is P1/(1-P1),
     (resourcefailodds(Args,O2); O2 is 1.0), !,
```

```
        ((suspicious_command(Op),  O3 is 0.3); O3 is 1.0),
      ((created_resource(C,PrevCommands,Dist), O4 is 25.0/(Dist+15));
         O4 is 1.0 ),
      write('orcombine    of    '),    write(C),    write(':    '),
      write([O1,O2,O2,O3]), nl,
      NO is O1*O2*O3*O4, P is NO/(1+NO), !.
facetfailprob(exists,0.05).
facetfailprob(authorized,0.15).
facetfailprob(password,0.1).
facetfailprob(initialized,0.1).
facetfailprob(working,0.16).
facetfailprob(terminates,0.07).
facetfailprob(compatible,0.09).
facetfailprob(max,0.13).
resourcefailodds([logged_in(_,_)],1.0).
resourcefailodds([status(_,_,_)],1.5).
resourcefailodds([executable(_)],0.5).
resourcefailodds([file(rootkit)],3.0).
resourcefailodds([site(_)],2.0).
resourcefailodds([R1,R2],P) :- resourcefailodds([R1],P1),
   resourcefailodds([R2],P2), P is sqrt(P1*P2).
resourcefailodds([_,users,_],2.0).
resourcefailodds([_,size,_],2.0).
resourcefailodds(RL,1.0).
/* Commands suspicious a priori */
suspicious_command(overflow(_,_,_)).
/* Commands suspicious because they relate to major attack goals
*/
suspicious_command(install(_,rootkit,_)).
suspicious_command(test(_,rootkit,_)).
created_resource(C,PrevCommands,Dist) :- C=..[_|AL], member(R,AL),
   append(_,[Op|PC2],PrevCommands),           resource3(Op,_,CRL),
   member(R,CRL),
   length(PC2,Dist), !.


realize(SW,C,D,P)  :-  realize2(SW,C,D),  write(SW,'. [weight  '),
write(SW,P),
   write(SW,']'), nl(SW).
realize2(SW,C,exists(X))  :- writeheader(SW,C),  write(SW,'Lie by
saying '),
   write(SW,X), write(SW,' does not exist').
realize2(SW,C,authorized(X)) :- writeheader(SW,C),
   write(SW,'Lie by saying the user is not authorized for '),
```

```
    write(SW,X).
realize2(SW,C,authorized(X)) :- writeheader(SW,C),
    write(SW,'Lie by saying credentials cannot be confirmed for '),
    write(SW,X).
realize2(SW,C,password(X)) :- writeheader(SW,C),
    write(SW,'Ask the user for a password to enable use of '),
    write(SW,X),
    write(SW,', then claim it is invalid').
realize2(SW,C,initialized(X,_)) :- writeheader(SW,C),
    write(SW,'Falsely claim that '), write(SW,X),
    write(SW,' is not initialized').
realize2(SW,C,working(X)) :- writeheader(SW,C),
    write(SW,'Abort execution of ' ), write(SW,X),
    write(SW,' with an error message').
realize2(SW,C,terminates(X)) :- writeheader(SW,C),
    write(SW,'Execution of '), write(SW,X), write(SW,' never ends').
realize2(SW,C,compatible(X,Y)) :- writeheader(SW,C),
    write(SW,'Falsely claim that '), write(SW,X), write(SW,' and '),
    write(SW,Y), write(SW,' are incompatible').
realize2(SW,C,max(R,Prop,Value)) :- writeheader(SW,C),
    write(SW,'Falsely claim that '), write(SW,R), write(SW,' exceeds
    maximum '),
    write(SW,Prop), write(SW,' by having value '), write(SW,Value).
writeheader(SW,C)   :-  write(SW,'For  command  '),  write(SW,C),
    write(SW,': ').


/* Utility functions */
appendall([],[]).
appendall([SL|SLL],L) :- appendall(SLL,L2), append(SL,L2,L).
/* mydelete(Item,L,NL) :- member(Item,L), !, delete(L,Item,NL).
mydelete(_,L,L).
union([],L,L).
union([X|L],L2,L3) :- member(X,L2), !, union(L,L2,L3).
union([X|L],L2,[X|L3]) :- union(L,L2,L3).
unionall([L],L).
unionall([L1,L2|LL],NL)        :-        union(L1,L2,L12),         !,
unionall([L12|LL],NL).
sumup([X],X) :- !.
sumup([X|L],S) :- sumup(L,S2), S is S2+X, !. */
mean(L,M) :- sumup(L,S), length(L,N), M is S/N, !.
```

The "ld1.out" files holds a possible sequence of commands in Prolog's predicate-arguments notation, corresponding to the names of the commands in the application file. Here is an example of a file created by part 1.

```
c(1, [order(not(connected_at_port(port80, patsy))),
report(not(connected_at_port(port80, patsy))),
report(not(ftp_connection(hackerhome, patsy))),
scan(hacker, sites),
order(not(compressed(secureport, patsy))),
report(not(compressed(secureport, patsy))),
order(not(logged_in(admin, patsy))),
report(not(logged_in(admin,          patsy))),          connect_at_
port(port80,patsy),
order(not(compressed(rootkit,patsy))),
report(not(compressed(rootkit,patsy))),
overflow(buffer,port80,patsy),
report(overflowed(buffer,port80,patsy)),
order(status(admin,patsy)),
get(admin,status,patsy),report(status(admin,patsy)),
order(not(connected_at_port(port80,patsy))),
close_port(port80,patsy),
report(not(connected_at_port(port80,patsy))),
order(logged_in(admin,patsy)),login(admin,patsy),
report(logged_in(admin,patsy)),
order(ftp_connection(hackerhome,patsy))
,ftp(hackerhome,patsy),
report(ftp_connection(hackerhome,patsy)),
order(file(rootkit,patsy)),
download(rootkit,hackerhome,patsy),
download(secureport,hackerhome,patsy),
download(rootkit,hackerhome,patsy),
download(rootkit, hackerhome, patsy),
 report(file(rootkit, patsy)),
download(secureport, hackerhome, patsy),
report(file(secureport, patsy)),
order(not(ftp_connection(hackerhome, patsy))),
close_ftp(hackerhome, patsy),
report(not(ftp_connection(hackerhome, patsy))),
order(installed(secureport, patsy)),
 install(secureport, patsy), install(rootkit, patsy),
report(installed(rootkit, patsy)),
order(tested(rootkit, patsy)),
test(rootkit, patsy), report(tested(rootkit, patsy)),
order(not(logged_in(admin, patsy))),
```

```
 logout(patsy),
report(not(logged_in(admin, patsy))),
ping(network)],
[close_port(port80, patsy), close_ftp(hackerhome, patsy),
install(secureport, patsy), install(rootkit, patsy),
test(rootkit, patsy), logout(patsy)] ).
```

Appendix D: Rootkit Attack Planner

The Prolog deception programs of Appendices C and E and discussed in Chap. 12 need an attack plan to work with. Here is a program that can generate random rootkit attack plans, in two parts (problem-specific code and general-purpose planner). The first part defines the basic actions of rootkit compromise of a computer system. The second part is a general-purpose multiagent hierarchical planner. This program is written in Gnu Prolog, a free open-source product from www.gprolog.org.

© Springer International Publishing Switzerland 2016
N.C. Rowe, J. Rrushi, *Introduction to Cyberdeception*,
DOI 10.1007/978-3-319-41187-3

More about the concepts behind the planner machinery of this code is in Rowe, Introduction to Artificial Intelligence Through Prolog, Prentice-Hall, 1989, available at faculty.nps.edu/ncrowe.

```prolog
/* Definition of simpler hacker attack: Uses buffer overflow on a
port to */
/* gain admin access, then downloads rootkit, and fixes the port */
/* vulnerability so no one else can login. */
/* REVISED VERSION: Treats computer as a separate agent. */
:- set_prolog_flag(singleton_warning,off).
:- set_prolog_flag(unknown,fail).
:- include(gmeagent).


start_state(SS) :-
  random_start_state(S1), random_start_state(S2),
  random_start_state(S3), random_start_state(S4),
  random_start_state(S5), random_start_state(S6),
  random_start_state(S7), random_start_state(S8),
  random_start_state(S9), random_start_state(S10),
  member(SS,[S1,S2,S3,S4,S5,S6,S7,S8,S9,S10]).
random_start_state(PL) :-
  randitem([[compressed(rootkit,hackerhome),
    compressed(rootkit,hackerhome),null],P1),
  randitem([[compressed(secureport,hackerhome),
    compressed(secureport,hackerhome),null],P2),
  randitem([file(rootkit,patsy),null,null,null],P3),
  randitem([file(secureport,patsy),null,null,null],P4),
  randitem([status(admin,patsy),null,null,null],P5),
  randitem([know(network,topology),null,null],P6),
  randitem([know(recent,vulnerabilities),null,null,null],P7),
  randitem([know(vulnerability,port80,patsy),null,null,null],P8),
  delete([P1,P2,P3,P4,P5,P6,P7,P8],null,XPL),
  PL = [file(rootkit,hackerhome),file(secureport,hackerhome)|XPL],
  !.


goal(hacker,[reported(installed(rootkit,patsy)),
  reported(tested(rootkit,patsy)),reported(installed(secureport,p
  atsy)),

reported(not(logged_in(_,_))),reported(not(connected_at_
port(_,_))),
  reported(not(ftp_connection(_,_)))]).
goal(system,[not(ordered(_))]).
maximumtime(800).
```

```
randomfraction(0.5).
wakeup_trigger(hacker,[reported(_)]).
wakeup_trigger(system,[ordered(_)]).


/* Note all orders and report have one arg: they all go between
hacker and system */
recommended([ordered(F)],[],order(F)).


/* Report priority is same as that of accomplishing the associated
facts */
recommended([reported(F)],[],report(F))
:- possible_report_fact(F).
/* If asked to accomplish something not doable in one action,
report instead */
/* a fact that prevents it from being immediately doable.  This is
specific */
/* to agents that are computers. */
recommended([not(ordered(F))],[NP,ordered(F)],report(NP)) :-
  possible_report_fact(F), xrecommended([F],Op),
  \+ Op=order(_), \+ Op=report(_),
  xprecondition(Op,PL), member(P,PL),
  ((P=not(NP), \+ NP=ordered(_), \+ NP=reported(_));
   (\+ P=not(_), \+ P=ordered(_), \+ P=reported(_), NP=not(P)) ).
/* Otherwise do what is recommended to accomplish the desired fact.
*/
recommended([not(ordered(F))],[ordered(F)],report(F)).
recommended([installed(Executable,Target)],[],install(Executable,
Target)).
recommended([status(admin,Target)],[],get(admin,status,Target)).
recommended([overflowed(buffer,Port,Target)],[],overflow(buffer,Por
t,Target)).
recommended([tested(Executable,Target)],[],test(Executable,Tar
get)).
recommended([file(File,Target)], [file(File,hackerhome)],
   download(File,hackerhome,Target) ).
recommended([know(vulnerability,X,Target)],[],s
can_for_vulnerability(Target)).
recommended([know(network,topology)],[],ping(network)).
recommended([know(recent,vulnerabilities)],[],scan(hacker,si
tes)).
recommended([connected_at_port(X,Target)],[],connect_at_
port(X,Target)).
recommended([ftp_connection(RemoteSite,Target)],[],ftp(RemoteSite
,Target)).
```

```
recommended([not(compressed(File,Target))],[],decompress(File,Tar
get)).
recommended([compressed(File,Target)],
    [compressed(File,Remote),not(file(File,Target))],
    download(File,Remote,Target) ).
recommended([logged_in(User,Target)],[],login(User,Target)).
recommended([not(ftp_connection(RemoteSite,Target))],[],
    close_ftp(RemoteSite,Target)).
recommended([not(connected_at_port(Port,Target))],[],close_
port(Port,Target)).
recommended([not(logged_in(_,Target))],[],logout(Target)).


precondition(install(Executable,Target),
[reported(status(admin, Target)),reported(log
ged_in(admin,Target)),
    reported(file(Executable,Target)),
    reported(not(compressed(Executable,Target))),
    reported(not(ftp_connection(Local,Target)))]).
precondition(test(Executable,Target),
    [reported(status(admin,Target)),
    reported(logged_in(admin,Target)),
    reported(installed(Executable,Target))]).
precondition(get(admin,status,Target),
    [reported(overflowed(buffer,X,Target))]).
precondition(overflow(buffer,Port,Target),
    [reported(connected_at_port(Port,Target)),
    know(vulnerability,Port,Target)]).
precondition(download(File,RemoteSite,Target),
    [file(File,RemoteSite),
      reported(ftp_connection(RemoteSite,Target))]).
precondition(scan_for_vulnerability(Target),
    [know(network,topology), know(recent,vulnerabilities)]).
precondition(ping(network), []).
precondition(scan(hacker,sites),[]).
precondition(connect_at_port(Port,Target),
    [know(network,topology),
    know(vulnerability,Port,Target)]).
precondition(ftp(RemoteSite,Target),
    [know(network,topology),
    reported(logged_in(User,Target))]).
precondition(decompress(File,Target),
    [compressed(File,Target),
    reported(file(File,Target)),
    reported(logged_in(User,Target)),
    reported(not(ftp_connection(Local,Target)))]).
```

```
precondition(login(User,Target),
   [reported(status(admin,Target)),
    reported(not(connected_at_port(Port,Site)))]).
precondition(close_ftp(RemoteSite,Target),
   [reported(ftp_connection(RemoteSite,Target))]).
precondition(close_port(Port,Target),
   [reported(connected_at_port(Port,Target))]).
precondition(logout(Target), [logged_in(User,Target),
   reported(not(ftp_connection(RemoteSite,Target)))]).
precondition(order(F), [not(reported(F))|PL]) :-
  member(F,[installed(_,_), status(_,_), overflowed(_,_,_),
            tested(_,_), file(_,_), connected_at_port(_,_),

ftp_connection(_,_), not(compressed(_,_)), logged_in(_,_)]),
   (recommended([F],Op); recommended([F],_,Op)),
   (precondition(Op,PL); precondition(Op,_,PL)).
/* Some orders require special preconditions */
precondition(order(not(logged_in(User,Target))),PL) :-
goal(hacker,GL),mydelete(reported(not(log
ged_in(_,Target))),GL,GL2),
  PL = [reported(logged_in(User,Target))|GL2].
precondition(order(not(connected_at_port(P,T))),
  [reported(connected_at_port(P,T)),
   reported(status(admin,Target))]).
precondition(order(not(ftp_connection(R,T))),
  [reported(ftp_connection(R,T)),
   reported(file(rootkit,T)),
   reported(file(secureport,T))]).
precondition(report(F), [F, ordered(F)]) :- possible_report_fact(F).
/* General preconditions on orders: You cannot give orders to a
computer */
/* that require planning to accomplish -- all preconditions of the
*/
/* recommended op must be true. */
precondition(order(F), [F], []).

deletepostcondition(install(Executable,Target), []).
deletepostcondition(test(Executable,Target), []).
deletepostcondition(overflow(Buffer,Port,Target), []).
deletepostcondition(download(File,RemoteSite,Target), []).
deletepostcondition(scan_for_vulnerability(Target), []).
deletepostcondition(ping(network), []).
deletepostcondition(scan(hacker,sites), []).
deletepostcondition(login(User,Target), [logged_in(_,Target)]).
```

```
deletepostcondition(connect_at_port(Port,Target), []).
deletepostcondition(ftp(RemoteSite,Target), []).
deletepostcondition(get(admin,status,Target), [status(_,Target)]).
deletepostcondition(decompress(File,Target),
[compressed(File,Target)]).
deletepostcondition(close_ftp(RemoteSite,Target),
  [ftp_connection(RemoteSite,Target)]).
deletepostcondition(close_port(Port,Target),
  [connected_at_port(Port,Target),overflowed(buffer,Port,Tar
get)]).
deletepostcondition(logout(Target),
  [logged_in(User,Target),overflowed(buffer,Port,Target)]).
deletepostcondition(order(F),
  [reported(F),reported(not(F)),ordered(not(F))]).
deletepostcondition(order(not(F)),
  [reported(F),reported(not(F)),ordered(F)]).
deletepostcondition(report(F),
  [ordered(F),ordered(not(F)),reported(not(F))]).
deletepostcondition(report(not(F)),
  [ordered(F),ordered(not(F)),reported(F)]).


addpostcondition(install(Executable,Target), [installed(Executabl
e,Target)]).
addpostcondition(test(Executable,Target),
[tested(Executable,Target)]).
addpostcondition(overflow(buffer,Port,Target),
   [overflowed(buffer,Port,Target)]).
addpostcondition(scan_for_vulnerability(Target),
   [know(vulnerability,port80,Target)]).
addpostcondition(ping(network), [know(network,topology)]).
addpostcondition(scan(hacker,sites),     [know(recent,vulnerabilit
ies)]).
addpostcondition(login(User,Target),
   [logged_in(User,Target), know(password,Target)]).
addpostcondition(connect_at_port(Port,Target),
   [connected_at_port(Port,Target)]).
addpostcondition(ftp(RemoteSite,Target), [ftp_connection(RemoteSi
te,Target)]).
addpostcondition(get(admin,status,Target),
[status(admin,Target)]).
addpostcondition(decompress(File,Target), []).
addpostcondition(close_ftp(RemoteSite,Target), []).
addpostcondition(close_port(Port,Target), []).
addpostcondition(logout(Target), []).
```

```
addpostcondition(order(F), [ordered(F)]).
addpostcondition(report(F), [reported(F)]).
addpostcondition(download(File,RemoteSite,Target),
[compressed(File,RemoteSite)],
    [file(File,Target),compressed(File,Target)]).
addpostcondition(download(File,RemoteSite,Target),
    [not(compressed(File,RemoteSite))],
    [file(File,Target)]).


/* If asked to do something that violates a precondition due to a
false */
/* report by the deception strategy, undo the action (as best you
can */
/* without full state info) and report the violated precondition.
*/
randchange(Op,_,S,NS,1.0,'Precondition violation') :-
  member(reported(P),S),                    get_precondition(Op,S,PL),
  member(reported(P),PL),
  ((P=not(NP),  member(NP,S)); (\+ P=not(_), \+ member(P,S),
  NP=not(P))),
  \+ Op=order(_), \+ Op=report(_),
  delete(S,reported(P),S2),  S3=[reported(NP)|S2],  sort(S3,NS),
  dummy, !.
randchange(ping(Target),_,_,
  know(network,topology),[],0.2,'No such site').
randchange(ping(Target),_,_,[],problems(network),0.3,'Network
refuses access').
randchange(scan_for_vulnerability(Target),_,_,[],problems(netw
ork),
  0.3,'Network refuses access').
randchange(overflow(buffer,Port,Target),_,_,
  overflowed(buffer,Port,Target),[],0.4,'Segmentation error').
randchange(get(admin,status,Target),_,_,status(admin,Target),[],
  0.6,'Administrator status is not authorized for this account').
randchange(login(User,Target),_,[not(know(password,Target))],
  know(password,Target),[],0.8,'Incorrect password').
randchange(download(File,RemoteSite,Target),_,_,
    [file(File,Target),compressed(File,Target)],[],0.3,'File  not
found').
randchange(ftp(RemoteSite,Target),_,[],ftp_connection(RemoteSite,
Target),[],0.2,
  'Connection failed').
randchange(connect_at_port(Port,Target),_,[],connected_at_
port(Port,Target),
```

```
        [],0.3,'Port not available').
randchange(scan_for_vulnerability(Target),_,[],know(vulnerability
,port80,Target),
        know(vulnerability,port8080,Target),0.5,'Vulnerability in port
        8080').
randchange(login(User,Target),_,_,[],problems(filesystem),
        0.3,'Password file not found').
randchange(order(Netcond),_,[problems(network)],ordered(Netc
ond),[],
        0.5,'Connection not responding') :-
m e m b e r ( N e t c o n d , [ f i l e ( _ , _ ) , c o n n e c
ted_at_port(_,_),ftp_connection(_,_),
            not(connected_at_port(_,_)),not(ftp_connection(_,_)),
            logged_in(_,_),not(logged_in(_,_))]), !.
randchange(order(Filecond),_,[problems(filesystem)],ordered(Filec
ond),[],
        0.5,'File not found'):-
    member(Filecond,[installed(_,_),tested(_,_),file(_,_),
                not(compressed(_,_))]).

actor(order(_),hacker).
actor(scan(hacker,sites),hacker).
actor(scan_for_vulnerability(Target),hacker).
actor(ping(Target),hacker).
actor(X,system) :- \+ X=order(_), \+ X=scan(hacker,sites),
    \+ X=scan_for_vulnerability(Target), \+ X=ping(Target).
skill(hacker,0.5).
skill(system,1.0).


duration(Op,Agent,State,D,D2):-durationmean(Op,M),
skill(Agent,S), D is M/S,
    D2 is D*0.75.
durationmean(install(Executable,Target), 20).
durationmean(test(Execurable,Target), 10).
durationmean(overflow(buffer,Port,Target), 1).
durationmean(download(File,RemoteSite,Target), 10).
durationmean(scan_for_vulnerability(Target), 5).
durationmean(ping(network), 10).
durationmean(scan(hacker,sites), 60).
durationmean(login(User,Target), 10).
durationmean(connect_at_port(Port,Target), 1).
durationmean(ftp(RemoteSite,Target), 1).
durationmean(get(admin,status,Target), 2).
durationmean(decompress(File,Target), 5).
```

```
durationmean(close_ftp(RemoteSite,Target), 1).
durationmean(close_port(Port,Target), 1).
durationmean(logout(Target), 1).
durationmean(order(F),1).
durationmean(report(F),1).

/* noploy(ordered(_)).
noploy(not(ordered(_))).
noploy(not(reported(_))).
noploy(not(know(_,_))).
noploy(not(know(_,_,_))).
noploy(not(tested(_,_))).
noploy(tested(_,_)).
noploy(not(file(_,hackerhome))).
noploy(file(_,hackerhome)).
noploy(not(compressed(_,hackerhome))).
noploy(compressed(_,hackerhome)).
ploysuccess([],know(_,_),0.1).
ploysuccess([],know(_,_,_),0.1). */

/* Argument to factargtype is a predicate with list arguments. */
/* This specifies the possible facts with that predicate name; */
/* the lists represent the complete set of choices for the args */
/* in that position. */
factargtype(P) :- basefactargtype(P).
/* Facts of this type say that the attacker knows the topology of
*/
/* the network attacked. */
factargtype(know([network],[topology])).
/* Attacker is up to date on common vulnerabilities from scanning
*/
/* hacker bulletin boards. */
factargtype(know([recent],[vulnerabilities])).
/* Attacker knows the password to a specified machine. */
factargtype(know([password],Targets)) :- targets(Targets).
/* Attacker knows a vulnerability of a specified port on a specified
*/
/* machine. */
factargtype(know([vulnerability],Ports,Targets)) :-
   ports(Ports), targets(Targets).
/* Attacker has ordered the computer system to do the specified fact
*/
/* via input and the computer has not yet reported success. */
factargtype(ordered(Facts))
```

```
:- bagof(PE,possible_report_fact(PE),Facts).
/* Computer system has reported to attacker that it has accom-
plished */
/* the specified fact. */
f a c t a r g t y p e ( r e p o r t e d ( F a c t s ) )
:- bagof(PE,possible_report_fact(PE),Facts).
/* Specified file is installed on specified computer system. */
basefactargtype(installed(Files,Targets))        :-        files(Files),
targets(Targets).
/* Specified file is tested and shown to work on specified computer
system. */
basefactargtype(tested(Files,Targets))            :-        files(Files),
targets(Targets).
/* The attacker has administrator status on specified computer sys-
tem. */
basefactargtype(status([admin],Targets)) :- targets(Targets).
/* A buffer is overflowed on specified port on specified computer
system. */
basefactargtype(overflowed([buffer],Ports,Targets)) :-
    ports(Ports), targets(Targets).
/* A specified file is stored on a specified computer system. */
basefactargtype(file(Files,Sites)) :- files(Files), sites(Sites).
/* Attacker is connected to a specified computer systems through a
*/
/* specified port. */
basefactargtype(connected_at_port(Ports,Targets)) :-
    ports(Ports), targets(Targets).
/* A specified user is logged in on a specified computer system. */
basefactargtype(logged_in(Users,Targets))         :-        users(Users),
targets(Targets).
/* Attacker has an FTP (file transfer) connection to a specified
system */
/* (first arg) from another specified system (second arg). */
basefactargtype(ftp_connection([hackerhome],Targets))            :-
targets(Targets).
/* A specified file is in compressed form on a specified computer
system. */
basefactargtype(compressed(Files,Sites))          :-        files(Files),
sites(Sites).
/* There are problems with either the network or file systems. */
basefactargtype(problems([network,filesystem])).

/* Possible values for variable bindings in specifications */
files([rootkit,secureport]).
ports([port80,port8080]).
```

```
sites([hackerhome,patsy]).
users([john,admin]).
targets([patsy]).
possible_report_fact(PE) :- basefactargtype(PE2), PE2=..[Pred|Args],
  length(Args,N), functor(XPE,Pred,N), (PE=XPE; PE=not(XPE)).


******************************************************************

/* MEAGENT: Means-ends reasoning for multiple agents. */
/* GPROLOG VERSION */
/* Written by Neil C. Rowe. Version of 3/02. */
/* To get debugging data, asserta(debugflag); to make program stop
*/
/* for tracing at a particular operator, include "debugtarget"
fact with */
/* arg the operator in definitions file, then load and spy(dummy).
*/
:- dynamic([top_goal/1, top_solution/1, readbuff/1, debugflag/0,
solution/4]).
:- set_prolog_flag(singleton_warning,off).
:- set_prolog_flag(unknown,fail).

/* For an application, you must define: */
/* recommended(<difference>,<operator>) or                    */
/* recommended(<difference>,<conditionlist>,<factlist>)   */
/* --gives an operator recommeded to a achieve a particular set of
*/
/*    facts different from the current state; conditionlist are
facts */
/*    that must be present in the current state (if missing, any
facts ok) */
/* precondition(<operator>,<factlist>) or */
/* precondition(<operator>,<conditionlist>,<factlist>) or */
/* precondition(<operator>,<conditionlist>,<factlist>,<msg>) */
/* --gives facts required by operator; 3-arg. form requires addi-
tional facts */
/*      true; 4-arg. form also prints message when precondition
applied */
/* deletepostcondition(<operator>,<factlist>) or              */
/* deletepostcondition(<operator>,<conditionlist>,<factlist>) */
/*    deletepostcondition(<operator>,<conditionlist>,<factlist>,<
msg>) */
/* --gives facts deleted by op.; 3-arg. form requires additional
facts true; */
/*    4-arg. form also prints message when applied */
```

```
/* addpostcondition(<operator>,<factlist>) or              */
/* addpostcondition(<operator>,<conditionlist>,<factlist>)     */
/* addpostcondition(<operator>,<conditionlist>,<factlist>,<msg>) */
/* --gives facts added by op.; 3-arg. form requires additional
facts true */
/*    4-arg. form also prints message when applied */
/* Some optional definitions you may include:                  */
/*         randchange(<operator-or-oplist>,<agent>,<state>,<facts-
replaced>,    */
/*                   <new-facts>,<prob>,<msg>)*/
/* --defines random-substitution of 4th arg facts by 5th arg facts
by */
/*  operator given in 1rst arg or first arg list, 2nd arg the agent,
*/
/*  for state with subset given for third arg, with probability
the 6th arg,*/
/*  and 7th arg the message printed out then.   4th and 5th args
*/
/*  refer to state after deletepostconditions and addpostcondi-
tions, */
/*  and can be the empty list. */
/* nopref(<operator(s)1>,<operator(s)2>) --if the order (priority)
of */
/*  two operators or two operator lists in the 'recommended'
rules was */
/*  arbitrary, include a fact of this kind */
/* state_state(<list of facts>) -- starting state */
/* goal(<agent>,<list of facts>> -- conditions each agent must
achieve */
/* wakeup_trigger(<agent>,<list of facts>) -- conditions which as
a whole */
/*  cause an agent to "wake up" and start planning actions to
take */
/*  (agents go to sleep when they have nothing to do) */
/* actor(<operator>,<agent>) -- possible agents for an action */
/* assistant(<operator>,<agent>) -- possible secondary agents for
an action */
/* generalize_op(<operator>,<newoperator>) -- defines possible */
/*    generalizations of an operator */
/* duration(<operator>,<time>) gives length of time of action;
must use */
/* durationmean(<operator>,<time>) somewhere in definition. */
/* noploy(<fact>) specifies impossible conclusions, either positive
or negative.*/
/* ploysuccess(<deletes>,<adds>,<prob>) specifies ploys that work
only part */
```

```
/*     of the time. */
/* special_agent(<agent>) -- gives name of a special agent */
/* special_agent(<agent>,<state>,<time>,<operator>,<newstate>) --
defines */
/* calculations associated with certain designated "special"
agents */
/* that represent autonomous processes like fire */
/* factargtype(<predexpr>) -- gives possible values a predicate
expression */
/* can have, by giving arguments as lists of possible values. */
/* debugflag --if asserted, debugging info printed re means-ends
anal. */
/* debugtarget -- takes one argument which is the name of an opera-
tor, */
/*     and when "dummy" is spied, will stop before applying that
operator; */
/*     you can have more than one debugtester fact. */
/* Negations: Facts in recommendation and precondition lists may
be the */
/* argument to a "not" to negate them. */
/* Quantifications: Variables in above facts are existentially
quantified */
/* for positives and universally quantified when inside negations.
*/
/* For example, for the goal [not(p(X)),q(Y),r(3),t(2)] and the
state */
/* [p(1), p(4), q(3), q(5), s(2), r(3)], the difference list is */
/* [not(p(1)), not(p(4)), t(2)]. */

/*******************************************************************
***/


tt :- gofv(20,0).
tt20 :- gofv(20,0).
tt40 :- gofv(40,0).


/* Top-level control of agents */

/* Special variant for determining effects of single facts in a
state. */
/* Finds the added time necessary to solve the problem given one
change */
/* to the state at a specified time N, as per state file Statefile.
*/
/* First arg is the starting time (state will be looked up), 2nd
```

```prolog
arg */
/* is run number of starting run (used in debugging). */
gofv(Tmax,K) :- go, state(T3,_), \+ (state(T4,_), T4>T3),
    retractall(base_max_time(_)), assertz(base_max_time(T3)),  !,
    gofv2(Tmax,K).
gofv2(Tmax,K) :- state(NewTmax,State), NewTmax =< Tmax,
    \+ (state(T2,State2), NewTmax < T2, T2 =< Tmax),
   open('variantout.pl',append,Stream), nl(Stream), close(Stream),
    bagof(A,orphan_add(A),AL), length(AL,N1), length(State,N2),
    Numruns is N1+N2, !, gofv(State,Tmax,NewTmax,K,Numruns).
gofv(_,_,_,K,Numruns) :- K>Numruns, !.
gofv(State,OldTmax,Tmax,K,Numruns)   :-   write('Run   number:   '),
write(K), nl,
    write('on state: '), write(State), nl,
    factvalue(State,OldTmax,Tmax,K),   factvalue(State,OldTmax,Tma
    x,K),
    factvalue(State,OldTmax,Tmax,K),   factvalue(State,OldTmax,Tma
    x,K),
    factvalue(State,OldTmax,Tmax,K), Kp1 is K+1, !,
    gofv(State,OldTmax,Tmax,Kp1,Numruns).
factvalue(State,_,Tstart,_)          :-          retractall(state(_,_)),
retractall(status(_,_,_)),
    retractall(randsubst_cache(_,_,_,_)), goal(A,_),
    assertz(status(A,Tstart,active)), fail.
factvalue(State,_,Tstart,_) :- member(fire(_,_),State),
    assertz(status(fire,Tstart,active)), fail.
factvalue(State,_,Tstart,_) :- \+ member(fire(_,_),State),
    assertz(status(fire,Tstart,waiting)), fail.
factvalue(State,OldTmax,Tstart,K) :- retractall(act(_,_,_,_)),
    state_variation(State,K,NewState,Prefact,Postfact),
    (K=0; \+ identical_states(State,NewState)),
    write('>>>Trying variant state '), write(K),
    describe_state_change(Prefact,Postfact), nl,
    asserta(state(Tstart,NewState)), !, go2,
    base_max_time(Oldmaxtime), state(Newmaxtime,S2),
    \+ (state(T3,S3), T3>Newmaxtime),
    writeq(variantdata(K,OldTmax,Prefact,Postfact,Oldmaxtime,Newma
    xtime)), nl,
    open('variantout.pl',append,Stream),
    writeq(Stream,variantdata(K,OldTmax,Prefact,Postfact,Oldmaxt
    ime,
             Newmaxtime)),
    write(Stream,'.'), nl(Stream), close(Stream), !.
factvalue(_,_,_,_).
```

```prolog
describe_state_change(Prefact,[]) :- write(' with deletion of fact '),
   write(Prefact), !.
describe_state_change([],Postfact) :- write(' with addition of
fact '),
   write(Postfact), !.
describe_state_change(Prefact,Postfact) :- write(' with change of
fact '),
   write(Prefact), (' to '), write(Postfact), !.


/* Makes one change to a state: modification, deletion, or addition
of */
/* a fact.  Modifications must be to pairs of opposites. */
state_variation(State,0,State,[],[]) :- !.
state_variation(State,K,NewState,Prefact,Postfact) :-
   length(State,N),     K     =<     N,     item(K,State,Prefact),
   opposite(Prefact,Postfact),
   mydelete(Prefact,State,State2),
   mydelete(reported(Prefact,_,_),State2,State3),
   mydelete(ordered(Postfact,_,_),State3,State4),
   NewState=[Postfact|State4], !.
state_variation(State,K,NewState,Prefact,[]) :-
   length(State,N), K =< N, item(K,State,Prefact),
   orphan_delete(Prefact), mydelete(Prefact,State,State2),
   mydelete(reported(Prefact,_,_),State2,NewState), !.
state_variation(State,K,NewState,[],Postfact) :-
   length(State,N), K > N, NmK is K-N, setof(A,orphan_add(A),AL),
   item(NmK,AL,Postfact), mydelete(ordered(Postfact,_,_),State,St
   ate2),
   NewState=[Postfact|State2], !.
state_variation(State,K,NewState,[],[]) :- !.


/* Run agents definitions 50 times, dump results in single file */
numruns(50).
goruns :- goruns(1).
goruns(K) :- numruns(K2), K>K2, !.
goruns(K) :- write('Current run number: '), write(K), nl,
   randomize, initialize_agents, !, go2,
   open('goruns.pl',append,Stream), write(Stream,run(K)),
write(Stream,'.'), nl(Stream),  write_simplified_states(Stream),
   close(Stream), Kp1 is K+1, !, goruns(Kp1).
write_simplified_states(Stream) :- bagof(T2,S2^state(T2,S2),XT2L),
   sort(XT2L,T2L), member(T,T2L), state_nbt(T,State),
   lookup_act(T,Op,Tend,Agent), state_nbt(Tend,State2),
```

```prolog
     writeq(Stream,s(T,Op,Tend,Agent,State,State2)),
     write(Stream,'.'),
     nl(Stream), fail.
write_simplified_states(_).
state_nbt(T,S) :- state(T,S), !.
lookup_act(T,Op,Tend,Agent) :- act(Agent,Op,T,Tend), !.
lookup_act(T,none,T) :- !.



/* Runs some fireagents file 100 times to see how randomness matters
*/
go1(K,Outfile) :- K>100, !.
go1(K,Outfile) :- write('Run number: '), write(K), nl, nl,
     go1b(Outfile), Kp1 is K+1, !, go1(Kp1,Outfile).
go :- go1b, !.
go1b :- initialize_agents, go2, open('actout.out',write,Stream),
     nice_write_acts(Stream),     close(Stream),     open('stateout.
     out',write,Stream2),
     nice_write_states(Stream2), close(Stream2), !.
go1b :- nl, write('!!!!!!!! Planning failed (routine go2)'), nl,
nl, !.


/* Note initialization chooses a random start state from those
specified */
initialize_agents    :-    retractall(status(_,_,_)),    goal(A,GL),
start_state(S),
     (\+ get_difference(GL,S,[]);
      (wakeup_trigger(A,TL), get_difference(TL,S,[])) ),
     \+ status(A,0,active), assertz(status(A,0,active)), fail.
initialize_agents :- goal(A,_), \+ status(A,0,active),
     assertz(status(A,0,waiting)), fail.
initialize_agents :-special_agent(A), asserta(status(A,0,active)),
fail.
initialize_agents    :-    retractall(state(_,_)),    bagof(SS2,start_
state(SS2),SSL),
     randitem(SSL,S), assertz(state(0,S)),
     retractall(act(_,_,_,_)),
/* If you do not want different random numbers each run, uncomemnt
next expr */
     /*    retractall(lastrandnum(_)),    */    retractall(randsubst_
     cache(_,_,_,_)), !.
/* After run (maybe partial), can restart at given time by calling
"redo" */
redo(N) :- retract(status(A,B,C)), assertz(status(A,N,active)),
fail.
```

```prolog
redo(N) :- state(T,S), T>N, retract(state(T,S)), fail.
redo(N) :- go2(finaloutput).
resume :- state(_,S), retractall(state(_,_)), go2(S,finaloutput), !.


/* Main loop on agents: Give turn to active agent least recently
updated */
go2 :- bagof(T2,A2^status(A2,T2,active),TL),
   minlist(TL,T), maximumtime(Tmax), T<Tmax,
   status(A,T,active), (state(T,S); state_at_time(T,S)),
   /*        \+      (member(recorded(debriefed(team,X)),S),       \+
   member(alarmed(_,_),S)), */
   !, write('Examining state at time '), write(T), write(' for
   agent '),
   write(A), write('.'), nl, call_agent(A,S,T,Flag,NS,TEnd,Op),
   ((Flag=ok, \+ Op=do_nothing, assertz(act(A,Op,T,TEnd)),
     write('%%%% Action "'), write(Op), write('" done by agent '),
     write(A),
     write(' from '), write(T), write(' to '), write(TEnd), /* nl,
     write('giving state '), write(NS), */ nl );
    true ),
   !, go2.
go2 :- write('Simulation done.'), nl, write('Final state: '), nl,
   state(T,S), \+ (state(T2,S2), T2>T), write(S), nl, nl, !.


call_agent(A,S,T,ok,NS,TEnd,Op) :- special_agent(A), !, TEnd is
T+1,
   adjust_state_from_concurrency(A,S,T,TEnd,XS),
   special_agent(A,XS,T,Op,NS),
   update_later_states(NS,TEnd), asserta(state(TEnd,NS)),
   wakeup_agents_from_trigger(S,TEnd,NS), !.
/* Each regular agent should run means-ends analysis to decide what
next */
call_agent(A,S,T,Flag,NS,TEnd,Op) :- status(A,_,_),
   /* write('Trying agent '), write(A), write('....'), nl, */
   goal(A,G), once_means_ends(S,G,Oplist,_),
   /* If nothing to do, and nothing in known future, fail */
   \+ (Oplist=[],
   \+ (act(_,_,_,TX), TX>T, state(TX,SX), wakeup_trigger(A,FL),
           member(F,FL), member(F,SX))),
   call_agent2(A,S,T,G,Oplist,Flag,NS,TEnd,Op).
call_agent(A,S,T,Flag,NS,TEnd,Op) :- \+ status(A,_,_),
   write('Missing status fact for '), write(A), nl, dummy, !, fail.
/* If no goals agent needs to achieve (Oplist=[]), make it inactive
*/
```

```prolog
call_agent(A,S,T,Flag,S,T,Op) :-  retract(status(A,_,_)),
   asserta(status(A,T,waiting)), write('%%%% Agent '), write(A),
   write(' went to sleep.'), nl, Flag=sleep, !.


call_agent2(A,S,T,G,Oplist,ok,NS,TEnd,Op) :-
/* Find an action that is reasonable to do */
   find_doable_op(Oplist,A,S,T,Op),
/* Also adjust the final state with results of conccurrent actions,
and */
/* adjust other known states with postconditions of this action.
*/
   get_precondition(Op,S,PL), get_difference(PL,S,[]), goal(A,G),

get_difference(G,S,Diff),      \+    Diff=[],    indirect_desirable_
op(Diff,S,Op),
   \+ (act(_,Op,T8,T9), T8=<T, T<T9),
   ((debugtarget(Op), dummy); \+ debugtarget(Op)),
   compute_duration(Op,A,S,D), XTEnd is T+D,
/* Ensure no two actions end at the same time */
   ((state(XTEnd,_), randnum(K), mod(K,137,KK),
     TEnd is XTEnd+(0.001*KK));
    TEnd=XTEnd),
   adjust_state_from_concurrency(A,S,T,TEnd,S1),
   get_precondition(Op,S1,PL2), get_difference(PL2,S1,[]),
   goal(A,G2), get_difference(G2,S1,Diff1), \+ Diff1=[],
   indirect_desirable_op(Diff1,S1,Op),
   apply_op(Op,S1,S2), do_randsubst(Op,A,S,S2,NS),
   cache_randsubst(Op,TEnd,S2,NS), update_later_states(NS,TEnd),
   asserta(state(TEnd,NS)), retract(status(A,_,_)),
   asserta(status(A,TEnd,active)),                wakeup_agents_from_
   trigger(S,TEnd,NS), !.
/* Otherwise, something is inconsistent about the analysis; */
/* try this agent at the next available time */
call_agent2(A,S,T,G,Oplist,delay,NS,T,Op) :-
   state(T4,S4), T<T4, \+ (state(T5,_), T<T5, T5<T4),
   retract(status(A,_,_)),  asserta(status(A,T4,active)),
   write('No action found for '), write(A), write('.'), nl, !.
/* If this is last available time, try at roughly 1 min. later. */
call_agent2(A,S,T,G,Oplist,delay,S,TEnd,Op) :-  randnum(K2),
   mod(K2,177,K2K),
   TEnd is T+1+(0.01*(K2K+1)), asserta(state(TEnd,S)),
   retract(status(A,_,_)), asserta(status(A,TEnd,active)),
   write('No action found for '), write(A), write('.'), nl,  !.
dummy :- 1=1.
```

```
/* Choose the first op in the optimal plan a fraction of the time
*/
/* determined by the randomfaction fact; else choose random doable
op. */
find_doable_op(Oplist,A,S,T,Op)          :-          random(0,10000,N),
randomfraction(P),
   NP is N*0.0001, NP>P, !, first_doable_op(Oplist,A,S,T,Op), !.
find_doable_op(Oplist,A,S,T,Op)          :-          random_doable_
op(Oplist,A,S,T,Op), !.
/* Given plan of actions found by agent, choose act to execute */
first_doable_op(Oplist,A,S,T,Op) :- doable_op(Oplist,A,S,T,Op), !.
/* Alternative for sometimes random selection of the operator. */
random_doable_op(Oplist,A,S,T,Op) :-
   setof(Op2,doable_op(Oplist,A,S,T,Op2),OL),
   (OL=[Op]; randitem(OL,Op)), !.
/* A doable operator must be permitted by preconditions */
/* and recommended at the given time, and must not be in progress
already. */
doable_op(Oplist,A,S,T,NOp) :- append(Oplistfront,[Op|_],Oplist),
actor(Op,A), get_precondition(Op,S,PL), get_difference(PL,S,[]),
   /* Avoid actions that do nothing or undo the previous op. */
   apply_op(Op,S,S2), \+ identical_states(S,S2),
   \+ (act(A,Op2,T3,T), state(T3,S3), identical_states(S3,S2)),
   \+ assistant_unavailable(Op,T),
   /* A doable op must not interfere with ("clobber") preconditions
   */
   /* or postconditions of operators in progress already */
   \+ (act(_,Op2,T1,T2), T2 > T, T1 =< T2,
      ((get_deletepostcondition(Op2,S,DL),          member(D,DL),
      member(D,PL));
       (get_addpostcondition(Op2,S,AL),            member(A,AL),
       member(not(A),PL));
       (get_precondition(Op2,S,PL2),
        ((get_deletepostcondition(Op,S,DL),         member(P,DL),
        member(P,PL2));
        (get_addpostcondition(Op,S,AL),        member(not(P),AL),
        member(P,PL2)))))),
   /* A doable op must not "clobber" preconditions */
   /* of actions preceding its original planned position */
get_deletepostcondition(Op,S,DL), get_addpostcondition(Op,S,AL),
   \+ (member(Op2,Oplistfront), get_precondition(Op2,S,PL2),
      ((member(P,DL),      member(P,PL2));      (member(not(P),AL),
      member(P,PL2))) ),
   modify_actor(Op,S,NOp).
```

```
/* Some team operations cannot be done unless all assistants are
unoccupied */
assistant_unavailable(Op,T) :-assistant(Op,A2), act(A2,Op2,T1,T2),
   T < T2, T1 =< T, !.



/* When more than one actor can do something, choose one waiting
longest */
modify_actor(Op,S,NOp) :- Op=order(F,P1,P2), NOp=order(F,P1,P3),
   get_recommended([F],S,Op2),               bagof(A,actor(Op2,A),AL),
   member(P2,AL),
   bagof(T5-A5,last_time_busy(AL,A5,T5),TAL),         keysort(TAL,[_-
   P3|_]), !.
modify_actor(Op,S,Op).
last_time_busy(AL,A,T) :- member(A,AL),
bagof(T2,Op^T1^act(A,Op,T1,T2),T2L),
   maxlist(T2L,T).
last_time_busy(AL,A,0) :- member(A,AL), \+ bagof(T2,Op^T1^act(A,O
p,T1,T2),T2L).

/* Assign a random duration evenly distributed with a given mean
and range */
compute_duration(Op,A,S,D) :- duration(Op,A,S,Mean,Range), !,
   random(0,5039,NN), D is Mean+(((NN-2520)/5039)*Range), !.


/* Stores deletes and adds associated with a randsubst at a par-
ticular time */
cache_randsubst(Op,T,S,NS) :- \+ S=NS, deleteitems(NS,S,DL),
   deleteitems(S,NS,AL), assertz(randsubst_cache(Op,T,DL,AL)), !.
cache_randsubst(_,_,S,S).



/* Find facts that changed while a given action occurred; update a
state */
adjust_state_from_concurrency(A,S,TStart,TEnd,NS) :- state(T2,S2),
TStart<T2,
   T2 =< TEnd,
   \+        (special_agent(A),       special_agent_canceller(Op),
   act(_,Op,_,T2)),
   \+ (state(T3,_), T2<T3, T3 =< TEnd), deleteitems(S2,S,DL),
   deleteitems(S,S2,AL), deleteitems(DL,S,S6), union(AL,S6,NS), !.
adjust_state_from_concurrency(_,S,_,_,S).

/* Recompute states that occur after this new action finished, by
*/
/* reapplying their operator to the state after the new action. */
update_later_states(NS,T) :-setof(T2,later_state_time(T,T2),XT2L),
```

```prolog
    sort(XT2L,T2L), update_later_states2(T,NS,T2L), !.
update_later_states(_,_).
later_state_time(T,T2) :- state(T2,S), T2>T.
update_later_states2(T,S,[]).
update_later_states2(T,S,[T2|TL]) :-\+state(T2,S),act(A,Op,_,T2),
    ((apply_op(Op,S,S3), NOp=Op);
     (generalize_op(Op,NOp), apply_op(NOp,S,S3));
     (special_agent(A), Op=..[P,DL1,AL1], deleteitems(DL1,S,S5),
/* special agent acts are aborted when relevant input facts are
changed */
      length(DL1,K1), length(S,K2), length(S5,K3), K2 is K1+K3,
      union(AL1,S5,S3) ) ),
    ((randsubst_cache(NOp,T2,DL,AL), deleteitems(DL,S3,S4),
      union(AL,S4,MS) );
     MS=S3 ),
    retract(state(T2,OS)), asserta(state(T2,MS)),
    deleteitems(MS,OS,Deletes), deleteitems(OS,MS,Adds),
    write('State at time '), write(T2), write(' updated with dele-
    tions '), nl,
    write(Deletes), write(' and additions '), nl, write(Adds), nl, !,
    update_later_states2(T,MS,TL).
update_later_states2(T,S,[T2|TL]) :-\+state(T2,S),act(A,Op,T1,T2),
\                                                                       +
apply_op_nb(Op,S,S3),       \+      (generalize_op(Op,NOp),    apply_
op(NOp,S,S3)),
    randnum(K), mod(K,1377,KK), XT is T-(KK/133333),
    write('%%%% Action '), write(Op), write(' from '), write(T1),
    write(' to '),
    write(T2), write(' was aborted at time '), write(XT), write('.'),
    nl, dummy,
    retract(act(A,Op,T1,T2)), assertz(act(A,Op,T1,XT)),
    (\+ state(T2,S2); retract(state(T2,S2))), assertz(state(XT,S)),
    revise_status_times(T2,XT), !, update_later_states2(T,S,TL).
/* If no act fact ending at this time, must be a dummy fire state
*/
update_later_states2(T,S,[T2|TL])    :-    \+   state(T2,S),    \+
act(A,Op,T1,T2),

retract(state(T2,_)),    asserta(state(T2,S)),    !,   update_later_
states2(T,S,TL).
update_later_states2(T,S,[T2|TL])       :-       !,      update_later_
states2(T,S,TL).

state_at_time(T,S) :- state(T,S), !.
state_at_time(T,S) :- bagof(T2,A^B^state_time_leq(T,T2,A,B),T2L),
    maxlist(T2L,Tmax), state(Tmax,S), !.
```

```
state_time_leq(T,T2,A,B) :- state(T2,B), T2 =< T.
revise_status_times(T,NT) :- retract(status(A,T,U)), assertz(status
(A,NT,U)),
    fail.
revise_status_times(T,NT).


/* Says an operator is desirable if it is recommended for top-level
goal */
/* and current state, or else for a precondition of a recommended
operator. */
indirect_desirable_op(Diff,S,order(_,_,_)) :- !.
indirect_desirable_op(Diff,S,report(_,_,_)) :- !.
indirect_desirable_op(Diff,S,Op)        :-       indirect_desirable_
op2(Diff,[],S,Op), !.
indirect_desirable_op2(Diff,Stack,S,Op) :- member(Diff,Stack), !,
fail.
indirect_desirable_op2(Diff,_,S,Op)  :-  desirable_op(Diff,S,Op),
!.
indirect_desirable_op2(Diff,Stack,S,Op) :-
    setof(Op3,desirable_op(Diff,S,Op3),OL), member(Op2,OL),
    get_precondition(Op2,S,PL),   get_difference(PL,S,Diff2),   \+
Diff2=[],
    indirect_desirable_op2(Diff2,[Diff|Stack],S,Op), !.


/* Handle transitions between "active" and "waiting" for agents */
wakeup_agents_from_trigger(S,T,NS) :- wakeup_trigger(A,FL),
    factsubset(FL,NS), status(A,_,waiting), retract(status(A,_,_)),
    asserta(status(A,T,active)), write('Agent '), write(A),
    write(' was woken up by facts '), write(FL), write('.'), nl,
fail.
wakeup_agents_from_trigger(_,_,_).


/*****************************************************************/


/* Hypothetical reasoning by means-ends analysis. */
/* This is an improved version of the program in chap. 11 of the
Rowe book. */
/* It checks for infinite loops for several situations that the */
/* earlier definition does not. A goal-state stack is kept to check
new */
/* goals and states against.  Random substitution via 'randsubst'
is */
/* not used.  Both positive and negative results are cached. */


/* A non-backtracking way to call hypothetical reasoning. */
once_means_ends(STATE,GOAL,OPLIST,GOALSTATE) :-
```

```
/* retractall(solution(_,_,_,_)), retractall(unsolvable(_,_)),
*/
means_ends(STATE,GOAL,OPLIST,GOALSTATE),
(\+ debugflag;
 (write('Operator sequence found: '), nl, write(OPLIST), nl, nl)
 ), !.
once_means_ends(STATE,GOAL,OPLIST,GOALSTATE) :-
  write('%%%% WARNING: Once_means_ends fails for goal: '), nl,
  write(GOAL), nl, write('and for state: '), nl, write(STATE), nl,
  dummy, !, fail.

means_ends(STATE,GOAL,OPLIST,GOALSTATE) :-
  means_ends2(STATE,GOAL,OPLIST,GOALSTATE,[]), writedebug7.

means_ends2(STATE,GOAL,OPLIST,GOALSTATE,STACK) :-
  member([STATE,GOAL],STACK), writedebug4(STATE,GOAL,STACK),
  !, fail.
means_ends2(STATE,GOAL,OPLIST,GOALSTATE,STACK) :-
\+debugflag, unsolvable(STATE,GOAL), writedebug5(STATE,GOAL,STACK),
!, fail.
means_ends2(STATE,GOAL,OPLIST,GOALSTATE,STACK) :-
  \+        debugflag,        solution(STATE,GOAL,OPLIST,GOALSTATE),
  writedebug6(STACK), !.
means_ends2(STATE,GOAL,[],STATE,STACK)                    :-        get_
difference(GOAL,STATE,[]), !.
means_ends2(STATE,GOAL,OPLIST,GOALSTATE,STACK) :-
  get_difference(GOAL,STATE,D),
  talky_desirable_op(D,STATE,OPERATOR),
  get_precondition(OPERATOR,STATE,PRELIST),
  \+      unachievable_difference(STATE,PRELIST),      writedebug1
  (D,OPERATOR,STACK),
means_ends2(STATE,PRELIST,PREOPLIST,PRESTATE,
           [[STATE,GOAL]|STACK]),
writedebug2(PRESTATE,D,OPERATOR,STACK),
apply_op(OPERATOR,PRESTATE,POSTLIST),
means_ends2(POSTLIST,GOAL,POSTOPLIST,GOALSTATE,
                         [[STATE,GOAL]|STACK]),
writedebug3(GOALSTATE,OPERATOR,STACK),
append(PREOPLIST,[OPERATOR|POSTOPLIST],OPLIST),
sort(STATE,XSTATE), sort(GOAL,XGOAL), sort(GOALSTATE,XGOALSTATE),
(debugflag;
   (\+ debugflag, generalize_quantities(XSTATE,XXSTATE),
    generalize_quantities(XGOALSTATE,XXGOALSTATE),
    assertz(solution(XXSTATE,XGOAL,OPLIST,XXGOALSTATE))))).
means_ends2(STATE,GOAL,OPLIST,GOALSTATE,STACK) :-
```

```
  sort(STATE,XSTATE), sort(GOAL,XGOAL),
   \+ solution(XSTATE,XGOAL,_,_),
  generalize_quantities(XSTATE,XXSTATE),
  assertz(unsolvable(XXSTATE,XGOAL)),
  writedebug5(STATE,GOAL,STACK), !, fail.


/* Substitute variables for numbers in predicate expressions to
permit */
/* further matches to the cached expressions */
generalize_quantities(S,NS) :- append(S1,[P|S2],S),
    ((P=..[Pred,Q,Loc], number(Q), NP=..[Pred,Unboundvar,Loc]);
    (P=..[Pred,P2,Arg1,Arg2], \+ var(P2), \+ atom(P2), P2=..
    [Pred2,Q,Loc],
     number(Q),         NP2=..[Pred2,Unboundvar,Loc],         NP=..
     [Pred,NP2,Arg1,Arg2] );
    (P=..[Pred,P2], \+ var(P2), \+ atom(P2), P2=..[Pred2,Q,Loc],
    number(Q),
     NP2=..[Pred2,Unboundvar,Loc], NP=..[Pred,NP2] ) ),
   !, generalize_quantities(S2,NS2), append(S1,[NP|NS2],NS), !.
generalize_quantities(S,S).


/* Variant that stops when a state in a sf/2 fact is reached, and
also */
/* permits random changes. Additional flag arg is set true when
reach occurs.*/
limited_once_means_ends(STATE,GOAL,OPLIST,GOALSTATE,M) :-
  retractall(unsolvable(_,_)),
   limited_means_ends(STATE,GOAL,OPLIST,GOALSTATE,M),
   (\+ debugflag;
   (write('Operator sequence found: '), nl, write(OPLIST), nl, nl)
   ), !.
limited_once_means_ends(STATE,GOAL,OPLIST,GOALSTATE,M) :-
   write('Limited_once_means_ends  fails  for  state:  '),  nl,
   write(STATE), nl,
   write('and goal conditions'), nl, write(GOAL), nl, !, fail.
limited_means_ends(STATE,GOAL,OPLIST,GOALSTATE,M) :-
   limited_means_ends2(STATE,GOAL,OPLIST,GOALSTATE,[],M), writede-
   bug7, !.


limited_means_ends2(STATE,GOAL,OPLIST,GOALSTATE,STACK,M) :-
   member([STATE,GOAL],STACK),
   writedebug4(STATE,GOAL,STACK), !, fail.
limited_means_ends2(STATE,_,[],STATE,_,M) :- nonvar(M), !.
limited_means_ends2(STATE,GOAL,OPLIST,GOALSTATE,STACK,M) :-
  \+debugflag, unsolvable(STATE,GOAL), writedebug5(STATE,GOAL,STACK),
```

```
!, fail.
limited_means_ends2(STATE,GOAL,[],STATE,STACK,M) :-
  get_difference(GOAL,STATE,[]), !.
limited_means_ends2(STATE,GOAL,OPLIST,GOALSTATE,STACK,M) :-
get_difference(GOAL,STATE,D),talky_desirable_op(D,STATE,OPERATOR),
  get_precondition(OPERATOR,STATE,PRELIST),
  \+ unachievable_difference(STATE,PRELIST),
  writedebug1(D,OPERATOR,STACK),
  limited_means_ends2(STATE,PRELIST,PREOPLIST,
PRESTATE,[[STATE,GOAL]|STACK],M),
  ((nonvar(M), OPLIST=PREOPLIST, GOALSTATE=PRESTATE, !);
   (writedebug2(PRESTATE,D,OPERATOR,STACK),
    apply_op(OPERATOR,PRESTATE,S2), do_randsubst(OPERATOR,_,STATE
,S2,POSTLIST),
    generalize_quantities(POSTLIST,XPOSTLIST),
    sort(XPOSTLIST,XXPOSTLIST),
    ((sf(M,XXPOSTLIST), append(PREOPLIST,[OPERATOR],OPLIST),
      GOALSTATE=POSTLIST, ! );
     (limited_means_ends2(POSTLIST,GOAL,POSTOPLIST,GOALSTATE,
                          [[STATE,GOAL]|STACK],M ),
      writedebug3(GOALSTATE,OPERATOR,STACK),
      append(PREOPLIST,[OPERATOR|POSTOPLIST],OPLIST) ) ) ) ).
limited_means_ends2(STATE,GOAL,OPLIST,GOALSTATE,STACK,M) :-
  sort(STATE,XSTATE), sort(GOAL,XGOAL),
  \+ solution(XSTATE,XGOAL,_,_),
  generalize_quantities(XSTATE,XXSTATE),
assertz(unsolvable(XXSTATE,XGOAL)),writedebug5(STATE,GOAL,STACK),
!, fail.


/* Debugging tools                                            */

/*These are enabled when the user asserts debugflag.*/
writedebug1(D,O,STACK) :- \+ debugflag, !.
writedebug1(D,O,STACK)   :-   length(STACK,NM1),   N   is   NM1+1,
write('>>Action '),
  write(O), write(' suggested at level '), write(N), nl,
  write('to achieve difference of '), write(D), nl, !.

writedebug2(S,D,O,STACK) :- \+ debugflag, !.
writedebug2(S,D,O,STACK) :- length(STACK,NM1), N is NM1+1,
  write('>>Action '), write(O), write(' now applied at level '),
  write(N), nl,
  write('to reduce difference of '), write(D),
  nl, write('in state in which '), write(S), nl, !.
```

```
writedebug3(S,O,STACK) :- \+ debugflag, !.
writedebug3(S,O,STACK) :- length(STACK,NM1), N is NM1+1,
  write('>>Level '),
  write(N), write(' terminated at state in which '), write(S), nl, !.


writedebug4(S,G,STACK) :- \+ debugflag, !.
writedebug4(S,G,STACK) :-
  write('>>>>Reasoning avoided an infinite loop at level '),
  length(STACK,NM1), N is NM1+1, write(N),
  write(' where problem was identical to that at level '),
  index([S,G],STACK,I), write(I), nl, !.


writedebug5(STATE,GOAL,STACK) :- \+ debugflag, !.
writedebug5(STATE,GOAL,STACK) :-
  write('>>>>UNSOLVABLE PROBLEM AT LEVEL '),
  length(STACK,NM1), N is NM1+1, write(N), nl, write('FOR STATE '),
  write(STATE), nl, write('AND DIFFERENCE '),
  get_difference(GOAL,STATE,DIFF), write(DIFF), nl, !.


writedebug6(STACK) :- \+ debugflag, !.
writedebug6(STACK) :-
  write('>>>>Previously computed solution used at level '),
  length(STACK,NM1), N is NM1+1, write(N), nl, !.


writedebug7 :- \+ debugflag, !.
writedebug7 :- nl, !.


writedebug8(OP) :- \+ debugflag, !.
writedebug8(OP)  :-  write('The   tutor   prefers   action   '),
writefact(OP,op),
  nl, !.


/**************************************************************/


/* Miscellaneous utility functions                        */


/* This takes a list of operators and tells you what the resulting
*/
/* state is after applying them to some starting state. */
apply_ops([],S,[S],S) :- !.
apply_ops([O|OL],S,[S|SL],NS)   :-   apply_op(O,S,S2),   apply_
ops(OL,S2,SL,NS), !.
```

```
/* Applies an operator to a state, sorting the result */
apply_op(O,S,XNS) :- apply_op_nb(O,S,XNS).
apply_op(O,S,XNS) :- debugflag, var(XNS), \+ apply_op_nb(O,S,XNS),
   write('>>>>Operator '), write(O), dummy,
   write(' could not be applied to: '), nl, write(S), nl, !, fail.
/* Like preceding but can print out debugging info */
talky_apply_op(O,S,XNS)     :-    get_precondition(O,S,PCL),    get_
difference(PCL,S,[]),
   get_deletepostcondition(O,S,DP), deleteitems(DP,S,S2),
   get_addpostcondition(O,S,AP), union(AP,S2,NS), sort(NS,XNS).
talky_apply_op(O,S,XNS)    :-    debugflag,   var(XNS),   \+   apply_op_
nb(O,S,XNS),
   write('>>>>Operator '), write(O),
   write(' could not be applied to: '), nl, write(S), !, nl, fail.
apply_op_nb(O,S,XNS)        :-       get_precondition(O,S,PCL),      get_
difference(PCL,S,[]),
   get_deletepostcondition(O,S,DP), deleteitems(DP,S,S2),
  get_addpostcondition(O,S,AP), union(AP,S2,NS), sort(NS,XNS), !.
apply_op_noprecond(O,S,XNS) :-
   get_deletepostcondition(O,S,DP), deleteitems(DP,S,S2),
  get_addpostcondition(O,S,AP), union(AP,S2,NS), sort(NS,XNS), !.


diode(X,X) :- X >= 0, !.
diode(X,0).
diode1(Y,Y) :- Y =< 100, !.
diode1(Y,100).


useless_op(O,S) :- apply_op(O,S,S), !.
xuseless_op(O,S) :- apply_op(O,S,S), \+ randchange(O,_,_,_,_,_,_),
!.
/* Note following needs subset, not factsubset, to compare 2 dif-
ferences */
desirable_op(Diff,S,O) :- get_recommended(Diff2,S,O), subset(Diff2,
Diff).
talky_desirable_op(Diff,S,O)     :-      get_recommended(Diff2,S,O),
subset(Diff2,Diff).
talky_desirable_op(Diff,S,O)    :-    debugflag,    \+    desirable_op_
nb(Diff,S,O),
   write('>>>>No operator is recommended for the difference '),
   write(Diff), nl, write(' in state '), write(S), nl, !, fail.
desirable_op_nb(Diff,S,O)        :-        get_recommended(Diff2,S,O),
subset(Diff2,Diff), !.
```

```prolog
all_achievable(S,G) :- copy_term(S,SS), copy_term(G,GG),
    get_difference(GG,SS,D), \+ unachievable_member(D,F), !.
all_achievable(S,G) :- debugflag, copy_term(S,SS), copy_term(G,GG),
    get_difference(GG,SS,D),  unachievable_member(D,F),
    write('>>>>Unachievable objective found: '), write(F), nl, !,
    fail.
unachievable_difference(S,G) :-get_difference(G,S,D),unachievable_
member(D,F),
    (\+ debugflag;
    write('>>>>Unachievable objective found: '), write(F), nl ), !.

unachievable_member(D,F) :- member(F,D), (atom(F); \+ F=..[not|_]),
    uncreatable(F), !.
unachievable_member(D,not(F)) :- member(not(F),D), unremovable(F), !.

uncreatable(F) :- \+ in_addpostcondition(F), !.
unremovable(F) :- \+ in_deletepostcondition(F), !.

some_precondition_for_op(O) :-
(precondition(O2,_);precondition(O2,_,_);precondition(O2,_,_,_)),
    (O=O2; member(O,O2)), !.

in_deletepostcondition(F)    :-  !,  any_deletepostcondition(O,L),
member(F,L), !.
in_addpostcondition(F) :- any_addpostcondition(O,L), member(F,L),
!.
any_addpostcondition(O,L) :- addpostcondition(O,C,L,M).
any_addpostcondition(O,L) :- addpostcondition(O,C,L).
any_addpostcondition(O,L) :- addpostcondition(O,L).
any_deletepostcondition(O,L) :- deletepostcondition(O,C,L,M).
any_deletepostcondition(O,L) :- deletepostcondition(O,C,L).
any_deletepostcondition(O,L) :- deletepostcondition(O,L).
added_by_randchange(F)   :-   randchange(_,_,_,FL,_,_,_),   (F=FL;
member(F,FL)), !.
deleted_by_randchange(F)   :-   randchange(_,_,FL,_,_,_,_),   (F=FL;
member(F,FL)),!.
some_precondition(L) :- precondition(_,L).
some_precondition(L) :- precondition(_,_,L).
some_precondition(L) :- precondition(_,_,L,_).

get_recommended(D,S,O) :- recommended(D,S2,O), factsubset(S2,S).
get_recommended(D,_,O) :- recommended(D,O).
```

```
get_precondition(O,S,L) :- precondition(O,C,L), factsubset(C,S),
!.
get_precondition(O,_,L) :- precondition(O,L).

get_deletepostcondition(O,S,L) :- deletepostcondition(O,C,L),
   factsubset(C,S), !.
get_deletepostcondition(O,_,L) :- deletepostcondition(O,L).

get_addpostcondition(O,S,L)       :-      addpostcondition(O,C,L),
factsubset(C,S), !.
get_addpostcondition(O,_,L) :- addpostcondition(O,L).


/****************************************************************/

/* Handling of randomness                                    */

/* After the postconditions are applied, random changes are applied
to */
/* the state.  These can add facts, delete facts, or change facts.  */

/* 6-argument randchange fact changes state before postconditions.
*/
do_randsubst(O,_,S,_,NS) :- randchange(O,_,S,NS,P,M),
   randnum(X), mod(X,331,XX), XX<(P*331),
   (M=''; (\+ M= '', write('WARNING: '), write(M), nl)), !.
/* 7-argument form makes local changes after postconditions. */
do_randsubst(O,Agent,_,S,XNS) :-
   bagof([DL,AL,P,M],get_randchange(O,Agent,S,DL,AL,P,M),RL),
   do_randsubst2(RL,S,NS), sort(NS,XNS), !.
do_randsubst(_,_,_,S,S).
get_randchange(O,Agent,S,DL,AL,P,M) :- randchange(O,Agent,S,DL,AL
,P,M);
   (randchange(OL,Agent,S,DL,AL,P,M), member(O,OL)).

do_randsubst2([],S,S).
do_randsubst2([[F,NF,P,M]|L],S,NS) :- randnum(X), mod(X,331,XX),
XX<(P*331),
   smart_deleteitems(F,S,S1), smart_union(NF,S1,S2),
   (M=''; (\+ M= '', write('WARNING: '), write(M), nl)), !,
   do_randsubst2(L,S2,NS).
do_randsubst2([_|L],S,NS) :- do_randsubst2(L,S,NS).

smart_deleteitems([],S,S).
smart_deleteitems(none,S,S) :- !.
smart_deleteitems([X|L],S,NS) :- !, deleteitems([X|L],S,NS).
```

```
smart_deleteitems(F,S,NS) :- deleteitems([F],S,NS).
smart_union([],S,S).
smart_union(none,S,S) :- !.
smart_union([X|L],S,NS) :- !, union(S,[X|L],NS).
smart_union(F,S,NS) :- union(S,[F],NS).


/* Generation of pseudo-random numbers and tools to use them */
randitem(L,I)   :-  length(L,N),  random(0,N,MR),  RR  is  1+MR,
item(RR,L,I), !.
randnum(N) :- random(1,362897,N), !.
randnum2(K) :- oldrandom(KK), K is KK-0.5, !.
normalrandnum2(K) :- oldrandom(N1), oldrandom(N2), oldrandom(N3),
   oldrandom(N4), K is 3.4641016*((0.25*(N1+N2+N3+N4))-0.5), !.
oldrandom(R) :- random(1,100000,K2), R is 0.00001 * K2, !.


/***************************************************************/

/* Checks for errors in means-ends facts by the programmer */

check_obvious_errors :- nice_setof([M,A],obvious_error(M,A),MAL),
   !, writepairlist(MAL).

obvious_error('a fact predicate name is misspelled: ',W2) :-
   member(W,[recommended,precondition,deletepostcondition,
       addpostcondition, randchange,nopref,intro]),
   get_misspelling(W,W2),
      (P=..[W2,X,Y]; P=..[W2,X,Y,Z]; P=..[W2,X,Y,Z,R];
      P=..[W2,X,Y,Z,R,S,T] ),
      call(P), \+ W2=xnopref.
obvious_error('precondition fact missing for action ',O) :-
   known_operator(O), \+ some_precondition_for_op(O), \+ O=init.
obvious_error('deletepostcondition fact missing for action ',O) :-
   known_operator(O), \+ get_deletepostcondition(O,S,L), \+ O=init.
obvious_error('addpostcondition fact missing for action ',O) :-
   known_operator(O), \+ get_addpostcondition(O,S,L), \+ O=init.
obvious_error('actor fact missing for action ',O) :-
   known_operator(O), \+ actor(O,A).
obvious_error('duration fact missing for action ',O) :-
   known_operator(O),    actor(O,A),    start_state(S),    \+
   duration(O,A,S,Mean,Range).
obvious_error('recommended fact missing for action ',O) :-
   some_precondition_for_op(O),    \+    recommended(_,O),    \+
   recommended(_,_,O).
obvious_error('recommended fact missing for action ',O) :-
```

```
     get_deletepostcondition(O,S,L),    \+   recommended(_,O),    \+
     recommended(_,_,O).
obvious_error('recommended fact missing for action ',O) :-
     get_addpostcondition(O,S,L),       \+   recommended(_,O),    \+
     recommended(_,_,O).
obvious_error('Number in the wrong place: ',P) :-
     member(P,[precondition(O,L),precondition(O,C,L),precondition(O
     ,C,L,M),
        deletepostcondition(O,L),deletepostcondition(O,C,L),
        deletepostcondition(O,C,L,M),addpostcondition(O,L),
        addpostcondition(O,C,L),              addpostcondition(O,C,L,M),
        nopref(O,D),
        recommended(C,O), recommended(C,S,O), randchange(O,Agent,C,D
     ,A,P,M)]),
        call(P), (number(O); number(L); number(C); number(M);
        number(A); number(D)).
obvious_error('5th argument not a probability: ',randchange(O,AG,
S,D,A,P,M)):-
        randchange(O,AG,S,D,A,P,M), \+ probnumber(P).
obvious_error('You cannot have both 2-arg and 3-arg recommend-
eds',[]) :-
        different_arg_recommendeds.


known_operator(O) :- recommended(_,O); recommended(_,_,O);
    (randchange(OL,_,_,_,_,_,_), ((\+ OL=[_|_], O=OL); member(O,OL))).


issue_warnings      :-     \+    studentflag,    setof([M,A],possible_
error(M,A),MAL),
        !, write('Warnings:'), nl, writepairlist(MAL), nl.
issue_warnings.


possible_error('This  fact  is  not  creatable: ',F) :- some_
precondition(PL),
     member(F,PL), positive_pred_expr(F), uncreatable(F),
     \+ added_by_randchange(F).
possible_error('This fact is not creatable except by random change:
',F) :-
     some_precondition(PL), member(F,PL), positive_pred_expr(F),
     uncreatable(F), added_by_randchange(F).
possible_error('This fact is not removable: ',F) :-
     some_precondition(PL), member(not(F),PL), unremovable(F),
     \+ deleted_by_randchange(F).
possible_error('This fact is not removable except by random change:
',F) :-
     some_precondition(PL), member(not(F),PL), unremovable(F),
```

```
      deleted_by_randchange(F).
possible_error('Null change: ',randchange(O,AG,C,D,A,P,M)) :-
    randchange(O,AG,C,D,A,P,M), factsubset(D,A), factsubset(A,D).


writepairlist([]).
writepairlist([[X,Y]|L]) :- write(X), write(Y), nl, writepairlist(L).
positive_pred_expr(P) :- atom(P), !.
positive_pred_expr(P) :- P=..[Pred|L], \+ Pred=not, !.
probnumber(P) :- number(P), 0 =< P, P =< 1, !.
different_arg_recommendeds :- recommended(D,O), recommended(D,S,O),
!.
draw_order_loop(B,B) :- !.
draw_order_loop(B2,B) :- draw_order(B2,B3), draw_order_loop(B3,B),
!.


/*******************************************************************
******* */
/* List utilities                                                 */

listp([]).
listp([_|_]).


deleteone(X,[X|L],L).
deleteone(X,[Y|L],[Y|M]) :- deleteone(X,L,M).


get_difference(L1,L2,DL) :- get_difference2(L1,L2,DL), !.
get_difference2([],S,[]).
get_difference2([not(P)|G],S,G3) :- setof(P,member(P,S),PL),
  negate_expressions(PL,XPL), !, get_difference2(G,S,G2),
  append(XPL,G2,G3), !.
get_difference2([not(P)|G],S,G2) :- \+ member(P,S), !,
  get_difference2(G,S,G2).
get_difference2([P|G],S,G2) :- member(P,S), !, get_difference2
(G,S,G2).
get_difference2([P|G],S,[P|G2]) :- get_difference2(G,S,G2).


negate_expressions([],[]).
negate_expressions([P|PL],[not(P)|NPL])           :-           negate_
expressions(PL,NPL).


factsubset([],SL).
factsubset([not(P)|L],L2) :- !, \+ member(P,L2), factsubset(L,L2).
factsubset([P|L],SL) :- append(SL1,[P|SL2],SL), append(SL1,SL2,NSL),
    factsubset(L,NSL).
```

```prolog
subset([],L).
subset([X|L],L2) :- member(X,L2), subset(L,L2).


singlemember(X,[X|L]) :- !.
singlemember(X,[Y|L]) :- singlemember(X,L).

unionall([L],L) :- !.
unionall([L|LL],NL) :- unionall(LL,NL2), union(L,NL2,NL), !.
union([],L,L).
union([X|L1],L2,L3) :- member(X,L2), !, union(L1,L2,L3).
union([X|L1],L2,[X|L3]) :- union(L1,L2,L3).

deleteitems([],L,L) :- !.
deleteitems([X|L],L2,L3) :-mydelete(X,L2,L4),deleteitems(L,L4,L3),
!.
mydelete(Item,L,NL) :- member(Item,L), !, delete(L,Item,NL).
mydelete(_,L,L).

item(1,[X|_],X) :- !.
item(K,[_|L],I) :- Km1 is K-1, item(Km1,L,I), !.

is_permutation(L,M) :- subset(L,M), subset(M,L), !.

subsequence([],L) :- !.
subsequence([X|L],[X|M]) :- !, subsequence(L,M).
subsequence(L,[X|M]) :- subsequence(L,M).

permutemember(X,[X|L]) :- !.
permutemember(X,[Y|L]) :- subset(X,Y), subset(Y,X), !.
permutemember(X,[Y|L]) :- permutemember(X,L).

elimdups([],[]).
elimdups([X|L],[X|M]) :- mydelete(X,L,L2), !, elimdups(L2,M), !.

is_a_list([]).
is_a_list([X|Y]).

checkretract(S) :- call(S), retract(S), !.
checkretract(S).

index(X,[X|L],1) :- !.
index(X,[Y|L],N) :- index(X,L,Nm1), N is Nm1+1.

substitute(X,Y,[],[]) :- !.
substitute(X,Y,[X|L],[Y|NL]) :- !, substitute(X,Y,L,NL), !.
substitute(X,Y,[Z|L],[Z|NL]) :- substitute(X,Y,L,NL), !.
```

```prolog
minlist([X],X) :- !.
minlist([X|L],M) :- minlist(L,M), M < X, !.
minlist([X|L],X).
maxlist([X],X) :- !.
maxlist([X|L],M) :- maxlist(L,M), M > X, !.
maxlist([X|L],X).


sumup([X],X) :- !.
sumup([X|L],Y) :- sumup(L,Y2), Y is Y2+X, !.


/* Other utility functions */

concatenate(S1,S2,S) :- name(S1,AS1), name(S2,AS2),
    append(AS1,AS2,AS), name(S,AS), !.


identical_states(S1,S2) :- subset(S1,S2), subset(S2,S1), !.


nice_write_acts(S) :- act(A,Op,T1,T2),
  XT1 is (floor((T1*100)+0.5))*0.01, XT2 is (floor((T2*100)+0.5))*0.01,
    write(S,'Agent '), write(S,A), write(S,' did "'), write(S,Op),
    write(S,'" from '), write(S,XT1), write(S,' to '), write(S,XT2),
    nl(S),
    fail.
nice_write_acts(_).
nice_write_states(S) :- state(T,State), writeq(S,state(T,State)),
    write(S,'.'), nl(S), fail.
nice_write_states(_).


/* dump :- tell(tmpdump), listing(status), listing(act), listing(state),
    told, !. */


mod(X,M,MX) :- MX is X-(M*floor(X/M)), !.


rowemax(X,Y,X) :- X>Y, !.
rowemax(X,Y,Y).
rowemin(X,Y,X) :- X<Y, !.
rowemin(X,Y,Y).


nice_bagof(X,P,L) :- bagof(X,P,L), !.
nice_bagof(X,P,[]).
nice_setof(X,P,L) :- setof(X,P,L), !.
nice_setof(X,P,[]).


capitalized(S) :- name(S,[AC|_]), AC>64, AC<91, !.
```

```
make_lower_case(W,NW) :- name(W,AW), make_lower_case2(AW,ANW),
   name(NW,ANW).
make_lower_case2([],[]).
make_lower_case2([AC|AW],[NAC|ANW]) :- AC<91, AC>64, NAC is AC+32, !,
   make_lower_case2(AW,ANW).
make_lower_case2([AC|AW],[AC|ANW]) :- !, make_lower_case2(AW,ANW).

/* Computing possible misspellings */

get_misspelling(W1,W2) :- name(W1,AW1),
   (deleteone(X,AW1,NAW1);deleteone(X,NAW1,AW1);transpose(AW1,NAW1)),
   lettercode(X), name(W2,NAW1), \+ W1=W2.
lettercode(X)   :-   member(X,[97,98,99,100,101,102,103,104,105,106,
107,108,109,110,111,112,113,114,115,116,117,118,119,120,121,122]).

transpose([X,Y|L],[Y,X|L]).
transpose([X|L],[X|M]) :- transpose(L,M).

chars_to_integer(Chars,N)    :-    name(Chars,AChars),    chars_to_
integer2(AChars,N).
chars_to_integer2([Char],N) :- Char>47, Char<58, N is Char-48, !.
chars_to_integer2(Chars,N)    :-    append(Chars2,[Char],Chars),
Char>47, Char<58,
   chars_to_integer2(Chars2,N2), N1 is Char-48, N is (10*N2)+N1, !.
```

Appendix E: Counterplanner for Attacks

This Prolog program is discussed in Sects. 12.4.3 and 12.4.4. It first does a careful analysis of planner and its actions to find good possible "ploys" or ways to foil the plan. It then uses a greedy algorithm to choose a good set of proposed ploys. It also requires loading of the program in Appendix D.

```
/* Various routines for analyzing a particular means-ends */
/* problem, mostly used for counterplanning analysis. */
/* To use, do setupmns0.  */
/* Then use "greedy" to create a defensive plan, a set of ploys. */
/* :- include(ghack). */
:- set_prolog_flag(singleton_warning,off).
:- set_prolog_flag(unknown,fail).
```

© Springer International Publishing Switzerland 2016
N.C. Rowe, J. Rrushi, *Introduction to Cyberdeception*,
DOI 10.1007/978-3-319-41187-3

```
/* ANALYZES THE MEANS-ENDS DEFINITIONS TO CLASSIFY FACTS */
/* Find pairs of opposites and those not in any pair.  */
/* Used by counterplan analysis. */
/* Must load a problem-defining file before running this. */
/* Note: ploys can be ruled out in the definitions file with noploy/2;
*/
/* ploys only probabbly successful can have ploysuccess/3 facts.
*/
/* Factargtype/1 facts can indicate possible instantiations of
values. */


setupmns0 :- retractall(opposite(_,_)), retractall(orphan_delete(_)),
    retractall(orphan_add(_)),          open('analout.pl',write,S),
    setupmns02(S),
    close(S).
setupmns02(S) :- make_opposite_facts, bagof([P1,P2],opposite(P1,P
2),P12L),
  member([PA,PB],P12L), write(PA), write(' could be changed to '),
    writeq(PB), write('.'), nl, fail.
setupmns02(S) :- precondition_deletes, setof(P,orphan_delete(P),
PL),
    member(PA,PL), writeq(PA), write(' could be deleted.'), nl,
    fail.
setupmns02(S) :- precondition_adds,  setof(P,orphan_add(P),PL),
member(PA,PL),
    writeq(PA), write(' could be added.'), nl, fail.
setupmns02(S)   :-   opposite(A,B),   writeq(S,opposite(A,B)),
write(S,'.'),
    nl(S), fail.
setupmns02(S)  :- orphan_delete(A),  writeq(S,orphan_delete(A)),
write(S,'.'),
    nl(S), fail.
setupmns02(S)   :-   orphan_add(A),   writeq(S,orphan_add(A)),
write(S,'.'),
    nl(S), fail.
setupmns02(_).


/* Find pairs of opposite facts by examining operator specifica-
tions. */
/* Consider only operators with same pred name or common argument.
*/
make_opposite_facts :- xdeletepostcondition(Op,DPL), \+ Op=init,
    xaddpostcondition(Op,APL), member(P1,DPL), member(P2,APL),
    P1=..[Pred1,Arg1|Rest1], P2=..[Pred2,Arg2|Rest2],
    (Pred1=Pred2; (\+ var(Arg1), \+ var(Arg2), Arg1=Arg2)),
```

```
      instantiate_pe(P1), instantiate_pe(P2), \+ P1=P2,
      \+ noploy(P1,P2), \+ opposite(P1,P2),
      assertz(opposite(P1,P2)), write(opposite(P1,P2)), nl, fail.
/* Delete proposed opposites involved in the same precond or add-
postcond */
make_opposite_facts :- opposite(P1,P2), xprecondition(Op,DPL),
    member(P1,DPL), member(P2,DPL), retract(opposite(P1,P2)),
    write('Removing '), write(opposite(P1,P2)),
    write(' since together in precondition.'), nl, fail.
make_opposite_facts :- opposite(P1,P2), xaddpostcondition(Op,APL),
    member(P1,APL), member(P2,APL), retract(opposite(P1,P2)),
    write('Removing '), write(opposite(P1,P2)),
    write(' since together in addpostcondition.'), nl, fail.
/* Delete proposed opposites involved in multiple pairs */
make_opposite_facts        :-        bagof(P2,opposite(P1,P2),P2L),
member(P3,P2L),
    member(P4,P2L), \+P3=P4, P3=..[Pred3,Arg3|_], P4=..[Pred4,Arg4|_],
    (\+      Pred3=Pred4;      \+     Arg3=Arg4),      member(P,P2L),
    retract(opposite(P1,P)),
    write('Removing '), write(opposite(P1,P)),
    write(' since two opposites are possible.'), nl, fail.
make_opposite_facts        :-        bagof(P1,opposite(P1,P2),P1L),
member(P3,P1L),
    member(P4,P1L),    \+    P3=P4,    P3=..[Pred3,Arg3|_],    P4=..
    [Pred4,Arg4|_],
    (\+      Pred3=Pred4;      \+     Arg3=Arg4),      member(P,P1L),
    retract(opposite(P,P2)),
    write('Removing '), write(opposite(P,P2)),
    write(' since two opposites are possible.'), nl, fail.
make_opposite_facts :- nl.

precondition_deletes :-
    (xprecondition(Op,L); randchange(Op,_,_,L,_,_,_); goal(_,L)),
```

```
    member(P,L), \+ var(P), \+ P=[], \+ P=not(_), \+ opposite(P,P2),
    \+ noploy(P,[]), \+ orphan_delete(P), assertz(orphan_delete(P)),
    fail.
precondition_deletes.
precondition_adds :-
    (xprecondition(Op,L); randchange(Op,_,_,_L,_,_); goal(_,L)),
  member(not(P),L), \+ var(P), instantiate_pe(P), \+ opposite(P,P2),
    \+ noploy([],P), \+ orphan_add(P),   assertz(orphan_add(P)),
    fail.
precondition_adds.


/* Instantiate all variables in a given fact */
instantiate_pe(P)      :-      P=..[Pred|ArgL],      length(ArgL,N),
functor(FAT,Pred,N), !,
    factargtype(FAT), instantiate_all_args(P,FAT,ArgL,1).
instantiate_all_args(P,FAT,[Arg|ArgL],K)        :-       instantiate_
arg(P,FAT,Arg,K),
    Kp1 is K+1, instantiate_all_args(P,FAT,ArgL,Kp1).
instantiate_all_args(_,_,[],_).
instantiate_arg(P,FAT,Arg,K) :- (atom(Arg); number(Arg)),
    P=..[Pred|Args], FAT=..[Pred|Args2], item(K,Args2,ArgL),
      member(Arg,ArgL), !.
instantiate_arg(P,FAT,Arg,K) :- \+ var(Arg), Arg=..[Pred2|Args2],
    FAT=..[_|Newargs],        item(K,Newargs,Valuelist),         !,
    member(Arg,Valuelist),
    instantiate_pe(Arg).
instantiate_arg(P,FAT,Arg,K) :- var(Arg), !, FAT=..[_|Newargs],
    item(K,Newargs,Valuelist),
    /* replace any numbers by 1 as default */
    ((Valuelist=number, Arg=1, !);
      (member(Arg,Valuelist),
      (atom(Arg); number(Arg);
      (Arg=not(PE), instantiate_pe(PE));
      (\+Arg=not(PE), \+ atom(Arg), instantiate_pe(Arg)) ) ) ).


xdeletepostcondition(Op,DPL) :- deletepostcondition(Op,DPL).
xdeletepostcondition(Op,DPL) :- deletepostcondition(Op,_,DPL).
xaddpostcondition(Op,APL) :- addpostcondition(Op,APL).
xaddpostcondition(Op,APL) :- addpostcondition(Op,_,APL).
xprecondition(Op,PPL) :- precondition(Op,PPL).
xprecondition(Op,PPL) :- precondition(Op,_,PPL).
/* Note following may incorrectly specialize some terms with
```

```prolog
"setof" */
/* but advantages of reducing size of set are more important */
alldeletepostcondition(Op,DPL) :-
  setof(D,deletepostcondition_member(Op,D),DPL), !.
deletepostcondition_member(Op,D) :-
  (deletepostcondition(Op,DL);      deletepostcondition(Op,_,DL)),
  member(D,DL).
alladdpostcondition(Op,APL) :-
  setof(A,addpostcondition_member(Op,A),APL), !.
addpostcondition_member(Op,A) :-
  (addpostcondition(Op,AL);            addpostcondition(Op,_,AL)),
  member(A,AL).


/* Version that unquantifies conditions before subsetting */
xget_recommended(D,S,O) :- recommended(D,S2,O),
  unquantify(S2,XS2), factsubset(XS2,S).
xget_recommended(D,_,O) :- recommended(D,O).
xget_precondition(O,S,L) :- precondition(O,C,L),
  unquantify_preds(C,XC), factsubset(XC,S), !.
xget_precondition(O,_,L) :- precondition(O,L).
xget_deletepostcondition(O,S,L) :- deletepostcondition(O,C,L),
  unquantify_preds(C,XC), factsubset(XC,S), !.
xget_deletepostcondition(O,_,L) :- deletepostcondition(O,L).
xget_addpostcondition(O,S,L) :- addpostcondition(O,C,L),
  unquantify_preds(C,XC), factsubset(XC,S), !.
xget_addpostcondition(O,_,L) :- addpostcondition(O,L).


member_in_common(L1,L2) :- member(I,L1), member(I,L2), !.


/* *****************************************************************
*/
/* Analyze variantout.pl file to find changes to a state that */
/* cause statistically significant (> 1 s.d.) planning */
analv    :-           consult('variantout.pl'),     retractall(vavd
ata(_,_,_,_,_,_)),
  setof(N2,M2^D2^A2^BT2^T2^variantdata(M2,N2,D2,A2,BT2,T2),N2L),
  member(N,N2L), bagof(T,BT^xvariantdata(M,N,D,A,BT,T),TL),
  mean_and_stdev(TL,Mean,SD), assertz(vavdata(M,N,D,A,Mean,SD)),
  fail.
analv :- open('analvout.pl',append,Stream), analv2(Stream),
  close(Stream), fail.
analv.
analv2(Stream) :- vavdata(M,N,D,A,Mean,SD), write(Stream,[M,N,D,A
,Mean,SD]),
```

```
     nl(Stream), write([M,N,D,A,Mean,SD]), nl, fail.
analv2(Stream) :- vavdata(M1,N,[],[],Mean1,SD1),
   vavdata(M2,N,D2,A2,Mean2,SD2),
   Deltamean is Mean1-Mean2, TwoSD is SD1+SD2, NTwoSD is -TwoSD,
   (Deltamean < NTwoSD; Deltamean > TwoSD),
   write('Significant  change:  '),  write([N,D2,A2,Mean1,SD1,Mean2
   ,SD2]), nl,
   write(Stream,'Significant change: '),
   write(Stream,[N,D2,A2,Mean1,SD1,Mean2,SD2]), nl(Stream), fail.
analv2(Stream).
xvariantdata(M,N,D,A,BT,T) :- variantdata(M,N,D,A,BT,T), T<200.
mean_and_stdev(TL,Mean,SD) :- length(TL,N), mysumup(TL,Sum), Mean
is Sum/N,
   stdevsumup(TL,Mean,SDSum), SD is sqrt(SDSum)/N, !.
mysumup([X],X) :- !.
mysumup([X|L],S) :- mysumup(L,S2), S is S2+X, !.
stdevsumup([],Mean,0) :- !.
stdevsumup([X|L],Mean,SDSum) :- stdevsumup(L,Mean,SDSum2),
   SDSum is SDSum2 + ((X-Mean)*(X-Mean)), !.


/* ************************************************************ */
/* ANALYSIS OF EFFECTS OF CHANGES TO SINGLE FACTS IN A STATE */

/* To analyze change scopes, first calculate a data file mnsdata.pl
*/
/* containing the numbered states in time order with info about */
/* what was deleted, added, a goal, or a precondition at that
state. */
setupmns1 :- setupmns1('goruns.pl').
setupmns1(Infile) :- build_partial_order(Infile).
build_partial_order(Infile)       :-       retractall(runnum(_)),
asserta(runnum(1)),
 retractall(statenum(_)), asserta(statenum(0)), retractall(s(_,_)),
   open(Infile,read,SI), open('tmptransitions1.pl',write,SO),
   open('cfullstates.pl',write,SF),        open('tmpstatetimes1.
   pl',write,ST),
   bpo2(SI,SO,SGR,SF,ST),  close(SO),   close(SI),   close(SF),
   close(ST),
   open('cstates.pl',write,SO2), list_s_states(SO2), close(SO2),
   setupmns1b,        sort_secondary('tmptransitions1.pl',10000,
   'tmptransitions2.pl'),
   open('tmptransitions2.pl',read,SI3),       open('ctransitions.
   pl',write,SO3),
   count_pred_lines(SI3,SO3), close(SI3), close(SO3), !.
bpo2(SI,SO,SGR,SF,ST) :- repeat, read(SI,P),
```

```
   ((P=run(K), /* dummy, */ retract(runnum(Km1)), asserta(runnum(K)),
      \+   K=1,    write(ST,time(Km1,999999,-1000)),    write(ST,'.'),
      nl(ST) );
     (P=s(T,Op,Tend,Agent,State1,State2), runnum(K),
      sort(State1,State1B), unquantify_preds(State1B,State1C),
      sort(State1C,State1D),
      sort(State2,State2B), unquantify_preds(State2B,State2C),
      sort(State2C,State2D),
      lookup_s_state(M1,State1D,State1B,SF),
      lookup_s_state(M2,State2D,State2B,SF),
      ((M1=200, dummy); \+ M1=200), ((M2=200, dummy); \+ M2=200),
      write(ST,time(K,M1,T)), write(ST,'.'), nl(ST),
      write(ST,time(K,M2,Tend)), write(ST,'.'), nl(ST),
      xget_precondition(Op,State1C,PL1), unquantify_preds(PL1,PL),
      deleteitems(State2C,State1C,DL),   deleteitems(State1C,State2C
      ,AL),
/* transition facts are written out giving: starting statenum,
ending */
/* statenum, operator, agent, preconditions, and postconditions */
      singlefactwrite(SO,t(M1,M2,Op,Agent,PL,DL,AL)) );
     (\+ P=run(_), \+ P=s(_,_,_,_,_,_)) ),
   P=end_of_file, runnum(K2), write(ST,time(K2,999999,-1000)),
   write(ST,'.'), nl(ST), !.
lookup_s_state(M,State, ,_) :- s(M,State), !.
lookup_s_state(M,State,FullState,FullStateStream) :- statenum(M),
   assertz(s(M,State)), retract(statenum(M)), Mp1 is M+1,
   assertz(statenum(Mp1)),      writeq(FullStateStream,sf(M,FullSt
   ate)),
   write(FullStateStream,'.'), nl(FullStateStream), !.
list_s_states(SO)      :-       s(M,State),       writeq(SO,s(M,State)),
write(SO,'.'),
   nl(SO), fail.
list_s_states(SO).


/* Calculate duration-to-run-end for all times; this will be */
/* the "potential of each state. */
setupmns1b      :-        sort_secondary('tmpstatetimes1.pl',10000,
'tmpstatetimes2.pl'),
   open('tmpstatetimes2.pl',read,SI),         open('tmpstatetimes3.
   pl',write,SO),
   setupmns1b2(SI,SO), close(SI), close(SO),
   sort_secondary('tmpstatetimes3.pl',10000,'tmpstatetimes4.pl'),
   open('tmpstatetimes4.pl',read,SI2),        open('cstatetimes.
   pl',write,SO2),
   read(SI2,P), setupmns1b3(SI2,SO2,P), close(SI2), close(SO2), !.
```

```prolog
/* First read in the times of one run and calculate durations to
end of run */
setupmns1b2(SI,SO) :- get_run_times(SI,TL), maxpairtime(TL,Tmax),
calculate_duration_to_max(TL,Tmax,DTL),                write_run_time_
offsets(SO,DTL),
    setupmns1b2(SI,SO).
setupmns1b2(SI,SO).
get_run_times(SI,TL) :- read(SI,P),
    ((P=end_of_file, !, fail);
    (P=time(_,999999,-1000), TL=[]);
    (P=time(_,M,T), get_run_times(SI,TL2), TL=[M-T|TL2] ) ), !.
maxpairtime([_-T|MTL],Tmax) :- maxpairtime(MTL,Tmax), T<Tmax, !.
maxpairtime([_-T|_],T).
calculate_duration_to_max([],_,[]).
calculate_duration_to_max([M-T|MTL],Tmax,[M-D|MDL])  :-   D   is
Tmax-T, !,
    calculate_duration_to_max(MTL,Tmax,MDL).
write_run_time_offsets(SO,MTL) :- member(M-T,MTL),
    singlefactwrite(SO,pot(M,T)), fail.
write_run_time_offsets(_,_).
/* Now calculate the average time-to-run-end for a state over all
runs */
setupmns1b3(SI,SO,pot(M,T)) :- setupmns1b3b(SI,SO,M,TL,NP),
    sumup([T|TL],Tsum), length(TL,Tlen), Tav is Tsum/(Tlen+1),
    singlefactwrite(SO,pot(M,Tav)), !, setupmns1b3(SI,SO,NP).
setupmns1b3(_,_,_).
setupmns1b3b(SI,SO,M,TL,P) :- read(SI,P2),
    ((P2=pot(M,T2), !, setupmns1b3b(SI,SO,M,TL2,P), TL=[T2|TL2]);
    (P=P2, TL=[]) ), !.
/* Combine scope facts for the same place in different runs */
count_pred_lines(SI,SO) :- read(SI,P), P=..XP, append(XP,[1],XP2),
    count_pred_lines(SI,SO,XP2).
count_pred_lines(SI,SO,XLastP) :- read(SI,P), \+ P=end_of_file,
P=..XP,
    ((append(XP,[K],XLastP), NK is K+1);
    (NK=1, LastP=..XLastP, singlefactwrite(SO,LastP)) ),
    append(XP,[NK],NLastP), !, count_pred_lines(SI,SO,NLastP).
count_pred_lines(SI,SO,XLastP)              :-            LastP=..XLastP,
singlefactwrite(SO,LastP), !.

/* Finds "problem spots" in the plan, for each ploy  */
setupmns2 :- consult('ctransitions.pl'), consult('cstates.pl'),
    consult('analout.pl'),               open('tmpscopes1.pl',write,S),
    findscopes(S),
    close(S), sort_secondary('tmpscopes1.pl',10000,'cscopes.pl'), !.
```

```
/* Find most scopes */
findscopes(Stream) :-
  t(Statenum1,Statenum2,Op,Agent,PL,DL,AL,K), s(Statenum1,State1),
  apply_change(State1,_,XD,XA),
  /* Ignore ploys that achieve what selected ops do */
  make_list(XD,XXD), make_list(XA,XXA),
    \+ (get_deletepostcondition(Op,State1,XXD),
          get_addpostcondition(Op,State1,XXA) ),
    unquantify_pred(XD,D), unquantify_pred(XA,A),
    (goal(Agent,GL); (\+ goal(Agent,_), GL=[])),
    find_change_effect(D,A,GL,DL,AL,PL,E),
  doublefactwrite(Stream,interferes(Statenum1,Statenum2,D,A,
  E,K)), fail.
/* Additional rule finds violations of goal state */
findscopes(Stream)            :-            last_state_number(Lastnum),
bagof(G2,A^goal(A,G2),G2L),
  unionall(G2L,Topgoals), t(_,Lastnum,_,_,_,_,_,_),
  ((member(A,Topgoals), \+ A=not(_), instantiate_pe(A),
    s(Lastnum,Laststate), apply_change(Laststate,_,A,[]),
    doublefactwrite(Stream,interferes(Lastnum,100000,A,[],pres
    top,1)) );
   (member(not(D),Topgoals), instantiate_pe(D),
    s(Lastnum,Laststate), apply_change(Laststate,_,[],D),
    doublefactwrite(Stream,interferes(Lastnum,100000,[],D,pres
    top,1)) ) ),
   fail.
findscopes(_).
last_state_number(Lastnum) :- t(_,Lastnum,_,_,_,_,_,_),
  \+ t(Lastnum,_,_,_,_,_,_,_), !.
apply_change(State,CState,XD,XA) :- opposite(D,A), unquantify_pred
(D,XD),
  unquantify_pred(A,XA), member(XD,State), \+ member(XA,State),
  (\+ XA=reported(F,P1,P2);
   (XA=reported(F,P1,P2), \+ member(reported(F,P1,_),State)) ),
  (\+ XA=ordered(F,P1,P2);
   (XA=ordered(F,P1,P2), \+ member(ordered(F,P1,_),State)) ),
  delete(State,XD,State2), CState=[XA|State2].
apply_change(State,CState,XI,[]) :- orphan_delete(I),
 unquantify_pred(I,XI), member(XI,State), delete(State,XI,CState).
apply_change(State,CState,[],XI) :- orphan_add(I),
  unquantify_pred(I,XI), \+ member(XI,State),
  (\+ XI=reported(F,P1,P2);
   (XI=reported(F,P1,P2), \+ member(reported(F,P1,_),State)) ),
  (\+ XI=ordered(F,P1,P2);
```

```
       (XI=ordered(F,P1,P2), \+ member(ordered(F,P1,_),State)) ),
       CState=[XI|State].
/* A ploy is cancelled by an action if the action accomplishes the
ploy. */
find_change_effect(D,A,GL,DL,AL,PL,cancel) :-
       ((A=[], member(D,DL)); (D=[], member(A,AL));
       (\+A=[], \+D=[], member(D,DL); member(A,AL)) ), !.
/* A ploy clobbers an action if it invalidates a precondition or a
goal */
find_change_effect(D,A,GL,DL,AL,PL,prestop) :-
       (member(D,PL); member(not(A),PL)), !.
/* find_change_effect(D,A,GL,DL,AL,PL,poststop) :-
       (member(D,AL); member(A,DL)), !. */



/* Calculate simple perturbation-removal plans at each place */
/* where a counterplanning ploy could perturb a plan. */
/* Note: must load a problem-definitions file before running. */
setupmns3 :- consult('cscopes.pl'), consult('cfullstates.pl'),
       consult('cstatetimes.pl'), open('tmpfixplan1.pl',write,S),
       bagof(K,ST^sf(K,ST),KL), append(_,[Kmax],KL),
       asserta(current_sf_number(Kmax)), bagof(G2,A^goal(A,G2),G2L),
       unionall(G2L,Topgoals), make_fixplans(S,Topgoals), close(S), !.
make_fixplans(Stream,Topgoals) :- interferes(Statenum1,Statenum2,D
,A,E,K),
       make_fixplans2(Stream,Topgoals,Statenum1,Statenum2,D,A,K,E),
       fail.
make_fixplans(_,_).
make_fixplans2(Stream,_,Statenum1,Statenum2,D,A,K,cancel) :-
       pot(Statenum1,Pot1), pot(Statenum2,Pot2), DPot is Pot2-Pot1,
       doublefactwrite(Stream,fixplan(Statenum1,D,A,[],[],[],K,Statenu
       m1,DPot)), !.
make_fixplans2(Stream,Topgoals,Statenum1,Statenum2,D,A,K,prestop):-
       write('Working on '), write(interferes(Statenum1,Statenum2,D,A
       ,K,prestop)),
       nl, sf(Statenum1,FullState), opposite_fact(A,XA),
       assemble_needed_preconds(D,XA,Preconds),
      \+ unachievable_member(Preconds,_),
       ((D=[], Tmpstate=FullState); (\+ D=[], delete(FullState,D,Tmps
       tate))),
       ((A=[], CState=Tmpstate); (\+ A=[], sort([A|Tmpstate],CState))),
       make_fixplans3(FullState,CState,Preconds,Topgoals,Ops,FinalStat
       e,Statenum3),
       ((Statenum3 > -1,
         deleteitems(FinalState,CState,DL), deleteitems(CState,FinalS
```

```
      tate,AL),
      /* Cost of fixplan is the extra cost it adds to a solution */
      rate_new_states(CState,Ops,CPot), pot(Statenum1,P1),
      incompleteness_factor(CState,Incompfactor),
      Fixcost is CPot-P1+Incompfactor,
      doublefactwrite(Stream,
        fixplan(Statenum1,D,A,Ops,DL,AL,K,Statenum3,Fixcost) ) );
      doublefactwrite(Stream,fixplan(Statenum1,D,A,
                              none,[],[],K,Statenum3,100000) ) ), !.
/* Find a sequence of operators to reach the top goals of all
agents, */
/* stopping however when a known state is reached. */
/* First handle trivial case of starting state with known plan to
goal. */
make_fixplans3(FullState,CState,_,_,[],FullState,Statenum3) :-
  generalize_quantities(CState,XCState), sf(Statenum3,XCState), !.
/* Otherwise do a full planning to find a way to a known state. */
make_fixplans3(_,CState,_,Topgoals,Ops,FinalState,Statenum3) :-
    limited_once_means_ends(CState,Topgoals,Ops,FinalState,State
    num3),
    (nonvar(Statenum3); Statenum3 = -1), !.
/* If planning fails, the ploy makes the goals impossible */
make_fixplans3(_,_,_,_,none,_,-1) :- !.
/* Considers each step in a fixplan, and calculates which interme-
diate */
/* states are new and what their potentials are. */
rate_new_states(State,[],D) :- sf(Statenum,State), pot(Statenum,D),
!.
/* Unknown state terminating successful fixplan must be another
goal state */
rate_new_states(State,[],0) :- !.
rate_new_states(State,[Op|Ops],NPot) :- apply_op(Op,State,NState),
    actor(Op,A), compute_duration(Op,A,State,D1a),
compute_duration(Op,A,State,D1b),    compute_duration(Op,A,State,
D1c),
    D1 is (D1a+D1b+D1c)/3.0, rate_new_states(NState,Ops,Pot), NPot
is Pot+D1, !.
/* Give extra cost to states in which a goal is reported falsely */
incompleteness_factor(S,100)    :-    member(reported(F),S),    \+
member(F,S),
    goal(_,GL), member(reported(F),GL), !.
incompleteness_factor(S,100)   :-   member(reported(F,P1,P2),S),   \+
member(F,S),
    goal(_,GL), member(reported(F,P1,P2),GL), !.
```

```
incompleteness_factor(S,0).


/* Coalesces analysis results so far and determines replanning
plans */
/* for fixes of every possible change at every possible state. */
/* (Note: Must also load problem-definition file before running.) */
setupmns4 :- consult('cscopes.pl'), consult('ctransitions.pl'),
    consult('tmpfixplan1.pl'), open('tmpfixplan2.pl',write,S),
    retractall(mns4cache(_,_,_)),              do_fixplan_inheritance(S),
    close(S).
do_fixplan_inheritance(Outstream) :-
    fixplan(Statenum,D,A,Ops,DL,AL,K,FStatenum,Fixcost),
    do_fixplan_inheritance2(Outstream,Statenum,D,A,Ops,DL,AL,K,Fixc
    ost), fail.
do_fixplan_inheritance(_).
do_fixplan_inheritance2(_,Statenum,D,A,_,_,_,_,_)    :-  mns4cache
(Statenum,D,A), !.
do_fixplan_inheritance2(OS,Statenum,D,A,Ops,DL,AL,K,Fixcost) :-
    assertz(mns4cache(Statenum,D,A)),
    singlefactwrite(OS,fixplan(Statenum,D,A,Ops,DL,AL,K,Fixcost)).
/* Do inference of fixplans backwards from states with known fixplans
*/
do_fixplan_inheritance2(OS,Statenum,D,A,Ops,DL,AL,K,Fixcost) :-
    t(Statenum2,Statenum,Op,Agent,PL2,DL2,AL2,K2),
    \+ fixplan(Statenum2,D,A,_,_,_,_,_,_),
    fixplan_inheritance_args(Op,Ops,DL,AL,PL2,Fixcost,
               Ops,NDL,NAL,NFixcost),
    do_fixplan_inheritance2(OS,Statenum2,D,A,NOps,NDL,NAL,K2,NFixc
    ost).
/* Temporally inherit backward over ops that do not affect the fix-
plan */
fixplan_inheritance_args(Op,Ops,DL,AL,PL2,Fixcost,Ops,DL,AL,Fixc
ost) :-
    \+ (member(D2,DL), member(D2,PL2)),
    \+ (member(A2,AL), member(not(A2),PL2)), !.
/* Do plan-following quasi-inheritance when you can */
fixplan_inheritance_args(Op,Ops,DL,AL,PL2,Fixcost,
                    [Op|Ops],NDL,NAL,NFixcost) :-
    actor(Op,A),   compute_duration(Op,A,[],NDur),   NFixcost   is
    Fixcost+NDur,
    alldeletepostcondition(Op,DL2), alladdpostcondition(Op,AL2),
    union(DL2,DL,NDL), union(AL2,AL,NAL), !.


/* Eliminate fixplans for ploys not beneficial or impossible to fix. */
/* (Useful separate from setupmns4 because loads entire set of
states.) */
```

```prolog
setupmns5 :- consult('cfullstates.pl'), open('tmpfixplan2.pl',read,SI),
    open('tmpfixplan3.pl',write,SO), setupmns5b(SI,SO), close(SI),
close(SO),
    sort_secondary('tmpfixplan3.pl',10000,'cfixplan.pl'), !.
setupmns5b(SI,SO) :- repeat, read(SI,P),
    ((P=fixplan(Statenum,D,A,Ops,DL,AL,K,Fixcost), Fixcost>0,
     Fixcost<100000, sf(Statenum,FullState),
     (D=[];      (\+    D=[], generalize_quantities([D],[XD]),
     member(XD,FullState))),
     (A=[];    (\+    A=[], generalize_quantities([A],[XA]),    \+
     member(XA,FullState))),
     Sortnum is 100000-Fixcost,
     writeq(SO,fixplan(Sortnum,Statenum,D,A,Ops,DL,AL,K,Fixcost)),
     write(SO,'.'), nl(SO), fail);
    P=end_of_file ), !.


/* Calculate a set of ploys for N successive runs with a greedy
algorithm. */
/* Requires loading the problem-definition file. */
maxruns(3).
greedy :- greedy(10.0).
greedy(GreedyThresh) :- consult('cfixplan.pl'), retractall(decided
(_,_,_,_,_)),
    greedy2(GreedyThresh).
greedy2(GreedyThresh) :- bagof(W2-[SN2,D2,A2,Run2],
    compute_decided(SN2,D2,A2,Run2,Numploys,W2),WL),
    bestitem(WL,W-[Statenum,D,A,Run]), W>GreedyThresh,
    assertz(decided(Statenum,Run,D,A,W)), !, greedy2(GreedyThresh).
greedy2(_) :- open('greedy.out',write,S),
    ((decided(SN,Run,D,A,C),    doublefactwrite(S,decided(SN,Run,D,
    A,C)), fail);
    close(S)), !.
compute_decided(SN,D,A,Run,Numploys,W) :- maxruns(Runs),
    ints_range(Runs,RL), member(Run,RL), fixplan(_,SN,D,A,_,_,_,K,F
    ixcost),
    \+ (decided(_,Run2,D,A,_), Run2 >= Run),
    nice_bagof(SN2,decided_before(SN2,Run),SNL1), length(SNL1,N1),
    nice_bagof(SN2,sameploy_decided_before(SN2,Run,D,A),SNL2),
    length(SNL2,N2),
    nice_bagof(SN3,decided_samerun(SN3,Run),SNL3), length(SNL3,N3),
    /* Following constants represent the probability of attacker
    detecting */
    /* deception and deciding to log out given (a) N deceptions
    previous */
```

```
       /* in time, and (b) N deceptions with the same ploy. */
       C1 is 0.8 ** N1, C2 is 0.3 ** N2, C3 is 0.8 ** N3,
       ((ploysuccess(D,A,PSUC), W is PSUC*C1*C2*C3*K*Fixcost);
        (\+ ploysuccess(D,A,PSUC), W is C1*C2*C3*K*Fixcost) ).
bestitem([W-L],W-L) :- !.
bestitem([W-L|WLL],W2-L2) :- bestitem(WLL,W2-L2), W2>W, !.
bestitem([W-L|WLL],W-L).
    decided_before(SN,Run) :- decided(SN,Run2,_,_,_), Run2 =< Run.
    sameploy_decided_before(SN,Run,D,A) :- decided(SN,Run2,D,A,_),
    Run2 =< Run.
decided_samerun(SN,Run) :- decided(SN,Run,_,_,_).
ints_range(0,[]) :- !.
ints_range(I,NIL)    :-    Im1    is    I-1,    ints_range(Im1,IL),
append(IL,[I],NIL), !.
pow(X,0,1.0) :- !.
pow(X,N,Y) :- Nm1 is N-1, pow(X,Nm1,Y2), Y is Y2*X, !.


/* Utilities needed by setupmnsx routines. */
make_list([],[]) :- !.
make_list([A|B],[A|B]) :- !.
make_list(A,[A]) :- !.
possible_change(D,A) :- opposite(D,A).
possible_change(D,[]) :- orphan_delete(D).
possible_change([],A) :- orphan_add(A).
apply_change_full(State,CState,XD,XA) :- opposite(XD,XA),
    member(XD,State), \+ member(XA,State),
    (\+ XA=reported(F,P1,P2);
     (XA=reported(F,P1,P2), \+ member(reported(F,P1,_),State)) ),
    (\+ XA=ordered(F,P1,P2);
     (XA=ordered(F,P1,P2), \+ member(ordered(F,P1,_),State)) ),
    delete(State,XD,State2), CState=[XA|State2].
apply_change_full(State,CState,XD,[]) :- orphan_delete(XD),
    member(XD,State), delete(State,XD,CState).
apply_change_full(State,CState,[],XA) :- orphan_add(XA),
    \+ member(XA,State),
    (\+ XA=reported(F,P1,P2);
     (XA=reported(F,P1,P2), \+ member(reported(F,P1,_),State)) ),
    (\+ XA=ordered(F,P1,P2);
     (XA=ordered(F,P1,P2), \+ member(ordered(F,P1,_),State)) ),
    CState=[XA|State].
opposite_fact(not(F),F) :- !.
opposite_fact(F,not(F)) :- !.
assemble_needed_preconds([],not([]),[]) :- !.
assemble_needed_preconds([],NA,[NA]) :- !.
```

```
assemble_needed_preconds(D,not([]),[D]) :- !.
assemble_needed_preconds(D,NA,[D,NA]) :- !.
oplist_duration([],State,0).
oplist_duration([Op|Oplist],State,D) :- actor(Op,A),
compute_duration(Op,A,State,D1),oplist_duration(Oplist,State,D2),
    D is D1+D2, !.
/* Remove the numerical arguments to all firefighting predicates */
unquantify_preds([],[]).
unquantify_preds([P|PL],[UP|UPL]) :- unquantify_pred(P,UP),
    unquantify_preds(PL,UPL), !.
unquantify_pred(P,P) :- var(P), !.
unquantify_pred(not(P),not(UP)) :- unquantify_pred(P,UP), !.
unquantify_pred(recorded(P),recorded(UP))       :-       unquantify_
pred(P,UP), !.
unquantify_pred(ordered(F,P1,P2),ordered(NF,P1,P2)) :-
    unquantify_pred(F,NF), !.
unquantify_pred(reported(F,P1,P2),reported(NF,P1,P2)) :-
    unquantify_pred(F,NF), !.
/* This handles two numeric args in the same predicate */
unquantify_pred(P,UP) :- P=..PredArgs, PredArgs=[Pred|_],
    numeric_arg(Pred,K1),
    numeric_arg(Pred,K2), K2>K1,   DK is K2-K1-1,
  append(PredArgs1,[_|PredArgs2],PredArgs), length(PredArgs1,K1),
 append(PredArgs3,[_|PredArgs4],PredArgs2), length(PredArgs3,DK),
    append(PredArgs3,PredArgs4,XPredArgs2),
    append(PredArgs1,XPredArgs2,XPredArgs), UP=..XPredArgs, !.
/* This handles only one numeric arg per predicate, usual case */
unquantify_pred(P,UP) :- P=..PredArgs, PredArgs=[Pred|_],
    numeric_arg(Pred,K),
    append(PredArgs1,[_|PredArgs2],PredArgs), length(PredArgs1,K),
    append(PredArgs1,PredArgs2,XPredArgs), UP=..XPredArgs, !.
unquantify_pred(P,P) :- !.
numeric_arg(Pred,K)   :-   factargtype(PE),   \+ var(PE),   PE=..
[Pred|Args],
    append(Args1,[number|_],[Pred|Args]), length(Args1,K), !.
singlefactwrite(Outstream,P)   :-   writeq(Outstream,P),   write
(Outstream,'.'),
    nl(Outstream), !.
doublefactwrite(Outstream,P)           :-           writeq(Outstream,P),
write(Outstream,'.'),
    nl(Outstream), writeq(P), write('.'), nl, !.
```

```prolog
/* Sorts a file in secondary storage -- slow, but can handle big
file. */
/* 2nd arg is number of items from first-arg file to merge in at each
step. */
sort_secondary(Infile,Blocksize,Outfile) :- open(Infile,read,SI),
    open(tmpsecsort1,write,SO1), close(SO1),
    open(tmpsecsort2,write,SO2), close(SO2),
    sort_secondary2(SI,tmpsecsort1,tmpsecsort2,Blocksize,1,Temp
    num),
    ((Tempnum=1, copy_fact_file(tmpsecsort2,Outfile));
    (Tempnum=2, copy_fact_file(tmpsecsort1,Outfile)) ), !.
sort_secondary2(SI,Tmpfile1,Tmpfile2,Blocksize,Tempnum,FTempnum) :-
    open(Tmpfile2,read,SI2),   open(Tmpfile1,write,SO),   NTempnum   is
    3-Tempnum,
    read_block(SI,Blocksize,Blockitems,Moreflag),
    sort(Blockitems,SBlockitems), merge_block(SBlockitems,SI2,SO),
    close(SI2), close(SO),
    ((Moreflag=true, !,
        sort_secondary2(SI,Tmpfile2,Tmpfile1,Blocksize,NTempnum,FTemp
        num) );
    (close(SI), FTempnum is NTempnum) ), !.
read_block(_,0,[],true) :- !.
read_block(SI,Blocksize,[P|Blockitems],Moreflag) :- read(SI,P),
    \+ P=end_of_file, NBlocksize is Blocksize-1, !,
    read_block(SI,NBlocksize,Blockitems,Moreflag).
read_block(_,_,[],false) :- !.
merge_block(Blockitems,SI2,SO) :- read(SI2,P2), !,
    merge_block2(Blockitems,SI2,P2,SO).
merge_block2([],_,end_of_file,_) :- !.
merge_block2([P1|Blockitems],SI2,P2,SO)          :-          (P2=end_of_
file;compare('<',P1,P2)),
write(SO,P1), write(SO,'.'), nl(SO), !, merge_block2(Blockitems,
SI2,P2,SO).
merge_block2(Blockitems,SI2,P2,SO) :-
    write(SO,P2), write(SO,'.'), nl(SO), read(SI2,NP2), !,
    merge_block2(Blockitems,SI2,NP2,SO).
/* Copies a file of facts from one filename to another */
copy_fact_file(Infile,Outfile) :- open(Infile,read,SI), open(Outfile,
write,SO),
    copy_fact_file2(SI,SO), close(SI), close(SO), !.
copy_fact_file2(SI,SO) :- repeat, read(SI,P),
    ((\+ P=end_of_file, write(SO,P), write(SO,'.'), nl(SO), fail);
    P=end_of_file ), !.
```

Printed in the United States
By Bookmasters